The Ultima
Quotations

Compiled and Arranged
by
Joseph Demakis

Copyright © 2012, Joseph M. Demakis

All rights reserved. Except as permitted under the U.S. Copyright Act of 1976, no part of this publication may be reproduced, distributed or transmitted in any form or by any means, or stored in a database or retrieval system, without the prior written permission of the author.

Printed by CreateSpace, An Amazon.com Company

CreateSpace
Charleston, SC
United States of America

First Printing: November 2012

ISBN-13: 978-1481053020
ISBN-10: 1481053027

Visit the fan pages
http://www.josephdemakis.com
http://www.facebook.com/joseph.demakis

DEDICATION

For Jake, James, Johnny, Katie, and Jack
The best siblings in the World

CONTENTS

AGE 1

ANGER 9

ARCHITECTURE 13

ART 19

BEAUTY 33

BIRTHDAY 41

BUSINESS 46

CAR 58

CHANGE 64

COMPUTERS 69

DAD 77

DATING 86

DEATH 93

DESIGN 99

DIET 104

DREAMS 110

EDUCATION 118

ENVIRONMENTAL 124

EQUALITY 131

EXPERIENCE 137

FAITH 142

FAMILY 147

FINANCE	157
FITNESS	163
FOOD	170
FORGIVENESS	178
FRIENDSHIP	182
FUNNY	188
GARDENING	204
GOVERNMENT	209
GRADUATION	215
HAPPINESS	224
HEALTH	232
HISTORY	236
HOME	247
HUMOR	252
IMAGINATION	257
INSPIRATIONAL	262
INTELLIGENCE	268
LEADERSHIP	273
LEGAL	278
LIFE	283
LOVE	294
MARRIAGE	310
MEDICAL	321
MEN	326
MOM	334
MONEY	342

MOTIVATIONAL	349
MOVIES	355
MUSIC	360
NATURE	366
PARENTING	380
PATRIOTISM	387
PEACE	392
PET	397
POETRY	403
POLITICS	409
POWER	423
RELIGION	431
SCIENCE	437
SOCIETY	445
SPORTS	451
SUCCESS	463
TECHNOLOGY	468
TEEN	476
TIME	481
TRAVEL	485
TRUST	490
WAR	494
WEDDING	500
WISDOM	505
WOMEN	515
WORK	525

Joseph M. Demakis

ACKNOWLEDGMENTS

The Ultimate Book Of Quotations is an invaluable tool for writers, public speakers, coaches, business leaders or anyone who wishes to improve communications. This book is conveniently organized by subjects with over 500 pages of quotations for everyone. The book's organization makes finding quotes easy and user friendly.

AGE

A comfortable old age is the reward of a well-spent youth. Instead of its bringing sad and melancholy prospects of decay, it would give us hopes of eternal youth in a better world.
Maurice Chevalier

A diplomat is a man who always remembers a woman's birthday but never remembers her age.
Robert Frost

A man growing old becomes a child again.
Sophocles

Advice in old age is foolish; for what can be more absurd than to increase our provisions for the road the nearer we approach to our journey's end.
Marcus Tullius Cicero

After thirty, a body has a mind of its own.
Bette Midler

Age considers; youth ventures.
Rabindranath Tagore

After you're older, two things are possibly more important than any others: health and money.
Helen Gurley Brown

Age does not diminish the extreme disappointment of having a scoop of ice cream fall from the cone.
Jim Fiebig

Age is a very high price to pay for maturity.
Tom Stoppard

Age is an issue of mind over matter. If you don't mind, it doesn't matter.
Mark Twain

Age is how we determine how valuable you are.
Jane Elliot

Every man over forty is a scoundrel.
George Bernard Shaw

Age is not a particularly interesting subject. Anyone can get old. All you have to do is live long enough.
Don Marquis

Aging is not lost youth but a new stage of opportunity and strength.
Betty Friedan

Aging seems to be the only available way to live a long life.
Kitty O'Neill Collins

Alas, after a certain age every man is responsible for his face.
Albert Camus

All diseases run into one, old age.
Ralph Waldo Emerson

An archaeologist is the best husband a woman can have. The older she gets the more interested he is in her.
Agatha Christie

Anyone who stops learning is old, whether at twenty or eighty. Anyone who keeps learning stays young. The greatest thing in life is to keep your mind young.
Henry Ford

As I approve of a youth that has something of the old man in him, so I am no less pleased with an old man that has something of the youth. He that follows this rule may be old in body, but can never be so in mind.
Marcus Tullius Cicero

As I grow older, I pay less attention to what men say. I just watch what they do.
Andrew Carnegie

As men get older, the toys get more expensive.
Marvin Davis

As long as any adult thinks that he, like the parents and teachers of old, can become introspective, invoking his own youth to understand the youth before him, he is lost.
Margaret Mead

As you age naturally, your family shows more and more on your face. If you deny that, you deny your heritage.
Frances Conroy

Bashfulness is an ornament to youth, but a reproach to old age.
Aristotle

Forty is the old age of youth,
fifty is the youth of old age.
Hosea Ballou

Forty is the old age of youth;
fifty the youth of old age.
Victor Hugo

Growing old is no more than a
bad habit which a busy person
has no time to form.
Andre Maurois

He has a profound respect for
old age. Especially when it's
bottled.
Gene Fowler

How incessant and great are
the ills with which a prolonged
old age is replete.
C. S. Lewis

I don't believe one grows
older. I think that what
happens early on in life is that
at a certain age one stands still
and stagnates.
T. S. Eliot

I don't feel old. I don't feel
anything till noon. That's when
it's time for my nap.
Bob Hope

I don't want to fight aging; I
want to take good care of
myself, but plastic surgery and
all that? I'm not interested.
Christine Lahti

I find that a man is as old as his
work. If his work keeps him
from moving forward, he will
look forward with the work.
William Ernest Hocking

I get all fired up about aging in
America.
Willard Scott

I think when the full horror of
being fifty hits you, you should
stay home and have a good
cry.
Josh Billings

I think your whole life shows in
your face and you should be
proud of that.
Lauren Bacall

I want to get old gracefully. I
want to have good posture, I
want to be healthy and be an
example to my children.
Sting

I will never be an old man. To
me, old age is always 15 years
older than I am.
Francis Bacon

I'm happy to report that my
inner child is still ageless.
James Broughton

I'm not afraid of aging.
Shelley Duvall

I'm not interested in age. People who tell me their age are silly. You're as old as you feel.
Henri Frederic Amiel

In old age we are like a batch of letters that someone has sent. We are no longer in the past, we have arrived.
Knut Hamsun

In youth the days are short and the years are long. In old age the years are short and day's long.
Pope Paul VI

Middle age is youth without levity, and age without decay.
Doris Day

In youth we run into difficulties. In old age difficulties run into us.
Beverly Sills

Inflation is when you pay fifteen dollars for the ten-dollar haircut you used to get for five dollars when you had hair.
Sam Ewing

It is sad to grow old but nice to ripen.
Brigitte Bardot

It takes a long time to become young.
Pablo Picasso

No man is ever old enough to know better.
Holbrook Jackson

Like everyone else who makes the mistake of getting older, I begin each day with coffee and obituaries.
Bill Cosby

Middle age is the awkward period when Father Time starts catching up with Mother Nature.
Harold Coffin

Middle age is the time when a man is always thinking that in a week or two he will feel as good as ever.
Don Marquis

Middle age is when your age starts to show around your middle.
Bob Hope

No one can avoid aging, but aging productively is something else.
Katharine Graham

Nobody grows old merely by living a number of years. We grow old by deserting our ideals. Years may wrinkle the skin, but to give up enthusiasm wrinkles the soul.
Samuel Ullman

None are so old as those who have outlived enthusiasm.
Henry David Thoreau

Old age adds to the respect due to virtue, but it takes nothing from the contempt inspired by vice; it whitens only the hair.
Ira Gershwin

Old age comes on suddenly, and not gradually as is thought.
Emily Dickinson

Old age has deformities enough of its own. It should never add to them the deformity of vice.
Eleanor Roosevelt

Old age is a shipwreck.
Charles de Gaulle

Old age is no place for sissies.
Bette Davis

Old age is fifteen years older than I am.
Oliver Wendell Holmes

Old age is an excellent time for outrage. My goal is to say or do at least one outrageous thing every week.
Louis Kronenberger

Old age is like a plane flying through a storm. Once you're aboard, there's nothing you can do.
Golda Meir

Old age is like everything else. To make a success of it, you've got to start young.
Theodore Roosevelt

Old age is the most unexpected of all the things that can happen to a man.
James Thurber

Old age, believe me, is a good and pleasant thing. It is true you are gently shouldered off the stage, but then you are given such a comfortable front stall as spectator.
Confucius

Preparation for old age should begin not later than one's teens. A life which is empty of purpose until 65 will not suddenly become filled on retirement.
Dwight L. Moody

The aging process has you firmly in its grasp if you never get the urge to throw a snowball.
Doug Larson

The answer to old age is to keep one's mind busy and to go on with one's life as if it were interminable. I always admired Chekhov for building a new house when he was dying of tuberculosis.
Leon Edel

The denunciation of the young is a necessary part of the hygiene of older people, and greatly assists the circulation of the blood.
Logan P. Smith

The great secret that all old people share is that you really haven't changed in seventy or eighty years. Your body changes, but you don't change at all. And that, of course, causes great confusion.
Doris Lessing

The really frightening thing about middle age is the knowledge that you'll grow out of it.
Doris Day

The trick is growing up without growing old.
Casey Stengel

The tendency of old age to the body, say the physiologists, is to form bone. It is as rare as it is pleasant to meet with an old man whose opinions are not ossified.
Bob Wells

The whole business of marshaling one's energies becomes more and more important as one grows older.
Hume Cronyn

There is always some specific moment when we become aware that our youth is gone; but, years after, we know it was much later.
Mignon McLaughlin

There is an anti-aging possibility, but it has to come from within.
Susan Anton

There's no such thing as old age, there is only sorrow.
Fay Weldon

Those who love deeply never grow old; they may die of old age, but they die young.
Dorothy Canfield Fisher

To keep the heart unwrinkled, to be hopeful, kindly, cheerful, reverent that is to triumph over old age.
Amos Bronson Alcott

We pay when old for the excesses of youth.
J. B. Priestley

To resist the frigidity of old age, one must combine the body, the mind, and the heart. And to keep these in parallel vigor one must exercise, study, and love.
Alan Bleasdale

True terror is to wake up one morning and discover that your high school class is running the country.
Kurt Vonnegut

We should so provide for old age that it may have no urgent wants of this world to absorb it from meditation on the next. It is awful to see the lean hands of dotage making a coffer of the grave.
Pearl S. Buck

We've put more effort into helping folks reach old age than into helping them enjoy it.
Frank Howard Clark

What most persons consider as virtue, after the age of 40 is simply a loss of energy.
Voltaire

Whatever poet, orator or sage may say of it, old age is still old age.
Sinclair Lewis

When a noble life has prepared old age, it is not decline that it reveals, but the first days of immortality.
Muriel Spark

When grace is joined with wrinkles, it is adorable. There is an unspeakable dawn in happy old age.
Victor Hugo

When you become senile, you won't know it.
Bill Cosby

While one finds company in himself and his pursuits, he cannot feel old, no matter what his years may be.
Amos Bronson Alcott

Wrinkles should merely indicate where smiles have been.
Mark Twain

You can't help getting older, but you don't have to get old.
George Burns

You end up as you deserve. In old age you must put up with the face, the friends, the health, and the children you have earned.
Judith Viorst

You know you're getting old when all the names in your black book have M. D. after them.
Harrison Ford

Youth is the best time to be rich, and the best time to be poor.
Euripides

Youth is the gift of nature, but age is a work of art.
Stanislaw Lec

Youth is when you're allowed to stay up late on New Year's Eve. Middle age is when you're forced to.
Bill Vaughan

ANGER

A man that studieth revenge keeps his own wounds green.
Francis Bacon

A man who has never made a woman angry is a failure in life.
Christopher Morley

Always write angry letters to your enemies. Never mail them.
James Fallows

An angry man opens his mouth and shuts his eyes.
Cato

Anger and intolerance are the enemies of correct understanding.
Mahatma Gandhi

Anger and jealousy can no more bear to lose sight of their objects than love.
George Eliot

Anger dwells only in the bosom of fools.
Albert Einstein

Anger is one of the sinews of the soul.
Thomas Fuller

Anger is a killing thing: it kills the man who angers, for each rage leaves him less than he had been before - it takes something from him.
Louis L'Amour

Anger is a wind which blows out the lamp of the mind.
Robert Green Ingersoll

Anger is an acid that can do more harm to the vessel in which it is stored than to anything on which it is poured.
Mark Twain

Anger is a short madness.
Horace

Anger makes dull men witty, but it keeps them poor.
Francis Bacon

Anger, if not restrained, is frequently more hurtful to us than the injury that provokes it.
Lucius Annaeus Seneca

Be not angry that you cannot make others as you wish them to be, since you cannot make yourself as you wish to be.
Thomas Kempis

Anybody can become angry - that is easy, but to be angry with the right person and to the right degree and at the right time and for the right purpose, and in the right way - that is not within everybody's power and is not easy.
Aristotle

Bitterness is like cancer. It eats upon the host. But anger is like fire. It burns it all clean.
Maya Angelou

Don't get the impression that you arouse my anger. You see, one can only be angry with those he respects.
Richard M. Nixon

Every time you get angry, you poison your own system.
Alfred A. Montapert

Experts say you should never hit your children in anger. When is a good time? When you're feeling festive?
Roseanne Barr

Expressing anger is a form of public littering.
Willard Gaylin

Fair peace becomes men; ferocious anger belongs to beasts.
Ovid

He who angers you conquers you.
Elizabeth Kenny

For every minute you remain angry, you give up sixty seconds of peace of mind.
Ralph Waldo Emerson

Get mad, then get over it.
Colin Powell

Hatred is an affair of the heart; contempt that of the head.
Arthur Schopenhauer

He that would be angry and sin not, must not be angry with anything but sin.
John Ruskin

Heaven has no rage like love to hatred turned, nor hell a fury like a woman scorned.
William Congreve

Holding on to anger is like grasping a hot coal with the intent of throwing it at someone else; you are the one who gets burned.
Buddha

How much more grievous are the consequences of anger than the causes of it.
Marcus Aurelius

How often it is that the angry man rages denial of what his inner self is telling him.
Frank Herbert

Keep cool; anger is not an argument.
Daniel Webster

I know of no more disagreeable situation than to be left feeling generally angry without anybody in particular to be angry at.
Frank Moore Colby

If a small thing has the power to make you angry, does that not indicate something about your size?
Sydney J. Harris

It is impossible for you to be angry and laugh at the same time. Anger and laughter are mutually exclusive and you have the power to choose either.
Wayne Dyer

Let us not look back in anger, nor forward in
fear, but around in awareness.
James Thurber

Man should forget his anger before he lies down to sleep.
Mahatma Gandhi

Never contend with a man who has nothing to lose.
Baltasar Gracian

Never do anything when you are in a temper, for you will do everything wrong.
Baltasar Gracian

Never go to bed angry, stay up and fight.
William Congreve

Never go to bed mad. Stay up and fight.
Phyllis Diller

No man can think clearly when his fists are clenched.
George Jean Nathan

One should not lose one's temper unless one is certain of getting more and more angry to the end.
William Butler Yeats

Revenge is often like biting a dog because the dog bit you.
Austin O'Malley

Somebody hits me, I'm going to hit him back. Even if it does look like he hasn't eaten in a while.
Charles Barkley

Speak when you are angry - and you'll make the best speech you'll ever regret.
Laurence J. Peter

Speak when you are angry and you will make the best speech you will ever regret.
Ambrose Bierce

The world needs anger. The world often continues to allow evil because it isn't angry enough.
Bede Jarrett

There are two things a person should never be angry at, what they can help, and what they cannot.
Plato

There is nothing that so much gratifies an ill tongue as when it finds an angry heart.
Thomas Fuller

Usually when people are sad, they don't do anything. They just cry over their condition. But when they get angry, they bring about a change.
James Russell Lowell

Whatever is begun in anger ends in shame.
Benjamin Franklin

When anger rises, think of the consequences.
Confucius

When angry count to ten before you speak. If very angry, count to one hundred.
Thomas Jefferson

When angry, count to four; when very angry, swear.
Mark Twain

ARCHITECTURE

A building has integrity just like a man. And just as seldom.
Ayn Rand

A city building, you experience when you walk; a suburban building, you experience when you drive.
Helmut Jahn

A great building must begin with the unmeasurable, must go through measurable means when it is being designed and in the end must be unmeasurable.
Louis Kahn

A house is a machine for living in.
Le Corbusier

An architect's most useful tools are an eraser at the drafting board, and a wrecking bar at the site.
Frank Lloyd Wright

Architecture is a visual art, and the buildings speak for themselves.
Julia Morgan

Architecture is the art of how to waste space.
Philip Johnson

Architects in the past have tended to concentrate their attention on the building as a static object. I believe dynamics are more important: the dynamics of people, their interaction with spaces and environmental condition.
John Portman

Architecture arouses sentiments in man. The architect's task therefore, is to make those sentiments more precise.
Adolf Loos

Architecture is basically a container of something. I hope they will enjoy not so much the teacup, but the tea.
Yoshio Taniguchi

Architecture is not an inspirational business, it's a rational procedure to do sensible and hopefully beautiful things; that's all.
Harry Seidler

Architecture is the learned game, correct and magnificent, of forms assembled in the light.
Le Corbusier

Architecture is the reaching out for the truth.
Louis Kahn

Architecture should speak of its time and place, but yearn for timelessness.
Frank Gehry

Architecture starts when you carefully put two bricks together. There it begins.
Ludwig Mies van der Rohe

Architecture tends to consume everything else, it has become one's entire life.
Arne Jacobsen

As a designer, the mission with which we have been charged is simple: providing space at the right cost.
Harry von Zell

At a certain point, I just put the building and the art impulse together. I decided that building was a legitimate way to make sculpture.
Martin Puryear

Buildings should serve people, not the other way around.
John Portman

Building art is a synthesis of life in materialized form. We should try to bring in under the same hat not a splintered way of thinking, but all in harmony together.
Alvar Aalto

But the building's identity resided in the ornament.
Louis Sullivan

Cities are the greatest creations of humanity.
Daniel Libeskind

Color in certain places has the great value of making the outlines and structural planes seem more energetic.
Antonio Gaudi

Designed by architects with honorable intentions but hands of palsy.
Jimmy Breslin

Don't clap too hard - it's a very old building.
John Osborne

Even at the United Nations, where legend has it that the building was designed so that there could be no corner offices, the expanse of glass in individual offices is said to be a dead giveaway as to rank. Five windows are excellent, one window not so great.
Enid Nemy

Every building is a prototype. No two are alike.
Helmut Jahn

Form follows profit is the aesthetic principle of our times.
Richard Rogers

Every great architect is - necessarily - a great poet. He must be a great original interpreter of his time, his day, his age.
Frank Lloyd Wright

For many years, I have lived uncomfortably with the belief that most planning and architectural design suffers for lack of real and basic purpose. The ultimate purpose, it seems to me, must be the improvement of mankind.
James Rouse

Form follows function.
Louis Sullivan

Great buildings that move the spirit have always been rare. In every case they are unique, poetic, products of the heart.
Arthur Erickson

I am but an architectural composer.
Alexander Jackson Davis

I believe that the way people live can be directed a little by architecture.
Tadao Ando

I don't build in order to have clients. I have clients in order to build.
Ayn Rand

If I have a style, I am not aware of it.
Michael Graves

I don't divide architecture, landscape and gardening; to me they are one.
Luis Barragan

I hate vacations. If you can build buildings, why sit on the beach?
Philip Johnson

I have designed the most buildings of any living American architect.
Alexander Jackson Davis

I love building spaces: architecture, furniture, all of it, probably more than fashion. The development procedure is more tactile. It's about space and form and it's something you can share with other people.
Donna Karan

I try to give people a different way of looking at their surroundings. That's art to me.
Maya Lin

If you give people nothingness, they can ponder what can be achieved from that nothingness.
Tadao Ando

In any architecture, there is an equity between the pragmatic function and the symbolic function.
Michael Graves

In Los Angeles, by the time you're 35, you're older than most of the buildings.
Delia Ephron

It is not the beauty of a building you should look at; it's the construction of the foundation that will stand the test of time.
David Allan Coe

Less is more.
Ludwig Mies van der Rohe

Light, God's eldest daughter, is a principal beauty in a building.
Thomas Fuller

Make big plans; aim high in hope and work, remembering that a noble, logical diagram once recorded will not die.
Daniel Burnham

My buildings don't speak in words but by means of their own spaciousness.
Thom Mayne

My buildings will be my legacy... they will speak for me long after I'm gone.
Julia Morgan

My passion and great enjoyment for architecture, and the reason the older I get the more I enjoy it, is because I believe we - architects - can affect the quality of life of the people.
Richard Rogers

The loftier the building, the deeper must the foundation be laid.
Thomas Kempis

Not many architects have the luxury to reject significant things.
Rem Koolhaas

No architect troubled to design houses that suited people who were to live in them, because that would have meant building a whole range of different houses. It was far cheaper and, above all, timesaving to make them identical.
Michael Ende

Nothing requires the architect's care more than the due proportions of buildings.
Marcus V. Pollio

Proportions are what makes the old Greek temples classic in their beauty. They are like huge blocks, from which the air has been literally hewn out between the columns.
Arne Jacobsen

Rome has not seen a modern building in more than half a century. It is a city frozen in time.
Richard Meier

Space has always been the spiritual dimension of architecture. It is not the physical statement of the structure so much as what it contains that moves us.
Arthur Erickson

What people want, above all, is order.
Stephen Gardiner

The bungalow had more to do with how Americans live today than any other building that has gone remotely by the name of architecture in our history.
Russell Lynes

The dialogue between client and architect is about as intimate as any conversation you can have, because when you're talking about building a house, you're talking about dreams.
Robert A. M. Stern

The frightening thought that what you draw may become a building makes for reasoned lines.
Saul Steinberg

The higher the building the lower the morals.
Noel Coward

The interior of the house personifies the private world; the exterior of it is part of the outside world.
Stephen Gardiner

The Romans were not inventors of the supporting arch, but its extended use in vaults and intersecting barrel shapes and domes is theirs.
Harry Seidler

The work of art shows people new directions and thinks of the future. The house thinks of the present.
Adolf Loos

Those who look for the laws of Nature as a support for their new works collaborate with the creator.
Antonio Gaudi

To me, a building - if it's beautiful - is the love of one man, he's made it out of his love for space, materials, things like that.
Martha Graham

To provide meaningful architecture is not to parody history but to articulate it.
Daniel Libeskind

Warmth isn't what minimalists are thought to have.
Maya Lin

We build buildings which are terribly restless. And buildings don't go anywhere. They shouldn't be restless.
Minoru Yamasaki

We require from buildings two kinds of goodness: first, the doing their practical duty well: then that they be graceful and pleasing in doing it.
John Ruskin

We shape our buildings; thereafter they shape us.
Winston Churchill

We should concentrate our work not only to a separated housing problem but housing involved in our daily work and all the other functions of the city.
Alvar Aalto

Whatever good things we build end up building us.
Jim Rohn

ART

A good painting to me has always been like a friend. It keeps me company, comforts and inspires.
Hedy Lamarr

A great artist is always before his time or behind it.
George Edward Moore

A guilty conscience needs to confess. A work of art is a confession.
Albert Camus

A man paints with his brains and not with his hands.
Michelangelo

A painting that is well composed is half finished.
Pierre Bonnard

A picture is a poem without words.
Horace

A picture is worth a thousand words.
Napoleon Bonaparte

A work of art is the unique result of a unique temperament.
Oscar Wilde

A sculptor is a person who is interested in the shape of things, a poet in words, a musician by sounds.
Henry Moore

A writer should write with his eyes and a painter paint with his ears.
Gertrude Stein

Abstract art: a product of the untalented sold by the unprincipled to the utterly bewildered.
Al Capp

Ads are the cave art of the twentieth century.
Marshall McLuhan

Advertising is the greatest art form of the 20th century.
Marshall McLuhan

All art is autobiographical. The pearl is the oyster's autobiography.
Federico Fellini

All art is but imitation of nature.
Lucius Annaeus Seneca

An artist cannot fail; it is a success to be one.
Charles Horton Cooley

An artist is a dreamer consenting to dream of the actual world.
George Santayana

An artist is always alone - if he is an artist. No, what the artist needs is loneliness.
Henry Miller

An artist is never ahead of his time but most people are far behind theirs.
Edgard Varese

An artist is not paid for his labor but for his vision.
James Whistler

An artist is somebody who produces things that people don't need to have.
Andy Warhol

An artist never really finishes his work, he merely abandons it.
Paul Valery

Art begins with resistance - at the point where resistance is overcome. No human masterpiece has ever been created without great labor.
Andre Gide

Art consists of limitation. The most beautiful part of every picture is the frame.
Gilbert K. Chesterton

Art doesn't transform. It just plain forms.
Roy Lichtenstein

Art enables us to find ourselves and lose ourselves at the same time.
Thomas Merton

Art for art's sake is a philosophy of the well-fed.
Frank Lloyd Wright

Art hurts. Art urges voyages - and it is easier to stay at home.
Gwendolyn Brooks

Art in Nature is rhythmic and has a horror of constraint.
Robert Delaunay

Art is a collaboration between God and the artist, and the less the artist does the better.
Andre Gide

Art is a revolt against fate. All art is a revolt against man's fate.
Andre Malraux

Art is a step from what is obvious and well-known toward what is arcane and concealed.
Khalil Gibran

Art is an invention of aesthetics, which in turn is an invention of philosophers... What we call art is a game.
Octavio Paz

Art is either plagiarism or revolution.
Paul Gauguin

Art is magic delivered from the lie of being truth.
Theodor Adorno

Art is man's expression of his joy in labor.
Henry A. Kissinger

Art is not a study of positive reality, it is the seeking for ideal truth.
John Ruskin

Art is not a thing; it is a way.
Elbert Hubbard

Art is parasitic on life, just as criticism is parasitic on art.
Harry S. Truman

Art is science made clear.
Wilson Mizner

Art is subject to arbitrary fashion.
Kary Mullis

Art is the desire of a man to express himself, to record the reactions of his personality to the world he lives in.
Amy Lowell

Art is the most intense mode of individualism that the world has known.
Oscar Wilde

Art is the proper task of life.
Friedrich Nietzsche

Art is the only way to run away without leaving home.
Twyla Tharp

Art is the right hand of Nature. The latter has only given us being, the former has made us men.
Friedrich Schiller

Art is the stored honey of the human soul, gathered on wings of misery and travail.
Theodore Dreiser

Art is the unceasing effort to compete with the beauty of flowers - and never succeeding.
Gian Carlo Menotti

Art ought never to be considered except in its relations with its ideal beauty.
Alfred de Vigny

Art produces ugly things which frequently become more beautiful with time. Fashion, on the other hand, produces beautiful things which always become ugly with time.
Jean Cocteau

Art, in itself, is an attempt to bring order out of chaos.
Stephen Sondheim

Art, like morality, consists in drawing the line somewhere.
Gilbert K. Chesterton

Artists don't make objects. Artists make mythologies.
Anish Kapoor

Artists themselves are not confined, but their output is.
Robert Smithson

Artists who seek perfection in everything are those who cannot attain it in anything.
Gustave Flaubert

Beauty in art is often nothing but ugliness subdued.
Jean Rostand

By the work one knows the workman.
Jean de La Fontaine

Creativity is allowing yourself to make mistakes. Art is knowing which ones to keep.
Scott Adams

Culture is the arts elevated to a set of beliefs.
Thomas Wolfe

Drawing is like making an expressive gesture with the advantage of permanence.
Henri Matisse

Drawing is the honesty of the art. There is no possibility of cheating. It is either good or bad.
Salvador Dali

Even a true artist does not always produce art.
Carroll O'Connor

Every artist dips his brush in his own soul, and paints his own nature into his pictures.
Henry Ward Beecher

Every artist was first an amateur.
Ralph Waldo Emerson

Every artist writes his own autobiography.
Havelock Ellis

Every creator painfully experiences the chasm between his inner vision and its ultimate expression.
Isaac Bashevis Singer

Every good painter paints what he is.
Jackson Pollock

Every human is an artist. The dream of your life is to make beautiful art.
Miguel Angel Ruiz

Every other artist begins with a blank canvas, a piece of paper the photographer begins with the finished product.
Edward Steichen

Every production of an artist should be the expression of an adventure of his soul.
W. Somerset Maugham

Every time a student walks past a really urgent, expressive piece of architecture that belongs to his college, it can help reassure him that he does have that mind, does have that soul.
Louis Kahn

Fashion is only the attempt to realize art in living forms and social intercourse.
Francis Bacon

Fine art is that in which the hand, the head, and the heart of man go together.
John Ruskin

Great art picks up where nature ends.
Marc Chagall

I choose a block of marble and chop off whatever I don't need.
Auguste Rodin

I cry out for order and find it only in art.
Helen Hayes

I don't paint things. I only paint the difference between things.
Henri Matisse

I don't think there's any artist of any value who doesn't doubt what they're doing.
Francis Ford Coppola

I don't want to be interesting. I want to be good.
Ludwig Mies van der Rohe

I found I could say things with color and shapes that I couldn't say any other way - things I had no words for.
Georgia O'Keeffe

I like to pretend that my art has nothing to do with me.
Roy Lichtenstein

I paint with shapes.
Alexander Calder

I realize that protest paintings are not exactly in vogue, but I've done many.
Robert Indiana

I think about my work every minute of the day.
Jeff Koons

I think an artist's responsibility is more complex than people realize.
Jodie Foster

I think of my peace paintings as one long poem, with each painting being a single stanza.
Robert Indiana

I was the least Pop of all the Pop artists.
Robert Indiana

I'm afraid that if you look at a thing long enough, it loses all of its meaning.
Andy Warhol

I've been called many names like perfectionist, difficult and obsessive. I think it takes obsession, takes searching for the details for any artist to be good.
Barbra Streisand

I've never really had a hobby, unless you count art, which the IRS once told me I had to declare as a hobby since I hadn't made money with it.
Laurie Anderson

If a building becomes architecture, then it is art.
Arne Jacobsen

If we could but paint with the hand what we see with the eye.
Honore de Balzac

If you do not breathe through writing, if you do not cry out in writing, or sing in writing, then don't write, because our culture has no use for it.
Anais Nin

If you hear a voice within you say 'you cannot paint,' then by all means paint, and that voice will be silenced.
Vincent Van Gogh

Immature artists imitate. Mature artists steal.
Lionel Trilling

In art the best is good enough.
Johann Wolfgang von Goethe

In an artwork you're always looking for artistic decisions, so an ashtray is perfect. An ashtray has got life and death.
Damien Hirst

In art as in love, instinct is enough.
Anatole France

In art, the hand can never execute anything higher than the heart can imagine.
Ralph Waldo Emerson

It is a mistake for a sculptor or a painter to speak or write very often about his job. It releases tension needed for his work.
Henry Moore

Minimal art went nowhere.
Sol LeWitt

It is art that makes life, makes interest, makes importance and I know of no substitute whatever for the force and beauty of its process.
Max Eastman

Lesser artists borrow, great artists steal.
Igor Stravinsky

Life imitates art far more than art imitates Life.
Oscar Wilde

Life is painting a picture, not doing a sum.
Oliver Wendell Holmes

Light in Nature creates the movement of colors.
Robert Delaunay

Lying in bed would be an altogether perfect and supreme experience if only one had a colored pencil long enough to draw on the ceiling.
Gilbert K. Chesterton

Modern art is what happens when painters stop looking at girls and persuade themselves that they have a better idea.
John Ciardi

Mournful and yet grand is the destiny of the artist.
Franz Liszt

Murals in restaurants are on a par with the food in museums.
Peter De Vries

My hand is the extension of the thinking process - the creative process.
Tadao Ando

My imagination can picture no fairer happiness than to continue living for art.
Clara Schumann

My love of fine art increased - the more of it I saw, the more of it I wanted to see.
Paul Getty

My painting does not come from the easel.
Jackson Pollock

No great artist ever sees things as they really are. If he did, he would cease to be an artist.
Oscar Wilde

No heirloom of humankind captures the past as do art and language.
Theodore Bikel

Not everybody trusts paintings but people believe photographs.
Ansel Adams

Of all lies, art is the least untrue.
Gustave Flaubert

Painting is an infinitely minute part of my personality.
Salvador Dali

Painting is by nature a luminous language.
Robert Delaunay

Painting is easy when you don't know how, but very difficult when you do.
Edgar Degas

Painting is just another way of keeping a diary.
Pablo Picasso

Painting, n.: The art of protecting flat surfaces from the weather, and exposing them to the critic.
Ambrose Bierce

Personality is everything in art and poetry.
Johann Wolfgang von Goethe

Photograph: a picture painted by the sun without instruction in art.
Ambrose Bierce

Photography is a major force in explaining man to man.
Edward Steichen

Photography takes an instant out of time, altering life by holding it still.
Dorothea Lange

Pictures deface walls more often than they decorate them.
William Wordsworth

Pictures must not be too picturesque.
Ralph Waldo Emerson

Rationalism is the enemy of art, though necessary as a basis for architecture.
Arthur Erickson

Rules and models destroy genius and art.
William Hazlitt

So vast is art, so narrow human wit.
Alexander Pope

The essence of all art is to have pleasure in giving pleasure.
Dale Carnegie

Some painters transform the sun into a yellow spot, others transform a yellow spot into the sun.
Pablo Picasso

That's the motivation of an artist - to seek attention of some kind.
James Taylor

The aim of art is to represent not the outward appearance of things, but their inward significance.
Aristotle

The aim of every artist is to arrest motion, which is life, by artificial means and hold it fixed so that a hundred years later, when a stranger looks at it, it moves again since it is life.
William Faulkner

The art of art, the glory of expression and the sunshine of the light of letters, is simplicity.
Walt Whitman

The artist belongs to his work, not the work to the artist.
Novalis

The artist is a receptacle for emotions that come from all over the place: from the sky, from the earth, from a scrap of paper, from a passing shape, from a spider's web.
Pablo Picasso

The artist is nothing without the gift, but the gift is nothing without work.
Emile Zola

The artist one day falls through a hole in the brambles, and from that moment he is following the dark rapids of an underground river which may sometimes flow so near to the surface that the laughing picnic parties are heard above.
Cyril Connolly

The artist who aims at perfection in everything achieves it in nothing.
Eugene Delacroix

The artist's world is limitless. It can be found anywhere, far from where he lives or a few feet away. It is always on his doorstep.
Paul Strand

The arts are an even better barometer of what is happening in our world than the stock market or the debates in congress.
Hendrik Willem Van Loon

The beauty one can find in art is one of the pitifully few real and lasting products of human endeavor.
Paul Getty

The beginning is the most important part of the work.
Plato

The business of art is to reveal the relation between man and his environment.
David Herbert Lawrence

The creative act lasts but a brief moment, a lightning instant of give-and-take, just long enough for you to level the camera and to trap the fleeting prey in your little box.
Henri Cartier-Bresson

The essence of all beautiful art, all great art, is gratitude.
Friedrich Nietzsche

The highest art is always the most religious, and the greatest artist is always a devout person.
Abraham Lincoln

The history of art is the history of revivals.
Samuel Butler

The history of modern art is also the history of the progressive loss of art's audience. Art has increasingly become the concern of the artist and the bafflement of the public.
Paul Gauguin

The mediator of the inexpressible is the work of art.
Johann Wolfgang von Goethe

The moment you cheat for the sake of beauty, you know you're an artist.
David Hockney

The more horrifying this world becomes, the more art becomes abstract.
Ellen Key

The perfection of art is to conceal art.
Quintilian

The principle of art is to pause, not bypass.
Jerzy Kosinski

The principles of true art is not to portray, but to evoke.
Jerzy Kosinski

The purpose of art is washing the dust of daily life off our souls.
Pablo Picasso

The sculptor produces the beautiful statue by chipping away such parts of the marble block as are not needed - it is a process of elimination.
Elbert Hubbard

The task of art today is to bring chaos into order.
Theodor Adorno

The terrifying and edible beauty of Art Nouveau architecture.
Salvador Dali

The true work of art is but a shadow of the divine perfection.
Michelangelo

There is nothing worse than a sharp image of a fuzzy concept.
Ansel Adams

The very essence of the creative is its novelty, and hence we have no standard by which to judge it.
Carl Rogers

The waking mind is the least serviceable in the arts.
Henry Miller

The writer, when he is also an artist, is someone who admits what others don't dare reveal.
Elia Kazan

Things are beautiful if you love them.
Jean Anouilh

This world is but a canvas to our imagination.
Henry David Thoreau

Time extracts various values from a painter's work. When these values are exhausted the pictures are forgotten, and the more a picture has to give, the greater it is.
Henri Matisse

To an engineer, good enough means perfect. With an artist, there's no such thing as perfect.
Alexander Calder

To make pictures big is to make them more powerful.
Robert Mapplethorpe

To make us feel small in the right way is a function of art; men can only make us feel small in the wrong way.
E. M. Forster

To me, photography is the simultaneous recognition, in a fraction of a second, of the significance of an event.
Henri Cartier-Bresson

Trying to force creativity is never good.
Sarah McLachlan

To say that a work of art is good, but incomprehensible to the majority of men, is the same as saying of some kind of food that it is very good but that most people can't eat it.
Leo Tolstoy

To send light into the darkness of men's hearts - such is the duty of the artist.
Robert Schumann

Treat a work of art like a prince. Let it speak to you first.
Arthur Schopenhauer

Trifles make perfection, and perfection is no trifle.
Michelangelo

True art is characterized by an irresistible urge in the creative artist.
Albert Einstein

Very few people possess true artistic ability. It is therefore both unseemly and unproductive to irritate the situation by making an effort. If you have a burning, restless urge to write or paint, simply eat something sweet and the feeling will pass.
Fran Lebowitz

Vision is the art of seeing what is invisible to others.
Jonathan Swift

Vision is the true creative rhythm.
Robert Delaunay

Vitality is radiated from exceptional art and architecture.
Arthur Erickson

We have art in order not to die of the truth.
Friedrich Nietzsche

What art offers is space - a certain breathing room for the spirit.
John Updike

What makes photography a strange invention is that its primary raw materials are light and time.
John Berger

When I judge art, I take my painting and put it next to a God made object like a tree or flower. If it clashes, it is not art.
Paul Cezanne

When I make art, I think about its ability to connect with others, to bring them into the process.
Jim Hodges

When I think of art I think of beauty. Beauty is the mystery of life. It is not in the eye it is in the mind. In our minds there is awareness of perfection.
Agnes Martin

When I work, and in my art, I hold hands with God.
Robert Mapplethorpe

When that shutter clicks, anything else that can be done afterward is not worth consideration.
Edward Steichen

Wherever art appears, life disappears.
Robert Motherwell

Without art, the crudeness of reality would make the world unbearable.
George Bernard Shaw

Without freedom, no art; art lives only on the restraints it imposes on itself, and dies of all others.
Albert Camus

Without tradition, art is a flock of sheep without a shepherd. Without innovation, it is a corpse.
Winston Churchill

Works of art, in my opinion,
are the only objects in the
material universe to possess
internal order, and that is why,
though I don't believe that
only art matters, I do believe in
Art for Art's sake.
E. M. Forster

You begin with the possibilities
of the material.
Robert Rauschenberg

You don't take a photograph,
you make it.
Ansel Adams

BEAUTY

To love beauty is to see light.
Victor Hugo

Everything has beauty, but not everyone sees it.
Confucius

A woman whose smile is open and whose expression is glad has a kind of beauty no matter what she wears.
Anne Roiphe

A thing of beauty is a joy forever: its loveliness increases; it will never pass into nothingness.
John Keats

Beauty is only skin deep. If you go after someone just because she's beautiful but don't have anything to talk about, it's going to get boring fast. You want to look beyond the surface and see if you can have fun or if you have anything in common with this person.
Amanda Peet

A beauty is a woman you notice; a charmer is one who notices you.
Adlai E. Stevenson

People are like stained - glass windows. They sparkle and shine when the sun is out, but when the darkness sets in, their true beauty is revealed only if there is a light from within.
Elisabeth Kubler-Ross

The pursuit of truth and beauty is a sphere of activity in which we are permitted to remain children all our lives.
Albert Einstein

Never lose an opportunity of seeing anything beautiful, for beauty is God's handwriting.
Ralph Waldo Emerson

Beauty is eternity gazing at itself in a mirror.
Khalil Gibran

A witty woman is a treasure; a witty beauty is a power.
George Meredith

Love of beauty is taste. The creation of beauty is art.
Ralph Waldo Emerson

Beauty doesn't need ornaments. Softness can't bear the weight of ornaments.
Munshi Premchand

Beauty has a lot to do with character.
Kevyn Aucoin

A women's greatest asset is her beauty.
Alex Comfort

She got her looks from her father. He's a plastic surgeon.
Groucho Marx

Beauty is unbearable, drives us to despair, offering us for a minute the glimpse of an eternity that we should like to stretch out over the whole of time.
Albert Camus

Beauty is a manifestation of secret natural laws, which otherwise would have been hidden from us forever.
Johann Wolfgang von Goethe

The world's biggest power is the youth and beauty of a woman.
Chanakya

Think of all the beauty still left around you and be happy.
Anne Frank

Beauty is power; a smile is its sword.
John Ray

Life is full of beauty. Notice it. Notice the bumble bee, the small child, and the smiling faces. Smell the rain, and feel the wind. Live your life to the fullest potential, and fight for your dreams.
Ashley Smith

Beauty is worse than wine, it intoxicates both the holder and beholder.
Aldous Huxley

Beauty awakens the soul to act.
Dante Alighieri

Of life's two chief prizes, beauty and truth, I found the first in a loving heart and the second in a laborer's hand.
Khalil Gibran

I don't think of all the misery but of the beauty that still remains.
Anne Frank

The soul that sees beauty may sometimes walk alone.
Johann Wolfgang von Goethe

Beauty is in the heart of the beholder.
H. G. Wells

Beauty is not caused. It is.
Emily Dickinson

Beauty in things exists in the mind which contemplates them.
David Hume

Beauty is all very well at first sight; but who ever looks at it when it has been in the house three days?
George Bernard Shaw

Beauty is only temporary, but your mind lasts you a lifetime.
Alicia Machado

There is no definition of beauty, but when you can see someone's spirit coming through, something unexplainable, that's beautiful to me.
Liv Tyler

Beauty is everywhere a welcome guest.
Johann Wolfgang von Goethe

Since love grows within you, so beauty grows. For love is the beauty of the soul.
Saint Augustine

Beauty is a fragile gift.
Ovid

The problem with beauty is that it's like being born rich and getting poorer.
Joan Collins

Beauty and folly are old companions.
Benjamin Franklin

In every man's heart there is a secret nerve that answers to the vibrations of beauty.
Christopher Morley

Beauty, n: the power by which a woman charms a lover and terrifies a husband.
Ambrose Bierce

Flowers... are a proud assertion that a ray of beauty out values all the utilities of the world.
Ralph Waldo Emerson

I don't need plastic in my body to validate me as a woman.
Courtney Love

Beauty is variable, ugliness is constant.
Douglas Horton

'Handsome' means many things to many people. If people consider me handsome, I feel flattered - and have my parents to thank for it. Realistically, it doesn't hurt to be good-looking, especially in this business.
Richard Chamberlain

Beauty saves. Beauty heals. Beauty motivates. Beauty unites. Beauty returns us to our origins, and here lies the ultimate act of saving, of healing, of overcoming dualism.
Matthew Fox

God gave me a great body and it's my duty to take care of my physical temple.
Jean Claude Van Damme

Having inner beauty is something you develop on your own, and I like to think I have that.
Cindy Margolis

Beauty is less important than quality.
Eugene Ormandy

Beauty itself is but the sensible image of the Infinite.
Francis Bacon

Every year of my life I grow more convinced that it is wisest and best to fix our attention on the beautiful and the good, and dwell as little as possible on the evil and the false.
Richard Cecil

Imagination disposes of everything; it creates beauty, justice, and happiness, which are everything in this world.
Blaise Pascal

I define nothing. Not beauty, not patriotism. I take each thing as it is, without prior rules about what it should be.
Bob Dylan

Love built on beauty, soon as beauty, dies.
John Donne

Beauty is whatever gives joy.
Edna St. Vincent Millay

Beauty is the first present nature gives to women and the first it takes away.
Fay Weldon

There is a kind of beauty in imperfection.
Conrad Hall

Dear God! how beauty varies in nature and art. In a woman the flesh must be like marble; in a statue the marble must be like flesh.
Victor Hugo

Taking joy in living is a woman's best cosmetic.
Rosalind Russell

In youth and beauty, wisdom is but rare!
Homer

Heat cannot be separated from fire, or beauty from The Eternal.
Dante Alighieri

I gave my beauty and my youth to men. I am going to give my wisdom and experience to animals.
Brigitte Bardot

For me the greatest beauty always lies in the greatest clarity.
Gotthold Ephraim Lessing

Rare is the union of beauty and purity.
Juvenal

Beauty is the promise of happiness.
Edmund Burke

I'd like to grow up and be beautiful. I know it doesn't matter, but it doesn't hurt.
Kirsten Dunst

Beauty is only skin deep.
Thomas Overbury

Inner beauty should be the most important part of improving one's self.
Priscilla Presley

I sincerely feel that beauty largely comes from within.
Christy Turlington

The real sin against life is to abuse and destroy beauty, even one's own even more, one's own, for that has been put in our care and we are responsible for its well-being.
Katherine Anne Porter

Zest is the secret of all beauty. There is no beauty that is attractive without zest.
Christian Dior

Let us live for the beauty of our own reality.
Charles Lamb

How goodness heightens beauty!
Milan Kundera

We live in a wonderful world that is full of beauty, charm and adventure. There is no end to the adventures that we can have if only we seek them with our eyes open.
Jawaharlal Nehru

The plainer the dress, the greater luster does beauty appear.
Edward F. Halifax

Beauty is our weapon against nature; by it we make objects, giving them limit, symmetry, proportion. Beauty halts and freezes the melting flux of nature.
Camille Paglia

Our hearts were drunk with a beauty Our eyes could never see.
George William Russell

Some guys say beauty is only skin deep. But when you walk into a party, you don't see somebody's brain. The initial contact has to be the sniffing.
James Caan

O human beauty, what a dream art thou, that we should cast our life and hopes away on thee!
Barry Cornwall

Goodness is beauty in the best estate.
Christopher Marlowe

My mother always called me an ugly weed, so I never was aware of anything until I was older. Plain girls should have someone telling them they are beautiful. Sometimes this works miracles.
Hedy Lamarr

Because beauty isn't enough, there must be something more.
Eva Herzigova

What beauty is, I know not, though it adheres to many things.
Albrecht Durer

Though beauty gives you a weird sense of entitlement, it's rather frightening and threatening to have others ascribe such importance to something you know you're just renting for a while.
Candice Bergen

When virtue and modesty enlighten her charms, the lust of a beautiful woman is brighter than the stars of heaven, and the influence of her power it is in vain to resist.
Akhenaton

You can only perceive real beauty in a person as they get older.
Anouk Aimee

Integrity reveals beauty.
Thomas Leonard

Even in the centuries which appear to us to be the most monstrous and foolish, the immortal appetite for beauty has always found satisfaction.
Charles Baudelaire

Personal beauty is a greater recommendation than any letter of reference.
Aristotle

I can't live without my beauty products. I love to be in my bathroom with my candles lit, morning, noon and night. I like taking hot baths and hot showers, using my body scrubs and lotions.
Traci Bingham

Real beauty is to be true to oneself. That's what makes me feel good.
Laetitia Casta

Like charity, I believe glamour should begin at home.
Loretta Young

My dad had this philosophy that if you tell children they're beautiful and wonderful then they believe it, and they will be. So I never thought I was unattractive. But I was never one of the girls at school who had lots of boyfriends.
Emily Mortimer

Real beauty knocks you a little bit off kilter.
David Byrne

There is hope and a kind of beauty in there somewhere, if you look for it.
H. R. Giger

We are learning, too, that the love of beauty is one of Nature's greatest healers.
Ellsworth Huntington

There is no cosmetic for beauty like happiness.
Maria Mitchell

You can't really say what is beautiful about a place, but the image of the place will remain vividly with you.
Tadao Ando

The love of beauty in its multiple forms is the noblest gift of the human cerebrum.
Alexis Carrel

When everything else physical
and mental seems to diminish,
the appreciation of beauty is
on the increase.
Bernard Berenson

Beauty is the sole ambition,
the exclusive goal of Taste.
Charles Baudelaire

BIRTHDAY

God gave us the gift of life; it is up to us to give ourselves the gift of living well.
Voltaire

All the world is birthday cake, so take a piece, but not too much.
George Harrison

How old would you be if you didn't know how old you are?
Satchel Paige

I think, at a child's birth, if a mother could ask a fairy godmother to endow it with the most useful gift, that gift should be curiosity.
Eleanor Roosevelt

Every year on your birthday, you get a chance to start new.
Sammy Hagar

A gift consists not in what is done or given, but in the intention of the giver or doer.
Lucius Annaeus Seneca

I hate birthdays.
Zane Grey

My father gave me the greatest gift anyone could give another person, he believed in me.
Jim Valvano

A friend never defends a husband who gets his wife an electric skillet for her birthday.
Erma Bombeck

For my birthday I got a humidifier and a de-humidifier... I put them in the same room and let them fight it out.
Steven Wright

The greatest gift that you can give to others is the gift of unconditional love and acceptance.
Brian Tracy

I remember when the candle shop burned down. Everyone stood around singing 'Happy Birthday.'
Steven Wright

A gift, with a kind countenance, is a double present.
Thomas Fuller

Thirty was so strange for me. I've really had to come to terms with the fact that I am now a walking and talking adult.
C. S. Lewis

There are three hundred and sixty-four days when you might get un-birthday presents, and only one for birthday presents, you know.
Lewis Carroll

About astrology and palmistry: they are good because they make people vivid and full of possibilities. They are communism at its best. Everybody has a birthday and almost everybody has a palm.
Kurt Vonnegut

You know you're getting old when you get that one candle on the cake. It's like, 'See if you can blow this out.'
Jerry Seinfeld

It is lovely, when I forget all birthdays, including my own, to find that somebody remembers me.
Ellen Glasgow

The way I see it, you should live everyday like it's your birthday.
Paris Hilton

I cried on my 18th birthday. I thought 17 was such a nice age. You're young enough to get away with things, but you're old enough, too.
Liv Tyler

The more you praise and celebrate your life, the more there is in life to celebrate.
Oprah Winfrey

It was on my fifth birthday that Papa put his hand on my shoulder and said, 'Remember, my son, if you ever need a helping hand, you'll find one at the end of your arm.'
Sam Levenson

You know you're getting old when the candles cost more than the cake.
Bob Hope

I wanted to buy a candle holder, but the store didn't have one. So I got a cake.
Mitch Hedberg

Presents don't really mean much to me. I don't want to sound mawkish, but - it was the realization that I have a great many people in my life who really love me, and who I really love.
Gabriel Byrne

I often buy myself presents. Sometimes I will spend $100,000 in one day in a posh boutique.
Celine Dion

Let them eat cake.
Marie Antoinette

I'm not materialistic. I believe in presents from the heart, like a drawing that a child does.
Victoria Beckham

Most of us can remember a time when a birthday - especially if it was one's own - brightened the world as if a second sun has risen.
Robert Staughton Lynd

There is still no cure for the common birthday.
John Glenn

To me - old age is always ten years older than I am.
John Burroughs

Being seventy is not a sin.
Golda Meir

Like many women my age, I am 28 years old.
Mary Schmich

Your children need your presence more than your presents.
Jesse Jackson

Let us celebrate the occasion with wine and sweet words.
Plautus

Our birthdays are feathers in the broad wing of time.
Jean Paul

If you look over the years, the styles have changed - the clothes, the hair, the production, the approach to the songs. The icing to the cake has changed flavors. But if you really look at the cake itself, it's really the same.
John Oates

I had a birthday one night on a farm we were shooting on. I walked into the tent, and there were 150 people waiting for me, all wearing masks of my face.
Stephen Hopkins

New Year's Day is every man's birthday.
Charles Lamb

The only thing better than

singing is more singing.
Ella Fitzgerald

I do like to shock and surprise people. When it's all in good fun, of course.
Ruth Warrick

My biggest hero, Gregory Peck, was my birthday present on April 14, 1973. I just sat and stared at him.
Loretta Lynn

I binge when I'm happy. When everything is going really well, every day is like I'm at a birthday party.
Kirstie Alley

I quit high school on my birthday. It was my senior year and I didn't see the point. This was 1962, and I was ready to make music.
Barry White

We have to be able to grow up. Our wrinkles are our medals of the passage of life. They are what we have been through and who we want to be.
Lauren Hutton

Handmade presents are scary because they reveal that you have too much free time.
Doug Coupland

If you can give your child only one gift, let it be enthusiasm.
Bruce Barton

Love the giver more than the gift.
Brigham Young

Would ye both eat your cake and have your cake?
John Heywood

The return of my birthday, if I remember it, fills me with thoughts which it seems to be the general care of humanity to escape.
Samuel Johnson

The best way to remember your wife's birthday is to remember it once.
E. Joseph Cossman

We'll take the cake with the red cherry on top.
Navjot Singh Sidhu

I crashed my boyfriend's birthday when I was 12 years old. He didn't invite me and so I showed up.
Isla Fisher

My mother asked me what I wanted for my birthday, so I said I wanted to read poetry with her.
Guy Johnson

When someone asks if you'd like cake or pie, why not say you want cake and pie?
Lisa Loeb

To my surprise, my 70s are nicer than my 60s and my 60s than my 50s, and I wouldn't wish my teens and 20s on my enemies.
Lionel Blue

The main prank that we play with props is for people's birthdays. The special effects people will put a little explosive in the cake so it blows up in their face - that's always fun to play on a guest star, or one of the trainees or someone who's new.
Catherine Bell

Only then, approaching my fortieth birthday, I made philosophy my life's work.
Karl Jaspers

In 1993 my birthday present was a star on Hollywood's Walk of Fame.
Annette Funicello

When I turned 60, it didn't bother me at all.
Yoko Ono

I used to be good with kids, but as I get older, I'm grumpy and terrible with them. As for doing a gig at a 6-year old's birthday party, you couldn't pay me enough.
Johnny Vegas

When I was little I thought, isn't it nice that everybody celebrates on my birthday? Because it's July 4th.
Gloria Stuart

I'm amazed. When I was 40, I thought I'd never make 50. And at 50 I thought the frosting on the cake would be 60. At 60, I was still going strong and enjoying everything.
Gloria Stuart

This is a wonderful way to celebrate an 80th birthday... I wanted to be 65 again, but they wouldn't let me - Homeland Security.
Art Buchwald

BUSINESS

Whenever you find yourself on the side of the majority, it is time to pause and reflect.
Mark Twain

No enterprise is more likely to succeed than one concealed from the enemy until it is ripe for execution.
Niccolo Machiavelli

All lasting business is built on friendship.
Alfred A. Montapert

A budget tells us what we can't afford, but it doesn't keep us from buying it.
William Feather

It is not from the benevolence of the butcher, the brewer, or the baker that we expect our dinner, but from their regard to their own interest.
Adam Smith

The superior man understands what is right; the inferior man understands what will sell.
Confucius

I want to put a ding in the universe.
Steve Jobs

Hell, there are no rules here - we're trying to accomplish something.
Thomas A. Edison

A cardinal principle of Total Quality escapes too many managers: you cannot continuously improve interdependent systems and processes until you progressively perfect interdependent, interpersonal relationships.
Stephen Covey

Most of the important things in the world have been accomplished by people who have kept on trying when there seemed to be no hope at all.
Dale Carnegie

If one does not know to which port one is sailing, no wind is favorable.
Lucius Annaeus Seneca

And while the law of competition may be sometimes hard for the individual, it is best for the race, because it ensures the survival of the fittest in every department.
Andrew Carnegie

There is only one boss. The customer. And he can fire everybody in the company from the chairman on down, simply by spending his money somewhere else.
Sam Walton

An economist is an expert who will know tomorrow why the things he predicted yesterday didn't happen today.
Laurence J. Peter

Just because something doesn't do what you planned it to do doesn't mean it's useless.
Thomas A. Edison

The hardest thing to understand in the world is the income tax.
Albert Einstein

Effort only fully releases its reward after a person refuses to quit.
Napoleon Hill

Failure doesn't mean you are a failure it just means you haven't succeeded yet.
Robert H. Schuller

As a small businessperson, you have no greater leverage than the truth.
John Greenleaf Whittier

Business, more than any other occupation, is a continual dealing with the future; it is a continual calculation, an instinctive exercise in foresight.
Henry R. Luce

An advertising agency is 85 percent confusion and 15 percent commission.
Fred Allen

Business, that's easily defined - it's other people's money.
Peter Drucker

Anyone who has lost track of time when using a computer knows the propensity to dream, the urge to make dreams come true and the tendency to miss lunch.
Tim Berners-Lee

There are no secrets to success. It is the result of preparation, hard work, and learning from failure.
Colin Powell

Almost all quality improvement comes via simplification of design, manufacturing... layout, processes, and procedures.
Tom Peters

Don't let your ego get too close to your position, so that if your position gets shot down, your ego doesn't go with it.
Colin Powell

Sometimes when you innovate, you make mistakes. It is best to admit them quickly, and get on with improving your other innovations.
Steve Jobs

Every day I get up and look through the Forbes list of the richest people in America. If I'm not there, I go to work.
Robert Orben

Corporation: An ingenious device for obtaining profit without individual responsibility.
Ambrose Bierce

Business is never so healthy as when, like a chicken, it must do a certain amount of scratching around for what it gets.
Henry Ford

About the time we can make the ends meet, somebody moves the ends.
Herbert Hoover

Do more than is required. What is the distance between someone who achieves their goals consistently and those who spend their lives and careers merely following? The extra mile.
Gary Ryan Blair

If you owe the bank $100 that's your problem. If you owe the bank $100 million, that's the bank's problem.
J. Paul Getty

If you listen to your fears, you will die never knowing what a great person you might have been.
Robert H. Schuller

If you cannot work with love but only with distaste, it is better that you should leave your work.
Khalil Gibran

The majority of men meet with failure because of their lack of persistence in creating new plans to take the place of those which fail.
Napoleon Hill
Business is a combination of

war and sport.
Andre Maurois

Ask five economists and you'll get five different answers - six if one went to Harvard.
Edgar R. Fiedler

In this world nothing can be said to be certain, except death and taxes.
Benjamin Franklin

Economic depression cannot be cured by legislative action or executive pronouncement. Economic wounds must be healed by the action of the cells of the economic body - the producers and consumers themselves.
Herbert Hoover

Every young man would do well to remember that all successful business stands on the foundation of morality.
Henry Ward Beecher

It's easy to make a buck. It's a lot tougher to make a difference.
Tom Brokaw

Cannibals prefer those who have no spines.
Stanislaw Lem

Happiness does not come from doing easy work but from the afterglow of satisfaction that comes after the achievement of a difficult task that demanded our best.
Theodore Isaac Rubin

A group or an artist shouldn't get his money until his boss gets his.
Bobby Darin

I am certainly not one of those who need to be prodded. In fact, if anything, I am the prod.
Winston Churchill

The secret of business is to know something that nobody else knows.
Aristotle Onassis

There is no time for cut-and-dried monotony. There is time for work. And time for love. That leaves no other time!
Coco Chanel

An economist's guess is liable to be as good as anybody else's.
Will Rogers

Blessed is he who has found his work; let him ask no other blessedness.
Thomas Carlyle

If there is anything that a man can do well, I say let him do it. Give him a chance.
Abraham Lincoln

Don't worry about people stealing your ideas. If your ideas are any good, you'll have to ram them down people's throats.
Howard Aiken

When in doubt, mumble; when in trouble, delegate; when in charge, ponder.
James H. Boren

I was told to avoid the business all together because of the rejection. People would say to me, 'Don't you want to have a normal job and a normal family?' I guess that would be good advice for some people, but I wanted to act.
Jennifer Aniston

Most of what we call management consists of making it difficult for people to get their work done.
Peter Drucker

Informed decision-making comes from a long tradition of guessing and then blaming others for inadequate results.
Scott Adams

The consumer isn't a moron; she is your wife.
David Ogilvy

The man who will use his skill and constructive imagination to see how much he can give for a dollar, instead of how little he can give for a dollar, is bound to succeed.
Henry Ford

Employees make the best dates. You don't have to pick them up and they're always tax-deductible.
Andy Warhol

I buy when other people are selling.
J. Paul Getty

High achievement always takes place in the framework of high expectation.
Charles Kettering

It takes more than capital to swing business. You've got to have the A. I. D. degree to get by - Advertising, Initiative, and Dynamics.
Isaac Asimov

In modern business it is not the crook who is to be feared most, it is the honest man who doesn't know what he is doing.
William Wordsworth

We succeed in enterprises which demand the positive qualities we possess, but we excel in those which can also make use of our defects.
Alexis de Tocqueville

Profit in business comes from repeat customers, customers that boast about your project or service, and that bring friends with them.
W. Edwards Deming

My son is now an 'entrepreneur.' That's what you're called when you don't have a job.
Ted Turner

The first responsibility of a leader is to define reality. The last is to say thank you. In between, the leader is a servant.
Max de Pree

The genius of a good leader is to leave behind him a situation which common sense, without the grace of genius, can deal with successfully.
Walter Lippmann

The buck stops with the guy who signs the checks.
Rupert Murdoch

Carpe per diem - seize the check.
Robin Williams

In the business world, everyone is paid in two coins: cash and experience. Take the experience first; the cash will come later.
Harold S. Geneen

If you don't drive your business, you will be driven out of business.
B. C. Forbes

Disneyland is a work of love. We didn't go into Disneyland just with the idea of making money.
Walt Disney

I find it rather easy to portray a businessman. Being bland, rather cruel and incompetent comes naturally to me.
John Cleese

Web users ultimately want to get at data quickly and easily. They don't care as much about attractive sites and pretty design.
Tim Berners-Lee

Wise are those who learn that the bottom line doesn't always have to be their top priority.
William Arthur Ward

So little done, so much to do.
Cecil Rhodes

Do not trust people. They are capable of greatness.
Stanislaw Lem

Perpetual optimism is a force multiplier.
Colin Powell

Time is the scarcest resource and unless it is managed nothing else can be managed.
Peter Drucker

Nothing so conclusively proves a man's ability to lead others as what he does from day to day to lead himself.
Thomas J. Watson

Business is in itself a power.
Garet Garrett

The invisible hand of the market always moves faster and better than the heavy hand of government.
Mitt Romney

If you can build a business up big enough, it's respectable.
Will Rogers

Regard it as just as desirable to build a chicken house as to build a cathedral.
Frank Lloyd Wright

It usually takes me more than three weeks to prepare a good impromptu speech.
Mark Twain

The way to get things done is not to mind who gets the credit for doing them.
Benjamin Jowett

One of the tests of leadership is the ability to recognize a problem before it becomes an emergency.
Arnold H. Glasow

The final test of a leader is that he leaves behind him in other men the conviction and the will to carry on.
Walter Lippmann

Reason and judgment are the qualities of a leader.
Tacitus

Don't simply retire from something; have something to retire to.
Harry Emerson Fosdick

The fastest way to succeed is to look as if you're playing by somebody else's rules, while quietly playing by your own.
Michael Korda

If all the economists were laid end to end, they'd never reach a conclusion.
George Bernard Shaw

Our work is the presentation of our capabilities.
Edward Gibbon

I'm not a driven businessman, but a driven artist. I never think about money. Beautiful things make money.
Lord Acton

I rate enthusiasm even above professional skill.
Edward Appleton

Punctuality is one of the cardinal business virtues: always insist on it in your subordinates.
Don Marquis

Try, try, try, and keep on trying is the rule that must be followed to become an expert in anything.
W. Clement Stone

There are two kinds of companies, those that work to try to charge more and those that work to charge less. We will be the second.
Jeff Bezos

Our favorite holding period is forever.
Warren Buffett

Inside every working anarchy, there's an Old Boy Network.
Mitchell Kapor

Definition of Statistics: The science of producing unreliable facts from reliable figures.
Evan Esar

The herd instinct among forecasters makes sheep look like independent thinkers.
Edgar R. Fiedler

What we actually learn, from any given set of circumstances, determines whether we become increasingly powerless or more powerful.
Blaine Lee

Our business is infested with idiots who try to impress by using pretentious jargon.
David Ogilvy

People will buy anything that is 'one to a customer.'
Sinclair Lewis

It's not what you pay a man, but what he costs you that counts.
Will Rogers

The gambling known as business looks with austere disfavor upon the business known as gambling.
Ambrose Bierce

The best measure of a man's honesty isn't his income tax return. It's the zero adjust on his bathroom scale.
Arthur C. Clarke

Remind people that profit is the difference between revenue and expense. This makes you look smart.
Scott Adams

Only a monopolist could study a business and ruin it by giving away products.
Scott McNealy

It's called a pen. It's like a printer, hooked straight to my brain.
Dale Dauten

We don't have a monopoly. We have market share. There's a difference.
Steve Ballmer

The leader who exercises power with honor will work from the inside out, starting with himself.
Blaine Lee

The great leaders are like the best conductors - they reach beyond the notes to reach the magic in the players.
Blaine Lee

The most important quality in a leader is that of being acknowledged as such. All leaders whose fitness is questioned are clearly lacking in force.
Andre Maurois

To command is to serve, nothing more and nothing less.
Andre Malraux

One's mind has a way of making itself up in the background, and it suddenly becomes clear what one means to do.
A. C. Benson

Real riches are the riches possessed inside.
B. C. Forbes

The incestuous relationship between government and big business thrives in the dark.
Jack Anderson

The meek shall inherit the Earth, but not its mineral rights.
J. Paul Getty

Every few seconds it changes - up an eighth, down an eighth - it's like playing a slot machine. I lose $20 million, I gain $20 million.
Ted Turner

I get to play golf for a living. What more can you ask for - getting paid for doing what you love.
Tiger Woods

I think that there is nothing, not even crime, more opposed to poetry, to philosophy, ay, to life itself than this incessant business.
Henry David Thoreau

Government in the U.S. today is a senior partner in every business in the country.
Norman Cousins

What's the subject of life - to get rich? All of those fellows out there getting rich could be dancing around the real subject of life.
Paul A. Volcker

The work of the individual still remains the spark that moves mankind ahead even more than teamwork.
Igor Sikorsky

I don't think meals have any business being deductible. I'm for separation of calories and corporations.
Ralph Nader

The work an unknown good man has done is like a vein of water flowing hidden underground, secretly making the ground green.
Thomas Carlyle

Sooner or later, those who win are those who think they can.
Paul Tournier

If the career you have chosen has some unexpected inconvenience, console yourself by reflecting that no career is without them.
Jane Fonda

Like dogs in a wheel, birds in a cage, or squirrels in a chain, ambitious men still climb and climb, with great labor, and incessant anxiety, but never reach the top.
Robert Browning

If you aren't playing well, the game isn't as much fun. When that happens I tell myself just to go out and play as I did when I was a kid.
Thomas J. Watson

Look at growth, look at how much time people spend on the Net and look at the variety of things that they are doing. It's all really good, so I am actually encouraged by the fundamentals that underlie usage growth on the Net.
Meg Whitman

What we've gone through in the last several years has caused some people to question 'Can we trust Microsoft?'
Steve Ballmer

To think that the new economy is over is like somebody in London in 1830 saying the entire industrial revolution is over because some textile manufacturers in Manchester went broke.
Alvin Toffler

Not for nothing is their motto TGIF - 'Thank God It's Friday.' They live for the weekends, when they can go do what they really want to do.
Richard Nelson Bolles

Definition of a Statistician: A man who believes figures don't lie, but admits than under analysis some of them won't stand up either.
Evan Esar

If you have to forecast, forecast often.
Edgar R. Fiedler

Whenever an individual or a business decides that success has been attained, progress stops.
Thomas J. Watson

Success or failure in business is caused more by the mental attitude even than by mental capacities.
Walter Scott

You can't operate a company by fear, because the way to eliminate fear is to avoid criticism. And the way to avoid criticism is to do nothing.
Steve Ross

Meetings are indispensable when you don't want to do anything.
John Kenneth Galbraith

I've never felt like I was in the cookie business. I've always been in a feel good feeling business. My job is to sell joy. My job is to sell happiness. My job is to sell an experience.
Debbi Fields

Family farms and small businesses are the backbone of our communities.
Tom Allen

When did it become a problem to be a small businessman and become successful? The small businessman - like my father, or like me?
Glenn Beck

CAR

I spent a lot of money on booze, birds and fast cars. The rest I just squandered.
George Best

There was a time in my life when I thought I had everything - millions of dollars, mansions, cars, nice clothes, beautiful women, and every other materialistic thing you can imagine. Now I struggle for peace.
Richard Pryor

If GM had kept up with technology like the computer industry has, we would all be driving $25 cars that got 1,000 MPG.
Bill Gates

I had to stop driving my car for a while... the tires got dizzy.
Steven Wright

I hooked up my accelerator pedal in my car to my brake lights. I hit the gas, people behind me stop, and I'm gone.
Steven Wright

I replaced the headlights in my car with strobe lights, so it looks like I'm the only one moving.
Steven Wright

In less enlightened times, the best way to impress women was to own a hot car. But women wised up and realized it was better to buy their own hot cars so they wouldn't have to ride around with jerks.
Scott Adams

Car designers are just going to have to come up with an automobile that outlasts the payments.
Erma Bombeck

I would have probably stolen cars - it would have given me the same adrenaline rush as racing.
Valentino Rossi

But my passion is racing cars. It's what I like to do in my off time.
Mark-Paul Gosselaar

Americans are the only people in the world known to me whose status anxiety prompts them to advertise their college and university affiliations in the rear window of their automobiles.
Paul Fussell

It's like driving a car at night. You never see further than your headlights, but you can make the whole trip that way.
E. L. Doctorow

Drive-in banks were established so most of the cars today could see their real owners.
E. Joseph Cossman

The automobile engine will come, and then I will consider my life's work complete.
Rudolf Diesel

In Japan, they have TV sets in cars right now, where you can punch up traffic routes, weather, everything! You can get Internet access already in cars in Japan, so within the next 2 to 3 years it's gonna be so crazy!
Glenn Danzig

A car for every purse and purpose.
Alfred P. Sloan

When you are fitted in a racing car and you race to win, second or third place is not enough.
Ayrton Senna

My boyfriend keeps telling me I've got to own things. So, first I bought this car. And then he told me I oughta get a house. 'Why a house?' 'Well, you gotta have a place to park the car.'
Julia Roberts

Perhaps people, and kids especially, are spoiled today, because all the kids today have cars, it seems. When I was young you were lucky to have a bike.
James Cagney

It's a never ending battle of making your cars better and also trying to be better yourself.
Dale Earnhardt

We approach people the same way we approach our cars. We take the poor kid to a doctor and ask, What's wrong with him, how much will it cost, and when can I pick him up?
James Hillman

I think we have to act like stars because it is expected of us. So we drive our big cars and live in our smart houses.
Maurice Gibb

Auto racing is boring except when a car is going at least 172 miles per hour upside down.
Dave Barry

The greatest pleasure when I started making money was not buying cars or yachts but finding myself able to have as many freshly typed drafts as possible.
Gore Vidal

If all the cars in the United States were placed end to end, it would probably be Labor Day Weekend.
Doug Larson

When it comes to cars, only two varieties of people are possible - cowards and fools.
Russell Baker

My mom said the only reason men are alive is for lawn care and vehicle maintenance.
Tim Allen

Fast cars are my only vice.
Michael Bay

I've got two old Volvos, two old Subarus, and an old Ford Ranger. If you've got an old car, you've gotta have at least several old cars, 'cause one's always gonna be in the garage.
Rip Torn

No illusion is more crucial than the illusion that great success and huge money buy you immunity from the common ills of mankind, such as cars that won't start.
Larry McMurtry

I liken myself to Henry Ford and the auto industry, I give you 90 percent of what most people need.
Adam Osborne

Well, I always had a chauffeur, because I have never driven a car in my life. I still can't drive.
Bud Abbott

See, what you're meant to do when you have a mid-life crisis is buy a fast car, aren't you? Well, I've always had fast cars. It's not that. It's the fear that you're past your best. It's the fear that the stuff you've done in the past is your best work.
Robbie Coltrane

We need to become good citizens in the global village, instead of competing. What are we competing for - to drive more cars, eat more steaks? That will destroy the world.
Yuan T. Lee

I have a need to make these sorts of connections literal sometimes, and a vehicle often helps to do that. I have a relationship to car culture. It isn't really about loving cars. It's sort of about needing them.
Matthew Barney

Remote villages and communities have lost their identity, and their peace and charm have been sacrificed to that worst of abominations, the automobile.
James Norman Hall

You have to wait six months to purchase a fuel efficient automobile made from overseas.
Ed Markey

Family trips to Yellowstone and to what are now national parks in Southern Utah, driving the primitive roads and cars of that day, were real adventures.
Paul D. Boyer

We often attribute 'understanding' and other cognitive predicates by metaphor and analogy to cars, adding machines, and other artifacts, but nothing is proved by such attributions.
John Searle

Back in the mid-1970s, we adopted some fairly ambitious goals to improve efficiency of our cars. What did we get? We got a tremendous boost in efficiency.
Jay Inslee

You talk about German technocracy and you get automobiles.
Gordon Sinclair

The automobile, both a cause and an effect of this decentralization, is ideally suited for our vast landscape and our generally confused and contrary commuting patterns.
Brock Yates

I admit to wasting my life messing around with fast cars and motorcycles.
Brock Yates

More books, more racing and more foolishness with cars and motorcycles are in the works.
Brock Yates

We're just into toys, whether it's motorcycles or race cars or computers. I've got the Palm Pilot right here with me, I've got the world's smallest phone. Maybe it's just because I'm still a big little kid and I just love toys, you know?
Catherine Bell

There's three things men always talk about - women, sports, and cars.
Mario Lopez

I never rode in an automobile until I was 12.
Loretta Lynn

Ikea people do not drive flashy cars or stay at luxury hotels.
Ingvar Kamprad

I love fast cars... and to go too fast in them.
Lara Flynn Boyle

I had more clothes than I had closets, more cars than garage space, but no money.
Sammy Davis, Jr.

I've always had an inquisitive mind about everything from flowers to television sets to motor cars. Always pulled them apart - couldn't put 'em back, but always extremely interested in how things work.
Craig Johnston

I would never kill a living thing, although I probably have inadvertently while driving automobiles.
Don Van Vliet

Not having to own a car has made me realize what a waste of time the automobile is.
Diane Johnson

The cars we drive say a lot about us.
Alexandra Paul

I had never been able to get a car that said how much I cared about the environment until I drove electric.
Alexandra Paul

Environmentalists have a very conflicted relationship with their cars.
Tom-Arnold

Societies need rules that make no sense for individuals. For example, it makes no difference whether a single car drives on the left or on the right. But it makes all the difference when there are many cars!
Marvin Minsky

But to personally satisfy my own adrenalin needs, I've been racing cars a little bit, which has been fun.
Picabo Street

CHANGE

If you don't like something, change it. If you can't change it, change your attitude.
Maya Angelou

God grant me the serenity to accept the things I cannot change, the courage to change the things I can, and the wisdom to know the difference.
Reinhold Niebuhr

All changes, even the most longed for, have their melancholy; for what we leave behind us is a part of ourselves; we must die to one life before we can enter another.
Anatole France

Everyone thinks of changing the world, but no one thinks of changing himself.
Leo Tolstoy

Always remember that the future comes one day at a time.
Dean Acheson

Action and reaction, ebb and flow, trial and error, change - this is the rhythm of living. Out of our over-confidence, fear; out of our fear, clearer vision, fresh hope. And out of hope, progress.
Bruce Barton

Any change, even a change for the better, is always accompanied by drawbacks and discomforts.
Arnold Bennett

It may be hard for an egg to turn into a bird: it would be a jolly sight harder for it to learn to fly while remaining an egg. We are like eggs at present. And you cannot go on indefinitely being just an ordinary, decent egg. We must be hatched or go bad.
C. S. Lewis

All change is not growth, as all movement is not forward.
Ellen Glasgow

If there is no struggle, there is no progress.
Frederick Douglass

If there is anything that we wish to change in the child, we should first examine it and see whether it is not something that could better be changed in ourselves.
Carl Jung

If we don't change, we don't grow. If we don't grow, we aren't really living.
Gail Sheehy

Because things are the way they are, things will not stay the way they are.
Bertolt Brecht

Change means that what was before wasn't perfect. People want things to be better.
Esther Dyson

Change before you have to.
Jack Welch

Things do not change; we change.
Henry David Thoreau

He who rejects change is the architect of decay. The only human institution which rejects progress is the cemetery.
Harold Wilson

Only the wisest and stupidest of men never change.
Confucius

It's the most unhappy people who most fear change.
Mignon McLaughlin

If you're in a bad situation, don't worry it'll change. If you're in a good situation, don't worry it'll change.
John A. Simone, Sr.

Change in all things is sweet.
Aristotle

They must often change, who would be constant in happiness or wisdom.
Confucius

Change alone is eternal, perpetual, immortal.
Arthur Schopenhauer

Christians are supposed not merely to endure change, nor even to profit by it, but to cause it.
Harry Emerson Fosdick

Anyone who thinks there's safety in numbers hasn't looked at the stock market pages.
Irene Peter

The only way to make sense out of change is to plunge into it, move with it, and join the dance.
Alan Watts

Never believe that a few caring people can't change the world. For, indeed, that's all who ever have.
Margaret Mead

Without change, something sleeps inside us, and seldom awakens. The sleeper must awaken.
Frank Herbert

Just when I think I have learned the way to live, life changes.
Hugh Prather

Change brings opportunity.
Nido Qubein

Change is the only constant. Hanging on is the only sin.
Denise McCluggage

Lord, where we are wrong, make us willing to change; where we are right, make us easy to live with.
Peter Marshall

We live in a moment of history where change is so speeded up that we begin to see the present only when it is already disappearing.
R. D. Laing

Without accepting the fact that everything changes, we cannot find perfect composure. But unfortunately, although it is true, it is difficult for us to accept it. Because we cannot accept the truth of transience, we suffer.
Shunryu Suzuki

We all have big changes in our lives that are more or less a second chance.
Harrison Ford

He that will not apply new remedies must expect new evils; for time is the greatest innovator.
Francis Bacon

A lot of people get impatient with the pace of change.
James Levine

Just because everything is different doesn't mean anything has changed.
Irene Peter

Life belongs to the living, and he who lives must be prepared for changes.
Johann Wolfgang von Goethe

When you are through changing, you are through.
Bruce Barton

Not only is women's work never done, the definition keeps changing.
Bill Copeland

Relentless, repetitive self talk is what changes our self-image.
Denis Waitley

When you jump for joy, beware that no one moves the ground from beneath your feet.
Stanislaw Lec

The world hates change, yet it is the only thing that has brought progress.
Charles Kettering

The world is changing very fast. Big will not beat small anymore. It will be the fast beating the slow.
Rupert Murdoch

Things alter for the worse spontaneously, if they be not altered for the better designedly.
Francis Bacon

You must welcome change as the rule but not as your ruler.
Denis Waitley

I don't know if you can change things, but it's a drop in the ocean.
Julie Walters

We emphasize that we believe in change because we were born of it, we have lived by it, we prospered and grew great by it. So the status quo has never been our god, and we ask no one else to bow down before it.
Carl T. Rowan

Change is such hard work.
Billy Crystal

If you want to change the culture, you will have to start by changing the organization.
Mary Douglas

The mind has exactly the same power as the hands; not merely to grasp the world, but to change it.
Colin Wilson

You could always go on changing things but there comes a time when you have to decide to stop.
Peter Wright

If you can change three lives in 10, three lives in a hundred, that's got to be good, hasn't it?
Ian Botham

What we call progress is the exchange of one nuisance for another nuisance.
Havelock Ellis

There is a danger of changing too much in the search for perfection.
Agnetha Faltskog

In a progressive country change is constant; change is inevitable.
Benjamin Disraeli

COMPUTERS

A computer once beat me at chess, but it was no match for me at kick boxing.
Emo Philips

Computers make it easier to do a lot of things, but most of the things they make it easier to do don't need to be done.
Andy Rooney

I think computer viruses should count as life. I think it says something about human nature that the only form of life we have created so far is purely destructive. We've created life in our own image.
Stephen Hawking

Computers are like Old Testament gods; lots of rules and no mercy.
Joseph Campbell

A wonderful thing about a book, in contrast to a computer screen, is that you can take it to bed with you.
Daniel J. Boorstin

I think it's fair to say that personal computers have become the most empowering tool we've ever created. They're tools of communication, they're tools of creativity, and they can be shaped by their user.
Bill Gates

Computers are useless. They can only give you answers.
Pablo Picasso

I do not fear computers. I fear the lack of them.
Isaac Asimov

Never trust a computer you can't throw out a window.
Steve Wozniak

Computers are magnificent tools for the realization of our dreams, but no machine can replace the human spark of spirit, compassion, love, and understanding.
Louis Gerstner

Personally, I rather look forward to a computer program winning the world chess championship. Humanity needs a lesson in humility.
Richard Dawkins

Treat your password like your toothbrush. Don't let anybody else use it, and get a new one every six months.
Clifford Stoll

The real danger is not that computers will begin to think like men, but that men will begin to think like computers.
Sydney J. Harris

Computing is not about computers any more. It is about living.
Nicholas Negroponte

Part of the inhumanity of the computer is that, once it is competently programmed and working smoothly, it is completely honest.
Isaac Asimov

Access to computers and the Internet has become a basic need for education in our society.
Kent Conrad

Security is, I would say, our top priority because for all the exciting things you will be able to do with computers - organizing your lives, staying in touch with people, being creative - if we don't solve these security problems, then people will hold back.
Bill Gates

Computer science is no more about computers than astronomy is about telescopes.
Edsger Dijkstra

No one ever said on their deathbed, 'Gee, I wish I had spent more time alone with my computer'.
Danielle Berry

Computers may save time but they sure waste a lot of paper. About 98 percent of everything printed out by a computer is garbage that no one ever reads.
Andy Rooney

The computer is a moron.
Peter Drucker

Home computers are being called upon to perform many new functions, including the consumption of homework formerly eaten by the dog.
Doug Larson

I am not the only person who uses his computer mainly for the purpose of diddling with his computer.
Dave Barry

Many of our own people here in this country do not ask about computers, telephones and television sets. They ask - when will we get a road to our village.
Thabo Mbeki

I am regularly asked what the average Internet user can do to ensure his security. My first answer is usually 'Nothing; you're screwed'.
Bruce Scheneier

There is no reason for any individual to have a computer in his home.
Ken Olsen

I happen to think that computers are the most important thing to happen to musicians since the invention of cat-gut which was a long time ago.
Robert Moog

Computers are famous for being able to do complicated things starting from simple programs.
Seth Lloyd

Because I believe that humans are computers, I conjectured that computers, like people, can have left- and right-handed versions.
Philip Emeagwali

You couldn't have fed the '50s into a computer and come out with the '60s.
Paul Kantner

The digital revolution is far more significant than the invention of writing or even of printing.
Douglas Engelbart

The Internet is not just one thing, it's a collection of things - of numerous communications networks that all speak the same digital language.
Jim Clark

The Internet: transforming society and shaping the future through chat.
Dave Barry

It's been my policy to view the Internet not as an 'information highway,' but as an electronic asylum filled with babbling loonies.
Mike Royko

Bill Gates is the pope of the personal computer industry. He decides who's going to build.
Larry Ellison

What do we want our kids to do? Sweep up around Japanese computers?
Walter F. Mondale

Think? Why think! We have computers to do that for us.
Jean Rostand

To err is human, but to really foul things up you need a computer.
Paul R. Ehrlich

I was afraid of the internet... because I couldn't type.
Jack Welch

To err is human - and to blame it on a computer is even more so.
Robert Orben

As a rule, software systems do not work well until they have been used, and have failed repeatedly, in real applications.
Dave Parnas

Reading computer manuals without the hardware is as frustrating as reading manuals without the software.
Arthur C. Clarke

Imagine if every Thursday your shoes exploded if you tied them the usual way. This happens to us all the time with computers, and nobody thinks of complaining.
Jef Raskin

The new information technology... Internet and e-mail... have practically eliminated the physical costs of communications.
Peter Drucker

Yet in this global economy, no jobs are safe. High-speed Internet connections and low-cost, skilled labor overseas are an explosive combination.
Bob Taft

If your computer speaks English, it was probably made in Japan.
Alan Perlis

In computing, turning the obvious into the useful is a living definition of the word "frustration".
Alan Perlis

The only legitimate use of a computer is to play games.
Eugene Jarvis

Right now, computers, which are supposed to be our servant, are oppressing us.
Jef Raskin

Software comes from heaven when you have good hardware.
Ken Olsen

The internet is not for sissies.
Paul Vixie

The good news about computers is that they do what you tell them to do. The bad news is that they do what you tell them to do.
Ted Nelson

I'm a '70s mom, and my daughter is a '90s mom. I know a lot of women my age who are real computer freaks.
Florence Henderson

It's hardware that makes a machine fast. It's software that makes a fast machine slow.
Craig Bruce

The future lies in designing and selling computers that people don't realize are computers at all.
Adam Osborne

People think computers will keep them from making mistakes. They're wrong. With computers you make mistakes faster.
Adam Osborne

Modern people are only willing to believe in their computers, while I believe in myself.
Alain Robert

The question of whether a computer can think is no more interesting than the question of whether a submarine can swim.
Edsger Dijkstra

One of the most feared expressions in modern times is 'The computer is down.'
Norman Ralph Augustine

Supercomputers will achieve one human brain capacity by 2010, and personal computers will do so by about 2020.
Ray Kurzweil

What I try to do is factor in how people use computers, what people's problems are, and how these technologies can get applied to those problems. Then I try to direct the various product groups to act on this information.
John Warnock

I've tried word processors, but I think I'm too old a dog to use one.
Dee Brown

I just became one with my browser software.
Bill Griffith

If you like overheads, you'll love PowerPoint.
Edward Tufte

We're entering a new world in which data may be more important than software.
Tim O'Reilly

We demand privacy, yet we glorify those that break into computers.
Bill McCollum

Every piece of software written today is likely going to infringe on someone else's patent.
Miguel de Icaza

Gee, I am a complete Luddite when it comes to computers, I can barely log on!
Jonathan Shapiro

Steve Wozniak and Steve Jobs founded Apple Inc, which set the computing world on its ear with the Macintosh in 1984.
Kevin Mitnick

I wouldn't know how to find eBay on the computer if my life depended on it.
Marc Jacobs

I got up with my wife, I sat down at the computer when she went to work, and I didn't stop until she got home.
George Stephen

I'm too old-fashioned to use a computer. I'm too old-fashioned to use a quill.
Christopher Plummer

I started on an Apple II, which I had bought at the very end of 1978 for half of my annual income. I made $4,500 a year, and I spent half of it on the computer.
Bill Budge

The power of the computer is starting to spread.
Bill Budge

The basis of computer work is predicated on the idea that only the brain makes decisions and only the index finger does the work.
Brian Eno

In the practical world of computing, it is rather uncommon that a program, once it performs correctly and satisfactorily, remains unchanged forever.
Niklaus Wirth

Man, I don't want to have nothing to do with computers. I don't want the government in my business.
Erykah Badu

You can't trust the internet.
Nicolette Sheridan

When I write software, I know that it will fail, either due to my own mistake, or due to some other cause.
Wietse Venema

It was a black and white only computer at the time, but it kept me fascinated.
Buffy Sainte-Marie

Computers have virtually replaced tape recorders.
Tony Visconti

If you could utilize the resources of the end users' computers, you could do things much more efficiently.
Niklas Zennstrom

What I was proud of was that I used very few parts to build a computer that could actually speak words on a screen and type words on a keyboard and run a programming language that could play games. And I did all this myself.
Steve Wozniak

Even when I work with computers, with high technology, I always try to put in the touch of the hand.
Issey Miyake

Nanotechnology will let us build computers that are incredibly powerful. We'll have more power in the volume of a sugar cube than exists in the entire world today.
Ralph Merkle

Shareware tends to combine the worst of commercial software with the worst of free software.
Linus Torvalds

To err is human but to really foul up requires a computer.
Dan Rather

Computers in classrooms are the filmstrips of the 1990s.
Clifford Stoll

If net neutrality goes away, it will fundamentally change everything about the Internet.
James Hilton

I got interested in computers and how they could be enslaved to the megalomaniac impulses of a teenager.
Eugene Jarvis

Even in the developing parts of the world, kids take to computers like fish to water.
Nicholas Negroponte

We can do things that we never could before. Stop-motion lets you build tiny little worlds, and computers make that world even more believable.
Nick Park

The Internet is a powerful way to make lots of money... But we are not going to buy Yahoo!
Sumner Redstone

What we did not imagine was a Web of people, but a Web of documents.
Dale Dougherty

I do two things. I design mobile computers and I study brains.
Jeff Hawkins

DAD

Dad, wherever you are, you are gone but you will never be forgotten.
Conrad Hall

When a father gives to his son, both laugh; when a son gives to his father, both cry.
William Shakespeare

It is a wise father that knows his own child.
William Shakespeare

Dad taught me everything I know. Unfortunately, he didn't teach me everything he knows.
Al Unser

When one has not had a good father, one must create one.
Friedrich Nietzsche

My father? I never knew him. Never even seen a picture of him.
Eminem

A father is a man who expects his son to be as good a man as he meant to be, A father is someone who carries pictures where his money used to be.
Frank Howard Clark

You don't have to deserve your mother's love. You have to deserve your father's.
Robert Frost

It is easier for a father to have children than for children to have a real father.
Pope John XXIII

Every parent is at some time the father of the unreturned prodigal, with nothing to do but keep his house open to hope.
John Ciardi

A father is always making his baby into a little woman. And when she is a woman he turns her back again.
Enid Bagnold

To a father growing old nothing is dearer than a daughter.
Euripides

I made a decision when my father passed away that I was going to be who God made me to be and not try to preach like my father.
Joel Osteen

I just wish I could understand my father.
Michael Jackson

Dad was the only adult male I ever trusted.
Michael Reagan

Fathers are biological necessities, but social accidents.
Margaret Mead

I have never been a material girl. My father always told me never to love anything that cannot love you back.
Imelda Marcos

Babies don't need fathers, but mothers do. Someone who is taking care of a baby needs to be taken care of.
Amy Heckerling

I stopped loving my father a long time ago. What remained was the slavery to a pattern.
Anais Nin

I am not ashamed to say that no man I ever met was my father's equal, and I never loved any other man as much.
Hedy Lamarr

It doesn't matter who my father was; it matters who I remember he was.
Anne Sexton

When I was 18, I thought my father was pretty dumb. After a while when I got to be 21, I was amazed to find out how much he'd learned in three years.
Frank Butler

Father told me that if I ever met a lady in a dress like yours, I must look her straight in the eyes.
Prince Charles

My father was my teacher. But most importantly he was a great dad.
Beau Bridges

Being a father, being a friend, those are the things that make me feel successful.
William Hurt

I kept my babies fed. I could have dumped them, but I didn't. I decided that whatever trip I was on, they were going with me. You're looking at a real daddy.
Barry White

One father is more than a hundred schoolmasters.
George Herbert

An angry father is most cruel towards himself.
Publilius Syrus

What harsh judges fathers are to all young men!
Terence

A man knows when he is growing old because he begins to look like his father.
Gabriel Garcia Marquez

It is much easier to become a father than to be one.
Kent Nerburn

I never had a speech from my father 'this is what you must do or shouldn't do' but I just learned to be led by example. My father wasn't perfect.
Adam Sandler

Whenever I fail as a father or husband... a toy and a diamond always works.
Shahrukh Khan

A father's disappointment can be a very powerful tool.
Michael Bergin

Being a father helps me be more responsible... you see more things than you've ever seen.
Kid Rock

But the love of adventure was in father's blood.
Buffalo Bill

As a little girl I used to daydream about my real father coming on a white horse to rescue me.
Christine Keeler

My father-in-law gets up at 5 o'clock in the morning and watches the Discovery Channel. I don't know why there's this big rush to do this.
Jeff Foxworthy

I know that I will never find my father in any other man who comes into my life, because it is a void in my life that can only be filled by him.
Halle Berry

Whoever does not have a good father should procure one.
Friedrich Nietzsche

A dramatic thing, the first time you stand up to your dad.
Lenny Kravitz

The place of the father in the modern suburban family is a very small one, particularly if he plays golf.
Bertrand Russell

If my father had hugged me even once, I'd be an accountant right now.
Ray Romano

There's sometimes a weird benefit to having an alcoholic, violent father. He really motivated me in that I never wanted to be anything like him.
Dean Koontz

Father or stepfather - those are just titles to me. They don't mean anything.
Oliver Hudson

It was my father who taught me to value myself. He told me that I was uncommonly beautiful and that I was the most precious thing in his life.
Dawn French

I decided in my life that I would do nothing that did not reflect positively on my father's life.
Sidney Poitier

I pressed my father's hand and told him I would protect his grave with my life. My father smiled and passed away to the spirit land.
Chief Joseph

As Daddy said, life is 95 percent anticipation.
Gloria Swanson

Feels good to try, but playing a father, I'm getting a little older. I see now that I'm taking it more serious and I do want that lifestyle.
Adam Sandler

I'm a father. It isn't just my life any more. I don't want my kid finding bottles in the house or seeing his father completely smashed.
Billie Joe Armstrong

Because of my father, we are that Shining City on a Hill.
Michael Reagan

My father taught me that the only way you can make good at anything is to practice, and then practice some more.
Pete Rose

I love my dad, although I'm definitely critical of him sometimes, like when his pants are too tight. But I love him so much and I try to be really supportive of him.
Liv Tyler

The surprising thing about fatherhood was finding my inner mush. Now I want to share it with the world.
Christopher Meloni

All the learnin' my father paid for was a bit o' birch at one end and an alphabet at the other.
George Eliot

My father was not a failure. After all, he was the father of a president of the United States.
Harry S. Truman

Humor is always based on a modicum of truth. Have you ever heard a joke about a father-in-law?
Dick Clark

No man is responsible for his father. That was entirely his mother's affair.
Margaret Turnbull

Undeservedly you will atone for the sins of your fathers.
Horace

That is the thankless position of the father in the family - the provider for all, and the enemy of all.
August Strindberg

To be as good as our fathers we must be better, imitation is not discipleship.
Wendell Phillips

The fundamental defect of fathers, in our competitive society, is that they want their children to be a credit to them.
Bertrand Russell

The time not to become a father is eighteen years before a war.
E. B. White

Rich men's sons are seldom rich men's fathers.
Herbert Kaufman

I'm a father; that's what matters most. Nothing matters more.
Gordon Brown

My father was an Episcopalian minister, and I've always been comforted by the power of prayer.
Anna Lee

I wanted to take up music, so my father bought me a blunt instrument. He told me to knock myself out.
Jay London

But I have to be careful not to let the world dazzle me so much that I forget that I'm a husband and a father.
Herbie Hancock

My father never raised his hand to any one of his children, except in self-defense.
Fred Allen

My father and I have a very good relationship. We always got along. But I always scold him.
Amy Sedaris

I would want my legacy to be that I was a great son, father and friend.
Dante Hall

So my father was a person who never lied to me. If I had a question, he answered it. I knew a lot of things at a young age because I was intrigued.
Nick Cannon

My father was always telling himself no one was perfect, not even my mother.
Broderick Crawford

My dad always said, 'Don't worry what people think, because you can't change it.'
Daisy Donovan

My grandfather, along with Carnegie, was a pioneer in philanthropy, which my father then practiced on a very large scale.
David Rockefeller

Fathers in today's modern families can be so many things.
Oliver Hudson

Child-rearing is my main interest now. I'm a hands-on father.
Sean Penn

My father was the guy on the block who said hi to everyone.
Damon Wayans

Employee fathers need to step up to the plate and put their family needs on the table.
James Levine

The most important influence in my childhood was my father.
DeForest Kelley

My father... had sharper eyes than the rest of our people.
Chief Joseph

I grew up not liking my father very much. I never saw him cry. But he must have. Everybody cries.
Charley Pride

No, I never thought about my father's money as my money.
Christie Hefner

I inherited that calm from my father, who was a farmer. You sow, you wait for good or bad weather, you harvest, but working is something you always need to do.
Miguel Indurain

One of my earliest memories is of my father carrying me in one arm with a picket sign in the other.
Camryn Manheim

When I was a kid, I used to imagine animals running under my bed. I told my dad, and he solved the problem quickly. He cut the legs off the bed.
Lou Brock

My father was something of a rainbow-chaser.
Marc Davis

My dad taught me true words you have to use in every relationship. Yes, baby.
Star Jones

My father wants me to be like my brother, but I can't be.
Robert Mapplethorpe

I would never have done what I'd done if I'd considered my father as somebody I wanted to please.
Robert Mapplethorpe

My father wouldn't get us a TV, he wouldn't allow a TV in the house.
Janis Joplin

I'm more comfortable with whatever's wrong with me than my father was whenever he felt he failed or didn't measure up to the standard he set.
John Malkovich

Thirteen, 13 children, and I love - I love them all. And I think I've been a good father to all of them.
Anthony Quinn

I have always thought of Walt Disney as my second father.
Annette Funicello

My father taught me how to substitute realities.
Mira Sorvino

I'm a fun father, but not a good father. The hard decisions always went to my wife.
John Lithgow

I wasn't anything special as a father. But I loved them and they knew it.
Sammy Davis, Jr.

I was punished for blowing the whistle on my father's lifestyle.
Tatum O'Neal

My father loved people, children and pets.
Tony Visconti

My father was grounded, a very meat-and-potatoes man. He was a baker.
Anthony Hopkins

Do you know that other than my father, I've never had a man take care of me?
Dionne Warwick

My father was the most rational and the most dispassionate of men.
Simon Newcomb

I love the comic opportunities that come up in the context of a father-son relationship.
Harrison Ford

I wanted to be a forest ranger or a coal man. At a very early age, I knew I didn't want to do what my dad did, which was work in an office.
Harrison Ford

Watching your husband become a father is really sexy and wonderful.
Cindy Crawford

I hope I am remembered by my children as a good father.
Orson Scott Card

My father, he was like the rock, the guy you went to with every problem.
Gwyneth Paltrow

My father was never anti-anything in our house.
Errol Flynn

It is impossible to please all the world and one's father.
Jean de La Fontaine

Nobody ever asks a father how he manages to combine marriage and a career.
Sam Ewing

I was raised by free-spirited people, though my father gave me a very strong work ethic.
Diane Lane

My father invented a cure for which there was no disease and unfortunately my mother caught it and died of it.
Victor Borge

When a father, absent during the day, returns home at six, his children receive only his temperament, not his teaching.
Robert Bly

The best money advice ever given me was from my father. When I was a little girl, he told me, 'Don't spend anything unless you have to.'
Dinah Shore

There is too much fathering going on just now and there is no doubt about it fathers are depressing.
Gertrude Stein

Sons have always a rebellious wish to be disillusioned by that which charmed their fathers.
Aldous Huxley

The child is father of the man.
William Wordsworth

Aeneas carried his aged father on his back from the ruins of Troy and so do we all, whether we like it or not, perhaps even if we have never known them.
Angela Carter

Being a father to my family and a husband is to me much more important than what I did in the business.
Tom Bosley

DATING

Nothing is perfect. Life is messy. Relationships are complex. Outcomes are uncertain. People are irrational.
Hugh Mackay

I don't have a girlfriend. But I do know a woman who'd be mad at me for saying that.
Mitch Hedberg

Save a boyfriend for a rainy day - and another, in case it doesn't rain.
Mae West

Falling in love and having a relationship are two different things.
Keanu Reeves

Assumptions are the termites of relationships.
Henry Winkler

I'm not the girl who always has a boyfriend. I'm the girl who rarely has a boyfriend.
Taylor Swift

I like the bad-boy types. Generally the guy I'm attracted to is the guy in the club with all the tattoos and nail polish. He's usually the lead singer in a punk band and plays guitar. But my serious boyfriends are relatively clean-cut, nice guys. So it's strange.
Megan Fox

Treasure your relationships, not your possessions.
Anthony J. D'Angelo

A relationship requires a lot of work and commitment.
Greta Scacchi

Nothing defines humans better than their willingness to do irrational things in the pursuit of phenomenally unlikely payoffs. This is the principle behind lotteries, dating, and religion.
Scott Adams

Do not just look at your boyfriend as just a boyfriend. Look at him as a friend, too.
Vanessa Hudgens

Real magic in relationships means an absence of judgment of others.
Wayne Dyer

You can't stop loving or wanting to love because when its right it's the best thing in the world. When you're in a relationship and its good, even if nothing else in your life is right, you feel like your whole world is complete.
Keith Sweat

However successful you are, there is no substitute for a close relationship. We all need them.
Francesca Annis

If you don't have a valentine, hang out with your girlfriends, don't go looking for someone. When it's right, they'll come to you.
Carmen Electra

If there hadn't been women we'd still be squatting in a cave eating raw meat, because we made civilization in order to impress our girlfriends.
Orson Welles

I change my mind so much I need two boyfriends and a girlfriend.
Pink

I don't know the first real thing about the dating game. I don't know how to talk to a specific person and connect. I just think you have to go to person by person and do the best you can with people in general.
Jason Schwartzman

If you can lie, you can act, and if you can lie to crazy girlfriends, you can act under pressure.
Joe Rogan

I've never been Romeo who meets a girl and falls for her immediately. It's been a much slower process for me each time I've gone into a relationship.
Leonardo DiCaprio

You know, the man of my dreams might walk round the corner tomorrow. I'm older and wiser and I think I'd make a great girlfriend. I live in the realm of romantic possibility.
Stevie Nicks

Right now I'm pretty single... My career is my boyfriend.
Christina Aguilera

I'm dating a woman now who, evidently, is unaware of it.
Garry Shandling

I'm quite sensitive to women. I saw how my sister got treated by boyfriends. I read this thing that said when you are in a relationship with a woman, imagine how you would feel if you were her father. That's been my approach, for the most part.
Orlando Bloom

Everything I buy is vintage and smells funny. Maybe that's why I don't have a boyfriend.
Lucy Liu

It seems essential, in relationships and all tasks, that we concentrate only on what is most significant and important.
Soren Kierkegaard

People could rationally decide that prolonged relationships take up too much time and effort and that they'd much rather do other kinds of things. But most people are afraid of rejection.
Albert Ellis

We are constantly protecting the male ego, and it's a disservice to men. If a man has any sensitivity or intelligence, he wants to get the straight scoop from his girlfriend.
Betty Dodson

I suppose I was a little bit of what would be called today a nerd. I didn't have girlfriends, and really I wasn't a very social boy.
Charles Kuralt

I'm 31 now. I think I'm beginning to understand what life is, what romance is, and what a relationship means.
Adam Sandler

There's only two people in your life you should lie to... the police and your girlfriend.
Jack Nicholson

I am a hopeless romantic and I love to spoil my girlfriends.
Orlando Bloom

Personally, I don't like a girlfriend to have a husband. If she'll fool her husband, I figure she'll fool me.
Orson Welles

I don't understand the whole dating thing. I know right off the bat if I'm interested in someone, and I don't want them to waste their money on me and take me out to eat if I know I'm not interested in that person.
Britney Spears

I have a lot of boyfriends, I want you to write that. Every country I visit, I have a different boyfriend. And I kiss them all.
Anna Kournikova

At this year's Open, I'll have five boyfriends.
Anna Kournikova

My boyfriend calls me 'princess', but I think of myself more along the lines of 'monkey' and 'retard'.
Alicia Silverstone

I've been dating since I was fifteen. I'm exhausted. Where is he?
Kristin Davis

I fantasize about going back to high school with the knowledge I have now. I would shine. I would have a good time, I would have a girlfriend. I think that's where a lot of my pain comes from. I think I never had any teenage years to go back to.
Spalding Gray

You show your vulnerability through relationships, and those feelings are your soft spot. You need to have a soft spot.
Victoria Pratt

I can't even find someone for a platonic relationship, much less the kind where someone wants to see me naked.
Gilbert Gottfried

I didn't have a financial need, and I wasn't very gifted at relationships. I probably was more like what we think of boys as being: hard to pin down and wary of commitment.
Candice Bergen

Well, a girlfriend once told me never to fight with anybody you don't love.
Jack Nicholson

Which is, I'm an optimist that two people can be together to work out their conflicts. And that commitment, I think, might be what love is, because they both grow from their relationship.
Garry Shandling

I started dating older men, and I would fall in love with them. I thought they could teach me about life.
Daphne Zuniga

In a relationship you have to open yourself up.
Neil LaBute

I always say now that I'm in my blonde years. Because since the end of my marriage, all of my girlfriends have been blonde.
Hugh Hefner

My boyfriend and I broke up. He wanted to get married and I didn't want him to.
Rita Rudner

Rumors about me? Calista Flockhart, Pam Anderson, and Matt Damon. That's who I'm dating.
Ben Affleck

Watching your daughter being collected by her date feels like handing over a million dollar Stradivarius to a gorilla.
Jim Bishop

I used to be a real prince charming if I went on a date with a girl. But then I'd get to where I was likely to have a stroke from the stress of keeping up my act. I've since learned the key to a good date is to pay attention on her.
Matthew Perry

My girlfriend bought me a down jacket, she said it fit my personality.
Jay London

I have stepped off the relationship scene to come to terms with myself. I have spent most of my adult life being 'someone's girlfriend', and now I am happy being single.
Penelope Cruz

You know when I feel inwardly beautiful? When I am with my girlfriends and we are having a 'goddess circle'.
Jennifer Aniston

I think more dating stuff is scheduling. It's needing people who understand your work schedule.
Jennifer Love Hewitt

Appearance is something you should definitely consider when you're going out. Have your girlfriend clip your nails or something like that.
Usher Raymond

It's always been my personal feeling that unless you are married, there is something that is not very dignified about talking about who you are dating.
Luke Wilson

If your best friend has stolen your girlfriend, it does become life and death.
Ben Kingsley

I was dating this guy and we would spend all day text messaging each other. And he thought that he could tell that he liked me more because he actually spelt the word 'YOU' and I just put the letter 'U'.
Kelly Osbourne

Maybe the most that you can expect from a relationship that goes bad is to come out of it with a few good songs.
Marianne Faithfull

I think if I could have a boyfriend like my brothers I'd be really happy. But without the brother thing.
Patricia Velasquez

I'm not cynical about marriage or romance. I enjoyed being married. And although being single was fun for a while, there was always the risk of dating someone who'd owned a lunch box with my picture on it.
Shaun Cassidy

Thank God I never got in a fight. All of the jock dudes hated me, but all of their girlfriends thought I was nice so they wouldn't touch me. It was infuriating to them.
Mark Hoppus

It's weird, I never wish anything bad upon anybody, except two or three old girlfriends.
Carrot Top

It was just that we had this phenomenal honeymoon relationship that just kept on going.
James Levine

You are not alone with a guy until you are a proper age. You don't go to certain levels with men until you are married or you have a certain relationship.
Daisy Fuentes

Relationships in general make people a bit nervous. It's about trust. Do I trust you enough to go there?
Neil LaBute

I've had enough boyfriends and enough issues. I'd seen enough train wrecks.
Taylor Dayne

If you're a sports fan you realize that when you meet somebody, like a girlfriend, they kind of have to root for your team. They don't have a choice.
Jimmy Fallon

I don't know any of us who are in relationships that are totally honest - it doesn't exist.
Richard Gere

Practically all the relationships I know are based on a foundation of lies and mutually accepted delusion.
Kim Cattrall

I stopped dating for six months a year ago. Dating requires a lot of energy and focus.
Daphne Zuniga

Last year my boyfriend gave me a painting - a very personal one. I really prefer personal gifts or ones made by someone for me. Except diamonds. That's the exception to the rule.
Minnie Driver

What I remember most about junior homecoming was my date getting sick afterwards. That kinda sucked. Then, senior year, someone got gum in her hair when we were dancing. She had to get one of the chaperones to take her to the office and cut up her hair. I felt really bad for her, but it worked out fine.
James Lafferty

Things were a lot simpler in Detroit. I didn't care about anything but boyfriends.
Madonna Ciccone

DEATH

A man who won't die for something is not fit to live.
Martin Luther King, Jr.

To be idle is a short road to death and to be diligent is a way of life; foolish people are idle, wise people are diligent.
Buddha

Death is no more than passing from one room into another. But there's a difference for me, you know. Because in that other room I shall be able to see.
Helen Keller

What we have done for ourselves alone dies with us; what we have done for others and the world remains and is immortal.
Albert Pike

I have never killed a man, but I have read many obituaries with great pleasure.
Clarence Darrow

Life is hard. Then you die. Then they throw dirt in your face. Then the worms eat you. Be grateful it happens in that order.
David Gerrold

I am become death, the destroyer of worlds.
J. Robert Oppenheimer

I didn't attend the funeral, but I sent a nice letter saying I approved of it.
Mark Twain

A friend who dies, it's something of you who dies.
Gustave Flaubert

A dying man needs to die, as a sleepy man needs to sleep, and there comes a time when it is wrong, as well as useless, to resist.
Stewart Alsop

The fear of death follows from the fear of life. A man who lives fully is prepared to die at any time.
Mark Twain

While I thought that I was learning how to live, I have been learning how to die.
Leonardo da Vinci

The fear of death is the most unjustified of all fears, for there's no risk of accident for someone who's dead.
Albert Einstein

I decided to devote my life to telling the story because I felt that having survived I owe something to the dead. and anyone who does not remember betrays them again.
Elie Wiesel

Our dead are never dead to us, until we have forgotten them.
George Eliot

Some men are alive simply because it is against the law to kill them.
Edward W. Howe

From my rotting body, flowers shall grow and I am in them and that is eternity.
Edvard Munch

Die, v.: To stop sinning suddenly.
Elbert Hubbard

Call no man happy till he is dead.
Aeschylus

Death most resembles a prophet who is without honor in his own land or a poet who is a stranger among his people.
Khalil Gibran

No one can confidently say that he will still be living tomorrow.
Euripides

Suicide is man's way of telling God, "You can't fire me - I quit."
Bill Maher

Death will be a great relief. No more interviews.
Katharine Hepburn

Because of indifference, one dies before one actually dies.
Elie Wiesel

Nothing that is really good and God-like dies.
Ernst Moritz Arndt

For death is no more than a turning of us over from time to eternity.
William Penn

Birth and death; we all move between these two unknowns.
Bryant H. McGill

Death is the last enemy: once we've got past that I think everything will be alright.
Alice Thomas Ellis

Cursed is the man who dies, but the evil done by him survives.
Abu Bakr

A man does not die of love or his liver or even of old age; he dies of being a man.
Miguel de Unamuno

Let no one weep for me, or celebrate my funeral with mourning; for I still live, as I pass to and fro through the mouths of men.
Quintus Ennius

All our knowledge merely helps us to die a more painful death than animals that know nothing.
Maurice Maeterlinck

Some people are so afraid do die that they never begin to live.
Henry Van Dyke

Everything that gets born dies.
Morrie Schwartz

Dying is easy, it's living that scares me to death.
Annie Lennox

Millions long for immortality who don't know what to do with themselves on a rainy Sunday afternoon.
Susan Ertz

Do not fear death so much but rather the inadequate life.
Bertolt Brecht

They tell us that suicide is the greatest piece of cowardice... that suicide is wrong; when it is quite obvious that there is nothing in the world to which every man has a more unassailable title than to his own life and person.
Arthur Schopenhauer

Death is a very dull, dreary affair, and my advice to you is to have nothing whatsoever to do with it.
W. Somerset Maugham

Life is better than death, I believe, if only because it is less boring, and because it has fresh peaches in it.
Alice Walker

The life of the dead is placed in the memory of the living.
Marcus Tullius Cicero

Any man who has $10,000 left when he dies is a failure.
Errol Flynn

I've told my children that when I die, to release balloons in the sky to celebrate that I graduated. For me, death is a graduation.
Elisabeth Kubler-Ross

The day which we fear as our last is but the birthday of eternity.
Lucius Annaeus Seneca

I had seen birth and death but had thought they were different.
T. S. Eliot

Death is always around the corner, but often our society gives it inordinate help.
Carter Burwell

Death borders upon our birth, and our cradle stands in the grave.
Joseph Hall

The idea is to die young as late as possible.
Ashley Montagu

To himself everyone is immortal; he may know that he is going to die, but he can never know that he is dead.
Samuel Butler

I shall not die of a cold. I shall die of having lived.
Willa Cather

Healthy children will not fear life if their elders have integrity enough not to fear death.
Erik H. Erikson

Of all the gods only death does not desire gifts.
Aeschylus

Love and death are the two great hinges on which all human sympathies turn.
B. R. Hayden

He who doesn't fear death dies only once.
Giovanni Falcone

All architects want to live beyond their deaths.
Philip Johnson

Man always dies before he is fully born.
Erich Fromm

Since the day of my birth, my death began its walk. It is walking toward me, without hurrying.
Jean Cocteau

If you don't have any fight in you, you might as well be dead.
Scott Caan

He who is completely sanctified, or cleansed from all sin, and dies in this state, is fit for glory.
Adam Clarke

We cannot banish dangers, but we can banish fears. We must not demean life by standing in awe of death.
David Sarnoff

Men fear death as children fear to go in the dark; and as that natural fear in children is increased by tales, so is the other.
Francis Bacon

'Tis very certain the desire of life prolongs it.
Lord Byron

Time rushes towards us with its hospital tray of infinitely varied narcotics, even while it is preparing us for its inevitably fatal operation.
Tennessee Williams

Death is the tyrant of the imagination.
Barry Cornwall

Death's in the good-bye.
Anne Sexton

For me, habit is just a synonym for death.
Juliette Binoche

It is possible to provide security against other ills, but as far as death is concerned, we men live in a city without walls.
Epicurus

When you're dead, you're dead. That's it.
Marlene Dietrich

I saw few die of hunger; of eating, a hundred thousand.
Benjamin Franklin

Man dies of cold, not of darkness.
Miguel de Unamuno

The words of a dead man are modified in the guts of the living.
W. H. Auden

Even at our birth, death does but stand aside a little. And every day he looks towards us and muses somewhat to himself whether that day or the next he will draw nigh.
Robert Bolt

Fling but a stone, the giant dies.
Matthew Green

Tradition demands that we not speak poorly of the dead.
Daniel Barenboim

John Candy knew he was going to die. He told me on his 40th birthday. He said, well, Maureen, I'm on borrowed time.
Maureen O'Hara

It was a time when only the dead smiled, happy in their peace.
Anna Akhmatova

When faith is lost, when honor dies, the man is dead.
John Greenleaf Whittier

Hell, madam, is to love no longer.
Georges Bernanos

The dead cannot cry out for justice. It is a duty of the living to do so for them.
Lois McMaster Bujold

Pale Death beats equally at the poor man's gate and at the palaces of kings.
Horace

The death of what's dead is the birth of what's living.
Arlo Guthrie

DESIGN

A designer knows he has achieved perfection not when there is nothing left to add, but when there is nothing left to take away.
Antoine de Saint-Exupery

Design is not just what it looks like and feels like. Design is how it works.
Steve Jobs

You can design and create, and build the most wonderful place in the world. But it takes people to make the dream a reality.
Walt Disney

I don't design clothes, I design dreams.
Ralph Lauren

Design is the method of putting form and content together. Design, just as art, has multiple definitions; there is no single definition. Design can be art. Design can be aesthetics. Design is so simple, that's why it is so complicated.
Paul Rand

Sometimes I can't figure designers out. It's as if they flunked human anatomy.
Erma Bombeck

I would be most content if my children grew up to be the kind of people who think decorating consists mostly of building enough bookshelves.
Anna Quindlen

I design for real people. I think of our customers all the time. There is no virtue whatsoever in creating clothing or accessories that are not practical.
Giorgio Armani

Color does not add a pleasant quality to design - it reinforces it.
Pierre Bonnard

Design is not making beauty, beauty emerges from selection, affinities, integration, love.
Louis Kahn

Some men give up their designs when they have almost reached the goal; While others, on the contrary, obtain a victory by exerting, at the last moment, more vigorous efforts than ever before.
Herodotus

Design works if it's authentic, inspired, and has a clear point of view. It can't be a collection of input.
Ron Johnson

Good buildings come from good people, ad all problems are solved by good design.
Stephen Gardiner

Designers are very fickle. I never wanted to be a victim of that. You're in one minute, out the next.
Tyra Banks

Design is not for philosophy it's for life.
Issey Miyake

What is design? It's where you stand with a foot in two worlds - the world of technology and the world of people and human purposes - and you try to bring the two together.
Mitchell Kapor

Good design is good business.
Thomas J. Watson

The design of each element should be thought out in order to be easy to make and easy to repair.
Leo Fender

A good designer must rely on experience, on precise, logic thinking; and on pedantic exactness. No magic will do.
Niklaus Wirth

I design for the woman who loves being a woman.
Diane von Furstenberg

Luck is the residue of design.
Branch Rickey

Great designers seldom make great advertising men, because they get overcome by the beauty of the picture - and forget that merchandise must be sold.
James Randolph Adams

About half my designs are controlled fantasy, 15 percent are total madness and the rest are bread-and-butter designs.
Manolo Blahnik

A designer is only as good as the star who wears her clothes.
Edith Head

It is only after years of preparation that the young artist should touch color - not color used descriptively, that is, but as a means of personal expression.
Henri Matisse

Outside of the chair, the teapot is the most ubiquitous and important design element in the domestic environment and almost everyone who has tackled the world of design has ended up designing one.
David McFadden

Many things difficult to design prove easy to performance.
Samuel Johnson

To design the future effectively, you must first let go of your past.
Charles J. Givens

Every contrivance of man, every tool, every instrument, every utensil, every article designed for use, of each and every kind, evolved from a very simple beginnings.
Robert Collier

Delay always breeds danger; and to protract a great design is often to ruin it.
Miguel de Cervantes

Recognizing the need is the primary condition for design.
Charles Eames

To whom does design address itself: to the greatest number, to the specialist of an enlightened matter, to a privileged social class? Design addresses itself to the need.
Charles Eames

Design is people.
Jane Jacobs

Design is everything. Everything!
Paul Rand

To design is to communicate clearly by whatever means you can control or master.
Milton Glaser

Design is directed toward human beings. To design is to solve human problems by identifying them and executing the best solution.
Ivan Chermayeff

Design must reflect the practical and aesthetic in business but above all... good design must primarily serve people.
Thomas J. Watson

Everyone designs who devises courses of action aimed at changing existing situations into preferred ones.
Herbert Simon

The proper study of mankind is the science of design.
Herbert Simon

I don't start with a design objective, I start with a communication objective. I feel my project is successful if it communicates what it is supposed to communicate.
Mike Davidson

In my opinion, no single design is apt to be optimal for everyone.
Donald Norman

Designs of purely arbitrary nature cannot be expected to last long.
Kenzo Tange

Good design doesn't date.
Harry Seidler

I think it's really important to design things with a kind of personality.
Marc Newson

The primary factor is proportions.
Arne Jacobsen

The details are the very source of expression in architecture. But we are caught in a vice between art and the bottom line.
Arthur Erickson

I would think twice about designing stuff for which there was no need and which didn't endure.
Robin Day

Design is an unknown.
Geoffrey Beene

The urge for good design is the same as the urge to go on living.
Harry Bertoia

I like the body. I like to design everything to do with the body.
Gianni Versace

I think there is a new awareness in this 21st century that design is as important to where and how we live as it is for museums, concert halls and civic buildings.
Daniel Libeskind

This is what I like about being a designer: You can't really get it until you see it.
Isaac Mizrahi

When I design buildings, I think of the overall composition, much as the parts of a body would fit together. On top of that, I think about how people will approach the building and experience that space.
Tadao Ando

Sacred spaces can be created in any environment.
Christy Turlington

So, to really execute design in its highest form and making people feel joy, that's a great reward.
Genevieve Gorder

Accessible design is good design.
Steve Ballmer

The artist in me cries out for design.
Robert Frost

Perhaps believing in good design is like believing in God, it makes you an optimist.
Terence

DIET

I never worry about diets. The only carrots that interest me are the number you get in a diamond.
Mae West

No disease that can be treated by diet should be treated with any other means.
Maimonides

Health food makes me sick.
Calvin Trillin

Adopting a new healthier lifestyle can involve changing diet to include more fresh fruit and vegetables as well as increasing levels of exercise.
Linford Christie

My doctor told me to stop having intimate dinners for four. Unless there are three other people.
Orson Welles

The best way to lose weight is to close your mouth - something very difficult for a politician. Or watch your food - just watch it, don't eat it.
Edward Koch

I told my doctor I get very tired when I go on a diet, so he gave me pep pills. Know what happened? I ate faster.
Joe E. Lewis

Do you know how many calories are in butter and cheese and ice cream? Would you get your dog up in the morning for a cup of coffee and a donut?
Jack LaLanne

Diets, like clothes, should be tailored to you.
Joan Rivers

An optimist is a person who starts a new diet on Thanksgiving Day.
Irv Kupcinet

Vegetables are a must on a diet. I suggest carrot cake, zucchini bread, and pumpkin pie.
Jim Davis

What some call health, if purchased by perpetual anxiety about diet, isn't much better than tedious disease.
Alexander Pope

The second day of a diet is always easier than the first. By the second day you're off it.
Jackie Gleason

Each of us should take personal responsibility for our diet, and our children's diet, and the government's role should be to make certain it provides the best information possible to help people stay healthy.
James Talent

I highly recommend worrying. It is much more effective than dieting.
William Powell

I don't believe in depriving myself of any food or being imprisoned by a diet.
Joely Fisher

We can all put weight on or lose weight.
Keith Emerson

I thought, you know the food and the diet thing is one way to start yourself onto a healthy lifestyle, but if you don't move, if you don't start exercising you're gonna deteriorate.
Warren Cuccurullo

I don't eat junk foods and I don't think junk thoughts.
Peace Pilgrim

And let's be clear: It's not enough just to limit ads for foods that aren't healthy. It's also going to be critical to increase marketing for foods that are healthy.
Michelle Obama

I refuse to spend my life worrying about what I eat. There is no pleasure worth forgoing just for an extra three years in the geriatric ward.
John Mortimer

French fries. I love them. Some people are chocolate and sweets people. I love French fries. That and caviar.
Cameron Diaz

If I like myself at this weight, then this is what I'm going to be. I don't have an eating disorder.
Courteney Cox

Feeding is a very important ritual for me. I don't trust people who don't like to eat.
Gina Gershon

It looks to me to be obvious that the whole world cannot eat an American diet.
Jerry Brown

I used to be hung up on my figure, but it's a waste of time. I don't believe in diets. Have four pints one night, be healthy the next.
Sophie Ellis Bextor

I have been dairy free for several years, and I started because I felt it was going to reduce my allergies, which it did, and help me lose weight, which it did.
Fran Drescher

As I mentioned previously, the tools that allow for optimum health are diet and exercise.
Bill Toomey

If you've got a big gut and you start doing sit-ups, you are going to get bigger because you build up the muscle. You've got to get rid of that fat! How do you get rid of fat? By changing your diet.
Jack LaLanne

The only way you get that fat off is to eat less and exercise more.
Jack LaLanne

Our society's strong emphasis on dieting and self-image can sometimes lead to eating disorders. We know that more than 5 million Americans suffer from eating disorders, most of them young women.
Tipper Gore

I'm lucky, I don't like sweets, not even chocolate.
Eva Herzigova

I started dieting. I dieted, dieted, dieted and tried all the diets and I would lose and then I would go back to normal eating and would put it on and then some.
Suzanne Somers

A systemic cleansing and detox is definitely the way to go after each holiday. It is the key to fighting high blood pressure, heart disease, cancer, and other health-related illnesses.
Lee Haney

The circuit training program along with a healthy clean diet is the way to excellent results.
Lee Haney

High-quality food is better for your health.
Michael Pollan

A safe and nutritionally adequate diet is a basic individual right and an essential condition for sustainable development, especially in developing countries.
Gro Harlem Brundtland

Such lifestyle factors such as cigarette smoking, excessive alcohol consumption, little physical activity and low dietary calcium intake are risk factors for osteoporosis as well as for many other non-communicable diseases.
Gro Harlem Brundtland

You can't be fat and fast, too; so lift, run, diet and work.
Hank Stram

A boxer's diet should be low in fat and high in proteins and sugar. Therefore you should eat plenty of lean meat, milk, leafy vegetables, and fresh fruit and ice cream for sugar.
Gene Tunney

I've been on a diet for two weeks and all I've lost is two weeks.
Totie Fields

As for those grapefruit and buttermilk diets, I'll take roast chicken and dumplings.
Hattie McDaniel

I am now in that happy comfortable state that I do not hesitate to indulge in any fancy in regard to diet, but watch the consequences, and do not continue any course which adds to weight or bulk and consequent discomfort.
William Banting

I followed the same diet for 20 years, eliminating starches, living on salads, lean meat, and small portions.
Gene Tierney

I don't believe in fad diets.
Jenny Craig

There are six components of wellness: proper weight and diet, proper exercise, breaking the smoking habit, control of alcohol, stress management and periodic exams.
Kenneth H. Cooper

So, when it comes to eating healthy, it's just doing the right thing. And it's not something you have to do 365 days a year, but I think it's something you have to do 25 days a month. Let's put it that way.
Mike Ditka

Some people are willing to pay the price and it's the same with staying healthy or eating healthy. There's some discipline involved. There's some sacrifices.
Mike Ditka

I don't believe in dieting.
Joan Collins

You see people who have been very heavy in their life who have taken that body, trimmed it down, firmed it up through discipline, exercise and being able to say no. Eating properly, that all comes into it.
Mike Ditka

I never diet. I smoke. I drink now and then. I never work out.
Naomi Campbell

Leave the table while you still feel you could eat a little more.
Helena Rubinstein

I am not naturally that thin, so I had to go through everything from using drugs to diet pills to laxatives to fasting. Those were my main ways of controlling my weight.
Carre Otis

My experience as a school nurse taught me that we need to make a concerted effort, all of us, to increase physical fitness activity among our children and to encourage all Americans to adopt a healthier diet that includes fruits and vegetables, but there is more.
Lois Capps

I'm very girly. I love to talk about diets, exercise, kids, make-up.
Rachel Hunter

Dieting is murder on the road. Show me a man who travels and I'll show you one who eats.
Bruce Froemming

It seems every year, people make the resolution to exercise and lose weight and get in shape.
Ed Smith

Cereal eating is almost a marker for a healthy lifestyle. It sets you up for the day, so you don't overeat.
Bruce Barton

I don't go long without eating. I never starve myself: I grab a healthy snack.
Vanessa Hudgens

People who shop in health food stores never look healthy.
Amy Sedaris

DREAMS

The future belongs to those who believe in the beauty of their dreams.
Eleanor Roosevelt

All our dreams can come true, if we have the courage to pursue them.
Walt Disney

All men dream, but not equally. Those who dream by night in the dusty recesses of their minds, wake in the day to find that it was vanity: but the dreamers of the day are dangerous men, for they may act on their dreams with open eyes, to make them possible.
T. E. Lawrence

A dreamer is one who can only find his way by moonlight, and his punishment is that he sees the dawn before the rest of the world.
Oscar Wilde

Deep into that darkness peering, long I stood there, wondering, fearing, doubting, dreaming dreams no mortal ever dared to dream before.
Edgar Allan Poe

Every great dream begins with a dreamer. Always remember, you have within you the strength, the patience, and the passion to reach for the stars to change the world.
Harriet Tubman

If one advances confidently in the direction of his dreams, and endeavors to live the life which he has imagined, he will meet with success unexpected in common hours.
Henry David Thoreau

Reality is wrong. Dreams are for real.
Tupac Shakur

There are those who look at things the way they are, and ask why... I dream of things that never were, and ask why not?
Robert Kennedy

A man is not old until regrets take the place of dreams.
John Barrymore

If you take responsibility for yourself you will develop a hunger to accomplish your dreams.
Les Brown

Dreams are today's answers to tomorrow's questions.
Edgar Cayce

Dream and give yourself permission to envision a You that you choose to be.
Joy Page

Dream no small dreams for they have no power to move the hearts of men.
Johann Wolfgang von

All of us failed to match our dreams of perfection. So I rate us on the basis of our splendid failure to do the impossible.
William Faulkner

Dreams pass into the reality of action. From the actions stems the dream again; and this interdependence produces the highest form of living.
Anais Nin

Dreams have only one owner at a time. That's why dreamers are lonely.
Erma Bombeck

Who looks outside, dreams; who looks inside, awakes.
Carl Jung

To accomplish great things, we must not only act, but also dream; not only plan, but also believe.
Anatole France

Dreams are necessary to life.
Anais Nin

You have to dream before your dreams can come true.
Abdul Kalam

All human beings are also dream beings. Dreaming ties all mankind together.
Jack Kerouac

In dreams begins responsibility.
William Butler Yeats

He was a dreamer, a thinker, a speculative philosopher... or, as his wife would have it, an idiot.
Douglas Adams

Dreams are the touchstones of our character.
Henry David Thoreau

I close my eyes, then I drift away, into the magic night I softly say. A silent prayer, like dreamers do, then I fall asleep to dream my dreams of you.
Roy Orbison

We all have dreams. But in order to make dreams come into reality, it takes an awful lot of determination, dedication, self-discipline, and effort.
Jesse Owens

Great dreams of great dreamers are always transcended.
Abdul Kalam

The best way to make your dreams come true is to wake up.
Paul Valery

All men of action are dreamers.
James Huneker

I stand for freedom of expression, doing what you believe in, and going after your dreams.
Madonna Ciccone

I'm a dreamer. I have to dream and reach for the stars, and if I miss a star then I grab a handful of clouds.
Mike Tyson

Dreams are true while they last, and do we not live in dreams?
Alfred Lord Tennyson

All the things one has forgotten scream for help in dreams.
Elias Canetti

Ideologies separate us. Dreams and anguish bring us together.
Eugene Ionesco

I don't use drugs, my dreams are frightening enough.
M. C. Escher

Dreams will get you nowhere, a good kick in the pants will take you a long way.
Baltasar Gracian

No one should negotiate their dreams. Dreams must be free to fly high. No government, no legislature, has a right to limit your dreams. You should never agree to surrender your dreams.
Jesse Jackson

The world needs dreamers and the world needs doers. But above all, the world needs dreamers who do.
Sarah Ban Breathnach

Yesterday is but today's memory, and tomorrow is today's dream.
Khalil Gibran

I tell people I'm too stupid to know what's impossible. I have ridiculously large dreams, and half the time they come true.
Debi Thomas

Dreaming or awake, we perceive only events that have meaning to us.
Jane Roberts

Myths are public dreams, dreams are private myths.
Joseph Campbell

Perhaps life is just that... a dream and a fear.
Joseph Conrad

I am accustomed to sleep and in my dreams to imagine the same things that lunatics imagine when awake.
Rene Descartes

The most pitiful among men is he who turns his dreams into silver and gold.
Khalil Gibran

It takes a lot of courage to show your dreams to someone else.
Erma Bombeck

Each man should frame life so that at some future hour fact and his dreaming meet.
Victor Hugo

I think we dream so we don't have to be apart so long. If we're in each other's dreams, we can play together all night.
Bill Watterson

So many of our dreams at first seem impossible, then they seem improbable, and then, when we summon the will, they soon become inevitable.
Christopher Reeve

Man is a genius when he is dreaming.
Akira Kurosawa

The dreamer can know no truth, not even about his dream, except by awaking out of it.
George Santayana

Judge of your natural character by what you do in your dreams.
Ralph Waldo Emerson

I am a dreamer. Seriously, I'm living on another planet.
Eva Green

Dreaming men are haunted men.
Stephen Vincent Benet

I've always said that one night, I'm going to find myself in some field somewhere, I'm standing on grass, and it's raining, and I'm with the person I love, and I know I'm at the very point I've been dreaming of getting to.
Drew Barrymore

We all dream; we do not understand our dreams, yet we act as if nothing strange goes on in our sleep minds, strange at least by comparison with the logical, purposeful doings of our minds when we are awake.
Erich Fromm

God's gifts put man's best dreams to shame.
Elizabeth Barrett Browning

Dreaming of a tomorrow, which tomorrow, will be as distant then as 'tis today.
Lope de Vega

I do not know whether I was then a man dreaming I was a butterfly, or whether I am now a butterfly dreaming I am a man.
Zhuangzi

Only in our dreams are we free. The rest of the time we need wages.
Terry Pratchett

Dream in a pragmatic way.
Aldous Huxley

Youth is a wonderful thing. What a crime to waste it on children.
George Bernard Shaw

I have always been amazed at the way an ordinary observer lends so much more credence and attaches so much more importance to waking events than to those occurring in dreams... Man... is above all the plaything of his memory.
Andre Breton

Dream manfully and nobly, and thy dreams shall be prophets.
Edward G. Bulwer-Lytton

Whatever you do, never stop dreaming.
Darren L. Johnson

When you cease to dream you cease to live.
Malcolm Forbes

Without leaps of imagination, or dreaming, we lose the excitement of possibilities. Dreaming, after all, is a form of planning.
Gloria Steinem

People are so busy dreaming the American Dream, fantasizing about what they could be or have a right to be, that they're all asleep at the switch. Consequently we are living in the Age of Human Error.
Florence King

I was always a dreamer, in childhood especially. People thought I was a little strange.
Charley Pride

Everybody's a dreamer.
John Lithgow

Sometimes, the only realists are the dreamers.
Paul Wellstone

Like all dreamers, I mistook disenchantment for truth.
Jean-Paul Sartre

One of the most adventurous things left us is to go to bed. For no one can lay a hand on our dreams.
E. V. Lucas

Those who have compared our life to a dream were right... we were sleeping wake, and waking sleep.
Michel de Montaigne

Take everything easy and quit dreaming and brooding and you will be well guarded from a thousand evils.
Amy Lowell

People need dreams, there's as much nourishment in 'em as food.
Dorothy Gilman

Strivers achieve what dreamers believe.
Usher Raymond

The world of men is dreaming, it has gone mad in its sleep, and a snake is strangling it, but it can't wake up.
David Herbert Lawrence

Writers write. Dreamers talk about it.
Jerry B. Jenkins

Was it only by dreaming or writing that I could find out what I thought?
Joan Didion

Living in dreams of yesterday, we find ourselves still dreaming of impossible future conquests.
Charles Lindbergh

My dreams were all my own; I accounted for them to nobody; they were my refuge when annoyed - my dearest pleasure when free.
Mary Wollstonecraft Shelley

Only the dreamer shall understand realities, though in truth his dreaming must be not out of proportion to his waking.
Margaret Fuller

We are near waking when we dream we are dreaming.
Novalis

I challenge you to be dreamers; I challenge you to be doers and let us make the greatest place in the world even better.
Brian Schweitzer

Only things the dreamers make live on. They are the eternal conquerors.
Herbert Kaufman

Oh, I was never a businessman. I was a visionary, a dreamer.
Jim Bakker

That's what keeps me going: dreaming, inventing, then hoping and dreaming some more in order to keep dreaming.
Joseph Barbera

We all keep dreaming, and luckily, dreams come true.
Katie Holmes

You can plant a dream.
Anne Campbell

You know, Willie Wonka said it best: we are the makers of dreams, the dreamers of dreams.
Herb Brooks

Married or unmarried, young or old, poet or worker, you are still a dreamer, and will one time know, and feel, that your life is but a dream.
Donald G. Mitchell

This is the city of dreamers and time and again it's the place where the greatest dream of all, the American dream, has been tested and has triumphed.
Michael Bloomberg

We should never discourage young people from dreaming dreams.
Lenny Wilkens

EDUCATION

Education is not the filling of a pail, but the lighting of a fire.
William Butler Yeats

An education isn't how much you have committed to memory, or even how much you know. It's being able to differentiate between what you know and what you don't.
Anatole France

Education is an admirable thing, but it is well to remember from time to time that nothing that is worth knowing can be taught.
Oscar Wilde

It is the mark of an educated mind to be able to entertain a thought without accepting it.
Aristotle

A human being is not attaining his full heights until he is educated.
Horace Mann

Education is the ability to listen to almost anything without losing your temper or your self-confidence.
Robert Frost

Develop a passion for learning. If you do, you will never cease to grow.
Anthony J. D'Angelo

In the first place, God made idiots. That was for practice. Then he made school boards.
Mark Twain

A liberal education is at the heart of a civil society, and at the heart of a liberal education is the act of teaching.
A. Bartlett Giamatti

Data is not information, information is not knowledge, knowledge is not understanding, understanding is not wisdom.
Clifford Stoll

An educated person is one who has learned that information almost always turns out to be at best incomplete and very often false, misleading, fictitious, mendacious - just dead wrong.
Russell Baker

He who opens a school door, closes a prison.
Victor Hugo

Education is not preparation for life; education is life itself.
John Dewey

Education is a progressive discovery of our own ignorance.
Will Durant

Education is a better safeguard of liberty than a standing army.
Edward Everett

Children have to be educated, but they have also to be left to educate themselves.
Ernest Dimnet

Education is the key to unlock the golden door of freedom.
George Washington Carver

The roots of education are bitter, but the fruit is sweet.
Aristotle

The only thing that interferes with my learning is my education.
Albert Einstein

An educated man is thoroughly inoculated against humbug, thinks for himself and tries to give his thoughts, in speech or on paper, some style.
Alan K. Simpson

The only person who is educated is the one who has learned how to learn and change.
Carl Rogers

Education is learning what you didn't even know you didn't know.
Daniel J. Boorstin

No one has yet realized the wealth of sympathy, the kindness and generosity hidden in the soul of a child. The effort of every true education should be to unlock that treasure.
Emma Goldman

America is becoming so educated that ignorance will be a novelty. I will belong to the select few.
Will Rogers

I'm not afraid of storms, for I'm learning to sail my ship.
Aeschylus

I would rather entertain and hope that people learned something than educate people and hope they were entertained.
Walt Disney

Education is simply the soul of a society as it passes from one generation to another.
Gilbert K. Chesterton

It is a thousand times better to have common sense without education than to have education without common sense.
Robert Green Ingersoll

Education is what survives when what has been learned has been forgotten.
B. F. Skinner

Education's purpose is to replace an empty mind with an open one.
Malcolm Forbes

Much education today is monumentally ineffective. All too often we are giving young people cut flowers when we should be teaching them to grow their own plants.
John W. Gardner

An educated people can be easily governed.
Frederick The Great

The illiterate of the future will not be the person who cannot read. It will be the person who does not know how to learn.
Alvin Toffler

America is the best half-educated country in the world.
Nicholas M. Butler

Some people will never learn anything, for this reason, because they understand everything too soon.
Alexander Pope

To the uneducated, an A is just three sticks.
A. A. Milne

The object of education is to prepare the young to educate themselves throughout their lives.
Robert M. Hutchins

Why should society feel responsible only for the education of children, and not for the education of all adults of every age?
Erich Fromm

If the Romans had been obliged to learn Latin, they would never have found time to conquer the world.
Heinrich Heine

Some people drink from the fountain of knowledge, others just gargle.
Robert Anthony

Good teaching is one-fourth preparation and three-fourths pure theatre.
Gail Godwin

I think everyone should go to college and get a degree and then spend six months as a bartender and six months as a cabdriver. Then they would really be educated.
Al McGuire

Learning is a result of listening, which in turn leads to even better listening and attentiveness to the other person. In other words, to learn from the child, we must have empathy, and empathy grows as we learn.
Alice Miller

I read Shakespeare and the Bible, and I can shoot dice. That's what I call a liberal education.
Tallulah Bankhead

Education is the transmission of civilization.
Will Durant

Education is all a matter of building bridges.
Ralph Ellison

Education... has produced a vast population able to read but unable to distinguish what is worth reading.
G. M. Trevelyan

Education, n.: That which discloses to the wise and disguises from the foolish their lack of understanding.
Ambrose Bierce

True, a little learning is a dangerous thing, but it still beats total ignorance.
Abigail Van Buren

If an ignorant person is attracted by the things of the world, that is bad. But if a learned person is thus attracted, it is worse.
Abu Bakr

I would like to learn, or remember, how to live.
Annie Dillard

The whole purpose of education is to turn mirrors into windows.
Sydney J. Harris

The more that learn to read the less learn how to make a living. That's one thing about a little education. It spoils you for actual work. The more you know the more you think somebody owes you a living.
Will Rogers

Learning is not attained by chance, it must be sought for with ardor and diligence.
Abigail Adams

To the extent that we are all educated and informed, we will be more equipped to deal with the gut issues that tend to divide us.
Caroline Kennedy Schlossberg

You can educate yourself right out of a relationship with God.
Tammy Faye Bakker

I learned more stuff in church than I did in the world.
Al Green

I know a lot of people think I'm dumb. Well, at least I ain't no educated fool.
Leon Spinks

Every educated person is a future enemy.
Martin Bormann

It has been said that 80% of what people learn is visual.
Allen Klein

The willingness to learn new skills is very high.
Angela Merkel

Responsibility educates.
Wendell Phillips

To me education is a leading out of what is already there in the pupil's soul. To Miss Mackay it is a putting in of something that is not there, and that is not what I call education. I call it intrusion.
Muriel Spark

When a subject becomes totally obsolete we make it a required course.
Peter Drucker

The simplest schoolboy is now familiar with truths for which Archimedes would have sacrificed his life.
Ernest Renan

I prefer the company of peasants because they have not been educated sufficiently to reason incorrectly.
Michel de Montaigne

The love of learning, the sequestered nooks, And all the sweet serenity of books.
Henry Wadsworth Longfellow

The only real failure in life is one not learned from.
Anthony J. D'Angelo

No man who worships education has got the best out of education... Without a gentle contempt for education no man's education is complete.
Gilbert K. Chesterton

Real education must ultimately be limited to men who insist on knowing, the rest is mere sheep-herding.
Ezra Pound

If I had learned education I would not have had time to learn anything else.
Cornelius Vanderbilt

Learning, n. The kind of ignorance distinguishing the studious.
Ambrose Bierce

The great difficulty in education is to get experience out of ideas.
George Santayana

Learn to think continentally.
Alexander Hamilton

It is always in season for old men to learn.
Aeschylus

Reading builds the educated and informed electorate so vital to our democracy.
Brad Henry

In the world today, a young lady who does not have a college education just is not educated.
Walter Annenberg

To be able to be caught up into the world of thought - that is being educated.
Edith Hamilton

So women are at the beginning of building a language, and not all women are conscious of it.
Judy Chicago

ENVIRONMENTAL

Never doubt that a small group of thoughtful, committed citizens can change the world; indeed, it's the only thing that ever has.
Margaret Mead

God has cared for these trees, saved them from drought, disease, avalanches, and a thousand tempests and floods. But he cannot save them from fools.
John Muir

Keep close to Nature's heart... and break clear away, once in awhile, and climb a mountain or spend a week in the woods. Wash your spirit clean.
John Muir

The environment is everything that isn't me.
Albert Einstein

When we try to pick out anything by itself, we find it hitched to everything else in the universe.
John Muir

Thank God men cannot fly, and lay waste the sky as well as the earth.
Henry David Thoreau

It is horrifying that we have to fight our own government to save the environment.
Ansel Adams

Birds are indicators of the environment. If they are in trouble, we know we'll soon be in trouble.
Roger Tory Peterson

All is connected... no one thing can change by itself.
Paul Hawken

We must return to nature and nature's god.
Luther Burbank

I see humanity now as one vast plant, needing for its highest fulfillment only love, the natural blessings of the great outdoors, and intelligent crossing and selection.
Luther Burbank

Conservation is a state of harmony between men and land.
Aldo Leopold

I did not become a vegetarian for my health, I did it for the health of the chickens.
Isaac Bashevis Singer

Every time I have some moment on a seashore, or in the mountains, or sometimes in a quiet forest, I think this is why the environment has to be preserved.
Bill Bradley

I think the environment should be put in the category of our national security. Defense of our resources is just as important as defense abroad. Otherwise what is there to defend?
Robert Redford

You will die but the carbon will not; its career does not end with you. It will return to the soil, and there a plant may take it up again in time, sending it once more on a cycle of plant and animal life.
Jacob Bronowski

We won't have a society if we destroy the environment.
Margaret Mead

Take a course in good water and air; and in the eternal youth of Nature you may renew your own. Go quietly, alone; no harm will befall you.
John Muir

Environmental degradation, overpopulation, refugees, narcotics, terrorism, world crime movements, and organized crime are worldwide problems that don't stop at a nation's borders.
Warren Christopher

After all, sustainability means running the global environment - Earth Inc. - like a corporation: with depreciation, amortization and maintenance accounts. In other words, keeping the asset whole, rather than undermining your natural capital.
Maurice Strong

If we do not permit the earth to produce beauty and joy, it will in the end not produce food, either.
Joseph Wood Krutch

I can find God in nature, in animals, in birds and the environment.
Pat Buckley

If people destroy something replaceable made by mankind, they are called vandals; if they destroy something irreplaceable made by God, they are called developers.
Joseph Wood Krutch

Not all is doom and gloom. We are beginning to understand the natural world and are gaining a reverence for life - all life.
Roger Tory Peterson

I don't think we're going to save anything if we go around talking about saving plants and animals only; we've got to translate that into what's in it for us.
Jim Fowler

They claim this mother of ours, the Earth, for their own use, and fence their neighbors away from her, and deface her with their buildings and their refuse.
Sitting Bull

Nuclear power will help provide the electricity that our growing economy needs without increasing emissions. This is truly an environmentally responsible source of energy.
Michael Burgess

If we gave up eating beef we would have roughly 20 to 30 times more land for food than we have now.
James Lovelock

I think Captain Cousteau might be the father of the environmental movement.
Ted Turner

Harmony with land is like harmony with a friend; you cannot cherish his right hand and chop off his left.
Aldo Leopold

In a few decades, the relationship between the environment, resources and conflict may seem almost as obvious as the connection we see today between human rights, democracy and peace.
Wangari Maathai

People blame their environment. There is only one person to blame - and only one - themselves.
Robert Collier

The Endangered Species Act is the strongest and most effective tool we have to repair the environmental harm that is causing a species to decline.
Norm Dicks

The only way forward, if we are going to improve the quality of the environment, is to get everybody involved.
Richard Rogers

Environmental concern is now firmly embedded in public life: in education, medicine and law; in journalism, literature and art.
Barry Commoner

Why are ecologists and environmentalists so feared and hated? This is because in part what they have to say is new to the general public, and the new is always alarming.
Garrett Hardin

We assume that everything's becoming more efficient, and in an immediate sense that's true; our lives are better in many ways. But that improvement has been gained through a massively inefficient use of natural resources.
Paul Hawken

Population, when unchecked, goes on doubling itself every 25 years or increases in a geometrical ratio.
Thomas Malthus

You may be able to fool the voters, but not the atmosphere.
Donella Meadows

Journey with me to a true commitment to our environment. Journey with me to the serenity of leaving to our children a planet in equilibrium.
Paul Tsongas

Within 10 years it will be impossible to travel to the North Pole by dog team. There will be too much open water.
Will Steger

By polluting clear water with slime you will never find good drinking water.
Aeschylus

I think the cost of energy will come down when we make this transition to renewable energy.
Al Gore

When a man wantonly destroys one of the works of man we call him a vandal. When he destroys one of the works of god we call him a sportsman.
Joseph Wood Krutch

If you violate Nature's laws
you are your own prosecuting
attorney, judge, jury, and
hangman.
Luther Burbank

Pushing production out of
America to nations without
our environmental standards
increases global environmental
risks.
Frank Murkowski

In today's world, it is no longer
unimaginable to think that
business can operate - and
even thrive - in an
environmentally-friendly
manner.
Olympia Snowe

No one should be able to enter
a wilderness by mechanical
means.
Garrett Hardin

I consider myself to have been
the bridge between the
shotgun and the binoculars in
bird watching. Before I came
along, the primary way to
observe birds was to shoot
them and stuff them.
Roger Tory Peterson

When we realize we can make
a buck cleaning up the
environment, it will be done!
Dennis Weaver

We learned that economic
growth and environmental
protection can and should go
hand in hand.
Christopher Dodd

Local innovation and initiative
can help us better understand
how to protect our
environment.
Gale Norton

Why has it seemed that the
only way to protect the
environment is with heavy-
handed government
regulation?
Gale Norton

There is no place where we
can safely store worn-out
reactors or their garbage. No
place!
David R. Brower

It seems that every time
mankind is given a lot of
energy, we go out and wreck
something with it.
David R. Brower

It is absolutely imperative that
we protect, preserve and pass
on this genetic heritage for
man and every other living
thing in as good a condition as
we received it.
David R. Brower

I firmly believe that we can have a healthy environment and a sustainable timber industry.
Frank Murkowski

The modern assault on the environment began about 50 years ago, during and immediately after World War II.
Barry Commoner

Earth Day 1970 was irrefutable evidence that the American people understood the environmental threat and wanted action to resolve it.
Barry Commoner

The government should set a goal for a clean environment but not mandate how that goal should be implemented.
Dixie Lee Ray

Mankind is considered (by the radical environmentalists) the lowest and the meanest of all species and is blamed for everything.
Dixie Lee Ray

People in Slow Food understand that food is an environmental issue.
Michael Pollan

If we bestow but a very little attention to the economy of the animal creation, we shall find manifest examples of premeditation, perseverance, resolution, and consumate artifice, in order to effect their purpose.
William Bartram

Maintaining healthy forests is essential to those who make a living from the land and for those of us who use them for recreational purposes.
Cathy McMorris

In a finite world this means that the per capita share of the world's goods must steadily decrease.
Garrett Hardin

Under the Environmental Protection Agency's Energy Star Program, homes are independently verified to be measurably more energy efficient than average houses.
Melissa Bean

I think the government has to reposition environment on top of their national and international priorities.
Brian Mulroney

We don't have to sacrifice a strong economy for a healthy environment.
Dennis Weaver

Unless we keep this planet healthy, everything else is for naught.
Victoria Principal

We are now heading down a centuries-long path toward increasing the productivity of our natural capital - the resource systems upon which we depend to live - instead of our human capital.
Paul Hawken

A knowledgeable and courageous U.S. president could help enormously in leading the world's nations toward saving the climate.
Donella Meadows

Liberals in Congress have spent the past three decades pandering to environmental extremists. The policies they have put in place are in large part responsible for the energy crunch we are seeing today. We have not built a refinery in this country for 30 years.
Marsha Blackburn

Industry is fortune's right hand, and frugality its left.
John Ray

Our world faces a true planetary emergency. I know the phrase sounds shrill, and I know it's a challenge to the moral imagination.
Al Gore

For me, going vegan was an ethical and environmental decision. I'm doing the right thing by the animals.
Alexandra Paul

EQUALITY

I have a dream that my four little children will one day live in a nation where they will not be judged by the color of their skin, but by the content of their character.
Martin Luther King, Jr.

Before God we are all equally wise - and equally foolish.
Albert Einstein

I have a dream that one day on the red hills of Georgia, the sons of former slaves and the sons of former slave owners will be able to sit together at the table of brotherhood.
Martin Luther King, Jr.

Coming generations will learn equality from poverty, and love from woes.
Khalil Gibran

All this talk about equality. The only thing people really have in common is that they are all going to die.
Bob Dylan

Fourscore and seven years ago our fathers brought forth on this continent, a new nation, conceived in Liberty, and dedicated to the proposition that all men are created equal.
Abraham Lincoln

I am free of all prejudices. I hate every one equally.
W. C. Fields

A woman who thinks she is intelligent demands the same rights as man. An intelligent woman gives up.
Sidonie Gabrielle Colette

The wisdom of man never yet contrived a system of taxation that would operate with perfect equality.
Andrew Jackson

From the equality of rights springs identity of our highest interests; you cannot subvert your neighbor's rights without striking a dangerous blow at your own.
Carl Schurz

Equality may perhaps be a right, but no power on earth can ever turn it into a fact.
Honore de Balzac

All men are created equal, it is only men themselves who place themselves above equality.
David Allan Coe

Equality, rightly understood as our founding fathers understood it, leads to liberty and to the emancipation of creative differences; wrongly understood, as it has been so tragically in our time, it leads first to conformity and then to despotism.
Barry Goldwater

All the people like us are we, and everyone else is They.
Rudyard Kipling

The emotional, sexual, and psychological stereotyping of females begins when the doctor says: It's a girl.
Shirley Chisholm

Democracy does not guarantee equality of conditions - it only guarantees equality of opportunity.
Irving Kristol

I believe in equality for everyone, except reporters and photographers.
Mahatma Gandhi

The sweltering summer of the Negro's legitimate discontent will not pass until there is an invigorating autumn of freedom and equality.
Martin Luther King, Jr.

To be successful, a woman has to be much better at her job than a man.
Golda Meir

In America everybody is of the opinion that he has no social superiors, since all men are equal, but he does not admit that he has no social inferiors, for, from the time of Jefferson onward, the doctrine that all men are equal applies only upwards, not downwards.
Bertrand Russell

To live anywhere in the world today and be against equality because of race or color is like living in Alaska and being against snow.
William Faulkner

These men ask for just the same thing, fairness, and fairness only. This, so far as in my power, they, and all others, shall have.
Abraham Lincoln

If any man claims the Negro should be content... let him say he would willingly change the color of his skin and go to live in the Negro section of a large city. Then and only then has he a right to such a claim.
Robert Kennedy

People are pretty much alike. It's only that our differences are more susceptible to definition than our similarities.
Linda Ellerbee

If liberty and equality, as is thought by some, are chiefly to be found in democracy, they will be best attained when all persons alike share in government to the utmost.
Aristotle

There can be no equality or opportunity if men and women and children be not shielded in their lives from the consequences of great industrial and social processes which they cannot alter, control, or singly cope with.
Woodrow Wilson

Do not call for black power or green power. Call for brain power.
Barbara Jordan

Equality is the soul of liberty; there is, in fact, no liberty without it.
Frances Wright

Equality is not in regarding different things similarly, equality is in regarding different things differently.
Tom Robbins

I know my country has not perfected itself. At times, we've struggled to keep the promise of liberty and equality for all of our people. We've made our share of mistakes, and there are times when our actions around the world have not lived up to our best intentions.
Barack Obama

Women are the only exploited group in history to have been idealized into powerlessness.
Erica Jong

As equality increases, so does the number of people struggling for predominance.
Mason Cooley

One of the things about equality is not just that you be treated equally to a man, but that you treat yourself equally to the way you treat a man.
Marlo Thomas

More countries have understood that women's equality is a prerequisite for development.
Kofi Annan

The battle for women's rights has been largely won.
Margaret Thatcher

If we were to select the most intelligent, imaginative, energetic, and emotionally stable third of mankind, all races would be present.
Franz Boas

All men are born equally free.
Salmon P. Chase

All imaginable futures are not equally possible.
Kevin Kelly

Women's rights is not only an abstraction, a cause; it is also a personal affair. It is not only about us; it is also about me and you. Just the two of us.
Toni Morrison

In order to get beyond racism, we must first take account of race. There is no other way. And in order to treat some persons equally, we must treat them differently.
Harry A. Blackmun

It is better that some should be unhappy rather than that none should be happy, which would be the case in a general state of equality.
Samuel Johnson

The cry of equality pulls everyone down.
Iris Murdoch

I am an aristocrat. I love liberty; I hate equality.
John Randolph

We who are liberal and progressive know that the poor are our equals in every sense except that of being equal to us.
Lionel Trilling

We are a model country where gender equality is concerned.
Tarja Halonen

Virtue can only flourish among equals.
Mary Wollstonecraft

Real equality is immensely difficult to achieve, it needs continual revision and monitoring of distributions. And it does not provide buffers between members, so they are continually colliding or frustrating each other.
Mary Douglas

Equal pay isn't just a women's issue; when women get equal pay, their family incomes rise and the whole family benefits.
Mike Honda

I want to organize so that women see ourselves as people who are entitled to power, entitled to leadership.
Patricia Ireland

Stewardesses are still paid so little that in many cases, new hires qualify for food stamps.
Patricia Ireland

Democratic principles are the result of equality of condition.
Mercy Otis Warren

Nobody really believes in equality anyway.
Warren Farrell

The extension of women's rights is the basic principle of all social progress.
Charles Fourier

Equality and development will not be achieved however if peace is not understood from women's' point of view.
Jenny Shipley

In the 1960s we were fighting to be recognized as equals in the marketplace, in marriage, in education and on the playing field. It was a very exciting, rebellious time.
Marlo Thomas

I refuse to consign the whole male sex to the nursery. I insist on believing that some men are my equals.
Brigid Brophy

Women have a lot to say about how to advance women's rights, and governments need to learn from that, listen to the movement and respond.
Charlotte Bunch

Until women learn to want economic independence, and until they work out a way to get this independence without denying themselves the joys of love and motherhood, it seems to me feminism has no roots.
Crystal Eastman

I want for myself what I want for other women, absolute

equality.
Agnes Macphail

Private religious speech can't be discriminated against. It has to be treated equally with secular speech.
Samuel Alito

EXPERIENCE

Life can only be understood backwards; but it must be lived forwards.
Soren Kierkegaard

A man who carries a cat by the tail learns something he can learn in no other way.
Mark Twain

A mind that is stretched by a new experience can never go back to its old dimensions.
Oliver Wendell Holmes, Jr.

A woman's life can really be a succession of lives, each revolving around some emotionally compelling situation or challenge, and each marked off by some intense experience.
Wallis Simpson

Do you know the difference between education and experience? Education is when you read the fine print; experience is what you get when you don't.
Pete Seeger

Experience is simply the name we give our mistakes.
Oscar Wilde

Excellence is not a skill. It is an attitude.
Ralph Marston

We are not human beings having a spiritual experience. We are spiritual beings having a human experience.
Pierre Teilhard de Chardin

The only source of knowledge is experience.
Albert Einstein

It has been my experience that folks who have no vices have very few virtues.
Abraham Lincoln

Experience is one thing you can't get for nothing.
Oscar Wilde

Bitter experience has taught us how fundamental our values are and how great the mission they represent.
Jan Peter Balkenende

Experience is the teacher of all things.
Julius Caesar

Man learns through experience, and the spiritual path is full of different kinds of experiences. He will encounter many difficulties and obstacles, and they are the very experiences he needs to encourage and complete the cleansing process.
Sai Baba

Every moment is an experience.
Jake Roberts

Everything has been said before, but since nobody listens we have to keep going back and beginning all over again.
Andre Gide

Experience enables you to recognize a mistake when you make it again.
Franklin P. Jones

Human beings, who are almost unique in having the ability to learn from the experience of others, are also remarkable for their apparent disinclination to do so.
Douglas Adams

All that I know I learned after I was thirty.
Georges Clemenceau

Nothing ever becomes real till it is experienced.
John Keats

The sky is the limit. You never have the same experience twice.
Frank McCourt

Deep experience is never peaceful.
Henry James

Life is the art of drawing without an eraser.
John W. Gardner

Good judgment comes from experience, and often experience comes from bad judgment.
Rita Mae Brown

All experience is an arch where through gleams that untraveled world whose margin fades forever and forever when I move.
Alfred Lord Tennyson

Good judgment comes from experience and experience comes from bad judgment.
Fred Brooks

Life is like playing a violin solo in public and learning the instrument as one goes on.
Samuel Butler

If we could sell our experiences for what they cost us, we'd all be millionaires.
Abigail Van Buren

Experience is a good school. But the fees are high.
Heinrich Heine

All experience is an arch, to build upon.
Henry B. Adams

Experience has taught me, when I am shaving of a morning, to keep watch over my thoughts, because, if a line of poetry strays into my memory, my skin bristles so that the razor ceases to act.
A. E. Housman

Nothing is a waste of time if you use the experience wisely.
Auguste Rodin

You cannot create experience. You must undergo it.
Albert Camus

The value of experience is not in seeing much, but in seeing wisely.
William Osler

Experience - the wisdom that enables us to recognize in an undesirable old acquaintance the folly that we have already embraced.
Ambrose Bierce

The years teach much which the days never know.
Ralph Waldo Emerson

My path has not been determined. I shall have more experiences and pass many more milestones.
Agnetha Faltskog

What one has not experienced, one will never understand in print.
Isadora Duncan

Conviction without experience makes for harshness.
Flannery O'Connor

Experience comprises illusions lost, rather than wisdom gained.
Joseph Roux

Experience is a great teacher.
John Legend

An optimist is a guy that has never had much experience.
Don Marquis

We are each responsible for all of our experiences.
Louise L. Hay

There's a beauty to wisdom and experience that cannot be faked. It's impossible to be mature without having lived.
Amy Grant

My experiences have taught me a lot and I'm happy with my learning's, if not with what I went through to learn.
Ally Sheedy

Experience teaches only the teachable.
Aldous Huxley

Experience is the child of thought, and thought is the child of action.
Benjamin Disraeli

Few people even scratch the surface, much less exhaust the contemplation of their own experience.
Randolph Bourne

There are many truths of which the full meaning cannot be realized until personal experience has brought it home.
John Stuart Mill

Judgment comes from experience - and experience comes from bad judgment.
Walter Wriston

Experience is the only prophecy of wise men.
Alphonse de Lamartine

The main thing experience has taught me is that one has to sort of hone their relationship to time, you know.
John Frusciante

I think we are a product of all our experiences.
Sanford I. Weill

Color is an intense experience on its own.
Jim Hodges

When you have really exhausted an experience you always reverence and love it.
Albert Camus

There is nothing so easy to learn as experience and nothing so hard to apply.
Josh Billings

Experiences are savings which a miser puts aside. Wisdom is an inheritance which a wastrel cannot exhaust.
Karl Kraus

Most of the images of reality on which we base our actions are really based on vicarious experience.
Albert Bandura

Information's pretty thin stuff unless mixed with experience.
Clarence Day

The experience of God, or in any case the possibility of experiencing God, is innate.
Alice Walker

Skill is the unified force of experience, intellect and passion in their operation.
John Ruskin

Real love is a permanently self-enlarging experience.
M. Scott Peck

Everything is discursive opinion instead of direct experience.
A. R. Ammons

Not the fruit of experience, but experience itself, is the end.
Walter Pater

FAITH

Be faithful in small things because it is in them that your strength lies.
Mother Teresa

Faith is taking the first step even when you don't see the whole staircase.
Martin Luther King, Jr.

Take the first step in faith. You don't have to see the whole staircase, just take the first step.
Martin Luther King, Jr.

All who call on God in true faith, earnestly from the heart, will certainly be heard, and will receive what they have asked and desired.
Martin Luther

Doubt is a pain too lonely to know that faith is his twin brother.
Khalil Gibran

Faith is a knowledge within the heart, beyond the reach of proof.
Khalil Gibran

As your faith is strengthened you will find that there is no longer the need to have a sense of control, that things will flow as they will, and that you will flow with them, to your great delight and benefit.
Emmanuel Teney

Faith is to believe what you do not see; the reward of this faith is to see what you believe.
Saint Augustine

Faith consists in believing when it is beyond the power of reason to believe.
Voltaire

That deep emotional conviction of the presence of a superior reasoning power, which is revealed in the incomprehensible universe, forms my idea of God.
Albert Einstein

A man of courage is also full of faith.
Marcus Tullius Cicero

Every tomorrow has two handles. We can take hold of it with the handle of anxiety or the handle of faith.
Henry Ward Beecher

A faith is a necessity to a man. Woe to him who believes in nothing.
Victor Hugo

God, our Creator, has stored within our minds and personalities, great potential strength and ability. Prayer helps us tap and develop these powers.
Abdul Kalam

He who has faith has... an inward reservoir of courage, hope, confidence, calmness, and assuring trust that all will come out well - even though to the world it may appear to come out most badly.
B. C. Forbes

Faith: not wanting to know what is true.
Friedrich Nietzsche

Be a sinner and sin strongly, but more strongly have faith and rejoice in Christ.
Martin Luther

Faith in oneself is the best and safest course.
Michelangelo

I have not lost faith in God. I have moments of anger and protest. Sometimes I've been closer to him for that reason.
Elie Wiesel

Faith is not belief without proof, but trust without reservation.
D. Elton Trueblood

Faith has to do with things that are not seen and hope with things that are not at hand.
Thomas Aquinas

To one who has faith, no explanation is necessary. To one without faith, no explanation is possible.
Thomas Aquinas

Faith is a passionate intuition.
William Wordsworth

Faith is the bird that feels the light when the dawn is still dark.
Rabindranath Tagore

Have faith in God; God has faith in you.
Edwin Louis Cole

Faith indeed tells what the senses do not tell, but not the contrary of what they see. It is above them and not contrary to them.
Blaise Pascal

Faith and doubt both are needed - not as antagonists, but working side by side to take us around the unknown curve.
Lillian Smith

In faith there is enough light for those who want to believe and enough shadows to blind those who don't.
Blaise Pascal

If patience is worth anything, it must endure to the end of time. And a living faith will last in the midst of the blackest storm.
Mahatma Gandhi

Faith is not something to grasp, it is a state to grow into.
Mahatma Gandhi

He wants you all to Himself to put His loving, divine arms around you.
Charles Stanley

Nor shall derision prove powerful against those who listen to humanity or those who follow in the footsteps of divinity, for they shall live forever. Forever.
Khalil Gibran

God... a being whose only definition is that he is beyond man's power to conceive.
Ayn Rand

Put your nose into the Bible everyday. It is your spiritual food. And then share it. Make a vow not to be a lukewarm Christian.
Kirk Cameron

If you have God on your side, everything becomes clear.
Ayrton Senna

Faith means belief in something concerning which doubt is theoretically possible.
William James

I hold that religion and faith are two different things.
Pat Buckley

We are twice armed if we fight with faith.
Plato

It takes vision and courage to create - it takes faith and courage to prove.
Owen D. Young

Your faithfulness makes you trustworthy to God.
Edwin Louis Cole

Reason is our soul's left hand, faith her right.
John Donne

I seek a deeper truth, but I don't think I have to go to a building designated for worship to find it.
Ted Lange

Faith and prayer are the vitamins of the soul; man cannot live in health without them.
Mahalia Jackson

Keep the faith, don't lose your perseverance and always trust your gut extinct.
Paula Abdul

Faith is spiritualized imagination.
Henry Ward Beecher

Worry is spiritual short sight. Its cure is intelligent faith.
Paul Brunton

Man, I just feel blessed... I was in a situation where the only way I could come out of it was by putting my faith in God. No matter how good my lawyers were, no matter how much celebrity I had, everything was just stacked up against me.
Puff Daddy

Faith is the very first thing you should pack in a hope chest.
Sarah Ban Breathnach

Our faith comes in moments; our vice is habitual.
Ralph Waldo Emerson

To me faith means not worrying.
John Dewey

Love, hope, fear, faith - these make humanity; These are its sign and note and character.
Robert Browning Hamilton

I die the king's faithful servant, but God's first.
Thomas More

Keep your faith in God, but keep your powder dry.
Oliver Cromwell

We are a long time in learning that all our strength and salvation is in God.
David Brainerd

It is truer to say that martyrs create faith more than faith creates martyrs.
Miguel de Unamuno

Faith is reason grown courageous.
Sherwood Eddy

My reason nourishes my faith and my faith my reason.
Norman Cousins

In the affairs of this world, men are saved not by faith, but by the want of it.
Benjamin Franklin

What does God the Father look like? Although I've never seen Him, I believe - as with the Holy Spirit - He looks like Jesus looked on earth.
Benny Hinn

The faith that stands on authority is not faith.
Ralph Waldo Emerson

Faith, to my mind, is a stiffening process, a sort of mental starch.
E. M. Forster

Faith is not contrary to reason.
Sherwood Eddy

The only faith that wears well and holds its color in all weathers is that which is woven of conviction and set with the sharp mordant of experience.
James Russell Lowell

Vision looks upward and becomes faith.
Stephen Samuel Wise

Only faith is sufficient.
Robert Ley

We can no more do without spirituality than we can do without food, shelter, or clothing.
Ernest Holmes

It was seldom that I attended any religious meetings, as my parents had not much faith in and were never so unfortunate as to unite themselves with any of the religious sects.
Orson Pratt

Knowledge is only one half. Faith is the other.
Novalis

The power of faith will often shine forth the most when the character is naturally weak.
Augustus Hare

No matter how old we become, we can still call them 'Holy Mother' and 'Father' and put a child-like trust in them.
Desmond Morris

Ultimately, blind faith is the only kind.
Mason Cooley

I think the greatest taboos in America are faith and failure.
Michael Malone

FAMILY

If a country is to be corruption free and become a nation of beautiful minds, I strongly feel there are three key societal members who can make a difference. They are the father, the mother and the teacher.
Abdul Kalam

The love of family and the admiration of friends is much more important than wealth and privilege.
Charles Kuralt

Family is not an important thing, it's everything.
Michael J. Fox

A man should never neglect his family for business.
Walt Disney

Family means no one gets left behind or forgotten.
David Ogden Stiers

A happy family is but an earlier heaven.
George Bernard Shaw

A family can develop only with a loving woman as its center.
Karl Wilhelm Friedrich Schlegel

He who is overly attached to his family members experiences fear and sorrow, for the root of all grief is attachment. Thus one should discard attachment to be happy.
Chanakya

Family is the most important thing in the world.
Princess Diana

A woman can take care of the family. It takes a man to provide structure, to provide stability.
Tom DeLay

I'll never stop dreaming that one day we can be a real family, together, all of us laughing and talking, loving and understanding, not looking at the past but only to the future.
LaToya Jackson

All of us grow up in particular realities - a home, family, a clan, a small town, a neighborhood. Depending upon how we're brought up, we are either deeply aware of the particular reading of reality into which we are born, or we are peripherally aware of it.
Chaim Potok

Cherish your human connections - your relationships with friends and family.
Barbara Bush

America cannot continue to lead the family of nations around the world if we suffer the collapse of the family here at home.
Mitt Romney

A family is a place where principles are hammered and honed on the anvil of everyday living.
Charles R. Swindoll

I was born into the most remarkable and eccentric family I could possibly have hoped for.
Maureen O'Hara

Without a family, man, alone in the world, trembles with the cold.
Andre Maurois

Family life itself, that safest, most traditional, most approved of female choices, is not a sanctuary: It is, perpetually, a dangerous place.
Margaret Drabble

Dignity is not negotiable. Dignity is the honor of the family.
Vartan Gregorian

The greatest thing in family life is to take a hint when a hint is intended-and not to take a hint when a hint isn't intended.
Robert Frost

If you cannot get rid of the family skeleton, you may as well make it dance.
George Bernard Shaw

Rarely do members of the same family grow up under the same roof.
Richard Bach

The family is the nucleus of civilization.
Will Durant

My family is my strength and my weakness.
Aishwarya Rai

Insanity runs in my family. It practically gallops.
Cary Grant

Both within the family and without, our sisters hold up our mirrors: our images of who we are and of who we can dare to be.
Elizabeth Fishel

I don't think anyone has a normal family.
Edward Furlong

I come from that society and there is a common thread, specifically family values - the idea that you do anything for your family, and the unconditional love for one's children.
Ednita Nazario

My family comes first. Maybe that's what makes me different from other guys.
Bobby Darin

When trouble comes, it's your family that supports you.
Guy Lafleur

I believe the world is one big family, and we need to help each other.
Jet Li

The family is one of nature's masterpieces.
George Santayana

The only rock I know that stays steady, the only institution I know that works, is the family.
Lee Iacocca

To us, family means putting your arms around each other and being there.
Barbara Bush

Spend some time this weekend on home improvement; improve your attitude toward your family.
Bo Bennett

I am the baby in the family, and I always will be. I am actually very happy to have that position. But I still get teased. I don't mind that.
Janet Jackson

If one is desperate for love, I suggest looking at one's friends and family and see if love is all around. If not, get a new set of friends, a new family.
Jasmine Guy

If we abandon marriage, we abandon the family.
Michael Enzi

My father used to play with my brother and me in the yard. Mother would come out and say, "You're tearing up the grass"; "We're not raising grass," Dad would reply. "We're raising boys".
Harmon Killebrew

I never did quite fit the glamour mode. It is life with my husband and family that is my high now.
Patty Duke

I have a family to support. And I'm not always going to be doing exactly what I want to do.
Patrick Warburton

For me, nothing has ever taken precedence over being a mother and having a family and a home.
Jessica Lange

The family is the first essential cell of human society.
Pope John XXIII

I am the family face; flesh perishes, I live on.
Thomas Hardy

It's not that our family has no taste, it's just that our family's taste is inconsistent.
Dave Eggers

Women's natural role is to be a pillar of the family.
Grace Kelly

One of the things that binds us as a family is a shared sense of humor.
Ralph Fiennes

I mean, I look at my dad. He was twenty when he started having a family, and he was always the coolest dad. He did everything for his kids, and he never made us feel like he was pressured. I know that it must be a great feeling to be a guy like that.
Adam Sandler

A woman should be home with the children, building that home and making sure there's a secure family atmosphere.
Mel Gibson

As a general thing, when a woman wears the pants in a family, she has a good right to them.
Josh Billings

People are pretty forgiving when it comes to other people's families. The only family that ever horrifies you is your own.
Doug Coupland

I've given it my all. I've done my best. Now, I'm ready with my family to begin the next phase of our lives.
Richard M. Daley

Happy is said to be the family which can eat onions together. They are, for the time being, separate, from the world, and have a harmony of aspiration.
Charles Dudley Warner

My family is more important than my party.
Zell Miller

I consider my mom and all my sisters my friends.
Alexa Vega

Pray in your family daily, that yours may be in the number of the families who call upon God.
Christopher Love

What must it be like for a little boy to read that daddy never loved mummy?
Princess Diana

You have to defend your honor. And your family.
Suzanne Vega

My family was my guide to my reality.
Haywood Nelson

Also, my mom and family are very important to me and I know that this is not expected.
Christina Milian

I grew up in a big family with a lot of kids around, and I definitely want to have children as well.
Heidi Klum

I realized my family was funny, because nobody ever wanted to leave our house.
Anthony Anderson

A woman can plan when to have her family and how to support a family.
Kathleen Turner

I've always put my family first and that's just the way it is.
Jamie Lee Curtis

I love my family.
Manute Bol

I am tortured when I am away from my family, from my children. I am horribly guilt-ridden.
Jessica Lange

I think togetherness is a very important ingredient to family life.
Barbara Bush

The family you come from isn't as important as the family you're going to have.
Ring Lardner

Give a little love to a child, and you get a great deal back.
John Ruskin

I love cooking for myself and cooking for my family.
Al Roker

It takes a lot of work to put together a marriage, to put together a family and a home.
Elizabeth Edwards

One's family is the most important thing in life. I look at it this way: One of these days I'll be over in a hospital somewhere with four walls around me. And the only people who'll be with me will be my family.
Robert Byrd

When I remember my family, I always remember their backs. They were always indignantly leaving places.
John Cheever

Family, nature and health all go together.
Olivia Newton-John

Maybe there is no actual place called hell. Maybe hell is just having to listen to our grandparents breathe through their noses when they're eating sandwiches.
Jim Carrey

When you start about family, about lineage and ancestry, you are talking about every person on earth.
Alex Haley

I would rather start a family than finish one.
Don Marquis

Tennis just a game, family is forever.
Serena Williams

The one thing that kept our family together was the music. The only thing that our family would share emotionally was to have our dad cry over something the kids did with music.
Dennis Wilson

The joke in our family is that we can cry reading the phone book.
Ron Reagan

Make a Goal Box, a chart of positive daily contact with a family when you are working with them.
Richard G. Scott

The most difficult is the first family, to bring someone out of the world.
Richard G. Scott

God did not intend the human family to be wafted to heaven on flowery beds of ease.
Frank Knox

I have these visions of myself being thirty, thirty-five, forty having a family.
Nastassja Kinski

We love to be with our family and friends and I can tell you that lots of eating will be involved.
Julia Barr

I grew up in a family in which political issues were often discussed, and debated intensely.
Joseph Stiglitz

At a certain point I'm going to want to have a family.
Gwen Stefani

When I'm ready, I plan to adopt. I still believe in family.
LaToya Jackson

We went to church every Sunday. When I was a kid, the only time I sang was around my family.
Darius Rucker

Some of the most important conversations I've ever had occurred at my family's dinner table.
Bob Ehrlich

There are things that you cannot talk to your mother and father about, there are things that you cannot talk to your children about.
Shirley Knight

I have a lot of very close girlfriends and sisters - I'm from an all female family. My father often quips that even the cat was neutered!
Shirley Manson

I find the family the most mysterious and fascinating institution in the world.
Amos Oz

I grew up in a very religious family. I could read the Qu'ran easily at the age of five.
Akhmad Kadyrov

Dad kept us out of school, but school comes and goes. Family is forever.
Charlie Sheen

Like all my family and class, I considered it a sign of weakness to show affection; to have been caught kissing my mother would have been a disgrace, and to have shown affection for my father would have been a disaster.
Agnes Smedley

I live quietly at home among my family and friends.
Antonio Tabucchi

Once I got married and had kids, I moved away from romantic roles, because it seemed wrong to have my 3-year-old wondering why Daddy was kissing someone else.
Chevy Chase

The foundation of family - that's where it all begins for me.
Faith Hill

Our family life was certainly not intellectual.
Douglass North

My family background was deeply Christian.
Abbe Pierre

I'm not much of a family man. I'm just not that into it. I love kids, I adore them, but I don't want to live my life for them.
Sting

The attempt to redefine the family as a purely voluntary arrangement grows out of the modern delusion that people can keep all their options open all the time.
Christopher Lasch

The left dismisses talk about the collapse of family life and talks instead about the emergence of the growing new diversity of family types.
Christopher Lasch

There's nothing I value more than the closeness of friends and family, a smile as I pass someone on the street.
Willie Stargell

For all of those willing to help me start a family, I am flattered. I will let you know when I need your help.
Paula Abdul

There is no such thing as fun for the whole family.
Jerry Seinfeld

My life comes down to three moments: the death of my father, meeting my husband, and the birth of my daughter. Everything I did previous to that just doesn't seem to add up to very much.
Gwyneth Paltrow

You leave home to seek your fortune and, when you get it, you go home and share it with your family.
Anita Baker

Little children are still the symbol of the eternal marriage between love and duty.
George Eliot

I stay in tune with my family and God.
Regina King

In every conceivable manner, the family is link to our past, bridge to our future.
Alex Haley

Parents need all the help they can get. The strongest as well as the most fragile family requires a vital network of social supports.
Bernice Weissbourd

It is extraordinary that when you are acquainted with a whole family you can forget about them.
Gertrude Stein

If I had no family, my wife and I would lead a much more romantic and nomadic existence.
David McCallum

I have frequently been questioned, especially by women, of how I could reconcile family life with a scientific career. Well, it has not been easy.
Marie Curie

I would love a family. I'm at the age where the wish for a child gets stronger. But who knows.
Cameron Diaz

It's very strange that most people don't care if their knowledge of their family history only goes back three generations.
Doug Coupland

I don't know if I believe in marriage. I believe in family, love and children.
Penelope Cruz

When I was younger, my family would go camping and fishing on our ranches. My dad loves being around all kinds of animals. He's the one who got me to be a really big animal lover.
Paris Hilton

We'll sort of get over the marriage first and then maybe look at the kids. But obviously we want a family so we'll have to start thinking about that.
Prince William

I love children and I get along with them great. It's just that I believe if you're going to be a parent, there has to be something inside you that says, 'I want a family.' I don't feel that sense of urgency.
George Clooney

FINANCE

I am favor of cutting taxes under any circumstances and for any excuse, for any reason, whenever it's possible.
Milton Friedman

Don't gamble; take all your savings and buy some good stock and hold it till it goes up, then sell it. If it don't go up, don't buy it.
Will Rogers

Money was never a big motivation for me, except as a way to keep score. The real excitement is playing the game.
Donald Trump

The propensity to truck, barter and exchange one thing for another is common to all men, and to be found in no other race of animals.
Adam Smith

Inflation is taxation without legislation.
Milton Friedman

A big part of financial freedom is having your heart and mind free from worry about the what-ifs of life.
Suze Orman

In the absence of the gold standard, there is no way to protect savings from confiscation through inflation. There is no safe store of value.
Alan Greenspan

It is a kind of spiritual snobbery that makes people think they can be happy without money.
Albert Camus

Your net worth to the world is usually determined by what remains after your bad habits are subtracted from your good ones.
Benjamin Franklin

Any informed borrower is simply less vulnerable to fraud and abuse.
Alan Greenspan

Owning a home is a keystone of wealth... both financial

affluence and emotional security.
Suze Orman

Surplus wealth is a sacred trust which its possessor is bound to administer in his lifetime for the good of the community.
Andrew Carnegie

Wealth consists not in having great possessions, but in having few wants.
Epictetus

Our incomes are like our shoes; if too small, they gall and pinch us; but if too large, they cause us to stumble and to trip.
John Locke

Under capitalism, man exploits man. Under communism, it's just the opposite.
John Kenneth Galbraith

A moderate addiction to money may not always be hurtful; but when taken in excess it is nearly always bad for the health.
Clarence Day

As sure as the spring will follow the winter, prosperity and economic growth will follow recession.
Bo Bennett

We cannot both preach and administer financial matters.
Saint Stephen

All money is a matter of belief.
Adam Smith

Do you know the only thing that gives me pleasure? It's to see my dividends coming in.
John D. Rockefeller

I don't think about financial success as the measurement of my success.
Christie Hefner

Money is like manure. You have to spread it around or it smells.
J. Paul Getty

The way to make money is to buy when blood is running in the streets.
John D. Rockefeller

Part of your heritage in this society is the opportunity to become financially independent.
Jim Rohn

I do not regard a broker as a member of the human race.
Honore de Balzac

We had a booming stock market in 1929 and then went into the world's greatest depression. We have a booming stock market in 1999. Will the bubble somehow burst, and then we enter depression? Well, some things are not different.
Jeffrey Sachs

Today, if you look at financial systems around the globe, more than half the population of the world - out of six billion people, more than three billion - do not qualify to take out a loan from a bank. This is a shame.
Muhammad Yunus

Thirty to 40 years ago, most financial decisions were fairly simple.
Scott Cook

I made my money by selling too soon.
Bernard Baruch

We at Chrysler borrow money the old-fashioned way. We pay it back.
Lee Iacocca

It's not the having, it's the getting.
Charles Spurgeon

The avoidance of taxes is the only intellectual pursuit that still carries any reward.
John Maynard Keynes

Money is to my social existence what health is to my body.
Mason Cooley

Starting out to make money is the greatest mistake in life. Do what you feel you have a flair for doing, and if you are good enough at it, the money will come.
Greer Garson

I finally know what distinguishes man from the other beasts: financial worries.
Jules Renard

For the merchant, even honesty is a financial speculation.
Charles Baudelaire

Wealth is not without its advantages and the case to the contrary, although it has often been made, has never proved widely persuasive.
John Kenneth Galbraith

Wealth, in even the most improbable cases, manages to convey the aspect of

intelligence.
John Kenneth Galbraith

The only way for a rich man to be healthy is by exercise and abstinence, to live as if he were poor.
William Temple

Security depends not so much upon how much you have, as upon how much you can do without.
Joseph Wood Krutch

The poor don't know that their function in life is to exercise our generosity.
Jean-Paul Sartre

The way to become rich is to put all your eggs in one basket and then watch that basket.
Andrew Carnegie

As a novelist, I tell stories and people give me money. Then financial planners tell me stories and I give them money.
Martin Cruz Smith

The rate of interest acts as a link between income-value and capital-value.
Irving Fisher

Thirteen thousand dollars a year is not enough to raise a family. That's not enough to pay your bills and save for their future. That's barely enough to provide for even the most basic needs.
Thomas Carper

I've always supported myself. I like the sense of knowing exactly where I stand financially, but there is a side of me that longs for a knight in shining armor.
Barbara Feldon

Under capitalism each individual engages in economic planning.
George Reisman

Capital is that part of wealth which is devoted to obtaining further wealth.
Alfred Marshall

I'm involved in the stock market, which is fun and, sometimes, very painful.
Regis Philbin

Money is the best rule of commerce.
William Petty

It is bad policy to regulate everything... where things may better regulate themselves and can be better promoted

by private exertions; but it is no less bad policy to let those things alone which can only be promoted by interfering social power.
Friedrich List

We've taken the view that if the rest of the world would democratize and create market economies, that would spread the benefits of prosperity around the world, and that it would enhance our own prosperity, and our own stability and security, as well.
Jeffrey Sachs

Rounding to the nearest cent is sufficiently accurate for practical purposes.
Alexander John Ellis

Poverty is unnecessary.
Muhammad Yunus

To beat the market you'll have to invest serious bucks to dig up information no one else has yet.
Merton Miller

You only need to make one big score in finance to be a hero forever.
Merton Miller

I wasn't a financial pro, and I paid the price.
Ruth Handler

The problem of how we finance the welfare state should not obscure a separate issue: if each person thinks he has an inalienable right to welfare, no matter what happens to the world, that's not equity, it's just creating a society where you can't ask anything of people.
Jacques Delors

The job of the Central Bank is to worry.
Alice Rivlin

The economy is a very sensitive organism.
Hjalmar Schacht

Gold and silver, like other commodities, have an intrinsic value, which is not arbitrary, but is dependent on their scarcity, the quantity of labour bestowed in procuring them, and the value of the capital employed in the mines which produce them.
David Ricardo

There can be no rise in the value of labour without a fall of profits.
David Ricardo

The only way that we can reduce our financial dependence on the inflow of funds from the rest of the

world is to reduce our trade deficit.
Martin Feldstein

It is incumbent upon each of us to improve spending and savings practices to ensure our own individual financial security and preserve the collective economic well-being of our great society.
Ron Lewis

Infinite growth of material consumption in a finite world is an impossibility.
E. F. Schumacher

One of the funny things about the stock market is that every time one person buys, another sells, and both think they are astute.
William Feather

The price of every thing rises and falls from time to time and place to place; and with every such change the purchasing power of money changes so far as that thing goes.
Alfred Marshall

Many people are in the dark when it comes to money, and I'm going to turn on the lights.
Suze Orman

FITNESS

Take care of your body. It's the only place you have to live.
Jim Rohn

Physical fitness is not only one of the most important keys to a healthy body, it is the basis of dynamic and creative intellectual activity.
John F. Kennedy

Bodybuilding is much like any other sport. To be successful, you must dedicate yourself 100% to your training, diet and mental approach.
Arnold Schwarzenegger

He who has health, has hope; and he who has hope, has everything.
Thomas Carlyle

Attention to health is life's greatest hindrance.
Plato

The first wealth is health.
Ralph Waldo Emerson

Exercise to stimulate, not to annihilate. The world wasn't formed in a day, and neither were we. Set small goals and build upon them.
Lee Haney

It is health that is real wealth and not pieces of gold and silver.
Mahatma Gandhi

Leave all the afternoon for exercise and recreation, which are as necessary as reading. I will rather say more necessary because health is worth more than learning.
Thomas Jefferson

A vigorous five-mile walk will do more good for an unhappy but otherwise healthy adult than all the medicine and psychology in the world.
Paul Dudley White

Fitness needs to be perceived as fun and games or we subconsciously avoid it.
Alan Thicke

If we could give every individual the right amount of nourishment and exercise, not too little and not too much, we would have found the safest way to health.
Hippocrates

If a man achieves victory over this body, who in the world can exercise power over him? He who rules himself rules over the whole world.
Vinoba Bhave

A runner must run with dreams in his heart, not money in his pocket.
Emil Zatopek

And I believe that the best buy in public health today must be a combination of regular physical exercise and a healthy diet.
Julie Bishop

Time and health are two precious assets that we don't recognize and appreciate until they have been depleted.
Denis Waitley

Jogging is very beneficial. It's good for your legs and your feet. It's also very good for the ground. If makes it feel needed.
Charles M. Schulz

Here's what I tell anybody and this is what I believe. The greatest gift we have is the gift of life. We understand that. That comes from our Creator. We're given a body. Now you may not like it, but you can maximize that body the best it can be maximized.
Mike Ditka

Our growing softness, our increasing lack of physical fitness, is a menace to our security.
John F. Kennedy

If it weren't for the fact that the TV set and the refrigerator are so far apart, some of us wouldn't get any exercise at all.
Joey Adams

The human body is the best picture of the human soul.
Ludwig Wittgenstein

Walking is the best possible exercise. Habituate yourself to walk very fast.
Thomas Jefferson

I think it's more important to be fit so that you can be healthy and enjoy activities than it is to have a good body.
Rachel Blanchard

Exercise is done against one's wishes and maintained only because the alternative is worse.
George A. Sheehan

Exercise is the chief source of improvement in our faculties.
Hugh Blair

The reason I exercise is for the quality of life I enjoy.
Kenneth H. Cooper

Find fitness with fun dancing. It is fun and makes you forget about the dreaded exercise.
Paula Abdul

Quit worrying about your health. It will go away.
Robert Orben

There's a lot of people in this world who spend so much time watching their health that they haven't the time to enjoy it.
Josh Billings

I would rather exercise than read a newspaper.
Kim Alexis

True enjoyment comes from activity of the mind and exercise of the body; the two are ever united.
Wilhelm von Humboldt

Happiness lies first of all in health.
George William Curtis

Clearly, society has a tremendous stake in insisting on a woman's natural fitness for the career of mother: the alternatives are all too expensive.
Ann Oakley

Muscles come and go; flab lasts.
Bill Vaughan

Exercise should be regarded as tribute to the heart.
Gene Tunney

I think exercise tests us in so many ways, our skills, our hearts, our ability to bounce back after setbacks. This is the inner beauty of sports and competition, and it can serve us all well as adult athletes.
Peggy Fleming

Personally, I need a high level of physical fitness in order to feel at ease.
Jurgen Klinsmann

I have been through various fitness regimes. I used to run about five miles a day and I did aerobics for a while.
Sting

Regularity in the hours of rising and retiring, perseverance in exercise, adaptation of dress to the variations of climate, simple and nutritious aliment, and temperance in all things are necessary branches of the regimen of health.
Lord Chesterfield

The only weights I lift are my dogs.
Olivia Newton-John

It's very important to have the right clothing to exercise in. If you throw on an old T-shirt or sweats, it's not inspiring for your workout.
Cheryl Tiegs

Never hurry. Take plenty of exercise. Always be cheerful. Take all the sleep you need. You may expect to be well.
James Freeman Clarke

You gotta have a body.
Jayne Mansfield

The groundwork of all happiness is health.
Leigh Hunt

Your body is the church where Nature asks to be reverenced.
Marquis de Sade

Exercise is labor without weariness.
Samuel Johnson

Health is the thing that makes you feel that now is the best time of the year.
Franklin P. Adams

Swimming is normal for me. I'm relaxed. I'm comfortable, and I know my surroundings. It's my home.
Michael Phelps

Looking after my health today gives me a better hope for tomorrow.
Anne Wilson Schaef

Like most people I can be lazy, so it's nice to have a goal or deadline or reason to work out. I feel better when I get to exercise, or when I'm outdoors. I like to hike, swim and run, and I love to play soccer.
Viggo Mortensen

And you know, the baby boomers are getting older, and those off the rack clothes are just not fitting right any longer, and so, tailor-made suits are coming back into fashion.
Amy Irving

You need to eat normally and healthfully, and you need to exercise. I'm so passionate about this because I think people spend their lives not happy in their bodies.
Courtney Thorne Smith

Tactics, fitness, stroke ability, adaptability, experience, and sportsmanship are all necessary for winning.
Fred Perry

I'm French, so I'm quite lazy about exercising, and I smoke. But I do love going for a run in the morning with my dog. That's all.
Eva Green

Once in a while I'll get moved to do some exercise. It's something I long for but the biggest problem is bending down and putting my tennis shoes on. Once I go out I'm OK.
David Soul

I concentrate on exercises from the waist down, since that is the laziest part of a woman's body.
Tina Louise

My bottom is so big it's got its own gravitational field.
Carol Vorderman

I like exercise. I like a healthy body.
Erin Gray

It's challenging, but you have to at least try to eat right and exercise.
Joely Fisher

In the midst of these hard times it is our good health and good sleep that are enjoyable.
Knute Nelson

It's not about weight, it's about fitness, and one component of being fit is to have relatively low body fat, because fat is not very efficient, whereas muscle is.
Deborah Bull

A year ago I had a back injury and followed a good nutrition program to help speed up my recovery. I focused on exercise and staying healthy in order to get back out on the ice.
Sasha Cohen

You must also give mental and physical fitness priority.
Jim Otto

For exercise, I now run with my chocolate Lab puppy, Oscar.
Daniela Pestova

Don't get me wrong, I think bikes are terrific. I own several of my own, including a trendy mountain style, and ride them for pleasure and light exercise.
Brock Yates

When I do get time, I like to hike and I take lots of vitamins and powders to keep healthy.
Catherine Bell

I love to swim for miles; I could just go back and forth.
Jill Clayburgh

Investing in health will produce enormous benefits.
Gro Harlem Brundtland

To enjoy the glow of good health, you must exercise.
Gene Tunney

I didn't have the same fitness or ability as the other girls, so I had to beat them with my mind.
Martina Hingis

It's been a long road back to health and fitness for me. I am just glad to have been given the opportunity to do what I love most.
Jonah Lomu

In terms of fitness and battling through cancer, exercise helps you stay strong physically and mentally.
Grete Waitz

I think if you exercise, your state of mind - my state of mind - is usually more at ease, ready for more mental challenges. Once I get the physical stuff out of the way it always seems like I have more calmness and better self-esteem.
Stone Gossard

So I've broadened the fitness concept to make it one of moderation and balance.
Kenneth H. Cooper

I'm still very professional about my fitness. I stay in trim as I always did.
Peter Shilton

I don't smoke, don't drink much, and go to the gym five times a week. I live a healthy lifestyle and feel great. I can run a marathon, you know.
Sarah Michelle Gellar

Training is such a vital part of preparation for a game, you really do train to play. It tops up your ability, like sharpening a carving knife. You can get away with not doing it for a while, as long as you have reached a certain standard of fitness.
Graeme Le Saux

Health is the vital principle of bliss, and exercise, of health.
James Thomson

FOOD

A man can live and be healthy without killing animals for food; therefore, if he eats meat, he participates in taking animal life merely for the sake of his appetite.
Leo Tolstoy

You better cut the pizza in four pieces because I'm not hungry enough to eat six.
Yogi Berra

It's okay to eat fish because they don't have any feelings.
Kurt Cobain

Animals are my friends... and I don't eat my friends.
George Bernard Shaw

I want my food dead. Not sick, not dying, dead.
Oscar Wilde

I don't like food that's too carefully arranged; it makes me think that the chef is spending too much time arranging and not enough time cooking. If I wanted a picture I'd buy a painting.
Andy Rooney

Once, during Prohibition, I was forced to live for days on nothing but food and water.
W. C. Fields

Anything is good if it's made of chocolate.
Jo Brand

Fettucini alfredo is macaroni and cheese for adults.
Mitch Hedberg

I won't eat anything green.
Kurt Cobain

A crust eaten in peace is better than a banquet partaken in anxiety.
Aesop

Beware the hobby that eats.
Benjamin Franklin

Gluttony is an emotional escape, a sign something is eating us.
Peter De Vries

If food were free, why work?
Douglas Horton

Man is the only animal that can remain on friendly terms with the victims he intends to eat until he eats them.
Samuel Butler

I come from a family where gravy is considered a beverage.
Erma Bombeck

Vegetarians are cool. All I eat are vegetarians - except for the occasional mountain lion steak.
Ted Nugent

Cultivation to the mind is as necessary as food to the body.
Marcus Tullius Cicero

It's difficult to believe that people are still starving in this country because food isn't available.
Ronald Reagan

Food for the body is not enough. There must be food for the soul.
Dorothy Day

Statistics show that of those who contract the habit of eating, very few survive.
George Bernard Shaw

Why does man kill? He kills for food. And not only food: frequently there must be a beverage.
Woody Allen

If you really want to make a friend, go to someone's house and eat with him... the people who give you their food give you their heart.
Cesar Chavez

I will not eat oysters. I want my food dead. Not sick. Not wounded. Dead.
Woody Allen

If you want to eat well in England, eat three breakfasts.
W. Somerset Maugham

Spaghetti can be eaten most successfully if you inhale it like a vacuum cleaner.
Sophia Loren

My weaknesses have always been food and men - in that order.
Dolly Parton

I eat a variety of foods like vegetables, fruit and beef for protein and iron.
Sasha Cohen

What I've enjoyed most, though, is meeting people who have a real interest in food and sharing ideas with them. Good food is a global thing and I find that there is always something new and amazing to learn - I love it!
Jamie Oliver

Health food may be good for the conscience but Oreos taste a hell of a lot better.
Robert Redford

Eating rice cakes is like chewing on a foam coffee cup, only less filling.
Dave Barry

The most remarkable thing about my mother is that for thirty years she served the family nothing but leftovers. The original meal has never been found.
Calvin Trillin

You can tell alot about a fellow's character by his way of eating jellybeans.
Ronald Reagan

I always knew that food and wine were vital, with my mother being Italian and a good cook.
Robert Mondavi

I can make dressing - or stuffing. Y'all call it stuffing up here, we call it dressing down there. It's really good dressing. That family recipe was passed on, and I love to make that.
Edie Brickell

Civilization as it is known today could not have evolved, nor can it survive, without an adequate food supply.
Norman Borlaug

So long as you have food in your mouth, you have solved all questions for the time being.
Franz Kafka

There is no sincerer love than the love of food.
George Bernard Shaw

More die in the United States of too much food than of too little.
John Kenneth Galbraith

Maybe a person's time would be as well spent raising food as raising money to buy food.
Frank Howard Clark

I said to my friends that if I was going to starve, I might as well starve where the food is good.
Virgil Thomson

An Englishman teaching an American about food is like the blind leading the one-eyed.
A. J. Liebling

Eating without conversation is only stoking.
Marcelene Cox

Like religion, politics, and family planning, cereal is not a topic to be brought up in public. It's too controversial.
Erma Bombeck

Food is our common ground, a universal experience.
James Beard

Human beings do not eat nutrients, they eat food.
Mary Catherine Bateson

It's easy for Americans to forget that the food they eat doesn't magically appear on a supermarket shelf.
Christopher Dodd

I do love Italian food. Any kind of pasta or pizza. My new pig out food is Indian food. I eat Indian food like three times a week. It's so good.
Jennifer Love Hewitt

I could talk food all day. I love good food.
Tom Brady

Food simply isn't important to me.
Alice Paul

Man seeks to change the foods available in nature to suit his tastes, thereby putting an end to the very essence of life contained in them.
Sai Baba

My idea of fast food is a mallard.
Ted Nugent

Food is your body's fuel. Without fuel, your body wants to shut down.
Ken Hill

You don't need a silver fork to eat good food.
Paul Prudhomme

Most vegetarians look so much like the food they eat that they can be classified as cannibals.
Finley Peter Dunne

I haven't eaten at a McDonald's since I became President.
William J. Clinton

Three things are needed for a good life, good friends, good food, and good song.
Jason Zebehazy

Venice is like eating an entire box of chocolate liqueurs in one go.
Truman Capote

One of the glories of New York is its ethnic food, and only McDonald's and Burger King equalize us all.
John Corry

I never eat in a restaurant that's over a hundred feet off the ground and won't stand still.
Calvin Trillin

The disparity between a restaurant's price and food quality rises in direct proportion to the size of the pepper mill.
Bryan Miller

More than any other in Western Europe, Britain remains a country where a traveler has to think twice before indulging in the ordinary food of ordinary people.
Joseph Lelyveld

He was a bold man that first eat an oyster.
Jonathan Swift

Is Elizabeth Taylor fat? Her favorite food is seconds.
Joan Rivers

Sharing food with another human being is an intimate act that should not be indulged in lightly.
M. F. K. Fisher

Never order food in excess of your body weight.
Erma Bombeck

If you're going to America, bring your own food.
Fran Lebowitz

One should eat to live, not live to eat.
Moliere

Our minds are like our stomachs; they are whetted by the change of their food, and variety supplies both with fresh appetite.
Quintilian

If you are ever at a loss to support a flagging conversation, introduce the subject of eating.
Leigh Hunt

We may find in the long run that tinned food is a deadlier weapon than the machine-gun.
George Orwell

Not eating meat is a decision, eating meat is an instinct.
Denis Leary

The food that enters the mind must be watched as closely as the food that enters the body.
Pat Buchanan

Confit is the ultimate comfort food, and trendy or not, it is dazzling stuff.
Sally Schneider

We provide food that customers love, day after day after day. People just want more of it.
Ray Kroc

Miss Child is never bashful with butter.
Phil Donahue

If I'm making a movie and get hungry, I call time-out and eat some crackers.
Carol Alt

I love spaghetti and meatballs... I eat a lot.
Susan Lucci

I love food and I love everything involved with food. I love the fun of it. I love restaurants. I love cooking, although I don't cook very much. I love kitchens.
Alma Guillermoprieto

I like to eat and I love the diversity of foods.
David Soul

LOVE: A word properly applied to our delight in particular kinds of food; sometimes metaphorically spoken of the favorite objects of all our appetites.
Henry Fielding

Get people back into the kitchen and combat the trend toward processed food and fast food.
Andrew Weil

The only think I like better than talking about Food is eating.
John Walters

My philosophy from day one is that I can sleep better at night if I can improve an individual's knowledge about food and wine, and do it on a daily basis.
Emeril Lagasse

We would load up the yellow Cutlass Supreme station wagon and pick blackberries during blackberry season or spring onions during spring onion season. For us, food was part of the fabric of our day.
Mario Batali

In America, I would say New York and New Orleans are the two most interesting food towns. In New Orleans, they don't have a bad deli. There's no mediocrity accepted.
Mario Batali

Food should be fun.
Thomas Keller

Chicken fat, beef fat, fish fat, fried foods - these are the foods that fuel our fat genes by giving them raw materials for building body fat.
Neal Barnard

If I could only have one type of food with me, I would bring soy sauce. The reason being that if I have soy sauce, I can flavor a lot of things.
Martin Yan

I think Australian food is probably some of the best in the world.
Karrie Webb

I always say centered food equals centered behavior.
Marilu Henner

The less food, the more time to talk, the more to talk about.
Damon Wayans

Sandwiches are wonderful. You don't need a spoon or a plate!
Paul Lynde

When I eat with my friends, it is a moment of real pleasure, when I really enjoy my life.
Monica Bellucci

Every major food company now has an organic division. There's more capital going into organic agriculture than ever before.
Michael Pollan

My favorite time of day is to get up and eat leftovers from dinner, especially spicy food.
David Byrne

Food can become such a point of anxiety - not because it's food, but just because you have anxiety. That's how eating disorders develop.
Vanessa Carlton

That's a big goal of mine, to try and grow as much of my own food as possible.
Daryl Hannah

Italy will always have the best food.
Diane von Furstenberg

Sitting down to a meal with an Indian family is different from sitting down to a meal with a British family.
Roland Joffe

I like food. I like eating. And I don't want to deprive myself of good food.
Sarah Michelle Gellar

Know how to garnish food so that it is more appealing to the eye and even more flavorful than before.
Marilyn vos Savant

I love food and feel that it is something that should be enjoyed. I eat whatever I want. I just don't overeat.
Tyra Banks

I love all kinds of bread. Whenever I crave junk food, I want salty things like peanuts or potato chips.
Tyra Banks

The most dangerous food is wedding cake.
James Thurber

The worst vice of the solitary is the worship of his food.
Cyril Connolly

Wine and cheese are ageless companions, like aspirin and aches, or June and moon, or good people and noble ventures.
M. F. K. Fisher

In Italy, they add work and life on to food and wine.
Robin Leach

FORGIVENESS

Forgive your enemies, but never forget their names.
John F. Kennedy

Always forgive your enemies - nothing annoys them so much.
Oscar Wilde

Forgiveness is the fragrance that the violet sheds on the heel that has crushed it.
Mark Twain

Forgiveness is the economy of the heart... forgiveness saves the expense of anger, the cost of hatred, the waste of spirits.
Hannah More

To err is human; to forgive, divine.
Alexander Pope

A mistake is always forgivable, rarely excusable and always unacceptable.
Robert Fripp

Forgiveness is a virtue of the brave.
Indira Gandhi

He that cannot forgive others breaks the bridge over which he must pass himself; for every man has need to be forgiven.
Thomas Fuller

Mistakes are always forgivable, if one has the courage to admit them.
Bruce Lee

Forgiveness is the final form of love.
Reinhold Niebuhr

When you forgive, you in no way change the past - but you sure do change the future.
Bernard Meltzer

Forgiveness is the answer to the child's dream of a miracle by which what is broken is made whole again, what is soiled is made clean again.
Dag Hammarskjold

The weak can never forgive. Forgiveness is the attribute of the strong.
Mahatma Gandhi

When I was a kid I used to pray every night for a new bicycle. Then I realised that the Lord doesn't work that way so I stole one and asked Him to forgive me.
Emo Philips

Forgiveness means letting go of the past.
Gerald Jampolsky

You will know that forgiveness has begun when you recall those who hurt you and feel the power to wish them well.
Lewis B. Smedes

Forgiveness is a funny thing. It warms the heart and cools the sting.
William Arthur Ward

Forgiveness is the remission of sins. For it is by this that what has been lost, and was found, is saved from being lost again.
Saint Augustine

Forgiveness is a gift you give yourself.
Suzanne Somers

People can be more forgiving than you can imagine. But you have to forgive yourself. Let go of what's bitter and move on.
Bill Cosby

I can forgive, but I cannot forget, is only another way of saying, I will not forgive. Forgiveness ought to be like a cancelled note - torn in two, and burned up, so that it never can be shown against one.
Henry Ward Beecher

Genuine forgiveness does not deny anger but faces it head-on.
Alice Duer Miller

How does one know if she has forgiven? You tend to feel sorrow over the circumstance instead of rage, you tend to feel sorry for the person rather than angry with him. You tend to have nothing left to say about it all.
Clarissa Pinkola Estes

Never forget the three powerful resources you always have available to you: love, prayer, and forgiveness.
H. Jackson Brown, Jr.

It takes one person to forgive, it takes two people to be reunited.
Lewis B. Smedes

Forgiveness is the key to action and freedom.
Hannah Arendt

Thank you, God, for this good life and forgive us if we do not love it enough.
Garrison Keillor

Once a woman has forgiven her man, she must not reheat his sins for breakfast.
Marlene Dietrich

It is easier to forgive an enemy than to forgive a friend.
William Blake

Forgive many things in others; nothing in yourself.
Ausonius

Forgiveness is like faith. You have to keep reviving it.
Mason Cooley

To forgive is to set a prisoner free and discover that the prisoner was you.
Lewis B. Smedes

There is no love without forgiveness, and there is no forgiveness without love.
Bryant H. McGill

One forgives to the degree that one loves.
Francois de La Rochefoucauld

God will forgive me. It's his job.
Heinrich Heine

Forgotten is forgiven.
F. Scott Fitzgerald

Without forgiveness, there's no future.
Desmond Tutu

The practice of forgiveness is our most important contribution to the healing of the world.
Marianne Williamson

When women love us, they forgive us everything, even our crimes; when they do not love us, they give us credit for nothing, not even our virtues.
Honore de Balzac

Life is an adventure in forgiveness.
Norman Cousins

How unhappy is he who cannot forgive himself.
Publilius Syrus

Forgive, son; men are men; they needs must err.
Euripides

Humanity is never so beautiful as when praying for forgiveness, or else forgiving another.
Jean Paul

There is no revenge so complete as forgiveness.
Josh Billings

The public is wonderfully tolerant. It forgives everything except genius.
Oscar Wilde

It is very east to forgive others their mistakes; it takes more grit and gumption to forgive them for having witnessed your own.
Jessamyn West

Forgiveness is the giving, and so the receiving, of life.
George MacDonald

My desire is to be a forgiving, non-judgmental person.
Janine Turner

I do not bring forgiveness with me, nor forgetfulness. The only ones who can forgive are dead; the living have no right to forget.
Chaim Herzog

To understand is to forgive, even oneself.
Alexander Chase

It is often easier to ask for forgiveness than to ask for permission.
Grace Hopper

If there is something to pardon in everything, there is also something to condemn.
Friedrich Nietzsche

The ineffable joy of forgiving and being forgiven forms an ecstasy that might well arouse the envy of the gods.
Elbert Hubbard

It's said in Hollywood that you should always forgive your enemies - because you never know when you'll have to work with them.
Lana Turner

To be social is to be forgiving.
Robert Frost

It's far easier to forgive an enemy after you've got even with him.
Olin Miller

I shall be an autocrat, that's my trade; and the good Lord will forgive me, that's his.
Catherine the Great

FRIENDSHIP

An insincere and evil friend is more to be feared than a wild beast; a wild beast may wound your body, but an evil friend will wound your mind.
Buddha

Don't walk behind me; I may not lead. Don't walk in front of me; I may not follow. Just walk beside me and be my friend.
Albert Camus

A friend should be one in whose understanding and virtue we can equally confide, and whose opinion we can value at once for its justness and its sincerity.
Robert Hall

A friend is one who knows you and loves you just the same.
Elbert Hubbard

Be courteous to all, but intimate with few, and let those few be well tried before you give them your confidence.
George Washington

A friendship can weather most things and thrive in thin soil; but it needs a little mulch of letters and phone calls and small, silly presents every so often - just to save it from drying out completely.
Pam Brown

A true friend never gets in your way unless you happen to be going down.
Arnold H. Glasow

A single rose can be my garden... a single friend, my world.
Leo Buscaglia

Friendship... is not something you learn in school. But if you haven't learned the meaning of friendship, you really haven't learned anything.
Muhammad Ali

A friend to all is a friend to none.
Aristotle

Lots of people want to ride with you in the limo, but what you want is someone who will take the bus with you when the limo breaks down.
Oprah Winfrey

Friendship is unnecessary, like philosophy, like art... It has no survival value; rather it is one of those things that give value to survival.
C. S. Lewis

But friendship is precious, not only in the shade, but in the sunshine of life, and thanks to a benevolent arrangement the greater part of life is sunshine.
Thomas Jefferson

I value the friend who for me finds time on his calendar, but I cherish the friend who for me does not consult his calendar.
Robert Brault

Friendship is a single soul dwelling in two bodies.
Aristotle

A hug is like a boomerang - you get it back right away.
Bil Keane

Friends and good manners will carry you where money won't go.
Margaret Walker

In everyone's life, at some time, our inner fire goes out. It is then burst into flame by an encounter with another human being. We should all be thankful for those people who rekindle the inner spirit.
Albert Schweitzer

A friendship founded on business is better than a business founded on friendship.
John D. Rockefeller

Let us be grateful to people who make us happy, they are the charming gardeners who make our souls blossom.
Marcel Proust

I don't need a friend who changes when I change and who nods when I nod; my shadow does that much better.
Plutarch

Friends are born, not made.
Henry B. Adams

Think where man's glory most begins and ends, and say my glory was I had such friends.
William Butler Yeats

True friends stab you in the front.
Oscar Wilde

When we honestly ask ourselves which person in our lives means the most to us, we often find that it is those who, instead of giving advice, solutions, or cures, have chosen rather to share our pain and touch our wounds with a warm and tender hand.
Henri Nouwen

Friends show their love in times of trouble.
Euripides

The friend who can be silent with us in a moment of despair or confusion, who can stay with us in an hour of grief and bereavement, who can tolerate not knowing... not healing, not curing... that is a friend who cares.
Henri Nouwen

Men kick friendship around like a football, but it doesn't seem to crack. Women treat it like glass and it goes to pieces.
Anne Morrow Lindbergh

If it's very painful for you to criticize your friends - you're safe in doing it. But if you take the slightest pleasure in it, that's the time to hold your tongue.
Alice Duer Miller

Never explain - your friends do not need it and your enemies will not believe you anyway.
Elbert Hubbard

Friendship and money: oil and water.
Mario Puzo

But friendship is the breathing rose, with sweets in every fold.
Oliver Wendell Holmes

It is one of the blessings of old friends that you can afford to be stupid with them.
Ralph Waldo Emerson

A man's growth is seen in the successive choirs of his friends.
Ralph Waldo Emerson

Fear makes strangers of people who would be friends.
Shirley MacLaine

I have friends in overalls whose friendship I would not swap for the favor of the kings of the world.
Thomas A. Edison

You can always tell a real friend: when you've made a fool of yourself he doesn't feel you've done a permanent job.
Laurence J. Peter

It's the friends you can call up at 4 a.m. that matter.
Marlene Dietrich

I always felt that the great high privilege, relief and comfort of friendship was that one had to explain nothing.
Katherine Mansfield

Friendship is one mind in two bodies.
Mencius

Silences make the real conversations between friends. Not the saying but the never needing to say is what counts.
Margaret Lee Runbeck

Friendship is held to be the severest test of character. It is easy, we think, to be loyal to a family and clan, whose blood is in your own veins.
Charles Alexander Eastman

There is nothing on this earth more to be prized than true friendship.
Thomas Aquinas

When you choose your friends, don't be short-changed by choosing personality over character.
W. Somerset Maugham

Nothing but heaven itself is better than a friend who is really a friend.
Plautus

She is a friend of mind. She gather me, man. The pieces I am, she gather them and give them back to me in all the right order. It's good, you know, when you got a woman who is a friend of your mind.
Toni Morrison

When a friend is in trouble, don't annoy him by asking if there is anything you can do. Think up something appropriate and do it.
Edward W. Howe

If instead of a gem, or even a flower, we should cast the gift of a loving thought into the heart of a friend, that would be giving as the angels give.
George MacDonald

It takes a long time to grow an old friend.
John Leonard

Friendship needs no words - it is solitude delivered from the anguish of loneliness.
Dag Hammarskjold

The language of friendship is not words but meanings.
Henry David Thoreau

The sincere friends of this world are as ship lights in the stormiest of nights.
Giotto di Bondone

It is not so much our friends' help that helps us, as the confidence of their help.
Epicurus

We call that person who has lost his father, an orphan; and a widower that man who has lost his wife. But that man who has known the immense unhappiness of losing a friend, by what name do we call him? Here every language is silent and holds its peace in impotence.
Joseph Roux

The most I can do for my friend is simply be his friend.
Henry David Thoreau

The friend is the man who knows all about you, and still likes you.
Elbert Hubbard

Wishing to be friends is quick work, but friendship is a slow ripening fruit.
Aristotle

He has no enemies, but is intensely disliked by his friends.
Oscar Wilde

The only way to have a friend is to be one.
Ralph Waldo Emerson

Yes'm, old friends is always best, 'less you can catch a new one that's fit to make an old one out of.
Sarah Orne Jewett

Rare as is true love, true friendship is rarer.
Jean de La Fontaine

Lovers have a right to betray you... friends don't.
Judy Holliday

Friendship multiplies the good of life and divides the evil.
Baltasar Gracian

Since there is nothing so well worth having as friends, never lose a chance to make them.
Francesco Guicciardini

Instead of loving your enemies - treat your friends a little better.
Edward W. Howe

The real test of friendship is: can you literally do nothing with the other person? Can you enjoy those moments of life that are utterly simple?
Eugene Kennedy

The bird a nest, the spider a web, man friendship.
William Blake

Friendship is certainly the finest balm for the pangs of disappointed love.
Jane Austen

Many a person has held close, throughout their entire lives, two friends that always remained strange to one another, because one of them attracted by virtue of similarity, the other by difference.
Emil Ludwig

It is important to our friends to believe that we are unreservedly frank with them, and important to friendship that we are not.
Mignon McLaughlin

Without wearing any mask we are conscious of, we have a special face for each friend.
Oliver Wendell Holmes

Love demands infinitely less than friendship.
George Jean Nathan

Never have a companion that casts you in the shade.
Baltasar Gracian

Mighty proud I am that I am able to have a spare bed for my friends.
Samuel Pepys

Life has no blessing like a prudent friend.
Euripides

Our friends interpret the world and ourselves to us, if we take them tenderly and truly.
Amos Bronson Alcott

One's friends are that part of the human race with which one can be human.
George Santayana

Nothing so fortifies a friendship as a belief on the part of one friend that he is superior to the other.
Honore de Balzac

FUNNY

A successful man is one who makes more money than his wife can spend. A successful woman is one who can find such a man.
Lana Turner

A word to the wise ain't necessary - it's the stupid ones that need the advice.
Bill Cosby

Behind every great man is a woman rolling her eyes.
Jim Carrey

A government that robs Peter to pay Paul can always depend on the support of Paul.
George Bernard Shaw

A day without sunshine is like, you know, night.
Steve Martin

Between two evils, I always pick the one I never tried before.
Mae West

A child of five would understand this. Send someone to fetch a child of five.
Groucho Marx

Any girl can be glamorous. All you have to do is stand still and look stupid.
Hedy Lamarr

A two-year-old is kind of like having a blender, but you don't have a top for it.
Jerry Seinfeld

Go to Heaven for the climate, Hell for the company.
Mark Twain

All right everyone, line up alphabetically according to your height.
Casey Stengel

A friend doesn't go on a diet because you are fat.
Erma Bombeck

As a child my family's menu consisted of two choices: take it or leave it.
Buddy Hackett

A stockbroker urged me to buy a stock that would triple its value every year. I told him, "At my age, I don't even buy green bananas."
Claude Pepper

I feel sorry for people who don't drink. When they wake up in the morning, that's as good as they're going to feel all day.
Frank Sinatra

When you are courting a nice girl an hour seems like a second. When you sit on a red-hot cinder a second seems like an hour. That's relativity.
Albert Einstein

A nickel ain't worth a dime anymore.
Yogi Berra

Do not take life too seriously. You will never get out of it alive.
Elbert Hubbard

Always end the name of your child with a vowel, so that when you yell the name will carry.
Bill Cosby

Get your facts first, then you can distort them as you please.
Mark Twain

A committee is a group that keeps minutes and loses hours.
Milton Berle

A pessimist is a person who has had to listen to too many optimists.
Don Marquis

Wine is constant proof that God loves us and loves to see us happy.
Benjamin Franklin

Everybody knows how to raise children, except the people who have them.
P. J. O'Rourke

A lot of baby boomers are baby bongers.
Kevin Nealon

Anyone who says he can see through women is missing a lot.
Groucho Marx

A vegetarian is a person who won't eat anything that can have children.
David Brenner

A waffle is like a pancake with a syrup trap.
Mitch Hedberg

Weather forecast for tonight: dark.
George Carlin

I have six locks on my door all in a row. When I go out, I lock every other one. I figure no matter how long somebody stands there picking the locks, they are always locking three.
Elayne Boosler

Happiness is having a large, loving, caring, close-knit family in another city.
George Burns

I refuse to join any club that would have me as a member.
Groucho Marx

I am not afraid of death, I just don't want to be there when it happens.
Woody Allen

I found there was only one way to look thin: hang out with fat people.
Rodney Dangerfield

I cook with wine, sometimes I even add it to the food.
W. C. Fields

I always wanted to be somebody, but now I realize I should have been more specific.
Lily Tomlin

Housework can't kill you, but why take a chance?
Phyllis Diller

I used to be Snow White, but I drifted.
Mae West

Cleanliness becomes more important when godliness is unlikely.
P. J. O'Rourke

Electricity is really just organized lightning.
George Carlin

A lot of people are afraid of heights. Not me, I'm afraid of widths.
Steven Wright

I intend to live forever. So far, so good.
Steven Wright

Do not worry about avoiding temptation. As you grow older it will avoid you.
Joey Adams

I like long walks, especially when they are taken by people who annoy me.
Fred Allen

If two wrongs don't make a right, try three.
Laurence J. Peter

I'm an idealist. I don't know where I'm going, but I'm on my way.
Carl Sandburg

All men are equal before fish.
Herbert Hoover

My fake plants died because I did not pretend to water them.
Mitch Hedberg

I did not have three thousand pairs of shoes, I had one thousand and sixty.
Imelda Marcos

Any kid will run any errand for you, if you ask at bedtime.
Red Skelton

California is a fine place to live - if you happen to be an orange.
Fred Allen

The only time a woman really succeeds in changing a man is when he is a baby.
Natalie Wood

A sure cure for seasickness is to sit under a tree.
Spike Milligan

I buy expensive suits. They just look cheap on me.
Warren Buffett

My grandmother started walking five miles a day when she was sixty. She's ninety-seven now, and we don't know where the hell she is.
Ellen DeGeneres

I distrust camels, and anyone else who can go a week without a drink.
Joe E. Lewis

If love is the answer, could you please rephrase the question?
Lily Tomlin

Because of their size, parents may be difficult to discipline properly.
P. J. O'Rourke

I haven't spoken to my wife in years. I didn't want to interrupt her.
Rodney Dangerfield

One man's folly is another man's wife.
Helen Rowland

Food, love, career, and mothers, the four major guilt groups.
Cathy Guisewite

I have a new philosophy. I'm only going to dread one day at a time.
Charles M. Schulz

Be obscure clearly.
E. B. White

Fatherhood is pretending the present you love most is soap-on-a-rope.
Bill Cosby

Cross country skiing is great if you live in a small country.
Steven Wright

I have never been hurt by what I have not said.
Calvin Coolidge

Do not let a flattering woman coax and wheedle you and deceive you; she is after your barn.
Hesiod

Every man's dream is to be able to sink into the arms of a woman without also falling into her hands.
Jerry Lewis

He taught me housekeeping; when I divorce I keep the house.
Zsa Zsa Gabor

How many people here have telekenetic powers? Raise my hand.
Emo Philips

I would never die for my beliefs because I might be wrong.
Bertrand Russell

There cannot be a crisis next week. My schedule is already full.
Henry A. Kissinger

Never have more children than you have car windows.
Erma Bombeck

Best way to get rid of kitchen odors: Eat out.
Phyllis Diller

I drank some boiling water because I wanted to whistle.
Mitch Hedberg

I bought some batteries, but they weren't included.
Steven Wright

I love Mickey Mouse more than any woman I have ever known.
Walt Disney

Nobody ever went broke underestimating the taste of the American public.
H. L. Mencken

Don't forget Mother's Day. Or as they call it in Beverly Hills, Dad's Third Wife Day.
Jay Leno

Recession is when a neighbor loses his job. Depression is when you lose yours.
Ronald Reagan

All the candy corn that was ever made was made in 1911.
Lewis Black

Guilt: the gift that keeps on giving.
Erma Bombeck

I like children - fried.
W. C. Fields

I used to jog but the ice cubes kept falling out of my glass.
David Lee Roth

I never said most of the things I said.
Yogi Berra

I love to go to Washington - if only to be near my money.
Bob Hope

I knew I was an unwanted baby when I saw that my bath toys were a toaster and a radio.
Joan Rivers

My Father had a profound influence on me. He was a lunatic.
Spike Milligan

There are only three things women need in life: food, water, and compliments.
Chris Rock

Tragedy is when I cut my finger. Comedy is when you fall into an open sewer and die.
Mel Brooks

I wear a necklace, cause I wanna know when I'm upside down.
Mitch Hedberg

Everything that used to be a sin is now a disease.
Bill Maher

I never drink water because of the disgusting things that fish do in it.
W. C. Fields

Money won't buy happiness, but it will pay the salaries of a large research staff to study the problem.
Bill Vaughan

As I get older, I just prefer to knit.
Tracey Ullman

O Lord, help me to be pure, but not yet.
Saint Augustine

Older people shouldn't eat health food, they need all the preservatives they can get.
Robert Orben

Food is an important part of a balanced diet.
Fran Lebowitz

Experience is what you have after you've forgotten her name.
Milton Berle

Procrastination is the art of keeping up with yesterday.
Don Marquis

People always ask me, 'Were you funny as a child?' Well, no, I was an accountant.
Ellen DeGeneres

If God wanted us to bend over he'd put diamonds on the floor.
Joan Rivers

By trying we can easily endure adversity. Another man's, I mean.
Mark Twain

If truth is beauty, how come no one has their hair done in the library?
Lily Tomlin

I'm undaunted in my quest to amuse myself by constantly changing my hair.
Hillary Clinton

It is a scientific fact that your body will not absorb cholesterol if you take it from another person's plate.
Dave Barry

Never raise your hand to your children - it leaves your midsection unprotected.
Robert Orben

Brought up to respect the conventions, love had to end in marriage. I'm afraid it did.
Bette Davis

I have a love interest in every one of my films: a gun.
Arnold Schwarzenegger

Roses are red, violets are blue, I'm schizophrenic, and so am I.
Oscar Levant

Drawing on my fine command of the English language, I said nothing.
Robert Benchley

I'm sorry, if you were right, I'd agree with you.
Robin Williams

I'm writing a book. I've got the page numbers done.
Steven Wright

I think they should have a Barbie with a buzz cut.
Ellen DeGeneres

I don't think anyone should write their autobiography until after they're dead.
Samuel Goldwyn

I like marriage. The idea.
Toni Morrison

I was the kid next door's imaginary friend.
Emo Philips

The superfluous, a very necessary thing.
Voltaire

Have enough sense to know, ahead of time, when your skills will not extend to wallpapering.
Marilyn vos Savant

I have tried to know absolutely nothing about a great many things, and I have succeeded fairly well.
Robert Benchley

Fashions have done more harm than revolutions.
Victor Hugo

It's amazing that the amount of news that happens in the world every day always just exactly fits the newspaper.
Jerry Seinfeld

God did not intend religion to be an exercise club.
Naguib Mahfouz

My definition of an intellectual is someone who can listen to the William Tell Overture without thinking of the Lone Ranger.
Billy Connolly

I wanna make a jigsaw puzzle that's 40,000 pieces. And when you finish it, it says 'go outside.'
Demetri Martin

Boy, those French: they have a different word for everything!
Steve Martin

Communism is like one big phone company.
Lenny Bruce

In comic strips, the person on the left always speaks first.
George Carlin

I saw a woman wearing a sweatshirt with Guess on it. I said, Thyroid problem?
Arnold Schwarzenegger

What contemptible scoundrel has stolen the cork to my lunch?
W. Clement Stone

I don't need you to remind me of my age. I have a bladder to do that for me.
Stephen Fry

If it weren't for Philo T. Farnsworth, inventor of television, we'd still be eating frozen radio dinners.
Johnny Carson

Originality is the fine art of remembering what you hear but forgetting where you heard it.
Laurence J. Peter

I don't have a bank account because I don't know my mother's maiden name.
Paula Poundstone

Never floss with a stranger.
Joan Rivers

It's simple, if it jiggles, it's fat.
Arnold Schwarzenegger

When I go to a bar, I don't go looking for a girl who knows the capital of Maine.
David Brenner

Every man has his follies - and often they are the most interesting thing he has got.
Josh Billings

If you're going to do something tonight that you'll be sorry for tomorrow morning, sleep late.
Henny Youngman

I failed to make the chess team because of my height.
Woody Allen

I was sleeping the other night, alone, thanks to the exterminator.
Emo Philips

It is even harder for the average ape to believe that he has descended from man.
H. L. Mencken

I was so naive as a kid I used to sneak behind the barn and do nothing.
Johnny Carson

We'll love you just the way you are if you're perfect.
Alanis Morissette

I don't have to look up my family tree, because I know that I'm the sap.
Fred Allen

If you want to be thought a liar, always tell the truth.
Logan P. Smith

My father would take me to the playground, and put me on mood swings.
Jay London

One picture is worth 1,000 denials.
Ronald Reagan

Smoking kills. If you're killed, you've lost a very important part of your life.
Brooke Shields

I rant, therefore I am.
Dennis Miller

You can lead a man to Congress, but you can't make him think.
Milton Berle

I'd luv to kiss ya, but I just washed my hair.
Bette Davis

You're only as good as your last haircut.
Fran Lebowitz

The reason there are two senators for each state is so that one can be the designated driver.
Jay Leno

When I was a boy the Dead Sea was only sick.
George Burns

I'm not a real movie star. I've still got the same wife I started out with twenty-eight years ago.
Will Rogers

My theory is that all of Scottish cuisine is based on a dare.
Mike Myers

I've always wanted to go to Switzerland to see what the army does with those wee red knives.
Billy Connolly

Men don't care what's on TV. They only care what else is on TV.
Jerry Seinfeld

I don't deserve this award, but I have arthritis and I don't deserve that either.
Jack Benny

My life needs editing.
Mort Sahl

If I had to live my life again, I'd make the same mistakes, only sooner.
Tallulah Bankhead

Men are only as loyal as their options.
Bill Maher

Never fight an inanimate object.
P. J. O'Rourke

TV is chewing gum for the eyes.
Frank Lloyd Wright

I recorded my hair this morning, tonight I'm watching the highlights.
Jay London

Everything in life is somewhere else, and you get there in a car.
E. B. White

My one regret in life is that I am not someone else.
Woody Allen

I was a vegetarian until I started leaning toward the sunlight.
Rita Rudner

I spent a year in that town, one Sunday.
George Burns

I never expected to see the day when girls would get sunburned in the places they now do.
Will Rogers

Parents are the last people on earth who ought to have children.
Samuel Butler

I looked up my family tree and found out I was the sap.
Rodney Dangerfield

All my children inherited perfect pitch.
Chevy Chase

If you have a secret, people will sit a little bit closer.
Rob Corddry

Defy your own group. Rebel against yourself.
Cathy Guisewite

If God wanted us to fly, He would have given us tickets.
Mel Brooks

Progress was all right. Only it went on too long.
James Thurber

If it's the Psychic Network why do they need a phone number?
Robin Williams

When we talk to God, we're praying. When God talks to us, we're schizophrenic.
Jane Wagner

The world is full of magical things patiently waiting for our wits to grow sharper.
Bertrand Russell

Miami Beach is where neon goes to die.
Lenny Bruce

My uncle Sammy was an angry man. He had printed on his tombstone: What are you looking at?
Margaret Smith

I used to sell furniture for a living. The trouble was, it was my own.
Les Dawson

There's nothing wrong with being shallow as long as you're insightful about it.
Dennis Miller

Ever notice that Soup for One is eight aisles away from Party Mix?
Elayne Boosler

In Hollywood a marriage is a success if it outlasts milk.
Rita Rudner

If my films make one more person miserable, I'll feel I have done my job.
Woody Allen

I quit therapy because my analyst was trying to help me behind my back.
Richard Lewis

Who picks your clothes - Stevie Wonder?
Don Rickles

That's my only goal. Surround myself with funny people, and make sure everyone has a good time and works hard.
Joe Rogan

The next time you have a thought... let it go.
Ron White

There are lots of people who mistake their imagination for their memory.
Josh Billings

The IRS! They're like the Mafia, they can take anything they want!
Jerry Seinfeld

How long was I in the army? Five foot eleven.
Spike Milligan

I can speak Esperanto like a native.
Spike Milligan

I cannot sing, dance or act; what else would I be but a talk show host.
David Letterman

Television has brought back murder into the home - where it belongs.
Alfred Hitchcock

When I eventually met Mr. Right I had no idea that his first name was Always.
Rita Rudner

Until you walk a mile in another man's moccasins you can't imagine the smell.
Robert Byrne

I'm for whatever gets you through the night.
Frank Sinatra

There's no better feeling in the world than a warm pizza box on your lap.
Kevin James

It all started when my dog began getting free roll over minutes.
Jay London

I wish I had the nerve not to tip.
Paul Lynde

Polite conversation is rarely either.
Fran Lebowitz

If I have to lay an egg for my country, I'll do it.
Bob Hope

What's another word for Thesaurus?
Steven Wright

If you live to be one hundred, you've got it made. Very few people die past that age.
George Burns

Our national flower is the concrete cloverleaf.
Lewis Mumford

My wife has a slight impediment in her speech. Every now and then she stops to breathe.
Jimmy Durante

Flattery is like cologne water, to be smelt, not swallowed.
Josh Billings

This shirt is dry clean only. Which means... it's dirty.
Mitch Hedberg

I was born in very sorry circumstances. Both of my parents were very sorry.
Norman Wisdom

The digital camera is a great invention because it allows us to reminisce. Instantly.
Demetri Martin

The only time I ever enjoyed ironing was the day I accidentally got gin in the steam iron.
Phyllis Diller

I have just returned from Boston. It is the only thing to do if you find yourself up there.
Fred Allen

You see much more of your children once they leave home.
Lucille Ball

A James Cagney love scene is one where he lets the other guy live.
Bob Hope

Never put a sock in a toaster.
Eddie Izzard

The day I made that statement, about the inventing the internet, I was tired because I'd been up all night inventing the Camcorder.
Al Gore

Moderation is a virtue only in those who are thought to have an alternative.
Henry A. Kissinger

We need two kinds of acquaintances, one to complain to, while to the others we boast.
Logan P. Smith

Every cloud has its silver lining but it is sometimes a little difficult to get it to the mint.
Don Marquis

I think serial monogamy says it all.
Tracey Ullman

Parrots make great pets. They have more personality than goldfish.
Chevy Chase

I'm a misplaced American, but don't know where I was misplaced.
Ruby Wax

I would talk in iambic pentameter if it were easier.
Howard Nemerov

It is easy for me to love myself, but for ladies to do it is another question altogether.
Johnny Vegas

If you can't tell a spoon from a ladle, then you're fat!
Demetri Martin

Whoever is my relative, I will not be nice to them.
George Lopez

The four building blocks of the universe are fire, water, gravel and vinyl.
Dave Barry

Tell us your phobias and we will tell you what you are afraid of.
Robert Benchley

Retirement at sixty-five is ridiculous. When I was sixty-five I still had pimples.
George Burns

Why don't you get out of that wet coat and into a dry martini?
Robert Benchley

People say that life is the thing, but I prefer reading.
Logan P. Smith

There's a great power in words, if you don't hitch too many of them together.
Josh Billings

To attract men, I wear a perfume called "New Car Interior."
Rita Rudner

I've never been married, but I tell people I'm divorced so they won't think something's wrong with me.
Elayne Boosler

When the sun comes up, I have morals again.
Elayne Boosler

I like a woman with a head on her shoulders. I hate necks.
Steve Martin

Well, if I called the wrong number, why did you answer the phone?
James Thurber

The way taxes are, you might as well marry for love.
Joe E. Lewis

My mother was against me being an actress - until I introduced her to Frank Sinatra.
Angie Dickinson

There's no such thing as soy milk. It's soy juice.
Lewis Black

I grew up in Europe, where the history comes from.
Eddie Izzard

When you're in love it's the most glorious two and a half days of your life.
Richard Lewis

I have a very low level of recognition, which is fine by me.
Dylan Moran

I sang in the choir for years, even though my family belonged to another church.
Paul Lynde

I'd never been in play long enough for the flowers to die in the dressing room.
Mercedes McCambridge

I'm kidding about having only a few dollars. I might have a few dollars more.
James Brown

The one thing you shouldn't do is try to tell a cab driver how to get somewhere.
Jimmy Fallon

Why do they call it rush hour when nothing moves?
Robin Williams

Mail your packages early so the post office can lose them in time for Christmas.
Johnny Carson

Someone told me that when they go to Vermont, they feel like they're home. I'm that way at Saks.
Caroline Rhea

Smartphones. Who cares? Smartphones. I only have dummy phones.
Don Rickles

GARDENING

He plants trees to benefit another generation.
Caecilius Statius

If you have a garden and a library, you have everything you need.
Marcus Tullius Cicero

Remember that children, marriages, and flower gardens reflect the kind of care they get.
H. Jackson Brown, Jr.

What is a weed? A plant whose virtues have never been discovered.
Ralph Waldo Emerson

A weed is a plant that has mastered every survival skill except for learning how to grow in rows.
Doug Larson

Flowers always make people better, happier, and more helpful; they are sunshine, food and medicine for the soul.
Luther Burbank

Gardens are not made by singing 'Oh, how beautiful,' and sitting in the shade.
Rudyard Kipling

In search of my mother's garden, I found my own.
Alice Walker

A garden is a complex of aesthetic and plastic intentions; and the plant is, to a landscape artist, not only a plant - rare, unusual, ordinary or doomed to disappearance - but it is also a color, a shape, a volume or an arabesque in itself.
Roberto Burle Marx

Everything that slows us down and forces patience, everything that sets us back into the slow circles of nature, is a help. Gardening is an instrument of grace.
May Sarton

My neighbor asked if he could use my lawnmower and I told him of course he could, so long as he didn't take it out of my garden.
Eric Morecambe

I don't like formal gardens. I like wild nature. It's just the wilderness instinct in me, I guess.
Walt Disney

Someone's sitting in the shade today because someone planted a tree a long time ago.
Les Brown

A man has made at least a start on discovering the meaning of human life when he plants shade trees under which he knows full well he will never sit.
D. Elton Trueblood

A good garden may have some weeds.
Thomas Fuller

It will never rain roses: when we want to have more roses we must plant more trees.
George Eliot

Show me your garden and I shall tell you what you are.
Alfred Austin

Gardening is how I relax. It's another form of creating and playing with colors.
Oscar de la Renta

But if each man could have his own house, a large garden to cultivate and healthy surroundings - then, I thought, there will be for them a better opportunity of a happy family life.
George Cadbury

We must cultivate our own garden. When man was put in the garden of Eden he was put there so that he should work, which proves that man was not born to rest.
Voltaire

I think this is what hooks one to gardening: it is the closest one can come to being present at creation.
Phyllis Theroux

All gardening is landscape painting.
William Kent

The love of gardening is a seed once sown that never dies.
Gertrude Jekyll

What's a butterfly garden without butterflies?
Roy Rogers

Who loves a garden loves a greenhouse too.
William Cowper

How deeply seated in the human heart is the liking for gardens and gardening.
Alexander Smith

God Almighty first planted a garden. And indeed, it is the purest of human pleasures.
Francis Bacon

The best place to find God is in a garden. You can dig for him there.
George Bernard Shaw

Plants that wake when others sleep. Timid jasmine buds that keep their fragrance to themselves all day, but when the sunlight dies away let the delicious secret out to every breeze that roams about.
Thomas Moore

The glory of gardening: hands in the dirt, head in the sun, heart with nature. To nurture a garden is to feed not just on the body, but the soul.
Alfred Austin

I do some of my best thinking while pulling weeds.
Martha Smith

I grow plants for many reasons: to please my eye or to please my soul, to challenge the elements or to challenge my patience, for novelty or for nostalgia, but mostly for the joy in seeing them grow.
David Hobson

The secret of improved plant breeding, apart from scientific knowledge, is love.
Luther Burbank

Working with plants, trees, fences and walls, if they practice sincerely they will attain enlightenment.
Dogen Zenji

If we had paid no more attention to our plants than we have to our children, we would now be living in a jungle of weed.
Luther Burbank

Trees and plants always look like the people they live with, somehow.
Zora Neale Hurston

A garden must combine the poetic and he mysterious with a feeling of serenity and joy.
Luis Barragan

Help us to be ever faithful gardeners of the spirit, who know that without darkness nothing comes to birth, and without light nothing flowers.
May Sarton

What a man needs in gardening is a cast-iron back, with a hinge in it.
Charles Dudley Warner

Weather means more when you have a garden. There's nothing like listening to a shower and thinking how it is soaking in around your green beans.
Marcelene Cox

It is a golden maxim to cultivate the garden for the nose, and the eyes will take care of themselves.
Robert Louis Stevenson

It is like the seed put in the soil - the more one sows, the greater the harvest.
Orison Swett Marden

It is only the farmer who faithfully plants seeds in the Spring, who reaps a harvest in the Autumn.
B. C. Forbes

If a tree dies, plant another in its place.
Carolus Linnaeus

I am sure that if you plant the trees back again, it will do nothing but good.
Michael Fish

One lifetime is never enough to accomplish one's horticultural goals. If a garden is a site for the imagination, how can we be very far from the beginning?
Francis Cabot Lowell

A person cannot love a plant after he has pruned it, then he has either done a poor job or is devoid of emotion.
Liberty Hyde Bailey

Garden as though you will live forever.
William Kent

To dwell is to garden.
Martin Heidegger

Use plants to bring life.
Douglas Wilson

I loved to get all dusty and ride horses and plant potatoes and cotton.
Dorothy Malone

I love decorating my home. I'm a gardener too, so that's usually something I have to play catch up with.
Suzy Bogguss

When a finished work of 20th century sculpture is placed in an 18th century garden, it is absorbed by the ideal representation of the past, thus reinforcing political and social values that are no longer with us.
Robert Smithson

I plant a lot of trees. I am a great believer in planting things for future generations. I loathe the now culture where you just live for today.
Penelope Keith

The garden, by design, is concerned with both the interior and the land beyond the garden.
Stephen Gardiner

Gardening is not a rational act.
Margaret Atwood

Some men like to make a little garden out of life and walk down a path.
Jean Anouilh

Well tended garden is better than a neglected wood lot.
Dixie Lee Ray

The garden suggests there might be a place where we can meet nature halfway.
Michael Pollan

If you build up the soil with organic material, the plants will do just fine.
John Harrison

GOVERNMENT

Government is not reason; it is not eloquent; it is force. Like fire, it is a dangerous servant and a fearful master.
George Washington

Government "help" to business is just as disastrous as government persecution... the only way a government can be of service to national prosperity is by keeping its hands off.
Ayn Rand

The best argument against democracy is a five-minute conversation with the average voter.
Winston Churchill

Knowledge will forever govern ignorance; and a people who mean to be their own governors must arm themselves with the power which knowledge gives.
James Madison

Laws are like sausages, it is better not to see them being made.
Otto von Bismarck

We make a living by what we get, but we make a life by what we give.
Winston Churchill

Giving money and power to government is like giving whiskey and car keys to teenage boys.
P. J. O'Rourke

It is error alone which needs the support of government. Truth can stand by itself.
Thomas Jefferson

Government, even in its best state, is but a necessary evil; in its worst state, an intolerable one.
Thomas Paine

The government solution to a problem is usually as bad as the problem.
Milton Friedman

The genius of our ruling class is that it has kept a majority of the people from ever questioning the inequity of a system where most people drudge along, paying heavy taxes for which they get nothing in return.
Gore Vidal

Man will never be free until the last king is strangled with the entrails of the last priest.
Denis Diderot

If 'pro' is the opposite of 'con' what is the opposite of 'progress'?
Paul Harvey

The oppressed are allowed once every few years to decide which particular representatives of the oppressing class are to represent and repress them.
Karl Marx

So that the record of history is absolutely crystal clear. That there is no alternative way, so far discovered, of improving the lot of the ordinary people that can hold a candle to the productive activities that are unleashed by a free enterprise system.
Milton Friedman

Ancient Rome declined because it had a Senate, now what's going to happen to us with both a House and a Senate?
Will Rogers

For in reason, all government without the consent of the governed is the very definition of slavery.
Jonathan Swift

Democracy gives every man the right to be his own oppressor.
James Russell Lowell

Feeling good about government is like looking on the bright side of any catastrophe. When you quit looking on the bright side, the catastrophe is still there.
P. J. O'Rourke

Democracy is the art and science of running the circus from the monkey cage.
H. L. Mencken

It is to be regretted that the rich and powerful too often bend the acts of government to their own selfish purposes.
Andrew Jackson

The best minds are not in government. If any were, business would steal them away.
Ronald Reagan

Ninety eight percent of the adults in this country are decent, hardworking, honest Americans. It's the other lousy two percent that get all the publicity. But then, we elected them.
Lily Tomlin

The instant formal government is abolished, society begins to act. A general association takes place, and common interest produces common security.
Thomas Paine

That government is best which governs least.
Henry David Thoreau

No man is good enough to govern another man without that other's consent.
Abraham Lincoln

If men were angels, no government would be necessary.
James Madison

The government, which was designed for the people, has got into the hands of the bosses and their employers, the special interests. An invisible empire has been set up above the forms of democracy.
Woodrow Wilson

It's not the voting that's democracy; it's the counting.
Tom Stoppard

Whenever the people are well-informed, they can be trusted with their own government.
Thomas Jefferson

Our government... teaches the whole people by its example. If the government becomes the lawbreaker, it breeds contempt for law; it invites every man to become a law unto himself; it invites anarchy.
Louis D. Brandeis

This country has come to feel the same when Congress is in session as when the baby gets hold of a hammer.
Will Rogers

Economics is extremely useful as a form of employment for economists.
John Kenneth Galbraith

In the absence of justice, what is sovereignty but organized robbery?
Saint Augustine

I'm tired of hearing it said that democracy doesn't work. Of course it doesn't work. We are supposed to work it.
Alexander Woollcott

Talk is cheap - except when Congress does it.
Cullen Hightower

A corporation's primary goal is to make money. Government's primary role is to take a big chunk of that money and give it to others.
Larry Ellison

Majority rule only works if you're also considering individual rights. Because you can't have five wolves and one sheep voting on what to have for supper.
Larry Flynt

To rule is easy, to govern difficult.
Johann Wolfgang von Goethe

Laws too gentle are seldom obeyed; too severe, seldom executed.
Benjamin Franklin

People try to live within their income so they can afford to pay taxes to a government that can't live within its income.
Robert Half

The people are the government, administering it by their agents; they are the government, the sovereign power.
Andrew Jackson

Democracy is the only system that persists in asking the powers that be whether they are the powers that ought to be.
Sydney J. Harris

If human beings are fundamentally good, no government is necessary; if they are fundamentally bad, any government, being composed of human beings, would be bad also.
Fred Woodworth

You don't pay taxes - they take taxes.
Chris Rock

Government is a trust, and the officers of the government are trustees. And both the trust and the trustees are created for the benefit of the people.
Henry Clay

Bureaucracy gives birth to itself and then expects maternity benefits.
Dale Dauten

Democracy is an abuse of statistics.
Jorge Luis Borges

Let the people think they govern and they will be governed.
William Penn

To hear some men talk of the government, you would suppose that Congress was the law of gravitation, and kept the planets in their places.
Wendell Phillips

The fact that political ideologies are tangible realities is not a proof of their vitally necessary character. The bubonic plague was an extraordinarily powerful social reality, but no one would have regarded it as vitally necessary.
Wilhelm Reich

I have long believed taxpayers make better use of their money than the government ever could.
Kay Bailey Hutchison

Our nation is built on the bedrock principle that governments derive their just powers from the consent of the governed.
Adrian Cronauer

The way people in democracies think of the government as something different from themselves is a real handicap. And, of course, sometimes the government confirms their opinion.
Lewis Mumford

Ohio claims they are due a president as they haven't had one since Taft. Look at the United States, they have not had one since Lincoln.
Will Rogers

It is hard to feel individually responsible with respect to the invisible processes of a huge and distant government.
John W. Gardner

Washington is a place where politicians don't know which way is up and taxes don't know which way is down.
Robert Orben

The mistakes made by Congress wouldn't be so bad if the next Congress didn't keep trying to correct them.
Cullen Hightower

Government is an unnecessary evil. Human beings, when

accustomed to taking responsibility for their own behavior, can cooperate on a basis of mutual trust and helpfulness.
Fred Woodworth

The danger is not that a particular class is unfit to govern: every class is unfit to govern.
Lord Acton

Here is my first principle of foreign policy: good government at home.
William E. Gladstone

The worst thing in this world, next to anarchy, is government.
Henry Ward Beecher

The essence of good government is trust.
Kathleen Sebelius

Americans no longer look to government for economic security; rather, they look to their portfolios.
Bill Owens

As a governor, I am naturally inclined to focus on the domestic side of protecting the United States.
Bill Owens

Government alone cannot solve the problems we deal with in our correctional facilities, treatment centers, homeless shelters and crisis centers - we need our faith-based and community partners.
Dirk Kempthorne

But let us remember, at the same time, government is sacred, and not to be trifled with.
Jonathan Mayhew

There are three species of government: republican, monarchical, and despotic.
Charles de Secondat

What I worry about would be that you essentially have two chambers, the House and the Senate, but you have simply, majoritarian, absolute power on either side. And that's just not what the founders intended.
Barack Obama

GRADUATION

A graduation ceremony is an event where the commencement speaker tells thousands of students dressed in identical caps and gowns that 'individuality' is the key to success.
Robert Orben

Never go to your high school reunion pregnant or they will think that is all you have done since you graduated.
Erma Bombeck

God will not look you over for medals degrees or diplomas, but for scars.
Elbert Hubbard

I learned law so well, the day I graduated I sued the college, won the case, and got my tuition back.
Fred Allen

Being considerate of others will take your children further in life than any college degree.
Marian Wright Edelman

I was never a Certified Public Accountant. I just had a degree in accounting. It would require passing a test, which I would not have been able to do.
Bob Newhart

I always wanted to have my own album released before I graduated from high school.
Christina Aguilera

Everyone has a right to a university degree in America, even if it's in Hamburger Technology.
Clive James

You are educated. Your certification is in your degree. You may think of it as the ticket to the good life. Let me ask you to think of an alternative. Think of it as your ticket to change the world.
Tom Brokaw

It might be said now that I have the best of both worlds. A Harvard education and a Yale degree.
John F. Kennedy

College athletes used to get a degree in bringing your pencil.
Ruby Wax

Even though I disagree with many of the changes, when I see the privates graduate at the end of the day, when they walk off that drill field at the end of the ceremony, they are still fine privates; outstanding, well motivated privates.
R. Lee Ermey

We don't stop going to school when we graduate.
Carol Burnett

It makes little difference how many university courses or degrees a person may own. If he cannot use words to move an idea from one point to another, his education is incomplete.
Norman Cousins

In this outward and physical ceremony we attest once again to the inner and spiritual strength of our Nation. As my high school teacher, Miss Julia Coleman, used to say: 'We must adjust to changing times and still hold to unchanging principles.'
Jimmy Carter

You must realize that honorary degrees are given generally to people whose SAT scores were too low to get them into schools the regular way. As a matter of fact, it was my SAT scores that led me into my present vocation in life, comedy.
Neil Simon

One half who graduate from college never read another book.
G. M. Trevelyan

For a man to attain to an eminent degree in learning costs him time, watching, hunger, nakedness, dizziness in the head, weakness in the stomach, and other inconveniences.
Miguel de Cervantes

Earlier today, Arnold Schwarzenegger criticized the California school system, calling it disastrous. Arnold says California's schools are so bad that its graduates are willing to vote for me.
Conan O'Brien

The college graduate is presented with a sheepskin to cover his intellectual nakedness.
Robert M. Hutchins

When nearly a third of our high school students do not graduate on time with their peers, we have work to do. We must design our middle and high schools so that no student gets lost in the crowd and disconnected from his or her own potential.
Christine Gregoire

Our promise to our children should be this: if you do well in school, we will pay for you to obtain a college degree.
Ruth Ann Minner

I was going to be an architect. I graduated with a degree in architecture and I had a scholarship to go back to Princeton and get my Masters in architecture. I'd done theatricals in college, but I'd done them because it was fun.
James Stewart

When I graduated from Santa Monica High in 1927, I was voted the girl most likely to succeed. I didn't realize it would take so long.
Gloria Stuart

I have actually five honorary degrees.
Katherine Dunham

Really, the potential for, first of all, any college graduate today is enormously good. These are good times for anyone with a college degree today, particularly African Americans. With a college degree today, you really breach the unemployment rate.
Alexis Herman

Life is the most exciting opportunity we have. But we have one shot. You graduate from college once, and that's it. You're going out of that nest. And you have to find that courage that's deep, deep, deep in there. Every step of the way.
Andrew Shue

It is virtually impossible to compete in today's global economy without a college degree.
Bobby Scott

Yeah, I spent about 20 years in a dorm room. It took me a while to graduate.
Douglas Wilson

I'm not impressed by someone's degree... I'm impressed by them making movies.
Richard King

I dropped out of school for a semester, transferred to another college, switched to an art major, graduated, got married, and for a while worked as a graphic designer.
James Green Somerville

I was really desperate. I don't know if you can remember back that far, but when I went to graduate school they didn't want females in graduate school. They were very open about it. They didn't mince their words. But then I got in and I got my degree.
Shannon Lucid

I wrote a novel for my degree, and I'm very happy I didn't submit that to a publisher. I sympathize with my professors who had to read it.
David Eddings

I was the first boy in the Kennedy family to graduate from college.
Mark Kennedy

I didn't get my degree at NYU; I got it later, they gave me an honourary one.
Jim Jarmusch

I graduated a the top of my class in the '84 Olympic Games; I won a gold medal.
Scott Hamilton

Our record number of teenagers must become our record number of high school and college graduates and our record number of teachers, scientists, doctors, lawyers, and skilled professionals.
Ruben Hinojosa

We had times in '66 and '67 when we would pick up a platoon of privates out of the receiving barracks the week before we even graduated the platoon that we were on!
R. Lee Ermey

In the summer we graduated we flipped out completely, drinking beer, cruising in our cars and beating up each other. It was a crazy summer. That's when I started to be interested in girls.
Ed O'Neill

I don't look to find an educated person in the ranks of university graduates, necessarily. Some of the most educated people I know have never been near a university.
John Keegan

So in my uncertainty, I went to graduate school and there it all happened.
Ted Nelson

It is soooooo necessary to get the basic skills, because by the time you graduate, undergraduate or graduate, that field would have totally changed from your first day of school.
Leigh Steinberg

I first became interested in women and religion when I was one of the few women doing graduate work in Religious Studies at Yale University in the late 1960's.
Carol P. Christ

When I was a graduate student, the leading spirits at Harvard were interested in the history of ideas.
M. H. Abrams

Some go on to trade schools or get further training for jobs they are interested in. Some go into the arts, some are craftsmen, some take a little time out to travel, and some start their own businesses. But our graduates find and work at what they want to do.
Daniel Greenberg

My father, who was from a wealthy family and highly educated, a lawyer, Yale and Columbia, walked out with the benefit of a healthy push from my mother, a seventh grade graduate, who took a typing course and got a secretarial job as fast as she could.
George Weinberg

For students today, only 10 percent of children from working-class families graduate from college by the age of 24 as compared to 58 percent of upper-middle-class and wealthy families.
Patrick J. Kennedy

Catholic school graduates exhibit a wide variety of qualities that will not only help them in their careers but also in their family and community lives.
Joe Baca

ACT and SAT each have their own parts of the country. The GRE has its lock on graduate admissions. And so, one could blame the companies, but really, economically, they have no incentive to change things very much because they're getting the business.
Robert Sternberg

I teach one semester a year, and this year I'm just teaching one course during that semester, a writing workshop for older students in their late 20s and early 30s, people in our graduate program who are already working on a manuscript and trying to bring it to completion.
Tobias Wolff

I could be happy doing something like architecture. It would involve another couple of years of graduate school, but that's what I studied in college. That's what I always wanted to do.
Parker Stevenson

My main objective is to prepare candidates for professional baseball; however, the majority of our graduates will go home as much better qualified amateurs.
Jim Evans

In my second year in graduate school, I took a computer course and that was like lightening striking.
Ted Nelson

I received my undergraduate degree in engineering in 1939 and a Master of Science degree in mathematical physics in 1941 at Steven Institute of Technology.
Frederick Reines

When I was going for my graduate degree, I decided I was going to make a feature film as my thesis. That's what I was famous for-that I had my thesis film be a feature film, which was 'You're a Big Boy Now.'
Francis Ford Coppola

The idea of winning a doctor's degree gradually assumed the aspect of a great moral struggle, and the moral fight possessed immense attraction for me.
Elizabeth Blackwell

Yale places great stress on undergraduate and graduate teaching. I like teaching, and I do a lot of it.
James Tobin

Even though I didn't get a business degree, I enjoyed learning about economics.
Herb Ritts

I went to college at the University of Kansas, where I got a degree in political science.
Sara Paretsky

I got all my work done to graduate in two months and then they were like, I'm sorry, you have to take driver's ed. I just kind of went, Oh, forget it.
Fiona Apple

I took three years off. I differentiated myself from the industry. Found my identity - sort of... I haven't graduated yet. I'm not legitimately educated yet, but maybe one day.
Claire Danes

The essays in The Great Taos Bank Robbery were my project to win a Master of Arts degree in English when I quit being a newspaper editor and went back to college.
Tony Hillerman

Everybody wants you to do good things, but in a small town you pretty much graduate and get married. Mostly you marry, have children and go to their football games.
Faith Hill

I did graduate with a bachelor's degree in civil engineering in 1948.
Daniel J. Evans

I think I finally chose the graduate degree in engineering primarily because it only took one year and law school took three years, and I felt the pressure of being a little behind - although I was just 22.
Daniel J. Evans

I think young writers should get other degrees first, social sciences, arts degrees or even business degrees. What you learn is research skills, a necessity because a lot of writing is about trying to find information.
Irvine Welsh

In 1858 I received the degree of D. S. from the Lawrence Scientific School, and thereafter remained on the rolls of the university as a resident graduate.
Simon Newcomb

I did get a degree in special education.
Clay Aiken

I have no problems with private schools. I graduated from one and so did my mother. Private schools are useful and we often use public funds to pay for their infrastructures and other common needs.
Jim Clyburn

The knowledge of languages was very useful. I have a university degree in foreign languages and literature.
Emma Bonino

If a student takes the whole series of my folklore courses including the graduate seminars, he or she should learn something about fieldwork, something about bibliography, something about how to carry out library research, and something about how to publish that research.
Alan Dundes

Having a college degree gave me the opportunity to be... well-rounded. Also, the people I met at the university, most of them are still my colleagues now. People I've known for years are all in the industry together.
Jon Secada

My father was on the faculty in the Chemistry Department of Harvard University; my mother had one year of graduate work in physics before her marriage.
Kenneth G. Wilson

My graduate studies were carried out at the California Institute of Technology.
Kenneth G. Wilson

I went to military college in Canada and graduated as an officer in the Navy but also as an engineer.
Marc Garneau

I was about to get a degree in economics when I accepted that I'd be a lousy businessman, and if I didn't give acting a try I'd regret it for the rest of my life.
Peter Gallagher

At the School of Visual Arts in New York, you can get your degree in Net art, which is really a fantastic way of thinking of theater in new ways.
Laurie Anderson

Remember, half the doctors in this country graduated in the bottom half of their class.
Al McGuire

North Dakota State. What do you have to do there to graduate? Milk a cow with your left hand?
Bobby Heenan

Knowledge is invariably a matter of degree: you cannot put your finger upon even the simplest datum and say this we know.
T. S. Eliot

Each year India and China produce four million graduates compared with just over 250,000 in Britain.
Gordon Brown

The economy in the Valley will need to grow if students want to come back and work with their specialized degrees. We need to develop more to create more opportunities.
Frank Murphy

This man used to go to school with his dog. Then they were separated. His dog graduated!
Henny Youngman

My personal advice is to go to school first and get a liberal arts education, and then if you want to pursue acting, go to graduate school.
Jillian Bach

I think women as well as men are concerned about jobs and the economy and spending and, and other issues. They're concerned that when their kids graduate from college they have an economy and they have a future in this country and they, they have the same opportunity that we've had and our grandparents have had.
Ken Buck

HAPPINESS

Happiness often sneaks in through a door you didn't know you left open.
John Barrymore

Happiness is not something ready made. It comes from your own actions.
Dalai Lama

Some cause happiness wherever they go; others whenever they go.
Oscar Wilde

Action may not always bring happiness; but there is no happiness without action.
Benjamin Disraeli

Happiness is when what you think, what you say, and what you do are in harmony.
Mahatma Gandhi

Don't wait around for other people to be happy for you. Any happiness you get you've got to make yourself.
Alice Walker

Future. That period of time in which our affairs prosper, our friends are true and our happiness is assured.
Ambrose Bierce

Happiness depends upon ourselves.
Aristotle

The Constitution only gives people the right to pursue happiness. You have to catch it yourself.
Benjamin Franklin

Happiness in intelligent people is the rarest thing I know.
Ernest Hemingway

A sure way to lose happiness, I found, is to want it at the expense of everything else.
Bette Davis

Happiness doesn't depend on any external conditions, it is governed by our mental attitude.
Dale Carnegie

Money can't buy happiness, but it can make you awfully comfortable while you're being miserable.
Clare Boothe Luce

Happiness is nothing more than good health and a bad memory.
Albert Schweitzer

All happiness or unhappiness solely depends upon the quality of the object to which we are attached by love.
Baruch Spinoza

Everyone chases after happiness, not noticing that happiness is right at their Happiness depends more on how life strikes you than on what happens.
Andy Rooney

It is not how much we have, but how much we enjoy, that makes happiness.
Charles Spurgeon

A large income is the best recipe for happiness I ever heard of.
Jane Austen

Do not speak of your happiness to one less fortunate than yourself.
Plutarch

heels.
Bertolt Brecht

Happiness is not a goal; it is a by-product.
Eleanor Roosevelt

Happiness is like a kiss. You must share it to enjoy it.
Bernard Meltzer

If your happiness depends on what somebody else does, I guess you do have a problem.
Richard Bach

Love is trembling happiness.
Khalil Gibran

Always leave something to wish for; otherwise you will be miserable from your very happiness.
Baltasar Gracian

Happiness is the only good. The time to be happy is now. The place to be happy is here. The way to be happy is to make others so.
Robert Green Ingersoll

But what is happiness except the simple harmony between a man and the life he leads?
Albert Camus

There is only one way to happiness and that is to cease worrying about things which are beyond the power of our will.
Epictetus

All who joy would win must share it. Happiness was born a Twin.
Lord Byron

There are people who can do all fine and heroic things but one - keep from telling their happiness to the unhappy.
Mark Twain

An effort made for the happiness of others lifts above ourselves.
Lydia M. Child

Happiness is that state of consciousness which proceeds from the achievement of one's values.
Ayn Rand

Desire is individual. Happiness is common.
Julian Casablancas

Happiness comes only when we push our brains and hearts to the farthest reaches of which we are capable.
Leo Rosten

In order to have great happiness you have to have great pain and unhappiness - otherwise how would you know when you're happy?
Leslie Caron

Happiness is a continuation of happenings which are not resisted.
Deepak Chopra

Every gift from a friend is a wish for your happiness.
Richard Bach

Happiness is having a scratch for every itch.
Ogden Nash

Happiness is ideal, it is the work of the imagination.
Marquis de Sade

Happiness is like those palaces in fairy tales whose gates are guarded by dragons: we must fight in order to conquer it.
Alexandre Dumas

Anything you're good at contributes to happiness.
Bertrand Russell

There is only one happiness in this life, to love and be loved.
George Sand

Just do what must be done. This may not be happiness, but it is greatness.
George Bernard Shaw

Happiness makes up in height for what it lacks in length.
Robert Frost

True happiness comes from the joy of deeds well done, the zest of creating things new.
Antoine de Saint-Exupery

Happiness does not lie in happiness, but in the achievement of it.
Fyodor Dostoevsky

Happiness is a direction, not a place.
Sydney J. Harris

Never mind your happiness; do your duty.
Peter Drucker

What we call the secret of happiness is no more a secret than our willingness to choose life.
Leo Buscaglia

Happiness is found in doing, not merely possessing.
Napoleon Hill

Happiness is mostly a by-product of doing what makes us feel fulfilled.
Benjamin Spock

It is not easy to find happiness in ourselves, and it is not possible to find it elsewhere.
Agnes Repplier

Happiness isn't something you experience; it's something you remember.
Oscar Levant

Happiness includes chiefly the idea of satisfaction after full honest effort. No one can possibly be satisfied and no one can be happy who feels that in some paramount affairs he failed to take up the challenge of life.
Arnold Bennett

True happiness is... to enjoy the present, without anxious dependence upon the future.
Lucius Annaeus Seneca

Money can't buy you happiness, but it can buy you a yacht big enough to pull up right alongside it.
David Lee Roth

You must try to generate happiness within yourself. If you aren't happy in one place, chances are you won't be happy anyplace.
Ernie Banks

When what we are is what we want to be, that's happiness.
Malcolm Forbes

The two enemies of human happiness are pain and boredom.
Arthur Schopenhauer

Happiness is the interval between periods of unhappiness.
Don Marquis

Happiness is like a cloud, if you stare at it long enough, it evaporates.
Sarah McLachlan

Happiness does not consist in self-love.
Joseph Butler

Nothing prevents happiness like the memory of happiness.
Andre Gide

Happiness never lays its finger on its pulse.
Adam Smith

The first recipe for happiness is: Avoid too lengthy meditation on the past.
Andre Maurois

Happiness is neither without us nor within us. It is in God, both without us and within us.
Blaise Pascal

If you wait for the perfect moment when all is safe and assured, it may never arrive. Mountains will not be climbed, races won, or lasting happiness achieved.
Maurice Chevalier

Happiness is composed of misfortunes avoided.
Alphonse Karr

It is the chiefest point of happiness that a man is willing to be what he is.
Desiderius Erasmus

Happiness grows at our own firesides, and is not to be picked in strangers' gardens.
Douglas William Jerrold

One of the keys to happiness is a bad memory.
Rita Mae Brown

The secret of happiness is to admire without desiring.
Carl Sandburg

True happiness consists not in the multitude of friends, but in the worth and choice.
Ben Jonson

You know it's love when all you want is that person to be happy, even if you're not part of their happiness.
Julia Roberts

If you hope for happiness in the world, hope for it from God, and not from the world.
David Brainerd

Happiness is a virtue, not its reward.
Baruch Spinoza

Happiness is itself a kind of gratitude.
Joseph Wood Krutch

Happiness: an agreeable sensation arising from contemplating the misery of another.
Ambrose Bierce

Happiness is a by-product. You cannot pursue it by itself.
Sam Levenson

The moments of happiness we enjoy take us by surprise. It is not that we seize them, but that they seize us.
Ashley Montagu

Happiness is brief. It will not stay. God batters at its sails.
Euripides

The person born with a talent they are meant to use will find their greatest happiness in using it.
Johann Wolfgang von Goethe

Growth itself contains the germ of happiness.
Pearl S. Buck

Your successes and happiness are forgiven you only if you generously consent to share them.
Albert Camus

The happiness of a man in this life does not consist in the absence but in the mastery of his passions.
Alfred Lord Tennyson

Happiness seems made to be shared.
Pierre Corneille

Love is the most terrible, and also the most generous of the passions; it is the only one which includes in its dreams the happiness of someone else.
Alphonse Karr

If you have easy self-contentment, you might have a very, very cheap source of happiness.
Leon Kass

Life everlasting in a state of happiness is the greatest desire of all men.
Joseph Franklin Rutherford

We possess only the happiness we are able to understand.
Maurice Maeterlinck

There is something curiously boring about somebody else's happiness.
Aldous Huxley

The greatest of follies is to sacrifice health for any other kind of happiness.
Arthur Schopenhauer

Our happiness depends on wisdom all the way.
Sophocles

To be without some of the things you want is an indispensable part of happiness.
Bertrand Russell

There is no worse sorrow than remembering happiness in the day of sorrow.
Alfred de Musset

Satisfaction of one's curiosity is one of the greatest sources of happiness in life.
Linus Pauling

Lovers who love truly do not write down their happiness.
Anatole France

There is only one passion, the passion for happiness.
Denis Diderot

Life in common among people who love each other is the ideal of happiness.
George Sand

To describe happiness is to diminish it.
Stendhal

Happiness is the harvest of a quiet eye.
Austin O'Malley

Happiness is hard to recall.

Its just a glow.
Frank McCourt

There is happiness in duty, although it may not seem so.
Jose Marti

The secret of happiness is to admire without desiring. And that is not happiness.
F. H. Bradley

People let their own hang-ups become the obstacles between them and personal happiness.
Lucinda Williams

The right to happiness is fundamental.
Anna Pavlova

To buy happiness is to sell soul.
Douglas Horton

Happiness will come from materialism, not from meaning.
Andrei Platonov

Unquestionably, it is possible to do without happiness; it is done involuntarily by nineteen-twentieths of mankind.
John Stuart Mill

To attain happiness in another world we need only to believe something, while to secure it in this world we must do something.
Charlotte Perkins Gilman

HEALTH

The wish for healing has always been half of health.
Lucius Annaeus Seneca

To keep the body in good health is a duty... otherwise we shall not be able to keep our mind strong and clear.
Buddha

Everybody needs beauty as well as bread, places to play in and pray in, where nature may heal and give strength to body and soul.
John Muir

A healthy attitude is contagious but don't wait to catch it from others. Be a carrier.
Tom Stoppard

Healing is a matter of time, but it is sometimes also a matter of opportunity.
Hippocrates

I have the body of an eighteen year old. I keep it in the fridge.
Spike Milligan

I made a commitment to completely cut out drinking and anything that might hamper me from getting my mind and body together. And the floodgates of goodness have opened upon me - spiritually and financially.
Denzel Washington

If you're happy, if you're feeling good, then nothing else matters.
Robin Wright Penn

The way you think, the way you behave, the way you eat, can influence your life by 30 to 50 years.
Deepak Chopra

Your body hears everything your mind says.
Naomi Judd

A healthy outside starts from the inside.
Robert Urich

I'm exhausted trying to stay healthy.
Steve Yzerman

I believe that if you're healthy, you're capable of doing everything. There's no one else who can give you health but God, and by being healthy I believe that God is listening to me.
Pedro Martinez

People who don't know how to keep themselves healthy ought to have the decency to get themselves buried, and not waste time about it.
Henrik Ibsen

I feel pretty good. My body actually looks like an old banana, but it's fine.
Mike Piazza

I really believe the only way to stay healthy is to eat properly, get your rest and exercise. If you don't exercise and do the other two, I still don't think it's going to help you that much.
Mike Ditka

I believe that how you feel is very important to how you look - that healthy equals beautiful.
Victoria Principal

True silence is the rest of the mind, and is to the spirit what sleep is to the body, nourishment and refreshment.
William Penn

Arguments are healthy. They clear the air.
John Deacon

My New Year's resolution is to stick to a good workout plan that will keep me healthy and happy.
James Lafferty

It takes more than just a good looking body. You've got to have the heart and soul to go with it.
Epictetus

Rest when you're weary. Refresh and renew yourself, your body, your mind, your spirit. Then get back to work.
Ralph Marston

Man needs difficulties; they are necessary for health.
Carl Jung

My body is like breakfast, lunch, and dinner. I don't think about it, I just have it.
Arnold Schwarzenegger

Cheerfulness is the best promoter of health and is as friendly to the mind as to the body.
Joseph Addison

You know, all that really matters is that the people you love are happy and healthy. Everything else is just sprinkles on the sundae.
Paul Walker

I became a fanatic about healthy food in 1944.
Gloria Swanson

'Tis healthy to be sick sometimes.
Henry David Thoreau

I stand before you a totally healthy person.
Melissa Etheridge

The trouble with always trying to preserve the health of the body is that it is so difficult to do without destroying the health of the mind.
Gilbert K. Chesterton

The body is a sacred garment.
Martha Graham

When you are young and healthy, it never occurs to you that in a single second your whole life could change.
Annette Funicello

I've made a promise to myself to be a 100% healthy person if nothing else.
Picabo Street

I believe it is important for people to create a healthy mental environment in which to accomplish daily tasks.
Darren L. Johnson

We can make a commitment to promote vegetables and fruits and whole grains on every part of every menu. We can make portion sizes smaller and emphasize quality over quantity. And we can help create a culture - imagine this - where our kids ask for healthy options instead of resisting them.
Michelle Obama

The average, healthy, well-adjusted adult gets up at seven-thirty in the morning feeling just plain terrible.
Jean Kerr

Liberty is to the collective body, what health is to every individual body. Without health no pleasure can be tasted by man; without liberty, no happiness can be enjoyed by society.
Henry St. John

Healthy people live with their world.
Anne Wilson Schaef

You know, true love really matters, friends really matter, family really matters. Being responsible and disciplined and healthy really matters.
Courtney Thorne Smith

I eat really healthy, and if I'm tired, I take a nap.
Casper Van Dien

I had my moments when I got very frightened that I would not recover.
Fran Drescher

What the public expects and what is healthy for an individual are two very different things.
Esther Williams

I'm still healthy as can be.
Darrell Royal

The minute anyone's getting anxious I say, You must eat and you must sleep. They're the two vital elements for a healthy life.
Francesca Annis

I have a healthy body, free of the chemicals that once controlled it.
Lorna Luft

My personal goals are to be happy, healthy and to be surrounded by loved ones.
Kiana Tom

My health may be better preserved if I exert myself less, but in the end doesn't each person give his life for his calling?
Clara Schumann

I sit on my duff, smoke cigarettes and watch TV. I'm not exactly a poster girl for healthy living.
Lexa Doig

Success doesn't mean that you are healthy, success doesn't mean that you're happy, success doesn't mean that you're rested. Success really doesn't mean that you look good, or feel good, or are good.
Victoria Principal

Man does not live by soap alone; and hygiene, or even health, is not much good unless you can take a healthy view of it or, better still, feel a healthy indifference to it.
Gilbert K. Chesterton

HISTORY

Our greatest glory is not in never falling, but in rising every time we fall.
Confucius

The dogmas of the quiet past are inadequate to the stormy present. The occasion is piled high with difficulty, and we must rise with the occasion. As our case is new, so we must think anew and act anew.
Abraham Lincoln

A small body of determined spirits fired by an unquenchable faith in their mission can alter the course of history.
Mahatma Gandhi

This is one small step for a man, one giant leap for mankind.
Neil Armstrong

I like the dreams of the future better than the history of the past.
Thomas Jefferson

If you are neutral in situations of injustice, you have chosen the side of the oppressor. If an elephant has its foot on the tail of a mouse and you say that you are neutral, the mouse will not appreciate your neutrality.
Desmond Tutu

Those who do not remember the past are condemned to repeat it.
George Santayana

I came, I saw, I conquered.
Julius Caesar

The test of our progress is not whether we add more to the abundance of those who have much it is whether we provide enough for those who have little.
Franklin D. Roosevelt

When you do the common things in life in an uncommon way, you will command the attention of the world.
George Washington Carver

History is a relentless master. It has no present, only the past rushing into the future. To try to hold fast is to be swept aside.
John F. Kennedy

To wear your heart on your sleeve isn't a very good plan; you should wear it inside, where it functions best.
Margaret Thatcher

A pint of sweat, saves a gallon of blood.
George S. Patton

Observe good faith and justice toward all nations. Cultivate peace and harmony with all.
George Washington

History will be kind to me for I intend to write it.
Winston Churchill

Posterity: you will never know how much it has cost my generation to preserve your freedom. I hope you will make good use of it.
John Quincy Adams

Democratic nations must try to find ways to starve the terrorist and the hijacker of the oxygen of publicity on which they depend.
Margaret Thatcher

Americans love to fight. All real Americans love the sting of battle.
George S. Patton

If we cannot now end our differences, at least we can help make the world safe for diversity.
John F. Kennedy

We used to root for the Indians against the cavalry, because we didn't think it was fair in the history books that when the cavalry won it was a great victory, and when the Indians won it was a massacre.
Dick Gregory

Despise the enemy strategically, but take him seriously tactically.
Mao Tse-Tung

History is the version of past events that people have decided to agree upon.
Napoleon Bonaparte

A world without nuclear weapons would be less stable and more dangerous for all of us.
Margaret Thatcher

Being president is like being a jackass in a hailstorm. There's nothing to do but to stand there and take it.
Lyndon B. Johnson

90 percent of my time is spent on 10 percent of the world.
Colin Powell

Difficulty is the excuse history never accepts.
Edward R. Murrow

The chief condition on which, life, health and vigor depend on, is action. It is by action that an organism develops its faculties, increases its energy, and attains the fulfillment of its destiny.
Colin Powell

We cannot defend freedom abroad by deserting it at home.
Edward R. Murrow

If one morning I walked on top of the water across the Potomac River, the headline that afternoon would read: "President Can't Swim."
Lyndon B. Johnson

Chaos often breeds life, when order breeds habit.
Henry B. Adams

Following the light of the sun, we left the Old World.
Christopher Columbus

History is a vast early warning system.
Norman Cousins

We would like to live as we once lived, but history will not permit it.
John F. Kennedy

Glory is fleeting, but obscurity is forever.
Napoleon Bonaparte

What is history but a fable agreed upon?
Napoleon Bonaparte

The very ink with which history is written is merely fluid prejudice.
Mark Twain

History is a gallery of pictures in which there are few originals and many copies.
Alexis de Tocqueville

Civilization is a movement and not a condition, a voyage and not a harbor.
Arnold J. Toynbee

A truly American sentiment recognizes the dignity of labor and the fact that honor lies in honest toil.
Grover Cleveland

The world we see that seems so insane is the result of a belief system that is not working. To perceive the world differently, we must be willing to change our belief system, let the past slip away, expand our sense of now, and dissolve the fear in our minds.
William James

Failure is impossible.
Susan B. Anthony

Although... the Chief Magistrate must almost of necessity be chosen by a party and stand pledged to its principles and measures, yet in his official action he should not be the President of a party only, but of the whole people of the United States.
James K. Polk

The Marine Corps is the Navy's police force and as long as I am President that is what it will remain. They have a propaganda machine that is almost equal to Stalin's.
Harry S. Truman

I have noticed that nothing I never said ever did me any harm.
Calvin Coolidge

The greater the difficulty, the more the glory in surmounting it.
Epicurus

History is a pack of lies about events that never happened told by people who weren't there.
George Santayana

People are trapped in history and history is trapped in them.
James A. Baldwin

Seek freedom and become captive of your desires. Seek discipline and find your liberty.
Frank Herbert

Never doubt that you can change history. You already have.
Marge Piercy

People that are really very weird can get into sensitive positions and have a tremendous impact on history.
Dan Quayle

The past actually happened but history is only what someone wrote down.
A. Whitney Brown

History is a tool used by politicians to justify their intentions.
Ted Koppel

Historian: an unsuccessful novelist.
H. L. Mencken

History is a cyclic poem written by time upon the memories of man.
Percy Bysshe Shelley

I cannot lead you into battle. I do not give you laws or administer justice but I can do something else - I can give my heart and my devotion to these old islands and to all the peoples of our brotherhood of nations.
Elizabeth II

Be assured those will be thy worst enemies, not to whom thou hast done evil, but who have done evil to thee. And those will be thy best friends, not to whom thou hast done good, but who have done good to thee.
Tacitus

Be as a tower firmly set; Shakes not its top for any blast that blows.
Dante Alighieri

Fear of serious injury alone cannot justify oppression of free speech and assembly. Men feared witches and burnt women. It is the function of speech to free men from the bondage of irrational fears.
Louis D. Brandeis

We, therefore, here in Britain stand shoulder to shoulder with our American friends in this hour of tragedy, and we, like them, will not rest until this evil is driven from our world.
Tony Blair

All truly historical peoples have an idea they must realize, and when they have sufficiently exploited it at home, they export it, in a certain way, by war; they make it tour the world.
Victor Cousin

Human history becomes more and more a race between education and catastrophe.
H. G. Wells

I can see clearly now... that I was wrong in not acting more decisively and more forthrightly in dealing with Watergate.
Richard M. Nixon

History is more or less bunk.
Henry Ford

God cannot alter the past, though historians can.
Samuel Butler

History is the sum total of things that could have been avoided.
Konrad Adenauer

The past is really almost as much a work of the imagination as the future.
Jessamyn West

History is indeed little more than the register of the crimes, follies, and misfortunes of mankind.
Edward Gibbon

Why should we honour those that die upon the field of battle? A man may show as reckless a courage in entering into the abyss of himself.
William Butler Yeats

I come into the peace of wild things who do not tax their lives with forethought of grief...
For a time I rest in the grace of the world, and am free.
Wendell Berry

History is an account, mostly false, of events, mostly unimportant, which are brought about by rulers, mostly knaves, and soldiers, mostly fools.
Ambrose Bierce

I have tried to lift France out of the mud. But she will return to her errors and vomiting. I cannot prevent the French from being French.
Charles de Gaulle

Russians can give you arms but only the United States can give you a solution.
Anwar Sadat

The judicial system is the most expensive machine ever invented for finding out what happened and what to do about it.
Irving R. Kaufman

Could I have but a line a century hence crediting a contribution to the advance of peace, I would yield every honor which has been accorded by war.
Douglas MacArthur

The man who is swimming against the stream knows the strength of it.
Woodrow Wilson

There are no extraordinary men... just extraordinary circumstances that ordinary men are forced to deal with.
William Halsey

Time is my greatest enemy.
Evita Peron

What is sad for women of my generation is that they weren't supposed to work if they had families. What were they going to do when the children are grown - watch the raindrops coming down the window pane?
Jackie Kennedy

Beware of endeavoring to become a great man in a hurry. One such attempt in ten thousand may succeed. These are fearful odds.
Benjamin Disraeli

In the long term we can hope that religion will change the nature of man and reduce conflict. But history is not encouraging in this respect. The bloodiest wars in history have been religious wars.
Richard M. Nixon

You have to look at history as an evolution of society.
Jean Chretien

Friendship is a word, the very sight of which in print makes the heart warm.
Augustine Birrell

It is the soothing thing about history that it does repeat itself.
Gertrude Stein

It takes an endless amount of history to make even a little tradition.
Henry James

You must pursue this investigation of Watergate even if it leads to the president. I'm innocent. You've got to believe I'm innocent. If you don't, take my job.
Richard M. Nixon

World War II was the last government program that really worked.
George Will

It is necessary for me to establish a winner image. Therefore, I have to beat somebody.
Richard M. Nixon

It's a very good historical book about history.
Dan Quayle

The future has a way of arriving unannounced.
George Will

The past is malleable and flexible, changing as our recollection interprets and re-explains what has happened.
Peter Berger

Legend: A lie that has attained the dignity of age.
H. L. Mencken

Hubert Humphrey talks so fast that listening to him is like trying to read Playboy magazine with your wife turning the pages.
Barry Goldwater

Peace, plenty, and contentment reign throughout our borders, and our beloved country presents a sublime moral spectacle to the world.
James K. Polk

In my view, far from deserving condemnation for their courageous reporting, the New York Times, the Washington Post and other newspapers should be commended for serving the purpose that the Founding Fathers saw so clearly.
Hugo Black

Terrorism takes us back to ages we thought were long gone if we allow it a free hand to corrupt democratic societies and destroy the basic rules of international life.
Jacques Chirac

One who comes to the Court must come to adore, not to protest. That's the new gloss on the 1st Amendment.
William O. Douglas

Tell the FBI that the kidnappers should pick out a judge that Nixon wants back.
William O. Douglas

I wouldn't attach too much importance to these student riots. I remember when I was a student at the Sorbonne in Paris, I used to go out and riot occasionally.
John Foster Dulles

The most terrible job in warfare is to be a second lieutenant leading a platoon when you are on the battlefield.
Dwight D. Eisenhower

History is a vision of God's creation on the move.
Arnold J. Toynbee

The 1st Amendment protects the right to speak, not the right to spend.
Byron White

Remember, God provides the best camouflage several hours out of every 24.
David M. Shoup

They can shout down the head of the physics department at Cal Tech.
James Stockdale

I'm the only person of distinction who has ever had a depression named for him.
Herbert Hoover

Honor is not the exclusive property of any political party.
Herbert Hoover

No greater nor more affectionate honor can be conferred on an American than to have a public school named after him.
Herbert Hoover

You can't set a hen in one morning and have chicken salad for lunch.
George M. Humphrey

The Russians feared Ike. They didn't fear me.
Lyndon B. Johnson

To the extent that the judicial profession becomes the daily routine of deciding cases on the most secure precedents and the narrowest grounds available, the judicial mind atrophies and its perspective shrinks.
Irving R. Kaufman

The Supreme Court's only armor is the cloak of public trust; its sole ammunition, the collective hopes of our society.
Irving R. Kaufman

Dad, I'm in some trouble. There's been an accident and you're going to hear all sorts of things about me from now on. Terrible things.
Edward Kennedy

The more bombers, the less room for doves of peace.
Nikita Khrushchev

It was a Greek tragedy. Nixon was fulfilling his own nature. Once it started it could not end otherwise.
Henry A. Kissinger

They were afraid, never having learned what I taught myself: Defeat the fear of death and welcome the death of fear.
G. Gordon Liddy

They died hard, those savage men - like wounded wolves at bay. They were filthy, and they were lousy, and they stunk. And I loved them.
Douglas MacArthur

An Edwardian lady in full dress was a wonder to behold, and her preparations for viewing were awesome.
William Manchester

I haven't, in the 23 years that I have been in the uniformed services of the United States of America, ever violated an order - not one.
Oliver North

Statutes authorizing unreasonable searches were the core concern of the framers of the 4th Amendment.
Sandra Day O'Connor

Something as curious as the monarchy won't survive unless you take account of people's attitudes. After all, if people don't want it, they won't have it.
Prince Charles

When the rich think about the poor, they have poor ideas.
Evita Peron

The fleet sailed to its war base in the North Sea, headed not so much for some rendezvous with glory as for rendezvous with discretion.
Barbara Tuchman

France is delighted at this new opportunity to show the world that when one has the will one can succeed in joining peoples who have been brought close by history.
Francois Mitterrand

The real 1960s began on the afternoon of November 22, 1963. It came to seem that Kennedy's murder opened some malign trap door in American culture, and the wild bats flapped out.
Lance Morrow

Whether in chains or in laurels, liberty knows nothing but victories.
Wendell Phillips

It is impossible to predict the time and progress of revolution. It is governed by its own more or less mysterious laws.
Vladimir Lenin

Libraries are not made, they grow.
Augustine Birrell

Keeping books on social aid is capitalistic nonsense. I just use the money for the poor. I can't stop to count it.
Evita Peron

Most of the things worth doing in the world had been declared impossible before they were done.
Louis D. Brandeis

Open markets offer the only realistic hope of pulling billions of people in developing countries out of abject poverty, while sustaining prosperity in the industrialized world.
Kofi Annan

The deliberate and deadly attacks which were carried out yesterday against our country were more than acts of terror. They were acts of war.
George W. Bush

The construction of Europe is an art. It is the art of the possible.
Jacques Chirac

History never looks like history when you are living through it.
John W. Gardner

We peruse one ideal, that of bringing people together in peace, irrespective of race, religion and political convictions, for the benefit of mankind.
Juan Antonio Samaranch

That great dust-heap called 'history'.
Augustine Birrell

Generally speaking, historically in this country, the care of a child has been thought of as female business.
Eddie Bernice Johnson

September 11th was a moment when America had the sympathy of the world.
Tom Ford

We learned the value of research in World War II.
Amar Bose

Stonehenge was built possibly by the Minoans. It presents one of man's first attempts to order his view of the outside world.
Stephen Gardiner

To people who remember JFK's assassination, JFK Jr. will probably always be that boy saluting his father's coffin.
Michael Beschloss

HOME

Home is the place where, when you have to go there, they have to take you in.
Robert Frost

A house is not a home unless it contains food and fire for the mind as well as the body.
Benjamin Franklin

Human beings are the only creatures on earth that allow their children to come back home.
Bill Cosby

Where we love is home - home that our feet may leave, but not our hearts.
Oliver Wendell Holmes

Any woman who understands the problems of running a home will be nearer to understanding the problems of running a country.
Margaret Thatcher

God is at home, it's we who have gone out for a walk.
Meister Eckhart

Be grateful for the home you have, knowing that at this moment, all you have is all you need.
Sarah Ban Breathnach

If I were asked to name the chief benefit of the house, I should say: the house shelters day-dreaming, the house protects the dreamer, the house allows one to dream in peace.
Gaston Bachelard

There is nothing like staying at home for real comfort.
Jane Austen

Charity begins at home, but should not end there.
Thomas Fuller

I kiss the soil as if I placed a kiss on the hands of a mother, for the homeland is our earthly mother. I consider it my duty to be with my compatriots in this sublime and difficult moment.
Pope John Paul II

When you finally go back to your old home, you find it wasn't the old home you missed but your childhood.
Sam Ewing

Decorate your home. It gives the illusion that your life is more interesting than it really is.
Charles M. Schulz

Home is where the heart is.
Pliny the Elder

Any old place I can hang my hat is home sweet home to me.
William Jerome

Housework is what a woman does that nobody notices unless she hasn't done it.
Evan Esar

Home wasn't built in a day.
Jane Sherwood Ace

I'm the type who'd be happy not going anywhere as long as I was sure I knew exactly what was happening at the places I wasn't going to. I'm the type who'd like to sit home and watch every party that I'm invited to on a monitor in my bedroom.
Andy Warhol

You never know what events are going to transpire to get you home.
Og Mandino

Charity should begin at home, but should not stay there.
Phillips Brooks

Seek home for rest, for home is best.
Thomas Tusser

I feel like I've never had a home, you know? I feel related to the country, to this country, and yet I don't know exactly where I fit in... There's always this kind of nostalgia for a place, a place where you can reckon with yourself.
Sam Shepard

Never make your home in a place. Make a home for yourself inside your own head. You'll find what you need to furnish it - memory, friends you can trust, love of learning, and other such things. That way it will go with you wherever you journey.
Tad Williams

I do not recall a Jewish home without a book on the table.
Elie Wiesel

In our home there was always prayer - aloud, proud and unapologetic.
Lyndon B. Johnson

Where thou art, that is home.
Emily Dickinson

Home is any four walls that enclose the right person.
Helen Rowland

Home life is no more natural to us than a cage is natural to a cockatoo.
George Bernard Shaw

The worst feeling in the world is the homesickness that comes over a man occasionally when he is at home.
E. W. Howe

A man's home is his wife's castle.
Alexander Chase

Home interprets heaven. Home is heaven for beginners.
Charles Henry Parkhurst

A heart makes a good home for the friend.
Yunus Emre

If your house is burning, wouldn't you try and put out the fire?
Imran Khan

I love grocery shopping when I'm home. That's what makes me feel totally normal. I love both the idea of home as in being with my family and friends, and also the idea of exploration. I think those two are probably my great interests.
Yo-Yo Ma

The home is the chief school of human virtues.
William Ellery Channing

Home is one's birthplace, ratified by memory.
Henry Anatole Grunwald

The home should be the treasure chest of living.
Le Corbusier

Homesickness is nothing. Fifty percent of the people in the world are homesick all the time.
John Cheever

I am not quite sure where home is right now. I do have places in London and Milan, and a house in Spain. I guess I would say home is where my mother is, and she lives in Spain.
Sarah Brightman

The fellow that owns his own home is always just coming out of a hardware store.
Kin Hubbard

Kindness goes a long ways lots of times when it ought to stay at home.
Kin Hubbard

Home is the most popular, and will be the most enduring of all earthly establishments.
Channing Pollock

We know that when people are safe in their homes, they are free to pursue their dream for a brighter economic future for themselves and their families.
George Pataki

There are only two things we should fight for. One is the defense of our homes and the other is the Bill of Rights.
Smedley Butler

I'm lucky because I have a job I love. I really miss being away from home, being in my own bed, seeing my animals and siblings, having my moms cookies. I have a couple cats. I got a kitten about a year ago and now Im going on the road so I wont see him for a while. I feel bad.
Michelle Branch

There is something permanent, and something extremely profound, in owning a home.
Kenny Guinn

Since I travel so much, it's always great to be home. There's nothing like getting to raid my own refrigerator at two in the morning.
Amy Grant

Home is the place we love best and grumble the most.
Billy Sunday

The home to everyone is to him his castle and fortress, as well for his defence against injury and violence, as for his repose.
Edward Coke

When I go home, its an easy way to be grounded. You learn to realize what truly matters.
Tony Stewart

I grew up in a household where everybody lived at the top of his lungs.
Frank Langella

I'm a real Suzy Homemaker.
Suzy Bogguss

The house has to please everyone, contrary to the work of art which does not. The work is a private matter for the artist. The house is not.
Adolf Loos

A man's house is his castle.
James Otis

Run a home like you would a small business and treat it with the same seriousness.
Anthea Turner

I say, If everybody in this house lives where it's God first, friends and family second and you third, we won't ever have an argument.
Jeff Foxworthy

The prospect of going home is very appealing.
David Ginola

To be a queen of a household is a powerful thing.
Jill Scott

People who have good relationships at home are more effective in the marketplace.
Zig Ziglar

Home, nowadays, is a place where part of the family waits till the rest of the family brings the car back.
Earl Wilson

There is nothing more important than a good, safe, secure home.
Rosalynn Carter

I'm going to buy some green bananas because by the time I get home they'll be ripe.
Ryan Stiles

HUMOR

A person without a sense of humor is like a wagon without springs. It's jolted by every pebble on the road.
Henry Ward Beecher

A joke is a very serious thing.
Winston Churchill

A sense of humor... is needed armor. Joy in one's heart and some laughter on one's lips is a sign that the person down deep has a pretty good grasp of life.
Hugh Sidey

Common sense and a sense of humor are the same thing, moving at different speeds. A sense of humor is just common sense, dancing.
William James

Everywhere is within walking distance if you have the time.
Steven Wright

Humor is mankind's greatest blessing.
Mark Twain

Imagination was given to man to compensate him for what he is not; a sense of humor to console him for what he is.
Francis Bacon

Start every day off with a smile and get it over with.
W. C. Fields

A sense of humor is a major defense against minor troubles.
Mignon McLaughlin

A well-developed sense of humor is the pole that adds balance to your steps as you walk the tightrope of life.
William Arthur Ward

Like a welcome summer rain, humor may suddenly cleanse and cool the earth, the air and you.
Langston Hughes

Alimony is like buying hay for a dead horse.
Groucho Marx

A taste for irony has kept more hearts from breaking than a sense of humor, for it takes irony to appreciate the joke which is on oneself.
Jessamyn West

Comedy is simply a funny way of being serious.
Peter Ustinov

You can turn painful situations around through laughter. If you can find humor in anything, even poverty, you can survive it.
Bill Cosby

There is hope for the future because God has a sense of humor and we are funny to God.
Bill Cosby

A humorist is a person who feels bad, but who feels good about it.
Don Herold

Everything human is pathetic. The secret source of humor itself is not joy but sorrow. There is no humor in heaven.
Mark Twain

Analyzing humor is like dissecting a frog. Few people are interested and the frog dies of it.
E. B. White

Humor is reason gone mad.
Groucho Marx

Humor is laughing at what you haven't got when you ought to have it.
Langston Hughes

My computer beat me at checkers, but I sure beat it at kickboxing.
Emo Philips

A sense of humor is the ability to understand a joke - and that the joke is oneself.
Clifton Paul Fadiman

Humor is emotional chaos remembered in tranquility.
James Thurber

If I had no sense of humor, I would long ago have committed suicide.
Mahatma Gandhi

Humor brings insight and tolerance. Irony brings a deeper and less friendly understanding.
Agnes Repplier

Gags die, humor doesn't.
Jack Benny

A pun is the lowest form of humor, unless you thought of it yourself.
Doug Larson

When humor goes, there goes civilization.
Erma Bombeck

A laugh is a surprise. And all humor is physical. I was always athletic, so that came naturally to me.
Chevy Chase

Humor is perhaps a sense of intellectual perspective: an awareness that some things are really important, others not; and that the two kinds are most oddly jumbled in everyday affairs.
Christopher Morley

Humor is something that thrives between man's aspirations and his limitations. There is more logic in humor than in anything else. Because, you see, humor is truth.
Victor Borge

Humor is just another defense against the universe.
Mel Brooks

The secret to humor is surprise.
Aristotle

Wit is the lowest form of humor.
Alexander Pope

Comedy has to be based on truth. You take the truth and you put a little curlicue at the end.
Sid Caesar

I have a fine sense of the ridiculous, but no sense of humor.
Edward Albee

If you could choose one characteristic that would get you through life, choose a sense of humor.
Jennifer Jones

Humor is the affectionate communication of insight.
Leo Rosten

Humor is everywhere, in that there's irony in just about anything a human does.
Bill Nye

Humor does not diminish the pain - it makes the space around it get bigger.
Allen Klein

I think the next best thing to solving a problem is finding some humor in it.
Frank Howard Clark

Humor is the instinct for taking pain playfully.
Max Eastman

Humor is richly rewarding to the person who employs it. It has some value in gaining and holding attention, but it has no persuasive value at all.
John Kenneth Galbraith

One doesn't have a sense of humor. It has you.
Larry Gelbart

All I know about humor is that I don't know anything about it.
Fred Allen

Humor can alter any situation and help us cope at the very instant we are laughing.
Allen Klein

Comedy, we may say, is society protecting itself - with a smile.
J. B. Priestley

The satirist shoots to kill while the humorist brings his prey back alive and eventually releases him again for another chance.
Peter De Vries

The more I live, the more I think that humor is the saving sense.
Jacob August Riis

This I conceive to be the chemical function of humor: to change the character of our thought.
Lin Yutang

Great men are rarely isolated mountain peaks; they are the summits of ranges.
Thomas W. Higginson

What a strange world this would be if we all had the same sense of humor.
Bern Williams

Humor is a serious thing. I like to think of it as one of our greatest earliest natural resources, which must be preserved at all cost.
James Thurber

Humor distorts nothing, and only false gods are laughed off their earthly pedestals.
Agnes Repplier

Humor is merely tragedy standing on its head with its pants torn.
Irvin S. Cobb

There is no defense against adverse fortune which is so effectual as an habitual sense of humor.
Thomas W. Higginson

In conversation, humor is worth more than wit and easiness more than knowledge.
George Herbert

When a thought takes one's breath away, a grammar lesson seems an impertinence.
Thomas W. Higginson

Nothing is so galling to a people not broken in from the birth as a paternal, or in other words a meddling government, a government which tells them what to read and say and eat and drink and wear.
Thomas W. Higginson

Puns are a form of humor with words.
Guillermo Cabrera Infante

Get well cards have become so humorous that if you don't get sick you're missing half the fun.
Flip Wilson

Humor is by far the most significant activity of the human brain.
Edward de Bono

There seems to be no lengths to which humorless people will not go to analyze humor. It seems to worry them.
Robert Benchley

Wit - the salt with which the American humorist spoils his intellectual cookery by leaving it out.
Ambrose Bierce

IMAGINATION

Those who dream by day are cognizant of many things that escape those who dream only at night.
Edgar Allan Poe

I like nonsense, it wakes up the brain cells. Fantasy is a necessary ingredient in living, it's a way of looking at life through the wrong end of a telescope. Which is what I do, and that enables you to laugh at life's realities.
Dr. Seuss

Can you imagine what I would do if I could do all I can?
Sun Tzu

The saddest thing I can imagine is to get used to luxury.
Charlie Chaplin

If everyone is thinking alike, then somebody isn't thinking.
George S. Patton

I saw the angel in the marble and carved until I set him free.
Michelangelo

If you want a vision of the future, imagine a boot stamping on a human face - forever.
George Orwell

All successful people men and women are big dreamers. They imagine what their future could be, ideal in every respect, and then they work every day toward their distant vision, that goal or purpose.
Brian Tracy

I cannot imagine a God who rewards and punishes the objects of his creation and is but a reflection of human frailty.
Albert Einstein

The man who has no imagination has no wings.
Muhammad Ali

You can't depend on your eyes when your imagination is out of focus.
Mark Twain

Live out of your imagination, not your history.
Stephen Covey

All men who have achieved great things have been great dreamers.
Orison Swett Marden

Think left and think right and think low and think high. Oh, the thinks you can think up if only you try!
Dr. Seuss

Imagination rules the world.
Napoleon Bonaparte

I paint objects as I think them, not as I see them.
Pablo Picasso

I am imagination. I can see what the eyes cannot see. I can hear what the ears cannot hear. I can feel what the heart cannot feel.
Peter Nivio Zarlenga

A rock pile ceases to be a rock pile the moment a single man contemplates it, bearing within him the image of a cathedral.
Antoine de Saint-Exupery

Imagination will often carry us to worlds that never were. But without it we go nowhere.
Carl Sagan

I always imagined I could be what I wanted to be.
Chris Brown

Everything that is new or uncommon raises a pleasure in the imagination, because it fills the soul with an agreeable surprise, gratifies its curiosity, and gives it an idea of which it was not before possessed.
Joseph Addison

Our truest life is when we are in dreams awake.
Henry David Thoreau

To imagine is everything, to know is nothing at all.
Anatole France

Fiction reveals truths that reality obscures.
Jessamyn West

Trust that little voice in your head that says 'Wouldn't it be interesting if...'; And then do it.
Duane Michals

Imagine for yourself a character, a model personality, whose example you determine to follow, in private as well as in public.
Epictetus

I used to lie in bed in my flat and imagine what would happen if there was a zombie attack.
Simon Pegg

I believe in the imagination. What I cannot see is infinitely more important than what I can see.
Duane Michals

People who lean on logic and philosophy and rational exposition end by starving the best part of the mind.
William Butler Yeats

I have always imagined that Paradise will be a kind of library.
Jorge Luis Borges

The lunatic, the lover, and the poet, are of imagination all compact.
William Shakespeare

I am better able to imagine hell than heaven; it is my inheritance, I suppose.
Elinor Wylie

It is impossible to imagine the universe run by a wise, just and omnipotent God, but it is quite easy to imagine it run by a board of gods.
H. L. Mencken

Some stories are true that never happened.
Elie Wiesel

I believed in myself. I never imagined myself as just an ordinary player.
Imran Khan

There is a boundary to men's passions when they act from feelings; but none when they are under the influence of imagination.
Edmund Burke

Imagination and fiction make up more than three quarters of our real life.
Simone Weil

I imagine that yes is the only living thing.
e. e. cummings

There are no rules of architecture for a castle in the clouds.
Gilbert K. Chesterton

I doubt that the imagination can be suppressed. If you truly eradicated it in a child, he would grow up to be an eggplant.
Ursula K. Le Guin

Imagination is at the root of much that passes for love.
Gilbert Parker

Imagination grows by exercise, and contrary to common belief, is more powerful in the mature than in the young.
W. Somerset Maugham

I never did very well in math - I could never seem to persuade the teacher that I hadn't meant my answers literally.
Calvin Trillin

Imagination has brought mankind through the dark ages to its present state of civilization. Imagination led Columbus to discover America. Imagination led Franklin to discover electricity.
L. Frank Baum

What we imagine is order is merely the prevailing form of chaos.
Kerry Thornley

They are ill discoverers that think there is no land, when they can see nothing but sea.
Francis Bacon

Personally, I would sooner have written Alice in Wonderland than the whole Encyclopedia Britannica.
Stephen Leacock

The imagination is man's power over nature.
Wallace Stevens

It is the eye of ignorance that assigns a fixed and unchangeable color to every object; beware of this stumbling block.
Paul Gauguin

The most imaginative people are the most credulous, for them everything is possible.
Alexander Chase

You have to imagine it possible before you can see something. You can have the evidence right in front of you, but if you can't imagine something that has never existed before, it's impossible.
Rita Dove

We imagine that we want to escape our selfish and commonplace existence, but we cling desperately to our chains.
Anne Sullivan Macy

One is never fortunate or as unfortunate as one imagines.
Francois de La Rochefoucauld

Imagination is the voice of daring. If there is anything Godlike about God it is that. He dared to imagine everything.
Henry Miller

You need imagination in order
to imagine a future that
doesn't exist.
Azar Nafisi

There are no shortcuts in life -
only those we imagine.
Frank Leahy

INSPIRATIONAL

It is during our darkest moments that we must focus to see the light.
Aristotle Onassis

Don't judge each day by the harvest you reap but by the seeds that you plant.
Robert Louis Stevenson

I have looked into your eyes with my eyes. I have put my heart near your heart.
Pope John XXIII

Clouds come floating into my life, no longer to carry rain or usher storm, but to add color to my sunset sky.
Rabindranath Tagore

Change your thoughts and you change your world.
Norman Vincent Peale

Believe you can and you're halfway there.
Theodore Roosevelt

Hope is a waking dream.
Aristotle

Happiness is not something you postpone for the future; it is something you design for the present.
Jim Rohn

God always gives His best to those who leave the choice with him.
Jim Elliot

A #2 pencil and a dream can take you anywhere.
Joyce A. Myers

Nothing is impossible, the word itself says 'I'm possible'!
Audrey Hepburn

Every moment and every event of every man's life on earth plants something in his soul.
Thomas Merton

Be faithful to that which exists within yourself.
Andre Gide

God sleeps in the minerals, awakens in plants, walks in animals, and thinks in man.
Arthur Young

Your present circumstances don't determine where you can go; they merely determine where you start.
Nido Qubein

Happiness resides not in possessions, and not in gold, happiness dwells in the soul.
Democritus

Every charitable act is a stepping stone toward heaven.
Henry Ward Beecher

Belief creates the actual fact.
William James

Health is the greatest possession. Contentment is the greatest treasure. Confidence is the greatest friend. Non-being is the greatest joy.
Lao Tzu

A compliment is something like a kiss through a veil.
Victor Hugo

Don't let the fear of striking out hold you back.
Babe Ruth

The glow of one warm thought is to me worth more than money.
Thomas Jefferson

The fact that I can plant a seed and it becomes a flower, share a bit of knowledge and it becomes another's, smile at someone and receive a smile in return, are to me continual spiritual exercises.
Leo Buscaglia

And now, this is the sweetest and most glorious day that ever my eyes did see.
Donald Cargill

Faith is love taking the form of aspiration.
William Ellery Channing

Give light and people will find the way.
Ella Baker

Put your heart, mind, and soul into even your smallest acts. This is the secret of success.
Swami Sivananda

A place for everything, everything in its place.
Benjamin Franklin

We can't help everyone, but everyone can help someone.
Ronald Reagan

For a gallant spirit there can never be defeat.
Wallis Simpson

In a gentle way, you can shake the world.
Mahatma Gandhi

Grace is the beauty of form under the influence of freedom.
Friedrich Schiller

Judge each day not by the harvest you reap but by the seeds you plant.
Robert Louis Stevenson

Hope is some extraordinary spiritual grace that God gives us to control our fears, not to oust them.
Vincent McNabb

The best way out is always through.
Robert Frost

I am prepared for the worst, but hope for the best.
Benjamin Disraeli

You change your life by changing your heart.
Max Lucado

If it were not for hopes, the heart would break.
Thomas Fuller

There is nothing stronger in the world than gentleness.
Han Suyin

On the recollection of so many and great favours and blessings, I now, with a high sense of gratitude, presume to offer up my sincere thanks to the Almighty, the Creator and Preserver.
William Bartram

There are two ways of spreading light: to be the candle or the mirror that reflects it.
Edith Wharton

Great hopes make great men.
Thomas Fuller

Show me your hands. Do they have scars from giving? Show me your feet. Are they wounded in service? Show me your heart. Have you left a place for divine love?
Fulton J. Sheen

Whoever is happy will make others happy too.
Anne Frank

Man never made any material as resilient as the human spirit.
Bern Williams

Look within. Within is the fountain of good, and it will ever bubble up, if thou wilt ever dig.
Marcus Aurelius

Enthusiasm moves the world.
Arthur Balfour

Gratitude is the fairest blossom which springs from the soul.
Henry Ward Beecher

I pray God may preserve your health and life many years.
Junipero Serra

Just what future the Designer of the universe has provided for the souls of men I do not know, I cannot prove. But I find that the whole order of Nature confirms my confidence that, if it is not like our noblest hopes and dreams, it will transcend them.
Henry Norris Russell

Wonder rather than doubt is the root of all knowledge.
Abraham Joshua Heschel

What great thing would you attempt if you knew you could not fail?
Robert H. Schuller

The truth is on the march and nothing will stop it.
Emile Zola

Happiness is the natural flower of duty.
Phillips Brooks

With self-discipline most anything is possible.
Theodore Roosevelt

It is only in sorrow bad weather masters us; in joy we face the storm and defy it.
Amelia Barr

How glorious a greeting the sun gives the mountains!
John Muir

It is by acts and not by ideas that people live.
Harry Emerson Fosdick

Of all human activities, man's listening to God is the supreme act of his reasoning and will.
Pope Paul VI

When deeds speak, words are nothing.
Pierre-Joseph Proudhon

It is always the simple that produces the marvelous.
Amelia Barr

The essential elements of giving are power and love - activity and affection - and the consciousness of the race testifies that in the high and appropriate exercise of these is a blessedness greater than any other.
Mark Hopkins

Love and desire are the spirit's wings to great deeds.
Johann Wolfgang von Goethe

It is not ignorance but knowledge which is the mother of wonder.
Joseph Wood Krutch

You don't look out there for God, something in the sky, you look in you.
Alan Watts

Tears of joy are like the summer rain drops pierced by sunbeams.
Hosea Ballou

Plant thy foot firmly in the prints which His foot has made before thee.
Joseph Barber Lightfoot

Nothing makes one feel so strong as a call for help.
Pope Paul VI

Ideas shape the course of history.
John Maynard Keynes

The only thing that ultimately matters is to eat an ice-cream cone, play a slide trombone, plant a small tree, good God, now you're free.
Ray Manzarek

Noble deeds that are concealed are most esteemed.
Blaise Pascal

The power of imagination makes us infinite.
John Muir

Thinking: the talking of the soul with itself.
Plato

Think with your whole body.
Taisen Deshimaru

Tears are often the telescope by which men see far into heaven.
Henry Ward Beecher

Let each man exercise the art he knows.
Aristophanes

I am deliberate and afraid of nothing.
Audre Lorde

Men must live and create. Live to the point of tears.
Albert Camus

Joy descends gently upon us like the evening dew, and does not patter down like a hailstorm.
Jean Paul

Our ideals are our better selves.
Amos Bronson Alcott

Nurture your minds with great thoughts. To believe in the heroic makes heroes.
Benjamin Disraeli

We convince by our presence.
Walt Whitman

Mankind is made great or little by its own will.
Friedrich Schiller

Thought is the wind, knowledge the sail, and mankind the vessel.
Augustus Hare

INTELLIGENCE

It's not that I'm so smart, it's just that I stay with problems longer.
Albert Einstein

The true sign of intelligence is not knowledge but imagination.
Albert Einstein

Failure is simply the opportunity to begin again, this time more intelligently.
Henry Ford

A woman has to be intelligent, have charm, a sense of humor, and be kind. It's the same qualities I require from a man.
Catherine Deneuve

I'm not offended by all the dumb blonde jokes because I know I'm not dumb... and I also know that I'm not blonde.
Dolly Parton

Action is the real measure of intelligence.
Napoleon Hill

Be as smart as you can, but remember that it is always better to be wise than to be smart.
Alan Alda

Common sense is not so common.
Voltaire

I choose my friends for their good looks, my acquaintances for their good characters, and my enemies for their intellects. A man cannot be too careful in the choice of his enemies.
Oscar Wilde

The test of a first-rate intelligence is the ability to hold two opposed ideas in mind at the same time and still retain the ability to function.
F. Scott Fitzgerald

Be what you are. This is the first step toward becoming better than you are.
Julius Charles Hare

Intelligence without ambition is a bird without wings.
Salvador Dali

All intelligent thoughts have already been thought; what is necessary is only to try to think them again.
Johann Wolfgang von Goethe

Character is higher than intellect. A great soul will be strong to live as well as think.
Ralph Waldo Emerson

The mind is not a vessel to be filled but a fire to be kindled.
Plutarch

An intellectual is someone whose mind watches itself.
Albert Camus

Being an intellectual creates a lot of questions and no answers.
Janis Joplin

A woman uses her intelligence to find reasons to support her intuition.
Gilbert K. Chesterton

If there are no stupid questions, then what kind of questions do stupid people ask? Do they get smart just in time to ask questions?
Scott Adams

Always be smarter than the people who hire you.
Lena Horne

Belief is the death of intelligence.
Robert Anton Wilson

Intelligence is the wife, imagination is the mistress, memory is the servant.
Victor Hugo

We should take care not to make the intellect our god; it has, of course, powerful muscles, but no personality.
Albert Einstein

Everyone is a genius at least once a year. The real geniuses simply have their bright ideas closer together.
Georg C. Lichtenberg

We have now sunk to a depth at which restatement of the obvious is the first duty of intelligent men.
George Orwell

Smartness runs in my family. When I went to school I was so smart my teacher was in my class for five years.
Gracie Allen

The surest sign that intelligent life exists elsewhere in the universe is that it has never tried to contact us.
Bill Watterson

Wit is educated insolence.
Aristotle

Genius is more often found in a cracked pot than in a whole one.
E. B. White

Genius ain't anything more than elegant common sense.
Josh Billings

Every true genius is bound to be naive.
Friedrich Schiller

Your intellect may be confused, but your emotions will never lie to you.
Roger Ebert

I'm not the smartest fellow in the world, but I can sure pick smart colleagues.
Franklin D. Roosevelt

The intelligent man is one who has successfully fulfilled many accomplishments, and is yet willing to learn more.
Ed Parker

The higher the voice the smaller the intellect.
Ernest Newman

I can't tell you if genius is hereditary, because heaven has granted me no offspring.
James Whistler

What a distressing contrast there is between the radiant intelligence of the child and the feeble mentality of the average adult.
Sigmund Freud

It's a poor sort of memory that only works backwards.
Lewis Carroll

I must have a prodigious quantity of mind; it takes me as much as a week sometimes to make it up.
Mark Twain

I not only use all the brains that I have, but all that I can borrow.
Woodrow Wilson

Small minds are concerned with the extraordinary, great minds with the ordinary.
Blaise Pascal

It is not worth an intelligent man's time to be in the majority. By definition, there are already enough people to do that.
G. H. Hardy

Intelligence is really a kind of taste: taste in ideas.
Susan Sontag

Man is the most intelligent of the animals - and the most silly.
Diogenes

There are only two races on this planet - the intelligent and the stupid.
John Fowles

Often the hands will solve a mystery that the intellect has struggled with in vain.
Carl Jung

It is better to have a fair intellect that is well used than a powerful one that is idle.
Bryant H. McGill

There is nobody so irritating as somebody with less intelligence and more sense than we have.
Don Herold

It is the mark of a truly intelligent person to be moved by statistics.
George Bernard Shaw

There are no great limits to growth because there are no limits of human intelligence, imagination, and wonder.
Ronald Reagan

Man becomes man only by his intelligence, but he is man only by his heart.
Henri Frederic Amiel

Ignorance is no excuse, it's the real thing.
Irene Peter

Mad, adj. Affected with a high degree of intellectual independence.
Ambrose Bierce

Intellectuals are too sentimental for me.
Margaret Anderson

The intellect of the wise is like glass; it admits the light of heaven and reflects it.
Augustus Hare

The bookful blockhead, ignorantly read With loads of learned lumber in his head.
Alexander Pope

Genius always finds itself a
century too early.
Ralph Waldo Emerson

There is no method but to be
very intelligent.
T. S. Eliot

There is no greater evidence of
superior intelligence than to
be surprised at nothing.
Josh Billings

To be able to fill leisure
intelligently is the last product
of civilization.
Arnold J. Toynbee

Intelligence is not a science.
Frank Carlucci

LEADERSHIP

If you think you can do a thing or think you can't do a thing, you're right.
Henry Ford

Be a yardstick of quality. Some people aren't used to an environment where excellence is expected.
Steve Jobs

Be careful the environment you choose for it will shape you; be careful the friends you choose for you will become like them.
W. Clement Stone

A man always has two reasons for doing anything: a good reason and the real reason.
J. P. Morgan

Effective leadership is putting first things first. Effective management is discipline, carrying it out.
Stephen Covey

Don't be afraid to give up the good to go for the great.
John D. Rockefeller

Don't find fault, find a remedy.
Henry Ford

A man who wants to lead the orchestra must turn his back on the crowd.
Max Lucado

Innovation distinguishes between a leader and a follower.
Steve Jobs

Leadership is the art of getting someone else to do something you want done because he wants to do it.
Dwight D. Eisenhower

He who is prudent and lies in wait for an enemy who is not, will be victorious.
Sun Tzu

Affirmation without discipline is the beginning of delusion.
Jim Rohn

High expectations are the key to everything.
Sam Walton

Everyone who's ever taken a shower has an idea. It's the person who gets out of the shower, dries off and does something about
it who makes a difference.
Nolan Bushnell

Good management is the art of making problems so interesting and their solutions so constructive that everyone wants to get to work and deal with them.
Paul Hawken

Getting in touch with your true self must be your first priority.
Tom Hopkins

Hold yourself responsible for a higher standard than anybody expects of you. Never excuse yourself.
Henry Ward Beecher

How we think shows through in how we act. Attitudes are mirrors of the mind. They reflect thinking.
David Joseph Schwartz

Leadership cannot really be taught. It can only be learned.
Harold S. Geneen

If a window of opportunity appears, don't pull down the shade.
Tom Peters

People who enjoy meetings should not be in charge of anything.
Thomas Sowell

Leaders must be close enough to relate to others, but far enough ahead to motivate them.
John C. Maxwell

Go as far as you can see; when you get there, you'll be able to see farther.
J. P. Morgan

Leadership is the capacity to translate vision into reality.
Warren G. Bennis

If you command wisely, you'll be obeyed cheerfully.
Thomas Fuller

Leadership is practiced not so much in words as in attitude and in actions.
Harold S. Geneen

Give whatever you are doing and whoever you are with the gift of your attention.
Jim Rohn

The task of the leader is to get his people from where they are to where they have not been.
Henry A. Kissinger

You have to think anyway, so why not think big?
Donald Trump

Doing is a quantum leap from imagining.
Barbara Sher

The cautious seldom err.
Confucius

People who don't take risks generally make about two big mistakes a year. People who do take risks generally make about two big mistakes a year.
Peter Drucker

If you want a quality, act as if you already had it.
William James

Without initiative, leaders are simply workers in leadership positions.
Bo Bennett

Get the best people and train them well.
Scott McNealy

Obstacles are things a person sees when he takes his eyes off his goal.
E. Joseph Cossman

Luck is a dividend of sweat. The more you sweat, the luckier you get.
Ray Kroc

Good enough never is.
Debbi Fields

The secret of my success is a two word answer: Know people.
Harvey S. Firestone

Millions saw the apple fall, but Newton was the one who asked why.
Bernard Baruch

The speed of the leader is the speed of the gang.
Mary Kay Ash

Making good decisions is a crucial skill at every level.
Peter Drucker

The amount of good luck coming your way depends on your willingness to act.
Barbara Sher

To succeed in business it is necessary to make others see things as you see them.
Aristotle Onassis

Every silver lining has a cloud.
Mary Kay Ash

No person will make a great business who wants to do it all himself or get all the credit.
Andrew Carnegie

The first man gets the oyster, the second man gets the shell.
Andrew Carnegie

Clarity affords focus.
Thomas Leonard

If you care enough for a result, you will most certainly attain it.
William James

What helps people, helps business.
Leo Burnett

Leaders grasp nettles.
David Ogilvy

My attitude is never to be satisfied, never enough, never.
Duke Ellington

Today a reader, tomorrow a leader.
Margaret Fuller

Strong convictions precede great actions.
James Freeman Clarke

If you have ideas, you have the main asset you need, and there isn't any limit to what you can do with your business and your life. Ideas are any man's greatest asset.
Harvey S. Firestone

The exercise of power is determined by thousands of interactions between the world of the powerful and that of the powerless, all the more so because these worlds are never divided by a sharp line: everyone has a small part of himself in both.
Vaclav Havel

The very exercise of leadership fosters capacity for it.
Cyril Falls

It is rare to find a business partner who is selfless. If you are lucky it happens once in a lifetime.
Michael Eisner

When your values are clear to you, making decisions becomes easier.
Roy E. Disney

Whatever ought to be, can be.
James Rouse

You have no power at all if you do not exercise constant power.
Major Owens

You're only as good as the people you hire.
Ray Kroc

Problems are only opportunities in work clothes.
Henry J. Kaiser

The great leaders have always stage-managed their effects.
Charles de Gaulle

I look for what needs to be done. After all, that's how the universe designs itself.
R. Buckminster Fuller

You have to have your heart in the business and the business in your heart.
An Wang

The employer generally gets the employees he deserves.
J. Paul Getty

Our business in life is not to get ahead of others, but to get ahead of ourselves.
E. Joseph Cossman

In fair weather prepare for foul.
Thomas Fuller

Think little goals and expect little achievements. Think big goals and win big success.
David Joseph Schwartz

The nicest thing about standards is that there are so many of them to choose from.
Ken Olsen

To succeed, one must be creative and persistent.
John H. Johnson

No matter how carefully you plan your goals they will never be more than pipe dreams unless you pursue them with gusto.
W. Clement Stone

Your most dangerous competitors are those that are most like you.
Bruce Henderson

LEGAL

I busted a mirror and got seven years bad luck, but my lawyer thinks he can get me five.
Steven Wright

Collecting more taxes than is absolutely necessary is legalized robbery.
Calvin Coolidge

Compromise is the best and cheapest lawyer.
Robert Louis Stevenson

Advertising is legalized lying.
H. G. Wells

Make crime pay. Become a lawyer.
Will Rogers

A successful lawsuit is the one worn by a policeman.
Robert Frost

Ignorance of the law excuses no man from practicing it.
Addison Mizner

Deceive not thy physician, confessor, nor lawyer.
George Herbert

Justice delayed is justice denied.
William E. Gladstone

The more laws, the less justice.
Marcus Tullius Cicero

Judges are the weakest link in our system of justice, and they are also the most protected.
Alan Dershowitz

A married woman has the same right to control her own body as does an unmarried woman.
Sol Wachtler

Lawyers are the only persons in whom ignorance of the law is not punished.
Jeremy Bentham

It is legal because I wish it.
Louis XIV

All ambitions are lawful except those which climb upward on the miseries or credulities of mankind.
Joseph Conrad

Lawyers are the first refuge of the incompetent.
Aaron Allston

Justice in the life and conduct of the State is possible only as first it resides in the hearts and souls of the citizens.
Plato

As a rule lawyers tend to want to do whatever they can to win.
Bill Williams

The law has no compassion. And justice is administered without compassion.
Christopher Darden

You can't learn everything you need to know legally.
John Irving

Obedience to lawful authority is the foundation of manly character.
Robert E. Lee

Laws are spider webs through which the big flies pass and the little ones get caught.
Honore de Balzac

If the laws could speak for themselves, they would complain of the lawyers in the first place.
Lord Halifax

Lawsuit: A machine which you go into as a pig and come out of as a sausage.
Ambrose Bierce

To force a lawyer on a defendant can only lead him to believe that the law contrives against him.
Potter Stewart

I used to want to be a lawyer, but I didn't want to have half my brain sucked out.
Max Walker

Lawyers, I suppose, were children once.
Charles Lamb

In law, nothing is certain but the expense.
Samuel Butler

He is no lawyer who cannot take two sides.
Charles Lamb

Avoid lawsuits beyond all things; they pervert your conscience, impair your health, and dissipate your property.
Jean de la Bruyere

A lean compromise is better than a fat lawsuit.
George Herbert

The trouble with law is lawyers.
Clarence Darrow

Where there is a will there is a lawsuit.
Addison Mizner

From your confessor, lawyer and physician, hide not your case on no condition.
John Harington

I never saw a lawyer yet who would admit he was making money.
Mary Roberts Rinehart

It is impossible to tell where the law stops and justice begins.
Arthur Baer

I come from a profession which has suffered greatly because of the lack of civility. Lawyers treat each other poorly and it has come home to haunt them. The public will not tolerate a lack of civility.
James E. Rogers

I decided I wanted to be a lawyer when I was 11 years of age.
Johnnie Cochran

A lawyer who does not know men is handicapped.
William Dunbar

People do not win people fights. Lawyers do.
Norman Ralph Augustine

Unfortunately, what many people forget is that judges are just lawyers in robes.
Tammy Bruce

They don't need a lawyer, they need a toastmaster.
Edward Bennett Williams

As for lawyers, it's more fun to play one than to be one.
Sam Waterston

I'm afraid I talk a lot, too much, perhaps. I should have been a lawyer or a college professor or a windy politician, though I'm glad I am not any of these.
Tom Glazer

The events of the day inspired me to become a lawyer.
Christopher Darden

The good lawyer is the great salesman.
Janet Reno

Frivolous lawsuits are booming in this county. The U.S. has more costs of litigation per person than any other industrialized nation in the world, and it is crippling our economy.
Jack Kingston

I would say that IQ is the strongest predictor of which field you can get into and hold a job in, whether you can be an accountant, lawyer or nurse, for example.
Daniel Goleman

Cagey trial lawyers have figured out there's a pretty good likelihood their case - no matter what its merit - will literally get its day in court because of favorable judges.
Dennis Hastert

Lawsuit abuse is a major contributor to the increased costs of healthcare, goods and services to consumers.
Charles W. Pickering

As a private lawyer, I could bill $750 an hour, but I don't.
Jay Alan Sekulow

I wouldn't pretend to tell you we don't pay our lawyers well.
Jay Alan Sekulow

A good lawyer is a bad Christian.
John Lothrop Motley

I have been surrounded by some of the smartest, brightest, most caring lawyers, by agents who are willing to risk their lives for others, by support staff that are willing to work as hard as they can.
Janet Reno

All the libel lawyers will tell you there's no libel any more, that everyone's given up.
Ian Hislop

The only people who benefit from lawsuits are lawyers. I think we made a couple of them rich.
Gavin Rossdale

We are led by lawyers who do not understand either technology or balance sheets.
Thomas Friedman

If somebody invented cigarettes today, the government would not legalize them.
Loni Anderson

I'm not sure I can say there is a clean line between me as an individual and me as a lawyer.
Anita Hill

One of the things I was taught in law school is that I'd never be able to think the same again - that being a lawyer is something that's part of who I am as an individual now.
Anita Hill

It costs a lot to sue a magazine, and it's too bad that we don't have a system where the losing team has to pay the winning team's lawyers.
Carol Burnett

I have a different approach. I don't file lawsuits because I really don't care.
Nicole Kidman
To some lawyers, all facts are created equal.
Felix Frankfurter

I'm trusting in the Lord and a good lawyer.
Oliver North

Lawyers spend a great deal of their time shoveling smoke.
Oliver Wendell Holmes, Jr.

Lawsuits should not be used to destroy a viable and independent distribution system. The solution lies in the marketplace and not the courtroom.
Don Henley

Misery is the company of lawsuits.
Francois Rabelais

People are getting smarter nowadays; they are letting lawyers, instead of their conscience, be their guide.
Will Rogers

I have been committed to carrying out my duties... in accordance with both the letter and spirit of all applicable rules of ethics and canons of conduct.
Samuel Alito

LIFE

In three words I can sum up everything I've learned about life: it goes on.
Robert Frost

Do not dwell in the past, do not dream of the future, concentrate the mind on the present moment.
Buddha

A life spent making mistakes is not only more honorable, but more useful than a life spent doing nothing.
George Bernard Shaw

All life is an experiment. The more experiments you make the better.
Ralph Waldo Emerson

A man who dares to waste one hour of time has not discovered the value of life.
Charles Darwin

Don't go around saying the world owes you a living. The world owes you nothing. It was here first.
Mark Twain

I still find each day too short for all the thoughts I want to think, all the walks I want to take, all the books I want to read, and all the friends I want to see.
John Burroughs

Any idiot can face a crisis - it's day to day living that wears you out.
Anton Chekhov

When I stand before God at the end of my life, I would hope that I would not have a single bit of talent left, and could say, 'I used everything you gave me'.
Erma Bombeck

A man sooner or later discovers that he is the master-gardener of his soul, the director of his life.
James Allen

A baby is God's opinion that life should go on.
Carl Sandburg

Never be bullied into silence. Never allow yourself to be made a victim. Accept no one's definition of your life; define yourself.
Harvey Fierstein

Believe that life is worth living and your belief will help create the fact.
William James

Every man dies. Not every man really lives.
William Wallace

I have a simple philosophy: Fill what's empty. Empty what's full. Scratch where it itches.
Alice Roosevelt Longworth

All the art of living lies in a fine mingling of letting go and holding on.
Havelock Ellis

I arise in the morning torn between a desire to improve the world and a desire to enjoy the world. This makes it hard to plan the day.
E. B. White

Change your life today. Don't gamble on the future, act now, without delay.
Simone de Beauvoir

You will never be happy if you continue to search for what happiness consists of. You will never live if you are looking for the meaning of life.
Albert Camus

Life is a dream for the wise, a game for the fool, a comedy for the rich, a tragedy for the poor.
Sholom Aleichem

Go confidently in the direction of your dreams. Live the life you have imagined.
Henry David Thoreau

Don't let life discourage you; everyone who got where he is had to begin where he was.
Richard L. Evans

Don't go through life, grow through life.
Eric Butterworth

He who has a why to live can bear almost any how.
Friedrich Nietzsche

Every creature is better alive than dead, men and moose and pine trees, and he who understands it aright will rather preserve its life than destroy it.
Henry David Thoreau

Everything has been figured out, except how to live.
Jean-Paul Sartre

A person will sometimes devote all his life to the development of one part of his body - the wishbone.
Robert Frost

Only a life lived for others is a life worthwhile.
Albert Einstein

Life is like dancing. If we have a big floor, many people will dance. Some will get angry when the rhythm changes. But life is changing all the time.
Miguel Angel Ruiz

I do not regret one moment of my life.
Lillie Langtry

A healthful hunger for a great idea is the beauty and blessedness of life.
Jean Ingelow

Here is the test to find whether your mission on Earth is finished: if you're alive, it isn't.
Richard Bach

Life is really simple, but we insist on making it complicated.
Confucius

I think I've discovered the secret of life - you just hang around until you get used to it.
Charles M. Schulz

Everything in life is luck.
Donald Trump

Begin at once to live, and count each separate day as a separate life.
Seneca

My formula for living is quite simple. I get up in the morning and I go to bed at night. In between, I occupy myself as best I can.
Cary Grant

Fortunately analysis is not the only way to resolve inner conflicts. Life itself still remains a very effective therapist.
Karen Horney

Life consists not in holding good cards but in playing those you hold well.
Josh Billings

It is not length of life, but depth of life.
Ralph Waldo Emerson

I love life because what more is there.
Anthony Hopkins

We must let go of the life we have planned, so as to accept the one that is waiting for us.
Joseph Campbell

It's all about quality of life and finding a happy balance between work and friends and family.
Philip Green

We must be willing to let go of the life we have planned, so as to have the life that is waiting for us.
E. M. Forster

Good friends, good books and a sleepy conscience: this is the ideal life.
Mark Twain

We need to give each other the space to grow, to be ourselves, to exercise our diversity. We need to give each other space so that we may both give and receive such beautiful things as ideas, openness, dignity, joy, healing, and inclusion.
Max de Pree

Our life is what our thoughts make it.
Marcus Aurelius

I have found that if you love life, life will love you back.
Arthur Rubinstein

An aim in life is the only fortune worth finding.
Robert Louis Stevenson

Life is 10 percent what you make it, and 90 percent how you take it.
Irving Berlin

The shoe that fits one person pinches another; there is no recipe for living that suits all cases.
Carl Jung

Look, I don't want to wax philosophic, but I will say that if you're alive you've got to flap your arms and legs, you've got to jump around a lot, for life is the very opposite of death, and therefore you must at very least think noisy and colorfully, or you're not alive.
Mel Brooks

The purpose of life is a life of purpose.
Robert Byrne

I love those who yearn for the impossible.
Johann Wolfgang von Goethe

The price of anything is the amount of life you exchange for it.
Henry David Thoreau

Life becomes harder for us when we live for others, but it also becomes richer and happier.
Albert Schweitzer

Most people have never learned that one of the main aims in life is to enjoy it.
Samuel Butler

Not life, but good life, is to be chiefly valued.
Socrates

Life is a succession of lessons which must be lived to be understood.
Helen Keller

Life is a series of collisions with the future; it is not the sum of what we have been, but what we yearn to be.
Jose Ortega y Gasset

Life loves the liver of it.
Maya Angelou

When we remember we are all mad, the mysteries disappear and life stands explained.
Mark Twain

Life is a long lesson in humility.
James M. Barrie

There are three constants in life... change, choice and principles.
Stephen Covey

This life is worth living, we can say, since it is what we make it.
William James

Life is a tragedy when seen in close-up, but a comedy in long-shot.
Charlie Chaplin

Life appears to me too short to be spent in nursing animosity, or registering wrongs.
Charlotte Bronte

Life is half spent before we know what it is.
George Herbert

We can't plan life. All we can do is be available for it.
Lauryn Hill

The aim of life is to live, and to live means to be aware, joyously, drunkenly, serenely, divinely aware.
Henry Miller

Maybe all one can do is hope to end up with the right regrets.
Arthur Miller

Unbeing dead isn't being alive.
e. e. cummings

Life is never easy for those who dream.
Robert James Waller

I take a simple view of life. It is keep your eyes open and get on with it.
Laurence Sterne

Life is something to do when you can't get to sleep.
Fran Lebowitz

The art of living is more like wrestling than dancing.
Marcus Aurelius

Kindness, I've discovered, is everything in life.
Isaac Bashevis Singer

Life is not a problem to be solved, but a reality to be experienced.
Soren Kierkegaard

What is important in life is life, and not the result of life.
Johann Wolfgang von Goethe

The privilege of a lifetime is being who you are.
Joseph Campbell

Nothing in life is to be feared, it is only to be understood. Now is the time to understand more, so that we may fear less.
Marie Curie

Who will tell whether one happy moment of love or the joy of breathing or walking on a bright morning and smelling the fresh air, is not worth all the suffering and effort which life implies.
Erich Fromm

To live a pure unselfish life, one must count nothing as one's own in the midst of abundance.
Buddha

The only disability in life is a bad attitude.
Scott Hamilton

For the happiest life, days should be rigorously planned, nights left open to chance.
Mignon McLaughlin

People living deeply have no fear of death.
Anais Nin

There is only one difference between a long life and a good dinner: that, in the dinner, the sweets come last.
Robert Louis Stevenson

Give me the luxuries of life and I will willingly do without the necessities.
Frank Lloyd Wright

My life is every moment of my life. It is not a culmination of the past.
Hugh Leonard

The great use of life is to spend it for something that will outlast it.
William James

Life is far too important a thing ever to talk seriously about.
Oscar Wilde

Life does not cease to be funny when people die any more than it ceases to be serious when people laugh.
George Bernard Shaw

The greatest pleasure of life is love.
Euripides

Life is but thought.
Sara Teasdale

Once you say you're going to settle for second, that's what happens to you in life.
John F. Kennedy

Life is largely a matter of expectation.
Horace

While there's life, there's hope.
Marcus Tullius Cicero

Life well spent is long.
Leonardo da Vinci

When I hear somebody sigh, 'Life is hard,' I am always tempted to ask, 'Compared to what?'
Sydney J. Harris

Life is wasted on the living.
Douglas Adams

Use your health, even to the point of wearing it out. That is what it is for. Spend all you have before you die; do not outlive yourself.
George Bernard Shaw

Every man regards his own life as the New Year's Eve of time.
Jean Paul

Life isn't a matter of milestones, but of moments.
Rose Kennedy

The greatest discovery of my generation is that a human being can alter his life by altering his attitudes.
William James

Life has meaning only if one barters it day by day for something other than itself.
Antoine de Saint-Exupery

Life is anything that dies when you stomp on it.
Dave Barry

I take care of my flowers and my cats. And enjoy food. And that's living.
Ursula Andress

My life is my message.
Mahatma Gandhi

To affect the quality of the day, that is the highest of arts.
Henry David Thoreau

Life is a moderately good play with a badly written third act.
Truman Capote

Life is too short to work so hard.
Vivien Leigh

Life is much shorter than I imagined it to be.
Abraham Cahan

May you live all the days of your life.
Jonathan Swift

There is just one life for each of us: our own.
Euripides

You have succeeded in life when all you really want is only what you really need.
Vernon Howard

The courage of life is often a less dramatic spectacle than the courage of a final moment; but it is no less a magnificent mixture of triumph and tragedy.
John F. Kennedy

I look back on my life like a good day's work, it was done and I am satisfied with it.
Grandma Moses

The main facts in human life are five: birth, food, sleep, love and death.
E. M. Forster

Life is not an exact science, it is an art.
Samuel Butler

Wrong life cannot be lived rightly.
Theodor Adorno

Life is like a trumpet - if you don't put anything into it, you don't get anything out of it.
William Christopher Handy

We are here to add what we can to life, not
to get what we can from life.
William Osler

There is no wealth but life.
John Ruskin

Life consists in what a man is thinking of all day.
Ralph Waldo Emerson

Life must be lived as play.
Plato

One way to get the most out of life is to look upon it as an adventure.
William Feather

The indispensable first step to getting the things you want out of life is this: decide what you want.
Ben Stein

The man who has no inner-life is a slave to his surroundings.
Henri Frederic Amiel

The basic fact about human existence is not that it is a tragedy, but that it is a bore. It is not so much a war as an endless standing in line.
H. L. Mencken

The true secret of happiness lies in taking a genuine interest in all the details of daily life.
William Morris

Life is pleasant. Death is peaceful. It's the transition that's troublesome.
Isaac Asimov

No man is a failure who is enjoying life.
William Feather

Not a shred of evidence exists in favor of the idea that life is serious.
Brendan Gill

Life is a succession of moments, to live each one is to succeed.
Corita Kent

The chief danger in life is that you may take too many precautions.
Alfred Adler

Life will always be to a large extent what we ourselves make it.
Samuel Smiles

Our entire life - consists ultimately in accepting ourselves as we are.
Jean Anouilh

The most exhausting thing in life is being insincere.
Anne Morrow Lindbergh

What a wonderful life I've had! I only wish I'd realized it sooner.
Sidonie Gabrielle Colette

While we are postponing, life speeds by.
Lucius Annaeus Seneca

To live is so startling it leaves little time for anything else.
Emily Dickinson

Seventy percent of success in life is showing up.
Woody Allen

The fear of life is the favorite disease of the 20th century.
William Lyon Phelps

The art of life is to know how to enjoy a little and to endure very much.
William Hazlitt

The less routine the more life.
Amos Bronson Alcott

Our life always expresses the result of our dominant thoughts.
Soren Kierkegaard

Wars and elections are both too big and too small to matter in the long run. The daily work - that goes on, it adds up.
Barbara Kingsolver

Life ought to be a struggle of desire toward adventures whose nobility will fertilize the soul.
Rebecca West

Life is the art of drawing sufficient conclusions from insufficient premises.
Samuel Butler

What we play is life.
Louis Armstrong

You don't have to be the Dalai Lama to tell people that life's about change.
John Cleese

The whole secret of life is to be interested in one thing profoundly and in a thousand things well.
Horace Walpole

Our business in life is not to succeed, but to continue to fail in good spirits.
Robert Louis Stevenson

Life itself still remains a very effective therapist.
Karen Horney

The person lives twice who lives the first
life well.
Robert Herrick

To know nothing is the happiest life.
Desiderius Erasmus

Life itself is the proper binge.
Julia Child

Unrest of spirit is a mark of life.
Karl A. Menninger

To be free is to have achieved your life.
Tennessee Williams

Life has a higher end, than to be amused.
William Ellery Channing

Variety's the very spice of life,
That gives it all its flavor.
William Cowper

LOVE

Affection is responsible for nine-tenths of whatever solid and durable happiness there is in our lives.
C. S. Lewis

Being deeply loved by someone gives you strength, while loving someone deeply gives you courage.
Lao Tzu

Love is composed of a single soul inhabiting two bodies.
Aristotle

A man reserves his true and deepest love not for the species of woman in whose company he finds himself electrified and enkindled, but for that one in whose company he may feel tenderly drowsy.
George Jean Nathan

A kiss is a lovely trick designed by nature to stop speech when words become superfluous.
Ingrid Bergman

Sometimes the heart sees what is invisible to the eye.
H. Jackson Brown, Jr.

A flower cannot blossom without sunshine, and man cannot live without love.
Max Muller

A woman knows the face of the man she loves as a sailor knows the open sea.
Honore de Balzac

A loving heart is the beginning of all knowledge.
Thomas Carlyle

For it was not into my ear you whispered, but into my heart. It was not my lips you kissed, but my soul.
Judy Garland

A kiss makes the heart young again and wipes out the years.
Rupert Brooke

A man is already halfway in love with any woman who listens to him.
Brendan Francis

I have found the paradox, that if you love until it hurts, there can be no more hurt, only more love.
Mother Teresa

Absence diminishes mediocre passions and increases great ones, as the wind extinguishes candles and fans fires.
Francois de La Rochefoucauld

Can miles truly separate you from friends... If you want to be with someone you love, aren't you already there?
Richard Bach

Immature love says: 'I love you because I need you.' Mature love says 'I need you because I love you.'
Erich Fromm

A very small degree of hope is sufficient to cause the birth of love.
Stendhal

At the touch of love everyone becomes a poet.
Plato

Come live in my heart, and pay no rent.
Samuel Lover

Let us always meet each other with smile, for the smile is the beginning of love.
Mother Teresa

All love shifts and changes. I don't know if you can be wholeheartedly in love all the time.
Julie Andrews

All my life, my heart has yearned for a thing I cannot name.
Andre Breton

A loving heart is the truest wisdom.
Charles Dickens

Gravitation is not responsible for people falling in love.
Albert Einstein

As soon go kindle fire with snow, as seek to quench the fire of love with words.
William Shakespeare

A part of kindness consists in loving people more than they deserve.
Joseph Joubert

If you live to be a hundred, I want to live to be a hundred minus one day so I never have to live without you.
A. A. Milne

A pair of powerful spectacles has sometimes sufficed to cure a person in love.
Friedrich Nietzsche

Friendship often ends in love; but love in friendship - never.
Charles Caleb Colton

If you press me to say why I loved him, I can say no more than because he was he, and I was I.
Michel de Montaigne

Love does not begin and end the way we seem to think it does. Love is a battle, love is a war; love is a growing up.
James A. Baldwin

Do all things with love.
Og Mandino

I was born with an enormous need for affection, and a terrible need to give it.
Audrey Hepburn

Love is a force more formidable than any other. It is invisible - it cannot be seen or measured, yet it is powerful enough to transform you in a moment, and offer you more joy than any material possession could.
Barbara de Angelis

Love is life. And if you miss love, you miss life.
Leo Buscaglia

I like not only to be loved, but also to be told I am loved.
George Eliot

A kiss is a rosy dot over the 'i' of loving.
Cyrano de Bergerac

I can live without money, but I cannot live without love.
Judy Garland

I was about half in love with her by the time we sat down. That's the thing about girls. Every time they do something pretty... you fall half in love with them, and then you never know where the hell you are.
J. D. Salinger

Love can sometimes be magic. But magic can sometimes... just be an illusion.
Javan

First love is only a little foolishness and a lot of curiosity.
George Bernard Shaw

We loved with a love that was more than love.
Edgar Allan Poe

Time is too slow for those who wait, too swift for those who fear, too long for those who grieve, too short for those who rejoice, but for those who love, time is eternity.
Henry Van Dyke

Faith makes all things possible... love makes all things easy.
Dwight L. Moody

Before I met my husband, I'd never fallen in love. I'd stepped in it a few times.
Rita Rudner

Love is like war: easy to begin but very hard to stop.
H. L. Mencken

Love is always bestowed as a gift - freely, willingly and without expectation. We don't love to be loved; we love to love.
Leo Buscaglia

Someday, after mastering the winds, the waves, the tides and gravity, we shall harness for God the energies of love, and then, for a second time in the history of the world, man will have discovered fire.
Pierre Teilhard de Chardin

If you want to be loved, be lovable.
Ovid

Love is the flower you've got to let grow.
John Lennon

Absence - that common cure of love.
Lord Byron

All mankind love a lover.
Ralph Waldo Emerson

Love is a game that two can play and both win.
Eva Gabor

If you wish to be loved, show more of your faults than your virtues.
Edward G. Bulwer-Lytton

The hunger for love is much more difficult to remove than the hunger for bread.
Mother Teresa

The best thing to hold onto in life is each other.
Audrey Hepburn

Love is an irresistible desire to be irresistibly desired.
Robert Frost

Once the realization is accepted that even between the closest human beings infinite distances continue, a wonderful living side by side can grow, if they succeed in loving the distance between them which makes it possible for each to see the other whole against the sky.
Rainer Maria Rilke

Love yourself first and everything else falls into line. You really have to love yourself to get anything done in this world.
Lucille Ball

How absurd and delicious it is to be in love with somebody younger than yourself. Everybody should try it.
Barbara Pym

I believe in the compelling power of love. I do not understand it. I believe it to be the most fragrant blossom of all this thorny existence.
Theodore Dreiser

It is difficult to know at what moment love begins; it is less difficult to know that it has begun.
Henry Wadsworth Longfellow

It's useless to hold a person to anything he says while he's in love, drunk, or running for office.
Shirley MacLaine

Don't brood. Get on with living and loving. You don't have forever.
Leo Buscaglia

Everything is clearer when you're in love.
John Lennon

Where there is love there is life.
Mahatma Gandhi

Love consists in this, that two solitudes protect and touch and greet each other.
Rainer Maria Rilke

The hours I spend with you I look upon as sort of a perfumed garden, a dim twilight, and a fountain singing to it. You and you alone make me feel that I am alive. Other men it is said have seen angels, but I have seen thee and thou art enough.
George Edward Moore

For small creatures such as we the vastness is bearable only through love.
Carl Sagan

You will find as you look back upon your life that the moments when you have truly lived are the moments when you have done things in the spirit of love.
Henry Drummond

'Tis better to have loved and lost than never to have loved at all.
Alfred Lord Tennyson

Love isn't something you find. Love is something that finds you.
Loretta Young

Love is being stupid together.
Paul Valery

It is sad not to love, but it is much sadder not to be able to love.
Miguel de Unamuno

In love the paradox occurs that two beings become one and yet remain two.
Erich Fromm

Blessed is the influence of one true, loving human soul on another.
George Eliot

Love is the beauty of the soul.
Saint Augustine

Love makes your soul crawl out from its hiding place.
Zora Neale Hurston

The one thing we can never get enough of is love. And the one thing we never give enough is love.
Henry Miller

Gestures, in love, are incomparably more attractive, effective and valuable than words.
Francois Rabelais

Be of love a little more careful than of anything.
e. e. cummings

Life is the flower for which love is the honey.
Victor Hugo

Life without love is like a tree without blossoms or fruit.
Khalil Gibran

The way to love anything is to realize that it may be lost.
Gilbert K. Chesterton

The best proof of love is trust.
Joyce Brothers

He is not a lover who does not love forever.
Euripides

There is a woman at the beginning of all great things.
Alphonse de Lamartine

We waste time looking for the perfect lover, instead of creating the perfect love.
Tom Robbins

Follow love and it will flee, flee love and it will follow thee.
John Gay

Looking back, I have this to regret, that too often when I loved, I did not say so.
David Grayson

We are not the same persons this year as last; nor are those we love. It is a happy chance if we, changing, continue to love a changed person.
W. Somerset Maugham

Love is a canvas furnished by nature and embroidered by imagination.
Voltaire

What we have once enjoyed we can never lose. All that we love deeply becomes a part of us.
Helen Keller

Love is the child of illusion and the parent of disillusion.
Miguel de Unamuno

Lord, grant that I might not so much seek to be loved as to love.
Francis of Assisi

Sometimes it's a form of love just to talk to somebody that you have nothing in common with and still be fascinated by their presence.
David Byrne

Love that is not madness is not love.
Pedro Calderon de la Barca

The moment you have in your heart this extraordinary thing called love and feel the depth, the delight, the ecstasy of it, you will discover that for you the world is transformed.
Jiddu Krishnamurti

True love is like ghosts, which everyone talks about and few have seen.
Francois de La Rochefoucauld

The greatest happiness of life is the conviction that we are loved; loved for ourselves, or rather, loved in spite of ourselves.
Victor Hugo

Love is my religion - I could die for it.
John Keats

To love oneself is the beginning of a lifelong romance.
Oscar Wilde

When love is not madness, it is not love.
Pedro Calderon de la Barca

Love is a smoke made with the fume of sighs.
William Shakespeare

Down on your knees, and thank heaven, fasting, for a good man's love.
Euripides

Love is a friendship set to music.
Joseph Campbell

Fortune and love favor the brave.
Ovid

Friendship is Love without his wings!
Lord Byron

The most powerful weapon on earth is the human soul on fire.
Ferdinand Foch

Love is supreme and unconditional; like is nice but limited.
Duke Ellington

If you could only love enough, you could be the most powerful person in the world.
Emmet Fox

Love knows not distance; it hath no continent; its eyes are for the stars.
Gilbert Parker

Love is but the discovery of ourselves in others, and the delight in the recognition.
Alexander Smith

We love life, not because we are used to living but because we are used to loving.
Friedrich Nietzsche

Love is what you've been through with somebody.
James Thurber

Love is a gross exaggeration of the difference between one person and everybody else.
George Bernard Shaw

Whatever our souls are made of, his and mine are the same.
Emily Bronte

Who, being loved, is poor?
Oscar Wilde

Do you have to have a reason for loving?
Brigitte Bardot

Falling in love consists merely in uncorking the imagination and bottling the common sense.
Helen Rowland

Come live with me and be my love, And we will all the pleasures prove, That valleys, groves, hills, and fields, Woods, or steeply mountain yields.
Christopher Marlowe

There is no remedy for love but to love more.
Henry David Thoreau

Love does not dominate; it cultivates.
Johann Wolfgang von Goethe

The degree of loving is measured by the degree of giving.
Edwin Louis Cole

What the world really needs is more love and less paper work.
Pearl Bailey

Love is all we have, the only way that each can help the other.
Euripides

Love means to commit yourself without guarantee.
Anne Campbell

One is loved because one is loved. No reason is needed for loving.
Paulo Coelho

Love is when you meet someone who tells you something new about yourself.
Andre Breton

He who loves, flies, runs, and rejoices; he is free and nothing holds him back.
Henri Matisse

Love is an act of endless forgiveness, a tender look which becomes a habit.
Peter Ustinov

To say "I love you" one must first be able to say the "I."
Ayn Rand

Love... it surrounds every being and extends slowly to embrace all that shall be.
Khalil Gibran

There is no limit to the power of loving.
John Morton

Love is the foundation from which your decisions about your life should be made.
Darren L. Johnson

There is no disguise which can hide love for long where it exists, or simulate it where it does not.
Francois de La Rochefoucauld

Take away love and our earth is a tomb.
Robert Browning

Love is the only sane and satisfactory answer to the problem of human existence.
Erich Fromm

Love is an emotion experienced by the many and enjoyed by the few.
George Jean Nathan

Sometimes it's hard to be a woman giving all your love to just one man.
Tammy Wynette

Love takes off masks that we fear we cannot live without and know we cannot live within.
James A. Baldwin

Love is that splendid triggering of human vitality the supreme activity which nature affords anyone for going out of himself toward someone else.
Jose Ortega y Gasset

Love conquers all.
Virgil

Each moment of a happy lover's hour is worth an age of dull and common life.
Aphra Behn

To fear love is to fear life, and those who fear life are already three parts dead.
Bertrand Russell

Love is only a dirty trick played on us to achieve continuation of the species.
W. Somerset Maugham

We are all born for love. It is the principle of existence, and its only end.
Benjamin Disraeli

Love means not ever having to say you're sorry.
Erich Segal

Love is the delusion that one woman differs from another.
H. L. Mencken

The giving of love is an education in itself.
Eleanor Roosevelt

Say what you will, 'tis better to be left than never to have been loved.
William Congreve

For love is immortality.
Emily Dickinson

Love is the word used to label the sexual excitement of the young, the habituation of the middle-aged, and the mutual dependence of the old.
John Ciardi

People think love is an emotion. Love is good sense.
Ken Kesey

Your words are my food, your breath my wine. You are everything to me.
Sarah Bernhardt

Love is the joy of the good, the wonder of the wise, the amazement of the Gods.
Plato

The way to know life is to love many things.
Vincent Van Gogh

The art of love is largely the art of persistence.
Albert Ellis

Love's greatest gift is its ability to make everything it touches sacred.
Barbara de Angelis

There are never enough I Love You's.
Lenny Bruce

The sweetest of all sounds is that of the voice of the woman we love.
Jean de la Bruyere

Stand by your man. Give him two arms to cling to and something warm to come to.
Tammy Wynette

The richest love is that which submits to the arbitration of time.
Lawrence Durrell

Love looks through a telescope; envy, through a microscope.
Josh Billings

There is no surprise more magical than the surprise of being loved: It is God's finger on man's shoulder.
Charles Morgan

When you love a man, he becomes more than a body. His physical limbs expand, and his outline recedes, vanishes. He is rich and sweet and right. He is part of the world, the atmosphere, the blue sky and the blue water.
Gwendolyn Brooks

Love is not only something you feel, it is something you do.
David Wilkerson

Love possesses not nor will it be possessed, for love is sufficient unto love.
Khalil Gibran

The only abnormality is the incapacity to love.
Anais Nin

Only do what your heart tells you.
Princess Diana

Love is the hardest habit to break, and the most difficult to satisfy.
Drew Barrymore

Nobody has ever measured, not even poets, how much the heart can hold.
Zelda Fitzgerald

Love is suffering. One side always loves more.
Catherine Deneuve

Sympathy constitutes friendship; but in love there is a sort of antipathy, or opposing passion. Each strives to be the other, and both together make up one whole.
Samuel Taylor Coleridge

Let no one who loves be unhappy, even love unreturned has its rainbow.
James M. Barrie

Though lovers be lost love shall not.
Dylan Thomas

Love is the triumph of imagination over intelligence.
H. L. Mencken

To love abundantly is to live abundantly, and to love forever is to live forever.
Henry Drummond

When we are in love we seem to ourselves quite different from what we were before.
Blaise Pascal

Love is the poetry of the senses.
Honore de Balzac

Love is a mutual self-giving which ends in self-recovery.
Fulton J. Sheen

When you're in love you never really know whether your elation comes from the qualities of the one you love, or if it attributes them to her; whether the light which surrounds her like a halo comes from you, from her, or from the meeting of your sparks.
Natalie Clifford Barney

Tell me who admires and loves you, and I will tell you who you are.
Antoine de Saint-Exupery

To love for the sake of being loved is human, but to love for the sake of loving is angelic.
Alphonse de Lamartine

The fact is that love is of two kinds, one which commands, and one which obeys. The two are quite distinct, and the passion to which the one gives rise is not the passion of the other.
Honore de Balzac

In every living thing there is the desire for love.
David Herbert Lawrence

If you wished to be loved, love.
Lucius Annaeus Seneca

Who would give a law to lovers? Love is unto itself a higher law.
Boethius

Love ceases to be a pleasure when it ceases to be a secret.
Aphra Behn

I long for the raised voice, the howl of rage or love.
Leslie Fiedler

You don't have to go looking for love when it's where you come from.
Werner Erhard

You never lose by loving. You always lose by holding back.
Barbara de Angelis

If thou must love me, let it be for naught except for love's sake only.
Elizabeth Barrett Browning

Only divine love bestows the keys of knowledge.
Arthur Rimbaud

What love we've given, we'll have forever. What love we fail to give, will be lost for all eternity.
Leo Buscaglia

Where there is great love, there are always wishes.
Willa Cather

Love is love's reward.
John Dryden

Love takes up where knowledge leaves off.
Thomas Aquinas

It is easier to love humanity as a whole than to love one's neighbor.
Eric Hoffer

Love is the only gold.
Alfred Lord Tennyson

But love's a malady without a cure.
John Dryden

Who ever loved that loved not at first sight?
Christopher Marlowe

Love is much nicer to be in than an automobile accident, a tight girdle, a higher tax bracket or a holding pattern over Philadelphia.
Judith Viorst

Love in its essence is spiritual fire.
Lucius Annaeus Seneca

Who so loves believes the impossible.
Elizabeth Barrett Browning

O, thou art fairer than the evening air clad in the beauty of a thousand stars.
Christopher Marlowe

Love is the great miracle cure. Loving ourselves works miracles in our lives.
Louise L. Hay

The quarrels of lovers are the renewal of love.
Jean Racine

Love is a springtime plant that perfumes everything with its hope, even the ruins to which it clings.
Gustave Flaubert

People who throw kisses are hopelessly lazy.
Bob Hope

There is only one terminal dignity - love.
Helen Hayes

If you would be loved, love, and be loveable.
Benjamin Franklin

Love is metaphysical gravity.
R. Buckminster Fuller

To love and be loved is to feel the sun from both sides.
David Viscott

Love is a hole in the heart.
Ben Hecht

The love we give away is the only love we keep.
Elbert Hubbard

There is always something left to love. And if you ain't learned that, you ain't learned nothing.
Lorraine Hansberry

Only love interests me, and I am only in contact with things that revolve around love.
Marc Chagall

Love is always being given where it is not required.
E. M. Forster

We perceive when love begins and when it declines by our embarrassment when alone together.
Jean de la Bruyere

Woe to the man whose heart has not learned while young to hope, to love - and to put its trust in life.
Joseph Conrad

More than kisses, letters mingle souls.
John Donne

Love is the magician that pulls man out of his own hat.
Ben Hecht

Love is blind.
Geoffrey Chaucer

Pains of love be sweeter far than all other pleasures are.
John Dryden

Love is the power to see similarity in the dissimilar.
Theodor Adorno

Oh, love will make a dog howl in rhyme.
Francis Beaumont

There is more pleasure in loving than in being beloved.
Thomas Fuller

It is very easy to love alone.
Gertrude Stein

When you love someone all your saved up wishes start coming out.
Elizabeth Bowen

Who loves, raves.
Lord Byron

There is only one kind of love, but there are a thousand imitations.
Francois de La Rochefoucauld

We love but once, for once only are we perfectly equipped for loving.
Cyril Connolly

In love there are two things - bodies and words.
Joyce Carol Oates

Ultimately love is everything.
M. Scott Peck

Love is like a faucet, it turns off and on.
Billie Holiday

True love is quiescent, except in the nascent moments of true humility.
Bryant H. McGill

One must not trifle with love.
Alfred de Musset

To good and true love fear is forever affixed.
Francois Rabelais

Love is an energy which exists of itself. It is its own value.
Thornton Wilder

The first magic of love is our ignorance that it can ever end.
Benjamin Disraeli

We can only learn to love by loving.
Iris Murdoch

To witness two lovers is a spectacle for the gods.
Johann Wolfgang von Goethe

Love shall be our token; love be yours and love be mine.
Christina Rossetti

There is room in the smallest cottage for a happy loving pair.
Friedrich Schiller

Love means to love that which is unlovable; or it is no virtue at all.
Gilbert K. Chesterton

We may give without loving, but we cannot love without giving.
Bernard Meltzer

To enlarge or illustrate this power and effect of love is to set a candle in the sun.
Robert Burton

With our love, we could save the world.
George Harrison

When love is at its best, one loves so much that he cannot forget.
Helen Hunt Jackson

We are most alive when we're in love.
John Updike

MARRIAGE

The critical period of matrimony is breakfast-time.
A. P. Herbert

A successful marriage requires falling in love many times, always with the same person.
Mignon McLaughlin

Before marriage, a girl has to make love to a man to hold him. After marriage, she has to hold him to make love to him.
Marilyn Monroe

A good marriage would be between a blind wife and a deaf husband.
Michel de Montaigne

How can a woman be expected to be happy with a man who insists on treating her as if she were a perfectly normal human being.
Oscar Wilde

Let the wife make the husband glad to come home, and let him make her sorry to see him leave.
Martin Luther

Don't marry the person you think you can live with; marry only the individual you think you can't live without.
James C. Dobson

A journey is like marriage. The certain way to be wrong is to think you control it.
John Steinbeck

A man in love is incomplete until he has married. Then he's finished.
Zsa Zsa Gabor

It is not a lack of love, but a lack of friendship that makes unhappy marriages.
Friedrich Nietzsche

The secret of a happy marriage remains a secret.
Henny Youngman

I'd marry again if I found a man who had fifteen million dollars, would sign over half to me, and guarantee that he'd be dead within a year.
Bette Davis

A dress that zips up the back will bring a husband and wife together.
James H. Boren

I love being married. It's so great to find that one special person you want to annoy for the rest of your life.
Rita Rudner

All men make mistakes, but married men find out about them sooner.
Red Skelton

I have learned that only two things are necessary to keep one's wife happy. First, let her think she's having her own way. And second, let her have it.
Lyndon B. Johnson

Do you know what it means to come home at night to a woman who'll give you a little love, a little affection, a little tenderness? It means you're in the wrong house, that's what it means.
Henny Youngman

Being divorced is like being hit by a Mack truck. If you live through it, you start looking very carefully to the right and to the left.
Jean Kerr

A successful marriage is an edifice that must be rebuilt every day.
Andre Maurois

Marriage is a wonderful institution, but who wants to live in an institution?
Groucho Marx

Sometimes I wonder if men and women really suit each other. Perhaps they should live next door and just visit now and then.
Katharine Hepburn

A husband is what is left of a lover, after the nerve has been extracted.
Helen Rowland

Bachelors know more about women than married men; if they didn't they'd be married too.
H. L. Mencken

All marriages are happy. It's the living together afterward that causes all the trouble.
Raymond Hull

An ideal wife is one who remains faithful to you but tries to be just as charming as if she weren't.
Sacha Guitry

Marriage is nature's way of keeping us from fighting with strangers.
Alan King

A man marries to have a home, but also because he doesn't want to be bothered with sex and all that sort of thing.
W. Somerset Maugham

A wedding is a funeral where you smell your own flowers.
Eddie Cantor

One advantage of marriage is that, when you fall out of love with him or he falls out of love with you, it keeps you together until you fall in again.
Judith Viorst

A psychiatrist asks a lot of expensive questions your wife asks for nothing.
Joey Adams

If I get married, I want to be very married.
Audrey Hepburn

Marriage is neither heaven nor hell, it is simply purgatory.
Abraham Lincoln

By our Heavenly Father and only because of God, only because of God. We're like other couples. We do not get along perfectly; we do not go without arguments and, as I call them, fights, and heartache and pain and hurting each other. But a marriage is three of us.
Barbara Mandrell

Almost no one is foolish enough to imagine that he automatically deserves great success in any field of activity; yet almost everyone believes that he automatically deserves success in marriage.
Sydney J. Harris

Basically my wife was immature. I'd be at home in the bath and she'd come in and sink my boats.
Woody Allen

Marriage is a great institution, but I'm not ready for an institution.
Mae West

In every marriage more than a week old, there are grounds for divorce. The trick is to find, and continue to find, grounds for marriage.
Robert Anderson

He's the kind of man a woman would have to marry to get rid of.
Mae West

For years my wedding ring has done its job. It has led me not into temptation. It has reminded my husband numerous times at parties that it's time to go home. It has been a source of relief to a dinner companion. It has been a status symbol in the maternity ward.
Erma Bombeck

Any intelligent woman who reads the marriage contract, and then goes into it, deserves all the consequences.
Isadora Duncan

Bachelors have consciences, married men have wives.
Samuel Johnson

Love is moral even without legal marriage, but marriage is immoral without love.
Ellen Key

Marriage, n: the state or condition of a community consisting of a master, a mistress, and two slaves, making in all, two.
Ambrose Bierce

Getting divorced just because you don't love a man is almost as silly as getting married just because you do.
Zsa Zsa Gabor

Marriage is a bribe to make the housekeeper think she's a householder.
Thornton Wilder

Love: A temporary insanity curable by marriage.
Ambrose Bierce

When marrying, ask yourself this question: Do you believe that you will be able to converse well with this person into your old age? Everything else in marriage is transitory.
Friedrich Nietzsche

In marriage there are no manners to keep up, and beneath the wildest accusations no real criticism. Each is familiar with that ancient child in the other who may erupt again. We are not ridiculous to ourselves. We are ageless. That is the luxury of the wedding ring.
Enid Bagnold

It's tough to stay married. My wife kisses the dog on the lips, yet she won't drink from my glass.
Rodney Dangerfield

The concept of two people living together for 25 years without a serious dispute suggests a lack of spirit only to be admired in sheep.
A. P. Herbert

It's not beauty but fine qualities, my girl, that keep a husband.
Euripides

There is nothing in the world like the devotion of a married woman. It is a thing no married man knows anything about.
Oscar Wilde

Marriage is good for those who are afraid to sleep alone at night.
St. Jerome

Do not put such unlimited power into the hands of husbands. Remember all men would be tyrants if they could.
Abigail Adams

There is nothing nobler or more admirable than when two people who see eye to eye keep house as man and wife, confounding their enemies and delighting their friends.
Homer

More marriages might survive if the partners realized that sometimes the better comes after the worse.
Doug Larson

Marriage resembles a pair of shears, so joined that they cannot be separated; often moving in opposite directions, yet always punishing anyone who comes between them.
Sydney Smith

I think women are natural caretakers. They take care of everybody. They take care of their husbands and their kids and their dogs, and don't spend a lot of time just getting back and taking time out.
Reese Witherspoon

If you want to sacrifice the admiration of many men for the criticism of one, go ahead, get married.
Katharine Hepburn

Marriage is an alliance entered into by a man who can't sleep with the window shut, and a woman who can't sleep with the window open.
George Bernard Shaw

Faithful women are all alike, they think only of their fidelity, never of their husbands.
Jean Giraudoux

If there is such a thing as a good marriage, it is because it resembles friendship rather than love.
Michel de Montaigne

Strike an average between what a woman thinks of her husband a month before she marries him and what she thinks of him a year afterward, and you will have the truth about him.
H. L. Mencken

When a man steals your wife, there is no better revenge than to let him keep her.
Sacha Guitry

The big difference between sex for money and sex for free is that sex for money usually costs a lot less.
Brendan Behan

Marriage: A word which should be pronounced "mirage".
Herbert Spencer

When a man opens a car door for his wife, it's either a new car or a new wife.
Prince Philip

Marriage should be a duet - when one sings, the other claps.
Joe Murray

Why does a woman work ten years to change a man's habits and then complain that he's not the man she married?
Barbra Streisand

He that loves not his wife and children feeds a lioness at home, and broods a nest of sorrows.
Jeremy Taylor

Protecting the institution of marriage safeguards, I believe, the American family.
John Boehner

I married the first man I ever kissed. When I tell this to my children, they just about throw up.
Barbara Bush

If you made a list of reasons why any couple got married, and another list of the reasons for their divorce, you'd have a hell of a lot of overlapping.
Mignon McLaughlin

Men who have a pierced ear are better prepared for marriage - they've experienced pain and bought jewelry.
Rita Rudner

The true index of a man's character is the health of his wife.
Cyril Connolly

My husband and I are either going to buy a dog or have a child. We can't decide whether to ruin our carpet or ruin our lives.
Rita Rudner

Daddy was real gentle with kids. That's why I expected so much out of marriage, figuring that all men should be steady and pleasant.
Loretta Lynn

Never feel remorse for what you have thought about your wife; she has thought much worse things about you.
Jean Rostand

On rare occasions one does hear of a miraculous case of a married couple falling in love after marriage, but on close examination it will be found that it is a mere adjustment to the inevitable.
Emma Goldman

If you want to read about love and marriage, you've got to buy two separate books.
Alan King

Never get married in college; it's hard to get a start if a prospective employer finds you've already made one mistake.
Elbert Hubbard

Marriage is the alliance of two people, one of whom never remembers birthdays and the other who never forgets them.
Ogden Nash

Where there's marriage without love, there will be love without marriage.
Benjamin Franklin

Love in marriage should be the accomplishment of a beautiful dream, and not, as it too often is, the end.
Alphonse Karr

I like getting married, but I don't like being married.
Don Adams

Marriage is an attempt to solve problems together which you didn't even have when you were on your own.
Eddie Cantor

I don't think my wife likes me very much, when I had a heart attack she wrote for an ambulance.
Frank Carson

Politics doesn't make strange bedfellows - marriage does.
Groucho Marx

The secret of a successful marriage is not to be at home too much.
Colin Chapman

Marriage is not about age; it's about finding the right person.
Sophia Bush

When a marriage works, nothing on earth can take its place.
Helen Gahagan

Love is often the fruit of marriage.
Moliere

Married men live longer than single men. But married men are a lot more willing to die.
Johnny Carson

She's been married so many times she has rice marks on her face.
Henny Youngman

It isn't tying himself to one woman that a man dreads when he thinks of marrying; it's separating himself from all the others.
Helen Rowland

Marriage - a book of which the first chapter is written in poetry and the remaining chapters in prose.
Beverley Nichols

Marriage, like money, is still with us; and, like money, progressively devalued.
Robert Graves

Staying married may have long-term benefits. You can elicit much more sympathy from friends over a bad marriage than you ever can from a good divorce.
P. J. O'Rourke

No man should marry until he has studied anatomy and dissected at least one woman.
Honore de Balzac

Marriage is an adventure, like going to war.
Gilbert K. Chesterton

Instead of getting married again, I'm going to find a woman I don't like and give her a house.
Lewis Grizzard

But, alas! what poor Woman is ever taught that she should have a higher Design than to get her a Husband?
Mary Astell

Many a man in love with a dimple makes the mistake of marrying the whole girl.
Stephen Leacock

The bonds of matrimony are like any other bonds - they mature slowly.
Peter De Vries

Only choose in marriage a man whom you would choose as a friend if he were a woman.
Joseph Joubert

The difficulty with marriage is that we fall in love with a personality, but must live with a character.
Peter De Vries

The majority of husbands remind me of an orangutan trying to play the violin.
Honore de Balzac

Marriage is a feast where the grace is sometimes better than the dinner.
Charles Caleb Colton

Marriage is a wonderful invention: then again, so is a bicycle repair kit.
Billy Connolly

Marrying for love may be a bit risky, but it is so honest that God can't help but smile on it.
Josh Billings

In olden times sacrifices were made at the altar - a practice which is still continued.
Helen Rowland

Well married a person has wings, poorly married shackles.
Henry Ward Beecher

It takes patience to appreciate domestic bliss; volatile spirits prefer unhappiness.
George Santayana

Marriage, for a woman at least, hampers the two things that made life to me glorious - friendship and learning.
Jane Harrison

Why in almost all societies have married women specialized in bearing and rearing children and in certain agricultural activities, whereas married men have done most of the fighting and market work?
Gary Becker

There's nothing like a good cheating song to make me want to run home to be with my wife.
Steven Curtis Chapman

Marriage is an institution fits in perfect harmony with the laws of nature; whereas systems of slavery and segregation were designed to brutally oppress people and thereby violated the laws of nature.
Jack Kingston

Married couples who work together to build and maintain a business assume broad responsibilities. Not only is their work important to our local and national economies, but their success is central to the well-being of their families.
Melissa Bean

Marriage is a gamble, let's be honest.
Yoko Ono

Caesar might have married Cleopatra, but he had a wife at home. There's always something.
Will Cuppy

When you have a baby, love is automatic, when you get married, love is earned.
Marie Osmond

Married people from my generation are like an endangered species!
Patrice Leconte

It destroys one's nerves to be amiable every day to the same human being.
Benjamin Disraeli

Marriage is a mistake every man should make.
George Jessel

Men have a much better time of it than women. For one thing, they marry later; for another thing, they die earlier.
H. L. Mencken

Marriage, a market which has nothing free but the entrance.
Michel de Montaigne

No man is regular in his attendance at the House of Commons until he is married.
Benjamin Disraeli

I married beneath me, all women do.
Nancy Astor

Quarrels often arise in marriages when the bridal gifts are excessive.
Antisthenes

The only good husbands stay bachelors: They're too considerate to get married.
Finley Peter Dunne

One was never married, and that's his hell; another is, and that's his plague.
Robert Burton

I've had an exciting time; I married for love and got a little money along with it.
Rose Kennedy

Plant and your spouse plants with you; weed and you weed alone.
Jean-Jacques Rousseau

If it were not for the presents, an elopement would be preferable.
George Ade

One should believe in marriage as in the immortality of the soul.
Honore de Balzac

The comfortable estate of widowhood is the only hope that keeps up a wife's spirits.
John Gay

They dream in courtship, but in wedlock wake.
Alexander Pope

The human brain starts working the moment you are born and never stops until you stand up to speak in public.
George Jessel

I wanted to marry a girl just like my mom.
Michael Bergin

Marriage is a financial contract; I have enough contracts already.
Linda Fiorentino

Marriage is an exercise in torture.
Frances Conroy

Marriage may be the closest thing to Heaven or Hell any of us will know on this earth.
Edwin Louis Cole

When I get married, it'll be no secret.
Elvis Presley

I've had two proposals since I've been a widow. I am a wonderful catch, you know. I have a lot of money.
Ruth Rendell

Never tell a secret to a bride or a groom; wait until they have been married longer.
E. W. Howe

Whoever, fleeing marriage and the sorrows that women cause, does not wish to wed comes to a deadly old age.
Hesiod

There is a time for all things - except marriage, my dear.
Thomas Chatterton

MEDICAL

I'm not feeling very well - I need a doctor immediately. Ring the nearest golf course.
Groucho Marx

A hospital bed is a parked taxi with the meter running.
Groucho Marx

Never go to a doctor whose office plants have died.
Erma Bombeck

Whenever a doctor cannot do good, he must be kept from doing harm.
Hippocrates

Modern medicine is a negation of health. It isn't organized to serve human health, but only itself, as an institution. It makes more people sick than it heals.
Ivan Illich

Doctors are just the same as lawyers; the only difference is that lawyers merely rob you, whereas doctors rob you and kill you too.
Anton Chekhov

In the name of Hypocrites, doctors have invented the most exquisite form of torture ever known to man: survival.
Edward Everett Hale

As a medical doctor, it is my duty to evaluate the situation with as much data as I can gather and as much expertise as I have and as much experience as I have to determine whether or not the wish of the patient is medically justified.
Jack Kevorkian

Medicine is my lawful wife and literature my mistress; when I get tired of one, I spend the night with the other.
Anton Chekhov

Getting out of the hospital is a lot like resigning from a book club. You're not out of it until the computer says you're out of it.
Erma Bombeck

Doctors will have more lives to answer for in the next world than even we generals.
Napoleon Bonaparte

The doctor sees all the weakness of mankind; the lawyer all the wickedness, the theologian all the stupidity.
Arthur Schopenhauer

All sorts of computer errors are now turning up. You'd be surprised to know the number of doctors who claim they are treating pregnant men.
Isaac Asimov

Some people think that doctors and nurses can put scrambled eggs back in the shell.
Cass Canfield

When I was born I was so ugly the doctor slapped my mother.
Rodney Dangerfield

Illness is the doctor to whom we pay most heed; to kindness, to knowledge, we make promise only; pain we obey.
Marcel Proust

The best doctor is the one you run to and can't find.
Denis Diderot

I was always shocked when I went to the doctor's office and they did my X-ray and didn't find that I had eight more ribs than I should have or that my blood was the color green.
Nicolas Cage

My doctor gave me six months to live, but when I couldn't pay the bill he gave me six months more.
Walter Matthau

The doctors x-rayed my head and found nothing.
Dizzy Dean

Medical liability reform is not a Republican or Democrat issue or even a doctor versus lawyer issue. It is a patient issue.
John Ensign

The physician's highest calling, his only calling, is to make sick people healthy - to heal, as it is termed.
Samuel Hahnemann

Flying back from New York, the flight attendant said 'God, I wished you were here yesterday, we had a stroke on the plane. I said, if I have a stroke on a plane, I hope the pretend doctor isn't the one on the plane. I want a real doctor.
Anthony Edwards

Mammograms are really sort of a gift. You can either catch something early or count your lucky stars because nothing was discovered. Either way, you're ahead of the game.
Charlotte Ross

The art of medicine was to be properly learned only from its practice and its exercise.
Thomas Sydenham

You can die of the cure before you die of the illness.
Michael Landon

Passion, you see, can be destroyed by a doctor. It cannot be created.
Peter Shaffer

You may not be able to read a doctor's handwriting and prescription, but you'll notice his bills are neatly typewritten.
Earl Wilson

Three-quarters of the sicknesses of intelligent people come from their intelligence. They need at least a doctor who can understand this sickness.
Marcel Proust

Medicine sometimes snatches away health, sometimes gives it.
Ovid

A physician's physiology has much the same relation to his power of healing as a cleric's divinity has to his power of influencing conduct.
Samuel Butler

Growing up, my dolls were doctors and on secret missions. I had Barbie Goes Rambo.
Zoe Saldana

When I told my doctor I couldn't afford an operation, he offered to touch-up my X-rays.
Henny Youngman

I was going to have cosmetic surgery until I noticed that the doctor's office was full of portraits by Picasso.
Rita Rudner

I got the bill for my surgery. Now I know what those doctors were wearing masks for.
James H. Boren

The great secret of doctors, known only to their wives, but still hidden from the public, is that most things get better by themselves; most things, in fact, are better in the morning.
Lewis Thomas

Doctors coin money when they do procedures but family medicine doesn't have any procedures.
David Jones

It is reasonable to expect the doctor to recognize that science may not have all the answers to problems of health and healing.
Norman Cousins

They certainly give very strange names to diseases.
Plato

I regret to this day that I never went to college. I feel I should have been a doctor.
Ty Cobb

When a man goes through six years training to be a doctor he will never be the same. He knows too much.
Enid Bagnold

Time is generally the best doctor.
Ovid

A pregnant woman facing the most dire circumstances must be able to count on her doctor to do what is medically necessary to protect her from serious physical harm.
Barbara Mikulski

America has the best doctors, the best nurses, the best hospitals, the best medical technology, the best medical breakthrough medicines in the world. There is absolutely no reason we should not have in this country the best health care in the world.
Bill Frist

One has a greater sense of degradation after an interview with a doctor than from any human experience.
Alice James

I went to the doctor and he said I had acute appendicitis, and I said compared to who?
Jay London

I'm by no means condemning prescription medicine for mental health. I've seen it save a lot of people's lives.
Zach Braff

I'm strongly for a patient Bill of Rights. Decisions ought to be made by doctors, not accountants.
Charles Schumer

I'm 86 and my doctor used to tell me to slow down - at least he did until he dropped dead.
Cesar Romero

People are so afraid of authority figures and doctors are authority figures.
Martha Beck

As a physician, I know many doctors want to utilize new technology, but they find the cost prohibitive.
Nathan Deal

Honestly, being a doctor could make you more close minded than regular people.
Alex Chiu

If you look at the human condition today, not everyone is well fed, has access to good medical care, or the physical basics that provide for a healthy and a happy life.
Ralph Merkle

In the sick room, ten cents' worth of human understanding equals ten dollars' worth of medical science.
Martin H. Fischer

MEN

It is easier to build strong children than to repair broken men.
Frederick Douglass

Without feelings of respect, what is there to distinguish men from beasts?
Confucius

Men always want to be a woman's first love - women like to be a man's last romance.
Oscar Wilde

A man's kiss is his signature.
Mae West

If you have men who will exclude any of God's creatures from the shelter of compassion and pity, you will have men who will deal likewise with their fellow men.
Francis of Assisi

The mass of men lead lives of quiet desperation.
Henry David Thoreau

A bachelor is a guy who never made the same mistake once.
Phyllis Diller

Boys will be boys, and so will a lot of middle-aged men.
Kin Hubbard

If so many men, so many minds, certainly so many hearts, so many kinds of love.
Leo Tolstoy

I look only to the good qualities of men. Not being faultless myself, I won't presume to probe into the faults of others.
Mahatma Gandhi

Men rise from one ambition to another: first, they seek to secure themselves against attack, and then they attack others.
Niccolo Machiavelli

The greatest deception men suffer is from their own opinions.
Leonardo da Vinci

Do not trust all men, but trust men of worth; the former course is silly, the latter a mark of prudence.
Democritus

The superior man is distressed by the limitations of his ability; he is not distressed by the fact that men do not recognize the ability that he has.
Confucius

I only have 'yes' men around me. Who needs 'no' men?
Mae West

Men are like steel. When they lose their temper, they lose their worth.
Chuck Norris

It's at the borders of pain and suffering that the men are separated from the boys.
Emil Zatopek

Honor is simply the morality of superior men.
H. L. Mencken

Man as an individual is a genius. But men in the mass form the headless monster, a great, brutish idiot that goes where prodded.
Charlie Chaplin

Man becomes great exactly in the degree in which he works for the welfare of his fellow-men.
Mahatma Gandhi

Beauty makes idiots sad and wise men merry.
George Jean Nathan

Men get to be a mixture of the charming mannerisms of the women they have known.
F. Scott Fitzgerald

I only like two kinds of men, domestic and imported.
Mae West

Men become much more attractive when they start looking older. But it doesn't do much for women, though we do have an advantage: make-up.
Bette Davis

Circumstances rule men; men do not rule circumstances.
Herodotus

Men, even when alone, lighten their labors by song, however rude it may be.
Quintilian

Passion makes idiots of the cleverest men, and makes the biggest idiots clever.
Francois de La Rochefoucauld

I am an agnostic; I do not pretend to know what many ignorant men are sure of.
Clarence Darrow

A lot of times, women don't get the male perspective in regards to a relationship, what men go through when they're not really dealing well.
Morris Chestnut

All men were made by the Great Spirit Chief. They are all brothers.
Chief Joseph

All men who have turned out worth anything have had the chief hand in their own education.
Walter Scott

I have always thought the actions of men the best interpreters of their thoughts.
John Locke

All men have an instinct for conflict: at least, all healthy men.
Hilaire Belloc

Liberty means responsibility. That is why most men dread it.
George Bernard Shaw

The first rule of business is: Do other men for they would do you.
Charles Dickens

Commitment means that it is possible for a man to yield the nerve center of his consent to a purpose or cause, a movement or an ideal, which may be more important to him than whether he lives or dies.
Howard Thurman

Men are more easily governed through their vices than through their virtues.
Napoleon Bonaparte

Men aren't necessities. They're luxuries.
Cher

Pride, envy, avarice - these are the sparks have set on fire the hearts of all men.
Dante Alighieri

Like all young men I set out to be a genius, but mercifully laughter intervened.
Lawrence Durrell

It is the privilege of the gods to want nothing, and of godlike men to want little.
Diogenes

Men do not quit playing because they grow old; they grow old because they quit playing.
Oliver Wendell Holmes

When a hundred men stand together, each of them loses his mind and gets another one.
Friedrich Nietzsche

Men are not against you; they are merely for themselves.
Gene Fowler

Either men will learn to live like brothers, or they will die like beasts.
Max Lerner

Nothing is as peevish and pedantic as men's judgments of one another.
Desiderius Erasmus

Certainly the best works, and of greatest merit for the public, have proceeded from the unmarried, or childless men.
Francis Bacon

By indignities men come to dignities.
Francis Bacon

Great men are seldom over-scrupulous in the arrangement of their attire.
Charles Dickens

Many men owe the grandeur of their lives to their tremendous difficulties.
Charles Spurgeon

Men tire themselves in pursuit of rest.
Laurence Sterne

Time destroys the speculation of men, but it confirms nature.
Marcus Tullius Cicero

Culture makes all men gentle.
Menander

I have always supported measures and principles and not men.
Davy Crockett

Men should strive to think much and know little.
Democritus

No nice men are good at getting taxis.
Katharine Whitehorn

The truth is found when men are free to pursue it.
Franklin D. Roosevelt

The less men think, the more they talk.
Charles de Montesquieu

Men must know their limitations.
Clint Eastwood

By nature, men love newfangledness.
Geoffrey Chaucer

Men shrink less from offending one who inspires love than one who inspires fear.
Niccolo Machiavelli

For tis not in mere death that men die most.
Elizabeth Barrett Browning

Women thrive on novelty and are easy meat for the commerce of fashion. Men prefer old pipes and torn jackets.
Anthony Burgess

Where all men think alike, no one thinks very much.
Walter Lippmann

If the world were a logical place, men would ride side-saddle.
Rita Mae Brown

For many men, the acquisition of wealth does not end their troubles, it only changes them.
Lucius Annaeus Seneca

For most men life is a search for the proper manila envelope in which to get themselves filed.
Clifton Paul Fadiman

Men give away nothing so liberally as their advice.
Francois de La Rochefoucauld

In life we shall find many men that are great, and some that are good, but very few men that are both great and good.
Charles Caleb Colton

Men of lofty genius when they are doing the least work are most active.
Leonardo da Vinci

When two men in business always agree, one of them is unnecessary.
Ezra Pound

There is always a type of man who says he loves his fellow men, and expects to make a living at it.
Edward W. Howe

Truth sits upon the lips of dying men.
Matthew Arnold

The beauty of a strong, lasting commitment is often best understood by men incapable of it.
Murray Kempton

Men are born to succeed, not to fail.
Henry David Thoreau

Men have as exaggerated an idea of their rights as women have of their wrongs.
Edward W. Howe

One must judge men not by their opinions, but by what their opinions have made of them.
Georg C. Lichtenberg

Neutral men are the devil's allies.
Edwin Hubbel Chapin

Men, as well as women, are much oftener led by their hearts than by their understandings.
Lord Chesterfield

Luck is not something you can mention in the presence of self-made men.
E. B. White

When men and women agree, it is only in their conclusions; their reasons are always different.
George Santayana

Men may live fools, but fools they cannot die.
Edward Young

There is no such thing as justice in the abstract; it is merely a compact between men.
Epicurus

Time takes away the grief of men.
Desiderius Erasmus

There are only two forces that unite men - fear and interest.
Napoleon Bonaparte

Deliberation is the work of many men. Action, of one alone.
Charles de Gaulle

Nothing great will ever be achieved without great men, and men are great only if they are determined to be so.
Charles de Gaulle

Men are not punished for their sins, but by them.
Kin Hubbard

There would be no great men if there were no little ones.
George Herbert

He was one of those men who possess almost every gift, except the gift of the power to use them.
Charles Kingsley

Women prefer to talk in twos, while men prefer to talk in threes.
Gilbert K. Chesterton

We should weep for men at their birth, not at their death.
Charles de Montesquieu

Men can only be happy when they do not assume that the object of life is happiness.
George Orwell

Men are only as good as their technical development allows them to be.
George Orwell

Stronger by weakness, wiser men become.
Edmund Waller

No gentleman ever discusses any relationship with a lady.
Keith Miller

Treat all men alike. Give them the same law. Give them an even chance to live and grow.
Chief Joseph

Men are different. When they are in love they may also have other girlfriends.
Zhang Ziyi

Men are often biased in their judgment on account of their sympathy and their interests.
George William Norris

Men are actually the weaker sex.
George Weinberg

Men, who are rogues individually, are in the mass very honorable people.
Charles de Secondat

Men and women have strengths

that complement each other.
Edwin Louis Cole

Men tend to feel threatened; women tend to feel guilty.
Edwin Louis Cole

You can't keep changing men, so you settle for changing your lipstick.
Heather Locklear

I have 20,000 girlfriends, all around the world.
Justin Timberlake

The duty of comedy is to correct men by amusing them.
Moliere

All men's gains are the fruit of venturing.
Herodotus

Men are like sheep, of which a flock is more easily driven than a single one.
Richard Whately

Men's arguments often prove nothing but their wishes.
Charles Caleb Colton

Human misery is too great for men to do without faith.
Heinrich Heine

Those men get along best with women who can get along best without them.
Charles Baudelaire

Most men, when they think they are thinking, are merely rearranging their prejudices.
Knute Rockne

Men do not fail; they give up trying.
Elihu Root

Law describes the way things would work if men were angels.
Christopher Dawson

Italian men do appreciate beautiful women. They're not afraid of the beauty, which is nice.
Eva Herzigova

One man that has a mind and knows it can always beat ten men who haven't and don't.
George Bernard Shaw

Men are freest when they are most unconscious of freedom. The shout is a rattling of chains, always was.
David Herbert Lawrence

Men often act knowingly against their interest.
David Hume

Whatever makes men good Christians, makes them good citizens.
Daniel Webster

Whenever ideas fail, men invent words.
Martin H. Fischer

Men won't read any email from a woman that's over 200 words

long.
Doug Coupland

MOM

Throughout my life, my mom has been the person that I've always looked up to.
Mike Krzyzewski

My mother was the most beautiful woman I ever saw. All I am I owe to my mother. I attribute all my success in life to the moral, intellectual and physical education I received from her.
George Washington

I remember my mother's prayers and they have always followed me. They have clung to me all my life.
Abraham Lincoln

My mother said to me, 'If you are a soldier, you will become a general. If you are a monk, you will become the Pope.' Instead, I was a painter, and became Picasso.
Pablo Picasso

A mother's arms are made of tenderness and children sleep soundly in them.
Victor Hugo

I got to grow up with a mother who taught me to believe in me.
Antonio Villaraigosa

Men are what their mothers made them.
Ralph Waldo Emerson

Mother's love is peace. It need not be acquired, it need not be deserved.
Erich Fromm

Children are the anchors of a mother's life.
Sophocles

I ask people why they have deer heads on their walls. They always say because it's such a beautiful animal. There you go. I think my mother is attractive, but I have photographs of her.
Ellen DeGeneres

I am sure that if the mothers of various nations could meet, there would be no more wars.
E. M. Forster

Only God Himself fully appreciates the influence of a Christian mother in the molding of character in her children.
Billy Graham

Mothers are fonder than fathers of their children because they are more certain they are their own.
Aristotle

I've been through it all, baby, I'm mother courage.
Elizabeth Taylor

Life began with waking up and loving my mother's face.
George Eliot

A mother's happiness is like a beacon, lighting up the future but reflected also on the past in the guise of fond memories.
Honore de Balzac

The natural state of motherhood is unselfishness. When you become a mother, you are no longer the center of your own universe. You relinquish that position to your children.
Jessica Lange

I am truly my mother's son.
David Geffen

Yes, Mother. I can see you are flawed. You have not hidden it. That is your greatest gift to me.
Alice Walker

My mother taught me to treat a lady respectfully.
Chris Brown

Sweater, n.: garment worn by child when its mother is feeling chilly.
Ambrose Bierce

Completeness? Happiness? These words don't come close to describing my emotions. There truly is nothing I can say to capture what motherhood means to me, particularly given my medical history.
Anita Baker

Mothers always find ways to fit in the work - but then when you're working, you feel that you should be spending time with your children and then when you're with your children, you're thinking about working.
Alice Hoffman

Every man must define his identity against his mother. If he does not, he just falls back into her and is swallowed up.
Camille Paglia

My mother used to tell me man gives the award, God gives the reward. I don't need another plaque.
Denzel Washington

Being a mother is hard and it wasn't a subject I ever studied.
Ruby Wax

Motherhood is priced Of God, at price no man may dare To lessen or misunderstand.
Helen Hunt Jackson

Of all the roles I've played, none has been as fulfilling as being a mother.
Annette Funicello

I was a brownie for a day. My mom made me stop. She didn't want me to conform.
Sandra Bullock

Just as a mother finds pleasure in taking her little child on her lap, there to feed and caress him, in like manner our loving God shows His fondness for His beloved souls who have given themselves entirely to Him and have placed all their hope in His goodness.
Alphonsus Liguori

The love of a mother is the veil of a softer light between the heart and the heavenly Father.
Samuel Taylor Coleridge

The Vatican is against surrogate mothers. Good thing they didn't have that rule when Jesus was born.
Elayne Boosler

Motherhood has a very humanizing effect. Everything gets reduced to essentials.
Meryl Streep

Only mothers can think of the future - because they give birth to it in their children.
Maxim Gorky

How simple a thing it seems to me that to know ourselves as we are, we must know our mothers names.
Alice Walker

I'm a Mommy's Girl - the strongest influence in my young life was my mom.
Susie Bright

Motherhood is... difficult and... rewarding.
Gloria Estefan

A woman must combine the role of mother, wife and politician.
Emma Bonino

Everyone checks out my mom. My mom's hot.
Ashley Scott

My mother taught me about the power of inspiration and courage, and she did it with a strength and a passion that I wish could be bottled.
Carly Fiorina

The fastest way to break the cycle of perfectionism and become a fearless mother is to give up the idea of doing it perfectly - indeed to embrace uncertainty and imperfection.
Arianna Huffington

I was raised by a single mother who made a way for me. She used to scrub floors as a domestic worker, put a cleaning rag in her pocketbook and ride the subways in Brooklyn so I would have food on the table. But she taught me as I walked her to the subway that life is about not where you start, but where you're going. That's family values.
Al Sharpton

There is nothing in the world of art like the songs mother used to sing.
Billy Sunday

My mom always said that there would be haters. Not everyone can love ya.
Joel Madden

I owe much to mother. She had an expert's understanding, but also approached art emotionally.
David Rockefeller

When motherhood becomes the fruit of a deep yearning, not the result of ignorance or accident, its children will become the foundation of a new race.
Margaret Sanger

Sometimes the strength of motherhood is greater than natural laws.
Barbara Kingsolver

If you ever become a mother, can I have one of the puppies?
Charles Pierce

Mothers are the necessity of invention.
Bill Watterson

The mother's heart is the child's schoolroom.
Henry Ward Beecher

Motherhood: All love begins and ends there.
Robert Browning

What do girls do who haven't any mothers to help them through their troubles?
Louisa May Alcott

What is free time? I'm a single mother. My free moments are filled with loving my little girl.
Roma Downey

I wanted to escape so badly. But of course I knew I couldn't just give up and leave school. It was only when I heard my mom's voice that I came out of my hiding place.
Zhang Ziyi

My parents, especially my mother, were no influence on me whatsoever.
Andy Partridge

I was always at peace because of the way my mom treated me.
Martina Hingis

I'd lose my mind if I heard my kid call the nanny Mommy.
Toni Braxton

I basically became a cheerleader because I had a very strict mom. That was my way of being a bad girl.
Sandra Bullock

I guess I was a mom so late in life, my daughter was the greatest thing since sliced bread.
Candice Bergen

I wish my mother had left me something about how she felt growing up. I wish my grandmother had done the same. I wanted my girls to know me.
Carol Burnett

Why do grandparents and grandchildren get along so well? The mother.
Claudette Colbert

If there were no schools to take the children away from home part of the time, the insane asylums would be filled with mothers.
Edward W. Howe

There are only two things a child will share willingly; communicable diseases and its mother's age.
Benjamin Spock

I may be the only mother in America who knows exactly what their child is up to all the time.
Barbara Bush

When you have a good mother and no father, God kind of sits in. It's not enough, but it helps.
Dick Gregory

Who in their infinite wisdom decreed that Little League uniforms be white? Certainly not a mother.
Erma Bombeck

Where there is a mother in the home, matters go well.
Amos Bronson Alcott

Mother is far too clever to understand anything she does not like.
Arnold Bennett

The babe at first feeds upon the mother's bosom, but it is always on her heart.
Henry Ward Beecher

Morality and its victim, the mother - what a terrible picture! Is there indeed anything more terrible, more criminal, than our glorified sacred function of motherhood?
Emma Goldman

Giving birth was easier than having a tattoo.
Nicole Appleton

I sing seriously to my mom on the phone. To put her to sleep, I have to sing "Maria" from West Side Story. When I hear her snoring, I hang up.
Adam Sandler

My mom taught us the Serenity Prayer at a young age.
Toby Keith

If my mom reads that I'm grammatically incorrect I'll have hell to pay.
Larisa Oleynik

My mother told me on several different occasions that she was livin' her dream vicariously through me. She once said that I was getting' to do all the things that she would have wanted to have done.
Buck Owens

My mother was a personal friend of God's. They had ongoing conversations.
Della Reese

Mothers don't let your daughters grow up to be models unless you're present.
Janice Dickinson

I'm sure that my mom would have been happy with any path I chose.
Joely Fisher

Motherhood is at its best when the tender chords of sympathy have been touched.
Paul Harris

What motivated me? My mother. My mother was an immigrant woman, a peasant woman, struggled all her life, worked in the garment center.
Al Lewis

My mom is definitely my rock.
Alicia Keys

Always it gave me a pang that my children had no lawful claim to a name.
Harriet Ann Jacobs

My mother thinks I could have even run a larger company.
Christie Hefner

Mommy smoked but she didn't want us to. She saw smoke coming out of the barn one time, so we got whipped.
Loretta Lynn

My mother worked in factories, worked as a domestic, worked in a restaurant, always had a second job.
Ed Bradley

I auditioned on my own. I tried to make a mark for myself without anybody's help, not even Mom's.
Kate Hudson

The man in our society is the breadwinner; the woman has enough to do as the homemaker, wife and mother.
Dorothy Fields

I am no mother, and I won't be one.
Brigitte Bardot

With what price we pay for the glory of motherhood.
Isadora Duncan

The woman is uniformly sacrificed to the wife and mother.
Elizabeth Cady Stanton

Motherhood is the strangest thing, it can be like being one's own Trojan horse.
Rebecca West

My mother taught me that we all have the power to achieve our dreams. What I lacked was the courage.
Clay Aiken

I stand fearlessly for small dogs, the American Flag, motherhood and the Bible. That's why people love me.
Art Linkletter

I think while all mothers deal with feelings of guilt, working mothers are plagued by guilt on steroids!
Arianna Huffington

Who's a boy gonna talk to if not his mother?
Donald E. Westlake

It is only in the act of nursing that a woman realizes her motherhood in visible and tangible fashion; it is a joy of every moment.
Honore De Balzac

Take motherhood: nobody ever thought of putting it on a moral pedestal until some brash feminists pointed out, about a century ago, that the pay is lousy and the career ladder nonexistent.
Barbara Ehrenreich

My sisters and mom raised me to respect women and open doors for them.
Milo Ventimiglia

My mother gets all mad at me if I stay in a hotel. I'm 31-years-old, and I don't want to sleep on a sleeping bag down in the basement. It's humiliating.
Ben Affleck

MONEY

A business that makes nothing but money is a poor business.
Henry Ford

A bank is a place that will lend you money if you can prove that you don't need it.
Bob Hope

The lack of money is the root of all evil.
Mark Twain

A little thought and a little kindness are often worth more than a great deal of money.
John Ruskin

I have no money, no resources, no hopes. I am the happiest man alive.
Henry Miller

All I ask is the chance to prove that money can't make me happy.
Spike Milligan

If women didn't exist, all the money in the world would have no meaning.
Aristotle Onassis

Honesty is the best policy - when there is money in it.
Mark Twain

I'd like to live as a poor man with lots of money.
Pablo Picasso

Don't stay in bed, unless you can make money in bed.
George Burns

He that is of the opinion money will do everything may well be suspected of doing everything for money.
Benjamin Franklin

There are people who have money and people who are rich.
Coco Chanel

I've got all the money I'll ever need, if I die by four o'clock.
Henny Youngman

A woman's best protection is a little money of her own.
Clare Boothe Luce

So you think that money is the root of all evil. Have you ever asked what is the root of all money?
Ayn Rand

For I can raise no money by vile means.
William Shakespeare

Money is better than poverty, if only for financial reasons.
Woody Allen

After a certain point, money is meaningless. It ceases to be the goal. The game is what counts.
Aristotle Onassis

Money is only a tool. It will take you wherever you wish, but it will not replace you as the driver.
Ayn Rand

A man is usually more careful of his money than of his principles.
Oliver Wendell Holmes, Jr.

A simple fact that is hard to learn is that the time to save money is when you have some.
Joe Moore

A man with money is no match against a man on a mission.
Doyle Brunson

Banks have a new image. Now you have 'a friend,' your friendly banker. If the banks are so friendly, how come they chain down the pens?
Alan King

A billion here, a billion there, and pretty soon you're talking about real money.
Everett Dirksen

It is not the creation of wealth that is wrong, but the love of money for its own sake.
Margaret Thatcher

A fool and his money are lucky enough to get together in the first place.
Stanley Weiser

Money is the barometer of a society's virtue.
Ayn Rand

A wise man should have money in his head, but not in his heart.
Jonathan Swift

All my life I knew that there was all the money you could want out there. All you have to do is go after it.
Curtis Carlson

If saving money is wrong, I don't want to be right!
William Shatner

It is money, money, money! Not ideas, not principles, but money that reigns supreme in American politics.
Robert Byrd

It doesn't matter about money; having it, not having it. Or having clothes, or not having them. You're still left alone with yourself in the end.
Billy Idol

An important lever for sustained action in tackling poverty and reducing hunger is money.
Gro Harlem Brundtland

If I can't get the girl, at least give me more money.
Alan Alda

A good reputation is more valuable than money.
Publilius Syrus

All riches have their origin in mind. Wealth is in ideas - not money.
Robert Collier

I'd rather lose my own money than someone else's.
Dean Kamen

Do what you love and the money will follow.
Marsha Sinetar

There was a time when a fool and his money were soon parted, but now it happens to everybody.
Adlai E. Stevenson

If you can count your money, you don't have a billion dollars.
J. Paul Getty

A fool and his money are soon parted.
Thomas Tusser

It's a kind of spiritual snobbery that makes people think they can be happy without money.
Albert Camus

Liking money like I like it, is nothing less than mysticism. Money is a glory.
Salvador Dali

Friendship is like money, easier made than kept.
Samuel Butler

The importance of money flows from it being a link between the present and the future.
John Maynard Keynes

Most men love money and security more, and creation and construction less, as they get older.
John Maynard Keynes

I don't mind that I'm fat. You still get the same money.
Marlon Brando

Anybody who thinks money will make you happy, hasn't got money.
David Geffen

Fame, I have already. Now I need the money.
Wilhelm Steinitz

What counts is what you do with your money, not where it came from.
Merton Miller

Don't judge me. I made a lot of money.
Samantha Bee

If the money we donate helps one child or can ease the pain of one parent, those funds are well spent.
Carl Karcher

It is a waste of money to help those who show no desire to help themselves.
Taylor Caldwell

Civilized countries generally adopt gold or silver or both as money.
Alfred Marshall

Money's a horrid thing to follow, but a charming thing to meet.
Henry James

No complaint... is more common than that of a scarcity of money.
Adam Smith

I've made all my money on my own without my family and I work very hard.
Paris Hilton

It is usually people in the money business, finance, and international trade that are really rich.
Robin Leach

If you make a living, if you earn your own money, you're free - however free one can be on this planet.
Theodore White

Sudden money is going from zero to two hundred dollars a week. The rest doesn't count.
Neil Simon

Money is always there but the pockets change; it is not in the same pockets after a change, and that is all there is to say about money.
Gertrude Stein

Many people take no care of their money till they come nearly to the end of it, and others do just the same with their time.
Johann Wolfgang von Goethe

It's a terribly hard job to spend a billion dollars and get your money's worth.
George M. Humphrey

Men make counterfeit money; in many more cases, money makes counterfeit men.
Sydney J. Harris

It is more rewarding to watch money change the world than watch it accumulate.
Gloria Steinem

Wealth flows from energy and ideas.
William Feather

Money differs from an automobile or mistress in being equally important to those who have it and those who do not.
John Kenneth Galbraith

All money means to me is a pride in accomplishment.
Ray Kroc

Art for art's sake, money for God's sake.
Simon Raven

Many folks think they aren't good at earning money, when what they don't know is how to use it.
Frank Howard Clark

Many good qualities are not sufficient to balance a single want - the want of money.
Johann Georg Zimmermann

In suggesting gifts: Money is appropriate, and one size fits all.
William Randolph Hearst

Marrying into money was not a good thing for me.
Anna Nicole Smith

Money is our madness, our vast collective madness.
David Herbert Lawrence

We've got to put a lot of money into changing behavior.
Bill Gates

I don't think business news is just for old white men with money.
Neil Cavuto

I think everything depends on money.
Alan Bean

You know, a lot of people are just interested in, in building a company so they can make money and get out.
Arthur Rock

Sooner or later, we sell out for money.
Tony Randall

I think that focusing on the money, on the business, is not enough.
Sergei Bubka

If money was my only motivation, I would organize myself differently.
Placido Domingo

If God has allowed me to earn so much money, it is because He knows I give it all away.
Edith Piaf

Money is a mechanism for control.
David Korten

Everyone needs a certain amount of money. Beyond that, we pursue money because we know how to obtain it. We don't necessarily know how to obtain happiness.
Gregg Easterbrook

It's all about the money.
Joseph Jackson

I am happy to make money. I want to make more money, make more music, eat Big Macs and drink Budweisers.
Kid Rock

I don't spend much money on clothes; I never did.
Lauren Hutton

It's easier to force feed people than it is to give 'em what they want. It makes more money.
Merle Haggard

If I have enough money to eat I'm good.
Shia LaBeouf

A fool and his money get a lot of publicity.
Al Bernstein

My goal wasn't to make a ton of money. It was to build good computers.
Steve Wozniak

Ben Franklin may have discovered electricity- but it is the man who invented the meter who made the money.
Earl Warren

Business is other people's money.
Delphine de Girardin

Isn't it a shame that future generations can't be here to see all the wonderful things we're doing with their money?
Earl Wilson

Money: power at its most liquid.
Mason Cooley

If American men are obsessed with money, American women are obsessed with weight. The men talk of gain, the women talk of loss, and I do not know which talk is the more boring.
Marya Mannes

Profit is sweet, even if it comes from deception.
Sophocles

It was an honor and privilege to arrive to this country 16 years ago with almost no money in my pocket. A lot has happened
since then.
Antonio Banderas

I am fiercely loyal to those willing to put their money where my mouth is.
Paul Harvey

MOTIVATIONAL

A creative man is motivated by the desire to achieve, not by the desire to beat others.
Ayn Rand

Believe in yourself! Have faith in your abilities! Without a humble but reasonable confidence in your own powers you cannot be successful or happy.
Norman Vincent Peale

Always continue the climb. It is possible for you to do whatever you choose, if you first get to know who you are and are willing to work with a power that is greater than ourselves to do it.
Ella Wheeler Wilcox

Be miserable. Or motivate yourself. Whatever has to be done, it's always your choice.
Wayne Dyer

Always do your best. What you plant now, you will harvest later.
Og Mandino

Act as if what you do makes a difference. It does.
William James

If you can dream it, you can do it.
Walt Disney

Even if you fall on your face, you're still moving forward.
Victor Kiam

Either you run the day or the day runs you.
Jim Rohn

I don't believe you have to be better than everybody else. I believe you have to be better than you ever thought you could be.
Ken Venturi

Do you want to know who you are? Don't ask. Act! Action will delineate and define you.
Thomas Jefferson

Expect problems and eat them for breakfast.
Alfred A. Montapert

If you don't design your own life plan, chances are you'll fall into someone else's plan. And guess what they have planned for you? Not much.
Jim Rohn

By failing to prepare, you are preparing to fail.
Benjamin Franklin

Always desire to learn something useful.
Sophocles

Follow your dreams, work hard, practice and persevere. Make sure you eat a variety of foods, get plenty of exercise and maintain a healthy lifestyle.
Sasha Cohen

The will to win, the desire to succeed, the urge to reach your full potential... these are the keys that will unlock the door to personal excellence.
Confucius

Determine never to be idle. No person will have occasion to complain of the want of time who never loses any. It is wonderful how much may be done if we are always doing.
Thomas Jefferson

Fear cannot be without hope nor hope without fear.
Baruch Spinoza

Learn from the past, set vivid, detailed goals for the future, and live in the only moment of time over which you have any control: now.
Denis Waitley

If you ask me what I came into this life to do, I will tell you: I came to live out loud.
Emile Zola

Crave for a thing, you will get it. Renounce the craving, the object will follow you by itself.
Swami Sivananda

Leap, and the net will appear.
John Burroughs

Be gentle to all and stern with yourself.
Saint Teresa of Avila

You are never too old to set another goal or to dream a new dream.
C. S. Lewis

If you want to conquer fear, don't sit home and think about it. Go out and get busy.
Dale Carnegie

The key is to keep company only with people who uplift you, whose presence calls forth your best.
Epictetus

When you reach the end of your rope, tie a knot in it and hang on.
Thomas Jefferson

Go big or go home. Because it's true. What do you have to lose?
Eliza Dushku

It's always too early to quit.
Norman Vincent Peale

I've worked too hard and too long to let anything stand in the way of my goals. I will not let my teammates down and I will not let myself down.
Mia Hamm

Begin to be now what you will be hereafter.
William James

Learning is the beginning of wealth. Learning is the beginning of health. Learning is the beginning of spirituality. Searching and learning is where the miracle process all begins.
Jim Rohn

Opportunity does not knock, it presents itself when you beat down the door.
Kyle Chandler

Set your sights high, the higher the better. Expect the most wonderful things to happen, not in the future but right now. Realize that nothing is too good. Allow absolutely nothing to hamper you or hold you up in any way.
Eileen Caddy

If you want to succeed you should strike out on new paths, rather than travel the worn paths of accepted success.
John D. Rockefeller

Things do not happen. Things are made to happen.
John F. Kennedy

Problems are not stop signs, they are guidelines.
Robert H. Schuller

Never complain and never explain.
Benjamin Disraeli

What you get by achieving your goals is not as important as what you become by achieving your goals.
Henry David Thoreau

The first step toward success is taken when you refuse to be a captive of the environment in which you first find yourself.
Mark Caine

In motivating people, you've got to engage their minds and their hearts. I motivate people, I hope, by example - and perhaps by excitement, by having productive ideas to make others feel involved.
Rupert Murdoch

Set your goals high, and don't stop till you get there.
Bo Jackson

You need to overcome the tug of people against you as you reach for high goals.
George S. Patton

The more man meditates upon good thoughts, the better will be his world and the world at large.
Confucius

Be thine own palace, or the world's thy jail.
John Donne

You can't wait for inspiration. You have to go after it with a club.
Jack London

The most effective way to do it, is to do it.
Amelia Earhart

The harder the conflict, the more glorious the triumph.
Thomas Paine

I can, therefore I am.
Simone Weil

Quality is not an act, it is a habit.
Aristotle

No matter how many goals you have achieved, you must set your sights on a higher one.
Jessica Savitch

You can never quit. Winners never quit, and quitters never win.
Ted Turner

Well done is better than well said.
Benjamin Franklin

What you do today can improve all your tomorrows.
Ralph Marston

Small deeds done are better than great deeds planned.
Peter Marshall

Setting goals is the first step in turning the invisible into the visible.
Tony Robbins

Do not weep; do not wax indignant. Understand.
Baruch Spinoza

The secret of getting ahead is getting started.
Agatha Christie

You can't build a reputation on what you are going to do.
Henry Ford

The wise does at once what the fool does at last.
Baltasar Gracian

One way to keep momentum going is to have constantly greater goals.
Michael Korda

The weeds keep multiplying in our garden, which is our mind ruled by fear. Rip them out and call them by name.
Sylvia Browne

I was motivated to be different in part because I was different.
Donna Brazile

Poverty was the greatest motivating factor in my life.
Jimmy Dean

Wherever you are - be all there.
Jim Elliot

When you fail you learn from the mistakes you made and it motivates you to work even harder.
Natalie Gulbis

Know or listen to those who know.
Baltasar Gracian

You can't expect to hit the jackpot if you don't put a few nickels in the machine.
Flip Wilson

If you've got a talent, protect it.
Jim Carrey

Only the educated are free.
Epictetus

What is called genius is the abundance of life and health.
Henry David Thoreau

The ultimate aim of the ego is not to see something, but to be something.
Muhammed Iqbal

There is nothing deep down inside us except what we have put there ourselves.
Richard Rorty

The dog that trots about finds a bone.
Golda Meir

To be a good loser is to learn how to win.
Carl Sandburg

Who seeks shall find.
Sophocles

Without hard work, nothing grows but weeds.
Gordon B. Hinckley

True happiness involves the full use of one's power and talents.
John W. Gardner

We make the world we live in and shape our own environment.
Orison Swett Marden

One may miss the mark by aiming too high as too low.
Thomas Fuller

You never know what motivates you.
Cicely Tyson

To know oneself, one should assert oneself.
Albert Camus

Perseverance is not a long race; it is many short races one after the other.
Walter Elliot

To be wholly devoted to some intellectual exercise is to have succeeded in life.
Robert Louis Stevenson

MOVIES

Am I a romantic? I've seen 'Wuthering Heights' ten times. I'm a romantic.
Johnny Depp

This film cost $31 million. With that kind of money I could have invaded some country.
Clint Eastwood

A film is - or should be - more like music than like fiction. It should be a progression of moods and feelings. The theme, what's behind the emotion, the meaning, all that comes later.
Stanley Kubrick

A story should have a beginning, a middle, and an end... but not necessarily in that order.
Jean-Luc Godard

You know what your problem is, it's that you haven't seen enough movies - all of life's riddles are answered in the movies.
Steve Martin

The length of a film should be directly related to the endurance of the human bladder.
Alfred Hitchcock

Movies can and do have tremendous influence in shaping young lives in the realm of entertainment towards the ideals and objectives of normal adulthood.
Walt Disney

A lot of movies are about life, mine are like a slice of cake.
Alfred Hitchcock

A film is never really good unless the camera is an eye in the head of a poet.
Orson Welles

Cinema is the most beautiful fraud in the world.
Jean-Luc Godard

Film spectators are quiet vampires.
Jim Morrison

It's the movies that have really been running things in America ever since they were invented. They show you what to do, how to do it, when to do it, how to feel about it, and how to look how you feel about it.
Andy Warhol

A wide screen just makes a bad film twice as bad.
Samuel Goldwyn

Cinema is a matter of what's in the frame and what's out.
Martin Scorsese

Movies are like an expensive form of therapy for me.
Tim Burton

I think cinema, movies, and magic have always been closely associated. The very earliest people who made film were magicians.
Francis Ford Coppola

Adding sound to movies would be like putting lipstick on the Venus de Milo.
Mary Pickford

A film is a petrified fountain of thought.
Jean Cocteau

Even if I set out to make a film about a fillet of sole, it would be about me.
Federico Fellini

I don't take the movies seriously, and anyone who does is in for a headache.
Bette Davis

Everything makes me nervous - except making films.
Elizabeth Taylor

So, where's the Cannes Film Festival being held this year?
Christina Aguilera

A good film is when the price of the dinner, the theatre admission and the babysitter were worth it.
Alfred Hitchcock

The secret to film is that it's an illusion.
George Lucas

Every great film should seem new every time you see it.
Roger Ebert

The movies we love and admire are to some extent a function of who we are when we see them.
Mary Schmich

You can map your life through your favorite movies, and no two people's maps will be the same.
Mary Schmich

If my films don't show a profit, I know I'm doing something right.
Woody Allen

Citizen Kane is perhaps the one American talking picture that seems as fresh now as the day it opened. It may seem even fresher.
Pauline Kael

Shoot a few scenes out of focus. I want to win the foreign film award.
Billy Wilder

Everybody's a filmmaker today.
John Milius

Most of us do not consciously look at movies.
Roger Ebert

The movies are the only business where you can go out front and applaud yourself.
Will Rogers

'Home Alone' was a movie, not an alibi.
Jerry Orbach

I don't think you should feel about a film. You should feel about a woman, not a movie. You can't kiss a movie.
Jean-Luc Godard

Film lovers are sick people.
Francois Truffaut

I'm married to the theater but my mistress is the films.
Oskar Werner

Why should people go out and pay money to see bad films when they can stay at home and see bad television for nothing?
Samuel Goldwyn

I never enjoyed working in a film.
Marlene Dietrich

Sometimes in movies, I still have to be the hero, but it's not all that important to me anymore.
Dennis Quaid

Everyone told me to pass on Speed because it was a 'bus movie.'
Sandra Bullock

Give me a couple of years, and I'll make that actress an overnight success.
Samuel Goldwyn

I was obsessed with romance. When I was in high school, I saw 'Doctor Zhivago' every day from the day it opened until the day it left the theater.
John Hughes

You read a script and its based on 'Reservoir Dogs' and 'Pulp Fiction', and it goes right in the bin.
Tim Roth

Movies are a complicated collision of literature, theatre, music and all the visual arts.
Yahoo Serious

I just like movies that somehow expose the world in a way that's different than you imagine it.
Alex Winter

Movies are an art form that is very available to the masses.
Richard King

Every single art form is involved in film, in a way.
Sydney Pollack

When you make a film you usually make a film about an idea.
Sydney Pollack

Nobody makes movies bad on purpose.
Roland Emmerich

It couldn't sound like a dog, because K9 isn't a dog, but I made it sound as mechanical as possible.
John Leeson

Movies are something people see all over the world because there is a certain need for it.
Wim Wenders

If you don't like my movies, don't watch them.
Dario Argento

And in movies you must be a gambler. To produce films is to gamble.
Douglas Sirk

Movies are not scripts - movies are films; they're not books, they're not the theatre.
Nicolas Roeg

There's an electrical thing about movies.
Oliver Stone

I make movies I want to see.
Neil LaBute

We are the movies and the movies are us.
David Ansen

There's only one thing that can kill the movies, and that's education.
Will Rogers

I've always been an animal lover. I've grown up with dogs my whole life. I think that is what helped me get the role on 'Lassie', I was comfortable around the dog, where many of the kids were afraid or intimidated by Lassie.
Will Estes

MUSIC

One good thing about music, when it hits you, you feel no pain.
Bob Marley

After silence, that which comes nearest to expressing the inexpressible is music.
Aldous Huxley

For me, singing sad songs often has a way of healing a situation. It gets the hurt out in the open into the light, out of the darkness.
Reba McEntire

I was born with music inside me. Music was one of my parts. Like my ribs, my kidneys, my liver, my heart. Like my blood. It was a force already within me when I arrived on the scene. It was a necessity for me-like food or water.
Ray Charles

If music be the food of love, play on.
William Shakespeare

I think music in itself is healing. It's an explosive expression of humanity. It's something we are all touched by. No matter what culture we're from, everyone loves music.
Billy Joel

Music doesn't lie. If there is something to be changed in this world, then it can only happen through music.
Jimi Hendrix

Music expresses that which cannot be said and on which it is impossible to be silent.
Victor Hugo

Music is a moral law. It gives soul to the universe, wings to the mind, flight to the imagination, and charm and gaiety to life and to everything.
Plato

Music was my refuge. I could crawl into the space between the notes and curl my back to loneliness.
Maya Angelou

Music is a higher revelation than all wisdom and philosophy.
Ludwig van Beethoven

Without music, life would be a mistake.
Friedrich Nietzsche

Music is my religion.
Jimi Hendrix

Music is everybody's possession. It's only publishers who think that people own it.
John Lennon

All good music resembles something. Good music stirs by its mysterious resemblance to the objects and feelings which motivated it.
Jean Cocteau

I don't make music for eyes. I make music for ears.
Adele

Music can change the world because it can change people.
Bono

I've said that playing the blues is like having to be black twice. Stevie Ray Vaughan missed on both counts, but I never noticed.
B. B. King

I don't know anything about music. In my line you don't have to.
Elvis Presley

Music in the soul can be heard by the universe.
Lao Tzu

It is cruel, you know, that music should be so beautiful. It has the beauty of loneliness of pain: of strength and freedom. The beauty of disappointment and never-satisfied love. The cruel beauty of nature and everlasting beauty of monotony.
Benjamin Britten

But when you get music and words together, that can be a very powerful thing.
Bryan Ferry

If you want to make beautiful music, you must play the black and the white notes together.
Richard M. Nixon

Music, in performance, is a type of sculpture. The air in the performance is sculpted into something.
Frank Zappa

In music the passions enjoy themselves.
Friedrich Nietzsche

It was my 16th birthday - my mom and dad gave me my Goya classical guitar that day. I sat down, wrote this song, and I just knew that that was the only thing I could ever really do - write songs and sing them to people.
Stevie Nicks

You are the music while the music lasts.
T. S. Eliot

Classical music is the kind we keep thinking will turn into a tune.
Kin Hubbard

Everywhere in the world, music enhances a hall, with one exception: Carnegie Hall enhances the music.
Isaac Stern

I don't care much about music. What I like is sounds.
Dizzy Gillespie

Music is the movement of sound to reach the soul for the education of its virtue.
Plato

Any good music must be an innovation.
Les Baxter

All music is beautiful.
Billy Strayhorn

Music washes away from the soul the dust of everyday life.
Berthold Auerbach

Music is forever; music should grow and mature with you, following you right on up until you die.
Paul Simon

If a composer could say what he had to say in words he would not bother trying to say it in music.
Gustav Mahler

Music is the shorthand of emotion.
Leo Tolstoy

Music is well said to be the speech of angels.
Thomas Carlyle

You can't stay the same. If you're a musician and a singer, you have to change, that's the way it works.
Van Morrison

Music has charms to sooth a savage breast, to soften rocks, or bend a knotted oak.
William Congreve

If you look deep enough you will see music; the heart of nature being everywhere music.
Thomas Carlyle

He has Van Gogh's ear for music.
Billy Wilder

There are more love songs than anything else. If songs could make you do something we'd all love one another.
Frank Zappa

Music is the best means we have of digesting time.
W. H. Auden

There's nothing like music to relieve the soul and uplift it.
Mickey Hart

Music is moonlight in the gloomy night of life.
Jean Paul

I wake up in the morning, I do a little stretching exercises, pick up the horn and play.
Herb Alpert

I asked my daughter when she was 16, What's the buzz on the street with the kids? She's going, to be honest, Dad, most of my friends aren't into Kiss. But they've all been told that it's the greatest show on Earth.
Ace Frehley

Music is love in search of a word.
Sidney Lanier

Composers shouldn't think too much - it interferes with their plagiarism.
Howard Dietz

The wise musicians are those who play what they can master.
Duke Ellington

The advice I am giving always to all my students is above all to study the music profoundly... music is like the ocean, and the instruments are little or bigger islands, very beautiful for the flowers and trees.
Andres Segovia

Secretly, I wanted to look like Jimi Hendrix, but I could never quite pull it off.
Bryan Ferry

Writing about music is like dancing about architecture.
Laurie Anderson

Hell is full of musical amateurs.
George Bernard Shaw

Music happens to be an art form that transcends language.
Herbie Hancock

Music should be your escape.
Missy Elliot

No good opera plot can be sensible, for people do not sing when they are feeling sensible.
W. H. Auden

You can never get silence anywhere nowadays, have you noticed?
Bryan Ferry

When words leave off, music begins.
Heinrich Heine

My music had roots which I'd dug up from my own childhood, musical roots buried in the darkest soil.
Ray Charles

Music is the fourth great material want, first food, then clothes, then shelter, then music.
Christian Nestell Bovee

Music is very spiritual, it has the power to bring people together.
Edgar Winter

Music is the soul of language.
Max Heindel

Who hears music feels his solitude peopled at once.
Robert Browning

Music is nothing else but wild sounds civilized into time and tune.
Thomas Fuller

Music is intended and designed for sentient beings that have hopes and purposes and emotions.
Jacques Barzun

Music when healthy, is the teacher of perfect order, and when depraved, the teacher of perfect disorder.
John Ruskin

Music is always changing and the changes are unpredictable.
Billy Sheehan

The iPod completely changed the way people approach music.
Karl Lagerfeld

There's a lot of music that sounds like it's literally computer-generated, totally divorced from a guy sitting down at an instrument.
Aimee Mann

The real art of conducting consists in transitions.
Gustav Mahler

Music is a performance and needs the audience.
Michael Tippett

Sometimes before we make a record I go back and listen to a few. It's equally humbling and uplifting.
Michael Stipe

Music's not like becoming a doctor, who can walk into a community and find people who need him.
Charlie Byrd

Music's staying power is a function of how timeless the lyrics, song and production are.
Gary Wright

My father used to sing to me in my mother's womb. I think I can name about any tune in two beats.
Yancy Butler

It is essential to do everything possible to attract young people to opera so they can see that it is not some antiquated art form but a repository of the most glorious music and drama that man has created.
Bruce Beresford

I was growing up listening to Queen. Freddie Mercury threw those incredible melodies into his songs.
Gary Cherone

My music, my songs are 100 percent inspired by girl power.
Paulina Rubio

NATURE

Green is the prime color of the world, and that from which its loveliness arises.
Pedro Calderon de la Barca

And the day came when the risk to remain tight in a bud was more painful than the risk it took to blossom.
Anais Nin

I thank you God for this most amazing day, for the leaping greenly spirits of trees, and for the blue dream of sky and for everything which is natural, which is infinite, which is yes.
e. e. cummings

And this, our life, exempt from public haunt, finds tongues in trees, books in the running brooks, sermons in stones, and good in everything.
William Shakespeare

Look deep into nature, and then you will understand everything better.
Albert Einstein

He is richest who is content with the least, for content is the wealth of nature.
Socrates

In the depth of winter I finally learned that there was in me an invincible summer.
Albert Camus

All my life I have tried to pluck a thistle and plant a flower wherever the flower would grow in thought and mind.
Abraham Lincoln

Wherever you go, no matter what the weather, always bring your own sunshine.
Anthony J. D'Angelo

A bird doesn't sing because it has an answer, it sings because it has a song.
Lou Holtz

Birds sing after a storm; why shouldn't people feel as free to delight in whatever remains to them?
Rose Kennedy

Keep your face to the sunshine and you cannot see a shadow.
Helen Keller

One of the most tragic things I know about human nature is that all of us tend to put off living. We are all dreaming of some magical rose garden over the horizon instead of enjoying the roses that are blooming outside our windows today.
Dale Carnegie

Forget not that the earth delights to feel your bare feet and the winds long to play with your hair.
Khalil Gibran

Sunshine is delicious, rain is refreshing, wind braces us up, snow is exhilarating; there is really no such thing as bad weather, only different kinds of good weather.
John Ruskin

A lot of people like snow. I find it to be an unnecessary freezing of water.
Carl Reiner

If you wish to make an apple pie from scratch, you must first invent the universe.
Carl Sagan

Autumn is a second spring when every leaf is a flower.
Albert Camus

Earth laughs in flowers.
Ralph Waldo Emerson

I still get wildly enthusiastic about little things... I play with leaves. I skip down the street and run against the wind.
Leo Buscaglia

Spring is nature's way of saying, "Let's party!"
Robin Williams

The butterfly counts not months but moments, and has time enough.
Rabindranath Tagore

What the caterpillar calls the end of the world the master calls a butterfly.
Richard Bach

All water has a perfect memory and is forever trying to get back to where it was.
Toni Morrison

Don't knock the weather; nine-tenths of the people couldn't start a conversation if it didn't change once in a while.
Kin Hubbard

A morning-glory at my window satisfies me more than the metaphysics of books.
Walt Whitman

Ah, summer, what power you have to make us suffer and like it.
Russell Baker

Rest is not idleness, and to lie sometimes on the grass under trees on a summer's day, listening to the murmur of the water, or watching the clouds float across the sky, is by no means a waste of time.
John Lubbock

All things are artificial, for nature is the art of God.
Thomas Browne

Come forth into the light of things, let nature be your teacher.
William Wordsworth

Fishes live in the sea, as men do a-land; the great ones eat up the little ones.
William Shakespeare

I love to think of nature as an unlimited broadcasting station, through which God speaks to us every hour, if we will only tune in.
George Washington Carver

The sun, with all those planets revolving around it and dependent on it, can still ripen a bunch of grapes as if it had nothing else in the universe to do.
Galileo Galilei

Let the rain kiss you. Let the rain beat upon your head with silver liquid drops. Let the rain sing you a lullaby.
Langston Hughes

A hen is only an egg's way of making another egg.
Samuel Butler

The clearest way into the Universe is through a forest wilderness.
John Muir

There is nothing in a caterpillar that tells you it's going to be a butterfly.
R. Buckminster Fuller

When I have a terrible need of - shall I say the word - religion. Then I go out and paint the stars.
Vincent Van Gogh

I think it pisses God off if you walk by the color purple in a field somewhere and don't notice it.
Alice Walker

I go to nature to be soothed and healed, and to have my senses put in order.
John Burroughs

Earth and sky, woods and fields, lakes and rivers, the mountain and the sea, are excellent schoolmasters, and teach some of us more than we can ever learn from books.
John Lubbock

The mountains are calling and I must go.
John Muir

By reading the scriptures I am so renewed that all nature seems renewed around me and with me. The sky seems to be a pure, a cooler blue, the trees a deeper green. The whole world is charged with the glory of God and I feel fire and music under my feet.
Thomas Merton

It is not light that we need, but fire; it is not the gentle shower, but thunder. We need the storm, the whirlwind, and the earthquake.
Frederick Douglass

A light wind swept over the corn, and all nature laughed in the sunshine.
Anne Bronte

We may brave human laws, but we cannot resist natural ones.
Jules Verne

Some people walk in the rain, others just get wet.
Roger Miller

Don't pray when it rains if you don't pray when the sun shines.
Satchel Paige

The trees that are slow to grow bear the best fruit.
Moliere

There are no passengers on spaceship earth. We are all crew.
Marshall McLuhan

I believe in God, only I spell it Nature.
Frank Lloyd Wright

Adapt or perish, now as ever, is nature's inexorable imperative.
H. G. Wells

And the heart that is soonest awake to the flowers is always the first to be touch'd by the thorns.
Thomas Moore

For in the true nature of things, if we rightly consider, every green tree is far more glorious than if it were made of gold and silver.
Martin Luther

There are always flowers for those who want to see them.
Henri Matisse

Everything is blooming most recklessly; if it were voices instead of colors, there would be an unbelievable shrieking into the heart of the night.
Rainer Maria Rilke

A woodland in full color is awesome as a forest fire, in magnitude at least, but a single tree is like a dancing tongue of flame to warm the heart.
Hal Borland

Flowers are the sweetest things God ever made and forgot to put a soul into.
Henry Ward Beecher

The world is mud-luscious and puddle-wonderful.
e. e. cummings

Spring is when you feel like whistling even with a shoe full of slush.
Doug Larson

Beauty for some provides escape, who gain a happiness in eyeing the gorgeous buttocks of the ape or Autumn sunsets exquisitely dying.
Langston Hughes

In all things of nature there is something of the marvelous.
Aristotle

Swans sing before they die - 'twere no bad thing should certain persons die before they sing.
Samuel Taylor Coleridge

As the poet said, 'Only God can make a tree,' probably because it's so hard to figure out how to get the bark on.
Woody Allen

Give me odorous at sunrise a garden of beautiful flowers where I can walk undisturbed.
Walt Whitman

To sit in the shade on a fine day and look upon verdure is the most perfect refreshment.
Jane Austen

Nature will bear the closest inspection. She invites us to lay our eye level with her smallest leaf, and take an insect view of its plain.
Henry David Thoreau

Let us learn to appreciate there will be times when the trees will be bare, and look forward to the time when we may pick the fruit.
Anton Chekhov

Forests, lakes, and rivers, clouds and winds, stars and flowers, stupendous glaciers and crystal snowflakes - every form of animate or inanimate existence, leaves its impress upon the soul of man.
Orison Swett Marden

Trees are the earth's endless effort to speak to the listening heaven.
Rabindranath Tagore

Solitary trees, if they grow at all, grow strong.
Winston Churchill

Just living is not enough... one must have sunshine, freedom, and a little flower.
Hans Christian Anderson

I believe a leaf of grass is no less than the journey-work of the stars.
Walt Whitman

The best thing one can do when it's raining is to let it rain.
Henry Wadsworth Longfellow

Nature, to be commanded, must be obeyed.
Francis Bacon

One touch of nature makes the whole world kin.
William Shakespeare

Nature teaches more than she preaches. There are no sermons in stones. It is easier to get a spark out of a stone than a moral.
John Burroughs

Every flower is a soul blossoming in nature.
Gerard De Nerval

I've made an odd discovery. Every time I talk to a savant I feel quite sure that happiness is no longer a possibility. Yet when I talk with my gardener, I'm convinced of the opposite.
Bertrand Russell

One must ask children and birds how cherries and strawberries taste.
Johann Wolfgang von Goethe

Let a hundred flowers bloom, let a hundred schools of thought contend.
Mao Tse-Tung

Breathless, we flung us on a windy hill, Laughed in the sun, and kissed the lovely grass.
Rupert Brooke

Nature always wears the colors of the spirit.
Ralph Waldo Emerson

Birds have wings; they're free; they can fly where they want when they want. They have the kind of mobility many people envy.
Roger Tory Peterson

Never measure the height of a mountain until you have reached the top. Then you will see how low it was.
Dag Hammarskjold

The flower is the poetry of reproduction. It is an example of the eternal seductiveness of life.
Jean Giraudoux

You can't be suspicious of a tree, or accuse a bird or a squirrel of subversion or challenge the ideology of a violet.
Hal Borland

To me a lush carpet of pine needles or spongy grass is more welcome than the most luxurious Persian rug.
Helen Keller

Winter is nature's way of saying, "Up yours."
Robert Byrne

Perhaps the truth depends on a walk around the lake.
Wallace Stevens

I like trees because they seem more resigned to the way they have to live than other things do.
Willa Cather

For every person who has ever lived there has come, at last, a spring he will never see. Glory then in the springs that are yours.
Pam Brown

I am two with nature.
Woody Allen

When nature has work to be done, she creates a genius to do it.
Ralph Waldo Emerson

Nothing is so beautiful as spring - when weeds, in wheels, shoot long and lovely and lush; Thrush's eggs look little low heavens, and thrush through the echoing timber does so rinse and wring the ear, it strikes like lightning to hear him sing.
Gerard Manley Hopkins

Should you shield the canyons from the windstorms you would never see the true beauty of their carvings.
Elisabeth Kubler-Ross

What would be ugly in a garden constitutes beauty in a mountain.
Victor Hugo

I believe that if one always looked at the skies, one would end up with wings.
Gustave Flaubert

We cannot command Nature except by obeying her.
Francis Bacon

Man has lost the capacity to foresee and to forestall. He will end by destroying the earth.
Albert Schweitzer

For myself I hold no preferences among flowers, so long as they are wild, free, spontaneous. Bricks to all greenhouses! Black thumb and cutworm to the potted plant!
Edward Abbey

The violets in the mountains have broken the rocks.
Tennessee Williams

Flowers are without hope. Because hope is tomorrow and flowers have no tomorrow.
Antonio Porchia

Ocean: A body of water occupying about two-thirds of a world made for man - who has no gills.
Ambrose Bierce

The bluebird carries the sky on his back.
Henry David Thoreau

Many a man curses the rain that falls upon his head, and knows not that it brings abundance to drive away the hunger.
Saint Basil

Yosemite Valley, to me, is always a sunrise, a glitter of green and golden wonder in a vast edifice of stone and space.
Ansel Adams

Let the gentle bush dig its root deep and spread upward to split the boulder.
Carl Sandburg

Like music and art, love of nature is a common language that can transcend political or social boundaries.
Jimmy Carter

It is only in the country that we can get to know a person or a book.
Cyril Connolly

To make a prairie it takes a clover and one bee, One clover, and a bee, And revery. The revery alone will do, If bees are few.
Emily Dickinson

Fall is my favorite season in Los Angeles, watching the birds change color and fall from the trees.
David Letterman

I knew, of course, that trees and plants had roots, stems, bark, branches and foliage that reached up toward the light. But I was coming to realize that the real magician was light itself.
Edward Steichen

If one way be better than another, that you may be sure is nature's way.
Aristotle

The sea is everything. It covers seven tenths of the terrestrial globe. Its breath is pure and healthy. It is an immense desert, where man is never lonely, for he feels life stirring on all sides.
Jules Verne

To be interested in the changing seasons is a happier state of mind than to be hopelessly in love with spring.
George Santayana

Understanding the laws of nature does not mean that we are immune to their operations.
David Gerrold

People from a planet without flowers would think we must be mad with joy the whole time to have such things about us.
Iris Murdoch

Nothing is more memorable than a smell. One scent can be unexpected, momentary and fleeting, yet conjure up a childhood summer beside a lake in the mountains.
Diane Ackerman

How strange that nature does not knock, and yet does not intrude!
Emily Dickinson

The poetry of the earth is never dead.
John Keats

In wilderness I sense the miracle of life, and behind it our scientific accomplishments fade to trivia.
Charles Lindbergh

In June as many as a dozen species may burst their buds on a single day. No man can heed all of these anniversaries; no man can ignore all of them.
Aldo Leopold

In some mysterious way woods have never seemed to me to be static things. In physical terms, I move through them; yet in metaphysical ones, they seem to move through me.
John Fowles

The mind, in proportion as it is cut off from free communication with nature, with revelation, with God, with itself, loses its life, just as the body droops when debarred from the air and the cheering light from heaven.
William Ellery Channing

The moment a little boy is concerned with which is a jay and which is a sparrow, he can no longer see the birds or hear them sing.
Eric Berne

It is not so much for its beauty that the forest makes a claim upon men's hearts, as for that subtle something, that quality of air that emanation from old trees, that so wonderfully changes and renews a weary spirit.
Robert Louis Stevenson

There is a muscular energy in sunlight corresponding to the spiritual energy of wind.
Annie Dillard

Knowing trees, I understand the meaning of patience. Knowing grass, I can appreciate persistence.
Hal Borland

What makes a river so restful to people is that it doesn't have any doubt - it is sure to get where it is going, and it doesn't want to go anywhere else.
Hal Boyle

Life has loveliness to sell, all beautiful and splendid things, blue waves whitened on a cliff, soaring fire that sways and sings, and children's faces looking up, holding wonder like a cup.
Sara Teasdale

Deep in their roots, all flowers keep the light.
Theodore Roethke

That which is not good for the bee-hive cannot be good for the bees.
Marcus Aurelius

I think that I shall never see a poem lovely as a tree.
Joyce Kilmer

Nature knows no pause in progress and development, and attaches her curse on all inaction.
Johann Wolfgang von Goethe

We do not see nature with our eyes, but with our understandings and our hearts.
William Hazlitt

Each blade of grass has its spot on earth whence it draws its life, its strength; and so is man rooted to the land from which he draws his faith together with his life.
Joseph Conrad

Having family responsibilities and concerns just has to make you a more understanding person.
Sandra Day O'Connor

Bats drink on the wing, like swallows, by sipping the surface, as they play over pools and streams.
Gilbert White

Mother Nature may be forgiving this year, or next year, but eventually she's going to come around and whack you. You've got to be prepared.
Geraldo Rivera

I'm very gregarious, but I love being in the hills on my own.
Norman MacCaig

Nature is so powerful, so strong. Capturing its essence is not easy - your work becomes a dance with light and the weather. It takes you to a place within yourself.
Annie Leibovitz

To cherish what remains of the Earth and to foster its renewal is our only legitimate hope of survival.
Wendell Berry

The sun, the moon and the stars would have disappeared long ago... had they happened to be within the reach of predatory human hands.
Havelock Ellis

There is nothing in which the birds differ more from man than the way in which they can build and yet leave a landscape as it was before.
Robert Wilson Lynd

I perhaps owe having become a painter to flowers.
Claude Monet

Hope is the only bee that makes honey without flowers.
Robert Green Ingersoll

It was one of those perfect English autumnal days which occur more frequently in memory than in life.
P. D. James

I am not bound for any public place, but for ground of my own where I have planted vines and orchard trees, and in the heat of the day climbed up into the healing shadow of the woods.
Wendell Berry

I remember a hundred lovely lakes, and recall the fragrant breath of pine and fir and cedar and poplar trees. The trail has strung upon it, as upon a thread of silk, opalescent dawns and saffron sunsets.
Hamlin Garland

I never saw a discontented tree. They grip the ground as though they liked it, and though fast rooted they travel about as far as we do.
John Muir

The groves were God's first temples.
William C. Bryant

Except during the nine months before he draws his first breath, no man manages his affairs as well as a tree does.
George Bernard Shaw

There's always a period of curious fear between the first sweet-smelling breeze and the time when the rain comes cracking down.
Don DeLillo

I decided that if I could paint that flower in a huge scale, you could not ignore its beauty.
Georgia O'Keeffe

The counterfeit and counterpart of Nature is reproduced in art.
Henry Wadsworth Longfellow

Unless a tree has borne blossoms in spring, you will vainly look for fruit on it in autumn.
Walter Scott

Sorrows gather around great souls as storms do around mountains; but, like them, they break the storm and purify the air of the plain beneath them.
Jean Paul

When I see a bird that walks like a duck and swims like a duck and quacks like a duck, I call that bird a duck.
James Whitcomb Riley

The Universe is one great kindergarten for man. Everything that exists has brought with it its own peculiar lesson.
Orison Swett Marden

Whenever the pressure of our complex city life thins my blood and numbs my brain, I seek relief in the trail; and when I hear the coyote wailing to the yellow dawn, my cares fall from me - I am happy.
Hamlin Garland

My recollection of a hundred lovely lakes has given me blessed release from care and worry and the troubled thinking of our modern day. It has been a return to the primitive and the peaceful.
Hamlin Garland

The ground we walk on, the plants and creatures, the clouds above constantly dissolving into new formations - each gift of nature possessing its own radiant energy, bound together by cosmic harmony.
Ruth Bernhard

The snow itself is lonely or, if you prefer, self-sufficient. There is no other time when the whole world seems composed of one thing and one thing only.
Joseph Wood Krutch

Love thou the rose, yet leave it on its stem.
Edward G. Bulwer-Lytton

Nature is wont to hide herself.
Heraclitus

Those little nimble musicians of the air, that warble forth their curious ditties, with which nature hath furnished them to the shame of art.
Izaak Walton

Maybe nature is fundamentally ugly, chaotic and complicated. But if it's like that, then I want out.
Steven Weinberg

Poor, dear, silly Spring, preparing her annual surprise!
Wallace Stevens

People in cities may forget the soil for as long as a hundred years, but Mother Nature's memory is long and she will not let them forget indefinitely.
Henry Cantwell Wallace

Occasionally I have come across a last patch of snow on top of a mountain in late May or June. There's something very powerful about finding snow in summer.
Andy Goldsworthy

Having contemplated this admirable grove, I proceeded towards the shrubberies on the banks of the river, and though it was now late in December, the aromatic groves appeared in full bloom.
William Bartram

My progress was rendered delightful by the sylvan elegance of the groves, chearful meadows, and high distant forests, which in grand order presented themselves to view.
William Bartram

The lake and the mountains have become my landscape, my real world.
Georges Simenon

There is no forgiveness in nature.
Ugo Betti

Mere goodness can achieve little against the power of nature.
Georg Wilhelm Friedrich Hegel

PARENTING

To enjoy good health, to bring true happiness to one's family, to bring peace to all, one must first discipline and control one's own mind. If a man can control his mind he can find the way to Enlightenment, and all wisdom and virtue will naturally come to him.
Buddha

A baby is born with a need to be loved - and never outgrows it.
Frank Howard Clark

A mother who is really a mother is never free.
Honore de Balzac

Even as kids reach adolescence, they need more than ever for us to watch over them. Adolescence is not about letting go. It's about hanging on during a very bumpy ride.
Ron Taffel

Telling a teenager the facts of life is like giving a fish a bath.
Arnold H. Glasow

Each day of our lives we make deposits in the memory banks of our children.
Charles R. Swindoll

Children are educated by what the grown-up is and not by his talk.
Carl Jung

The most important thing a father can do for his children is to love their mother.
Theodore Hesburgh

Every cliche about kids is true; they grow up so quickly, you blink and they're gone, and you have to spend the time with them now. But that's a joy.
Liam Neeson

Don't try to make children grow up to be like you, or they may do it.
Russell Baker

Never lend your car to anyone to whom you have given birth.
Erma Bombeck

How pleasant it is for a father to sit at his child's board. It is like an aged man reclining under the shadow of an oak which he has planted.
Voltaire

Let parents bequeath to their children not riches, but the spirit of reverence.
Plato

Few things are more satisfying than seeing your children have teenagers of their own.
Doug Larson

Mothers all want their sons to grow up to be president, but they don't want them to become politicians in the process.
John F. Kennedy

We never know the love of a parent till we become parents ourselves.
Henry Ward Beecher

To me luxury is to be at home with my daughter, and the occasional massage doesn't hurt.
Olivia Newton-John

Most American children suffer too much mother and too little father.
Gloria Steinem

Mothers - especially single mothers - are heroic in their efforts to raise our nation's children, but men must also take responsibility for their children and recognize the impact they have on their families' well-being.
Evan Bayh

Most children threaten at times to run away from home. This is the only thing that keeps some parents going.
Phyllis Diller

Having a baby changes the way you view your in-laws. I love it when they come to visit now. They can hold the baby and I can go out.
Matthew Broderick

There's really no point in having children if you're not going to be home enough to father them.
Anthony Edwards

Childhood obesity is best tackled at home through improved parental involvement, increased physical exercise, better diet and restraint from eating.
Bob Filner

Education, like neurosis, begins at home.
Milton Sapirstein

The interesting thing about being a mother is that everyone wants pets, but no one but me cleans the kitty litter.
Meryl Streep

What good mothers and fathers instinctively feel like doing for their babies is usually best after all.
Benjamin Spock

We are apt to forget that children watch examples better than they listen to preaching.
Roy L. Smith

Girls are the future mothers of our society, and it is important that we focus on their well-being.
Miriam Makeba

Children that are raised in a home with a married mother and father consistently do better in every measure of well-being than their peers who come from divorced or step-parent, single-parent, cohabiting homes.
Todd Tiahrt

I take my children everywhere, but they always find their way back home.
Robert Orben

I want to have children, but my friends scare me. One of my friends told me she was in labor for 36 hours. I don't even want to do anything that feels good for 36 hours.
Rita Rudner

I had no idea that mothering my own child would be so healing to my own sadness from my childhood.
Susie Bright

The well-being and welfare of children should always be our focus.
Todd Tiahrt

I figure that if the children are alive when I get home, I've done my job.
Roseanne Barr

My mother protected me from the world and my father threatened me with it.
Quentin Crisp

The family teaches us about the importance of knowledge, education, hard work and effort. It teaches us about enjoying ourselves, having fun, keeping fit and healthy.
Kamisese Mara

It's a huge change for your body. You don't even want to look in the mirror after you've had a baby, because your stomach is just hanging there like a Shar-Pei.
Cindy Crawford

Family life was wonderful. The streets were bleak. The playgrounds were bleak. But home was always warm. My mother and father had a great relationship. I always felt 'safe' there.
Robert Cormier

I've said it before, but it's absolutely true: My mother gave me my drive, but my father gave me my dreams. Thanks to him, I could see a future.
Liza Minelli

It's hard enough to work and raise a family when your kids are all healthy and relatively normal, but when you add on some kind of disability or disease, it can just be such a burden.
Patricia Heaton

If you're asking your kids to exercise, then you better do it, too. Practice what you preach.
Bruce Jenner

Parents should not smoke in order to discourage their kids from smoking. A child is more likely to smoke when they have been raised in the environment of a smoker.
Christy Turlington

Love is staying up all night with a sick child - or a healthy adult.
David Frost

The child supplies the power but the parents have to do the steering.
Benjamin Spock

I get whatever placidity I have from my father. But my mother taught me how to take it on the chin.
Norma Shearer

Fathers and mothers have lost the idea that the highest aspiration they might have for their children is for them to be wise... specialized competence and success are all that they can imagine.
Allan Bloom

It's a great mistake, I think, to put children off with falsehoods and nonsense, when their growing powers of observation and discrimination excite in them a desire to know about things.
Anne Sullivan

Parenthood and family come first for me, and when I'm not working I'm cool with the Teletubbies.
Clive Owen

I'd just as soon stay home and raise babies.
June Allyson

I don't think children's inner feelings have changed. They still want a mother and father in the very same house; they want places to play.
Beverly Cleary

You have to support your children to have a healthy relationship.
Connie Sellecca

I feel very blessed to have two wonderful, healthy children who keep me completely grounded, sane and throw up on my shoes just before I go to an awards show just so I know to keep it real.
Reese Witherspoon

It is a sad commentary of our times when our young must seek advice and counsel from "Dear Abby" instead of going to Mom and Dad.
Abigail Van Buren

Mama and Daddy King represent the best in manhood and womanhood, the best in a marriage, the kind of people we are trying to become.
Coretta Scott King

What feeling is so nice as a child's hand in yours? So small, so soft and warm, like a kitten huddling in the shelter of your clasp.
Marjorie Holmes

Parentage is a very important profession, but no test of fitness for it is ever imposed in the interest of the children.
George Bernard Shaw

We expect teachers to handle teenage pregnancy, substance abuse, and the failings of the family. Then we expect them to educate our children.
John Sculley

No fathers or mothers think their own children ugly.
Miguel de Cervantes

We criticize mothers for closeness. We criticize fathers for distance. How many of us have expected less from our fathers and appreciated what they gave us more? How many of us always let them off the hook?
Ellen Goodman

My mom's a Catholic, and my dad's a Jew, and they didn't want anything to do with anything.
Isabelle Huppert

The Internet is just bringing all kinds of information into the home. There's just a lot of distraction, a lot of competition for the parent's voice to resonate in the children's ears.
Phil McGraw

My father was a farmer and my mother was a farmer, but, my childhood was very good. I am very grateful for my childhood, because it was full of gladness and good humanity.
Roberto Benigni

My mother was the influence in my life. She was strong; she had great faith in the ultimate triumph of justice and hard work. She believed passionately in education.
John H. Johnson

We all have an interest in making sure teens grow up healthy and drug-free.
John Walters

My father wasn't really involved and my mom is the light in my life.
Marion Jones

There are 80 million moms in the United States. Forty million stay at home with their children.
Andrew Shue

Believe me, my children have more stamina than a power station.
Robbie Coltrane

That's my ideal day, time with my boys.
Kenny G

I regret not having had more time with my kids when they were growing up.
Tina Turner

There are some great questions to ask your doctor. If he says 'no,' then you find yourself a different doctor. There really has to be a change in how we medically look at women at this time. I mean, this is not just baby gloom.
Marie Osmond

Home life's great, man. The kids are great, happy and healthy. I've reached this sort of wonderful precipice.
Ryan Phillippe

I wasn't very good about juggling family and my career. I was interested in who was coming to the children's birthday party, what my son was writing. I was thinking about Legos.
Jill Clayburgh

I think I'm going to have to live vicariously through my daughter's rebellion because I certainly never did go through adolescence.
Brooke Shields

Studies show that children best flourish when one mom and one dad are there to raise them.
John Boehner

Mom and Dad would stay in bed on Sunday morning, but the kids would have to go to church.
Lynn Johnston

Family involvement is a valuable thing and playing together actively can be the '90s version of it. Instead of just watching, you can do it together... something we don't spend enough time on. We can motivate and excite each other about fitness.
Alan Thicke

Success for me its to raise happy, healthy human beings.
Kelly LeBrock

No one knows his true character until he has run out of gas, purchased something on the installment plan and raised an adolescent.
Marcelene Cox

PATRIOTISM

My fellow Americans, ask not what your country can do for you, ask what you can do for your country.
John F. Kennedy

Nationalism is an infantile disease. It is the measles of mankind.
Albert Einstein

Patriotism is supporting your country all the time, and your government when it deserves it.
Mark Twain

Heroism on command, senseless violence, and all the loathsome nonsense that goes by the name of patriotism - how passionately I hate them!
Albert Einstein

Guard against the impostures of pretended patriotism.
George Washington

Patriotism is the virtue of the vicious.
Oscar Wilde

I love America more than any other country in this world, and, exactly for this reason, I insist on the right to criticize her perpetually.
James A. Baldwin

A man's country is not a certain area of land, of mountains, rivers, and woods, but it is a principle and patriotism is loyalty to that principle.
George William Curtis

Dissent is the highest form of patriotism.
Howard Zinn

Patriot: the person who can holler the loudest without knowing what he is hollering about.
Mark Twain

It is lamentable, that to be a good patriot one must become the enemy of the rest of mankind.
Voltaire

137 years later, Memorial Day remains one of America's most cherished patriotic observances. The spirit of this day has not changed - it remains a day to honor those who died defending our freedom and democracy.
Doc Hastings

A real patriot is the fellow who gets a parking ticket and rejoices that the system works.
Bill Vaughan

Patriotism is not short, frenzied outbursts of emotion, but the tranquil and steady dedication of a lifetime.
Adlai E. Stevenson

Can anything be stupider than that a man has the right to kill me because he lives on the other side of a river and his ruler has a quarrel with mine, though I have not quarrelled with him?
Blaise Pascal

I am not an Athenian or a Greek, but a citizen of the world.
Diogenes

True patriotism hates injustice in its own land more than anywhere else.
Clarence Darrow

I only regret that I have but one life to lose for my country.
Nathan Hale

I have no country to fight for; my country is the earth, and I am a citizen of the world.
Eugene V. Debs

A nation is a society united by a delusion about its ancestry and by common hatred of its neighbours.
William Ralph Inge

Patriotism is when love of your own people comes first; nationalism, when hate for people other than your own comes first.
Charles de Gaulle

It was patriotism, not communism, that inspired me.
Ho Chi Minh

Patriotism consists not in waving the flag, but in striving that our country shall be righteous as well as strong.
James Bryce

On what rests the hope of the republic? One country, one language, one flag!
Alexander Henry

Patriotism is easy to understand in America. It means looking out for yourself by looking out for your country.
Calvin Coolidge

No matter that patriotism is too often the refuge of scoundrels. Dissent, rebellion, and all-around hell-raising remain the true duty of patriots.
Barbara Ehrenreich

The greater the state, the more wrong and cruel its patriotism, and the greater is the sum of suffering upon which its power is founded.
Leo Tolstoy

I realize that patriotism is not enough. I must have no hatred or bitterness towards anyone.
Edith Cavell

There is nothing wrong with America that cannot be cured with what is right in America.
William J. Clinton

Patriotism is a kind of religion; it is the egg from which wars are hatched.
Guy de Maupassant

It is the patriotic duty of every man to lie for his country.
Alfred Adler

Patriotism is your conviction that this country is superior to all others because you were born in it.
George Bernard Shaw

Patriotism is the willingness to kill and be killed for trivial reasons.
Bertrand Russell

You'll never have a quiet world till you knock the patriotism out of the human race.
George Bernard Shaw

It is not easy to see how the more extreme forms of nationalism can long survive when men have seen the Earth in its true perspective as a single small globe against the stars.
Arthur C. Clarke

Nationalism is a silly cock crowing on his own dunghill.
Richard Aldington

I have long believed that sacrifice is the pinnacle of patriotism.
Bob Riley

I distinguish, between nationalism and patriotism.
Michael Ignatieff

The very idea of true patriotism is lost, and the term has been prostituted to the very worst of purposes. A patriot, sir! Why, patriots spring up like mushrooms!
Robert Walpole

Gentlemen have talked a great deal of patriotism. A venerable word, when duly practiced.
Robert Walpole

I'm an advocate of the great Dr. Johnson, the English man of letters who said that patriotism was the last refuge of the scoundrel.
George Galloway

The highest patriotism is not a blind acceptance of official policy, but a love of one's country deep enough to call her to a higher plain.
George McGovern

Patriotism is often an arbitrary veneration of real estate above principles.
George Jean Nathan

The love of one's country is a splendid thing. But why should love stop at the border?
Pablo Casals

To me, it seems a dreadful indignity to have a soul controlled by geography.
George Santayana

The proper means of increasing the love we bear our native country is to reside some time in a foreign one.
William Shenstone

The most tragic paradox of our time is to be found in the failure of nation-states to recognize the imperatives of internationalism.
Earl Warren

Each nation feels superior to other nations. That breeds patriotism - and wars.
Dale Carnegie

We'll try to cooperate fully with the IRS, because, as citizens, we feel a strong patriotic duty not to go to jail.
Dave Barry

They are patriotic in time of war because it is to their interest to be so, but in time of peace they follow power and the dollar wherever they may lead.
Henry A. Wallace

The patriot blood of my father was warm in my veins.
Clara Barton

Patriotism is an instant reaction that fades away when the war starts.
Mick Jagger

The average American is nothing if not patriotic.
Herbert Croly

The tree of liberty needs to be watered from time to time with the blood of patriots and tyrants.
Lyn Nofziger

We do not consider patriotism desirable if it contradicts civilized behavior.
Friedrich Durrenmatt

PEACE

If we have no peace, it is because we have forgotten that we belong to each other.
Mother Teresa

An eye for an eye only ends up making the whole world blind.
Mahatma Gandhi

Those who make peaceful revolution impossible will make violent revolution inevitable.
John F. Kennedy

Imagine all the people living life in peace. You may say I'm a dreamer, but I'm not the only one. I hope someday you'll join us, and the world will be as one.
John Lennon

Peace begins with a smile.
Mother Teresa

A peace is of the nature of a conquest; for then both parties nobly are subdued, and neither party loser.
William Shakespeare

I believe in the religion of Islam. I believe in Allah and peace.
Muhammad Ali

A people free to choose will always choose peace.
Ronald Reagan

If you want to make peace with your enemy, you have to work with your enemy. Then he becomes your partner.
Nelson Mandela

Every goal, every action, every thought, every feeling one experiences, whether it be consciously or unconsciously known, is an attempt to increase one's level of peace of mind.
Sydney Madwed

I think that people want peace so much that one of these days government had better get out of their way and let them have it.
Dwight D. Eisenhower

It isn't enough to talk about peace. One must believe in it. And it isn't enough to believe in it. One must work at it.
Eleanor Roosevelt

He that would live in peace and at ease must not speak all he knows or all he sees.
Benjamin Franklin

I dream of an Africa which is in peace with itself.
Nelson Mandela

Let there be work, bread, water and salt for all.
Nelson Mandela

The most valuable possession you can own is an open heart. The most powerful weapon you can be is an instrument of peace.
Carlos Santana

I can promise you that women working together - linked, informed and educated - can bring peace and prosperity to this forsaken planet.
Isabel Allende

Nobody can bring you peace but yourself.
Ralph Waldo Emerson

Those who are at war with others are not at peace with themselves.
William Hazlitt

Peace cannot be achieved through violence, it can only be attained through understanding.
Ralph Waldo Emerson

I'm concentrating on staying healthy, having peace, being happy, remembering what is important, taking in nature and animals, spending time reading, trying to understand the universe, where science and the spiritual meet.
Joan Jett

Even peace may be purchased at too high a price.
Benjamin Franklin

One does not need buildings, money, power, or status to practice the Art of Peace. Heaven is right where you are standing, and that is the place to train.
Morihei Ueshiba

Peace is not an absence of war, it is a virtue, a state of mind, a disposition for benevolence, confidence, justice.
Baruch Spinoza

Complete peace equally reigns between two mental waves.
Swami Sivananda

Peace and friendship with all mankind is our wisest policy, and I wish we may be permitted to pursue it.
Thomas Jefferson

For behind all imperialism is ultimately the imperialistic individual, just as behind all peace is ultimately the peaceful individual.
Irving Babbitt

You cannot find peace by avoiding life.
Virginia Woolf

If they want peace, nations should avoid the pin-pricks that precede cannon shots.
Napoleon Bonaparte

It is an unfortunate fact that we can secure peace only by preparing for war.
John F. Kennedy

I think it's naive to pray for world peace if we're not going to change the form in which we live.
Godfrey Reggio

I don't know whether war is an interlude during peace, or peace an interlude during war.
Georges Clemenceau

It is madness for sheep to talk peace with a wolf.
Thomas Fuller

The pursuit of peace and progress cannot end in a few years in either victory or defeat. The pursuit of peace and progress, with its trials and its errors, its successes and its setbacks, can never be relaxed and never abandoned.
Dag Hammarskjold

The real and lasting victories are those of peace, and not of war.
Ralph Waldo Emerson

The simplification of life is one of the steps to inner peace. A persistent simplification will create an inner and outer well-being that places harmony in one's life.
Peace Pilgrim

Peace is a journey of a thousand miles and it must be taken one step at a time.
Lyndon B. Johnson

I happen to dig being able to use whatever mystique I have to further the idea of peace.
Garrett Morris

Peace is its own reward.
Mahatma Gandhi

It is easier to lead men to combat, stirring up their passion, than to restrain them and direct them toward the patient labors of peace.
Andre Gide

Peace and justice are two sides of the same coin.
Dwight D. Eisenhower

Peace hath higher tests of manhood, than battle ever knew.
John Greenleaf Whittier

The forces that are driving mankind toward unity and peace are deep-seated and powerful. They are material and natural, as well as moral and intellectual.
Arthur Henderson

Of one thing I am certain, the body is not the measure of healing, peace is the measure.
Phyllis McGinley

We make war that we may live in peace.
Aristotle

War will never cease until babies begin to come into the world with larger cerebrums and smaller adrenal glands.
H. L. Mencken

The quest for peace begins in the home, in the school and in the workplace.
Silvia Cartwright

To attain inner peace you must actually give your life, not just your possessions. When you at last give your life - bringing into alignment your beliefs and the way you live then, and only then, can you begin to find inner peace.
Peace Pilgrim

The only important thing I have to say is that my father never fought against his country.
Zinedine Zidane

Yes, we love peace, but we are not willing to take wounds for it, as we are for war.
John Andrew Holmes

Peace is the first thing the angels sang.
John Keble

You don't have to have fought in a war to love peace.
Geraldine Ferraro

Peace is rarely denied to the peaceful.
Friedrich Schiller

Peace is not only better than war, but infinitely more arduous.
George Bernard Shaw

The Dove, on silver pinions, winged her peaceful way.
James Montgomery

People always make war when they say they love peace.
David Herbert Lawrence

This enemy of peace in the world today is unlike any we have seen in the past, and our military is learning from, and building on, previous successes while carrying peace and freedom into the future.
Mark Kennedy

The business of peace requires more than showing up with paint brushes, foodstuffs and an oil pipeline or two.
Tony Snow

Peace is when time doesn't matter as it passes by.
Maria Schell

One cannot subdue a man by holding back his hands. Lasting peace comes not from force.
David Borenstein

Peace is liberty in tranquillity.
Marcus Tullius Cicero

Power to the peaceful!
Michael Franti

It has become impossible to give up the enterprise of disarmament without abandoning the whole great adventure of building up a collective peace system.
Arthur Henderson

We want to take good tidings home to our people, that they may sleep in peace.
Black Kettle

Nonviolence is the first article of my faith. It is also the last article of my creed.
Mahatma Gandhi

PET

A dog is the only thing on earth that loves you more than you love yourself.
Josh Billings

I am fond of pigs. Dogs look up to us. Cats look down on us. Pigs treat us as equals.
Winston Churchill

I wish I could write as mysterious as a cat.
Edgar Allan Poe

The better I get to know men, the more I find myself loving dogs.
Charles de Gaulle

Animals are such agreeable friends - they ask no questions; they pass no criticisms.
George Eliot

Dogs are not our whole life, but they make our lives whole.
Roger Caras

No matter how much cats fight, there always seem to be plenty of kittens.
Abraham Lincoln

The average dog is a nicer person than the average person.
Andy Rooney

Dogs are my favorite people.
Richard Dean Anderson

I wonder if other dogs think poodles are members of a weird religious cult.
Rita Rudner

Dachshunds are ideal dogs for small children, as they are already stretched and pulled to such a length that the child cannot do much harm one way or the other.
Robert Benchley

I looked up my family tree and found three dogs using it.
Rodney Dangerfield

Time spent with cats is never wasted.
Sigmund Freud

I kind of imagine myself at eighty, a cat lady.
Juliette Lewis

Women and cats will do as they please, and men and dogs should relax and get used to the idea.
Robert A. Heinlein

Do not make the mistake of treating your dogs like humans or they will treat you like dogs.
Martha Scott

There are two means of refuge from the miseries of life: music and cats.
Albert Schweitzer

If a dog will not come to you after having looked you in the face, you should go home and examine your conscience.
Woodrow Wilson

I have felt cats rubbing their faces against mine and touching my cheek with claws carefully sheathed. These things, to me, are expressions of love.
James Herriot

Cats have it all - admiration, an endless sleep, and company only when they want it.
Rod McKuen

A kitten is in the animal world what a rosebud is in the garden.
Robert Southey

Cats are intended to teach us that not everything in nature has a purpose.
Garrison Keillor

As anyone who has ever been around a cat for any length of time well knows, cats have enormous patience with the limitations of the human kind.
Cleveland Amory

I believe cats to be spirits come to earth. A cat, I am sure, could walk on a cloud without coming through.
Jules Verne

A dog teaches a boy fidelity, perseverance, and to turn around three times before lying down.
Robert Benchley

The trouble with a kitten is that eventually it becomes a cat.
Ogden Nash

Don't accept your dog's admiration as conclusive evidence that you are wonderful.
Ann Landers

I love cats because I enjoy my home; and little by little, they become its visible soul.
Jean Cocteau

Way down deep, we're all motivated by the same urges. Cats have the courage to live by them.
Jim Davis

What counts is not necessarily the size of the dog in the fight - it's the size of the fight in the dog.
Dwight D. Eisenhower

Dogs laugh, but they laugh with their tails.
Max Eastman

I poured spot remover on my dog. Now he's gone.
Steven Wright

Cat: a pygmy lion who loves mice, hates dogs, and patronizes human beings.
Oliver Herford

Cats are rather delicate creatures and they are subject to a good many different ailments, but I have never heard of one who suffered from insomnia.
Joseph Wood Krutch

Never wear anything that panics the cat.
P. J. O'Rourke

The dog is the god of frolic.
Henry Ward Beecher

Many who have spent a lifetime in it can tell us less of love than the child that lost a dog yesterday.
Thornton Wilder

To his dog, every man is Napoleon; hence the constant popularity of dogs.
Aldous Huxley

What a dog I got, his favorite bone is in my arm.
Rodney Dangerfield

People who keep dogs are cowards who haven't got the guts to bite people themselves.
August Strindberg

If a dog jumps into your lap, it is because he is fond of you; but if a cat does the same thing, it is because your lap is warmer.
Alfred North Whitehead

There is no psychiatrist in the world like a puppy licking your face.
Bern Williams

Scratch a dog and you'll find a permanent job.
Franklin P. Jones

I've got a new invention. It's a revolving bowl for tired goldfish.
Lefty Gomez

We've begun to long for the pitter-patter of little feet - so we bought a dog. Well, it's cheaper, and you get more feet.
Rita Rudner

There are all sorts of cute puppy dogs, but it doesn't stop people from going out and buying Dobermans.
Angus Young

A hungry dog hunts best. A hungrier dog hunts even better.
Norman Ralph Augustine

There's a saying. If you want someone to love you forever, buy a dog, feed it and keep it around.
Dick Dale

I live alone, with cats, books, pictures, fresh vegetables to cook, the garden, the hens to feed.
Jeanette Winterson

Just watching my cats can make me happy.
Paula Cole

I was a dog in a past life. Really. I'll be walking down the street and dogs will do a sort of double take. Like, Hey, I know him.
William H. Macy

Cats don't like change without their consent.
Roger Caras

Like all pure creatures, cats are practical.
William S. Burroughs

A kitten is chiefly remarkable for rushing about like mad at nothing whatever, and generally stopping before it gets there.
Agnes Repplier

Kittens are wide-eyed, soft and sweet. With needles in their jaws and feet.
Pam Brown

A happy arrangement: many people prefer cats to other people, and many cats prefer people to other cats.
Mason Cooley

Even cats grow lonely and anxious.
Mason Cooley

I had been told that the training procedure with cats was difficult. It's not. Mine had me trained in two days.
Bill Dana

Kittens can happen to anyone.
Paul Gallico

No one can feel as helpless as the owner of a sick goldfish.
Kin Hubbard

Never stand between a dog and the hydrant.
John Peers

Money can buy you a fine dog, but only love can make him wag his tail.
Kinky Friedman

If you are a dog and your owner suggests that you wear a sweater suggest that he wear a tail.
Fran Lebowitz

The trees in Siberia are miles apart, that is why the dogs are so fast.
Bob Hope

Cats seem to go on the principle that it never does any harm to ask for what you want.
Joseph Wood Krutch

It was so cold today that I saw a dog chasing a cat, and the dog was walking.
Mickey Rivers

We have three cats. It's like having children, but there is no tuition involved.
Ron Reagan

Perhaps it is because cats do not live by human patterns, do not fit themselves into prescribed behavior, that they are so united to creative people.
Andre Norton

Cats are connoisseurs of comfort.
James Herriot

Cats know how to obtain food without labor, shelter without confinement, and love without penalties.
W. L. George

I'm looking more like my dogs every day - it must be the shaggy fringe and the ears.
Christine McVie

Many cats are the death of the mouse.
Kaspar Hauser

I used to love dogs until I discovered cats.
Nafisa Joseph

Only very brave mouse makes nest in cat's ear.
Earl Derr Biggers

I've always been mad about cats.
Vivien Leigh

I love cats.
Dick Van Patten

There's just me and my wife and a dog and we feed him Healthy Choice also.
Mike Ditka

The world spends $40 billion a year on pet food.
Nicholas D. Kristof

It is impossible for a lover of cats to banish these alert, gentle, and discriminating friends, who give us just enough of their regard and complaisance to make us hunger for more.
Agnes Repplier

Cats are inquisitive, but hate to admit it.
Mason Cooley

I have studied many philosophers and many cats. The wisdom of cats is infinitely superior.
Hippolyte Taine

If cats were double the size they are now, they'd probably be illegal.
Doug Coupland

POETRY

A poem begins as a lump in the throat, a sense of wrong, a homesickness, a lovesickness.
Robert Frost

All bad poetry springs from genuine feeling.
Oscar Wilde

Poetry is what gets lost in translation.
Robert Frost

Genuine poetry can communicate before it is understood.
T. S. Eliot

A poet can survive everything but a misprint.
Oscar Wilde

A poet is, before anything else, a person who is passionately in love with language.
W. H. Auden

Poetry is when an emotion has found its thought and the thought has found words.
Robert Frost

Poetry is the rhythmical creation of beauty in words.
Edgar Allan Poe

I was reading the dictionary. I thought it was a poem about everything.
Steven Wright

Poetry is not a turning loose of emotion, but an escape from emotion; it is not the expression of personality, but an escape from personality. But, of course, only those who have personality and emotions know what it means to want to escape from these things.
T. S. Eliot

Poetry is an echo, asking a shadow to dance.
Carl Sandburg

The poets have been mysteriously silent on the subject of cheese.
Gilbert K. Chesterton

A poem is never finished, only abandoned.
Paul Valery

A poet's work is to name the unnameable, to point at frauds, to take sides, start arguments, shape the world, and stop it going to sleep.
Salman Rushdie

Poetry is just the evidence of life. If your life is burning well, poetry is just the ash.
Leonard Cohen

Poetry is a deal of joy and pain and wonder, with a dash of the dictionary.
Khalil Gibran

There's no money in poetry, but then there's no poetry in money, either.
Robert Graves

If you cannot be a poet, be the poem.
David Carradine

He who draws noble delights from sentiments of poetry is a true poet, though he has never written a line in all his life.
George Sand

Always be a poet, even in prose.
Charles Baudelaire

Poets are the unacknowledged legislators of the world.
Percy Bysshe Shelley

Painting is silent poetry, and poetry is painting that speaks.
Plutarch

No poem is easily grasped; so why should any reader expect fast results?
John Barton

A poem is true if it hangs together. Information points to something else. A poem points to nothing but itself.
E. M. Forster

A poet's autobiography is his poetry. Anything else is just a footnote.
Yevgeny Yevtushenko

Any healthy man can go without food for two days - but not without poetry.
Charles Baudelaire

Breathe-in experience, breathe-out poetry.
Muriel Rukeyser

God is the perfect poet.
Robert Browning

Poetry is nearer to vital truth than history.
Plato

Poetry is a mirror which makes beautiful that which is distorted.
Percy Bysshe Shelley

Poetry heals the wounds inflicted by reason.
Novalis

If Galileo had said in verse that the world moved, the inquisition might have let him alone.
Thomas Hardy

A poet looks at the world the way a man looks at a woman.
Wallace Stevens

A poem can have an impact, but you can't expect an audience to understand all the nuances.
Douglas Dunn

There is poetry as soon as we realize that we possess nothing.
John Cage

Everything one invents is true, you may be perfectly sure of that. Poetry is as precise as geometry.
Gustave Flaubert

Even when poetry has a meaning, as it usually has, it may be inadvisable to draw it out... Perfect understanding will sometimes almost extinguish pleasure.
A. E. Housman

Poetry is thoughts that breathe, and words that burn.
Thomas Gray

Children and lunatics cut the Gordian knot which the poet spends his life patiently trying to untie.
Jean Cocteau

A true poet does not bother to be poetical. Nor does a nursery gardener scent his roses.
Jean Cocteau

Poetry is ordinary language raised to the Nth power. Poetry is boned with ideas, nerved and blooded with emotions, all held together by the delicate, tough skin of words.
Paul Engle

Each memorable verse of a true poet has two or three times the written content.
Alfred de Musset

No poems can please for long or live that are written by water drinkers.
Horace

One merit of poetry few persons will deny: it says more and in fewer words than prose.
Voltaire

The moment of change is the only poem.
Adrienne Rich

Every single soul is a poem.
Michael Franti

If you read quickly to get through a poem to what it means, you have missed the body of the poem.
M. H. Abrams

To read a poem is to hear it with our eyes; to hear it is to see it with our ears.
Octavio Paz

Poetry is the synthesis of hyacinths and biscuits.
Carl Sandburg

We all write poems; it is simply that poets are the ones who write in words.
John Fowles

Publishing a volume of verse is like dropping a rose petal down the Grand Canyon and waiting for the echo.
Don Marquis

Poetry is an orphan of silence. The words never quite equal the experience behind them.
Charles Simic

Poetry is the art of creating imaginary gardens with real toads.
Marianne Moore

Poets are soldiers that liberate words from the steadfast possession of definition.
Eli Khamarov

Poetry should... should strike the reader as a wording of his own highest thoughts, and appear almost a remembrance.
John Keats

"Therefore" is a word the poet must not know.
Andre Gide

The poem is the point at which our strength gave out.
Richard Rosen

The poet doesn't invent. He listens.
Jean Cocteau

Wanted: a needle swift enough to sew this poem into a blanket.
Charles Simic

Poetry is the revelation of a feeling that the poet believes to be interior and personal which the reader recognizes as his own.
Salvatore Quasimodo

You will find poetry nowhere unless you bring some of it with you.
Joseph Joubert

You don't have to suffer to be a poet; adolescence is enough suffering for anyone.
John Ciardi

Poetry is all that is worth remembering in life.
William Hazlitt

Poetry is the art of uniting pleasure with truth.
Samuel Johnson

The poet is a liar who always speaks the truth.
Jean Cocteau

Poetry is language at its most distilled and most powerful.
Rita Dove

Poetry is plucking at the heartstrings, and making music with them.
Dennis Gabor

How do poems grow? They grow out of your life.
Robert Penn Warren

I like poems that are little games.
Peter Davison

The poem is a little myth of man's capacity of making life meaningful. And in the end, the poem is not a thing we see-it is, rather, a light by which we may see-and what we see is life.
Robert Penn Warren

The poet may be used as a barometer, but let us not forget that he is also part of the weather.
Lionel Trilling

To have great poets, there must be great audiences.
Walt Whitman

Poetry is the opening and closing of a door, leaving those who look through to guess about what is seen during the moment.
Carl Sandburg

There'll always be working people in my poems because I grew up with them, and I am a poet of memory.
Philip Levine

Everyone thinks they're going to write one book of poems or one novel.
Marilyn Hacker

I still read Donne, particularly his love poems.
Carol Ann Duffy

However, if a poem can be reduced to a prose sentence, there can't be much to it.
James Schuyler

One will never again look at a birch tree, after the Robert Frost poem, in exactly the same way.
Paul Muldoon

A poem conveys not a message so much as the provenance of a message, an advent of sense.
Thomas Harrison

A poem might be defined as thinking about feelings - about human feelings and frailties.
Anne Stevenson

Each word bears its weight, so you have to read my poems quite slowly.
Anne Stevenson

Sometimes poetry is inspired by the conversation entered into by reading other poems.
John Barton

Usually a life turned into a poem is misrepresented.
Mark Strand

Pain is filtered in a poem so that it becomes finally, in the end, pleasure.
Mark Strand

I sometimes talk about the making of a poem within the poem.
Howard Nemerov

You don't help people in your poems. I've been trying to help people all my life - that's my trouble.
Charles Olson

You don't make a poem with ideas, but with words.
Stephane Mallarme

Poetry: the best words in the best order.
Samuel Taylor Coleridge

The novel is born of disillusionment; the poem, of despair.
Jose Bergamin

To see clearly is poetry, prophecy and religion all in one.
John Ruskin

POLITICS

One of the penalties for refusing to participate in politics is that you end up being governed by your inferiors.
Plato

The modern conservative is engaged in one of man's oldest exercises in moral philosophy; that is, the search for a superior moral justification for selfishness.
John Kenneth Galbraith

If you put the federal government in charge of the Sahara Desert, in 5 years there'd be a shortage of sand.
Milton Friedman

Let us not seek the Republican answer or the Democratic answer, but the right answer. Let us not seek to fix the blame for the past. Let us accept our own responsibility for the future.
John F. Kennedy

If voting changed anything, they'd make it illegal.
Emma Goldman

Suppose you were an idiot, and suppose you were a member of Congress; but I repeat myself.
Mark Twain

Those who stand for nothing fall for anything.
Alexander Hamilton

The Democrats are the party that says government will make you smarter, taller, richer, and remove the crabgrass on your lawn. The Republicans are the party that says government doesn't work and then they get elected and prove it.
P. J. O'Rourke

In this world of sin and sorrow there is always something to be thankful for; as for me, I rejoice that I am not a Republican.
H. L. Mencken

A conservative is a man with two perfectly good legs who, however, has never learned how to walk forward.
Franklin D. Roosevelt

A fool and his money are soon elected.
Will Rogers

The whole aim of practical politics is to keep the populace alarmed (and hence clamorous to be led to safety) by menacing it with an endless series of hobgoblins, all of them imaginary.
H. L. Mencken

If we don't believe in freedom of expression for people we despise, we don't believe in it at all.
Noam Chomsky

The darkest places in hell are reserved for those who maintain their neutrality in times of moral crisis.
Dante Alighieri

There ain't no answer. There ain't gonna be any answer. There never has been an answer. That's the answer.
Gertrude Stein

If you have ten thousand regulations you destroy all respect for the law.
Winston Churchill

Any American who is prepared to run for president should automatically, by definition, be disqualified from ever doing so.
Gore Vidal

Only government can take perfectly good paper, cover it with perfectly good ink and make the combination worthless.
Milton Friedman

It is enough that the people know there was an election. The people who cast the votes decide nothing. The people who count the votes decide everything.
Joseph Stalin

A free America... means just this: individual freedom for all, rich or poor, or else this system of government we call democracy is only an expedient to enslave man to the machine and make him like it.
Frank Lloyd Wright

Politics have no relation to morals.
Niccolo Machiavelli

Healthy citizens are the greatest asset any country can have.
Winston Churchill

Always vote for principle, though you may vote alone, and you may cherish the sweetest reflection that your vote is never lost.
John Quincy Adams

If the United States of America or Britain is having elections, they don't ask for observers from Africa or from Asia. But when we have elections, they want observers.
Nelson Mandela

If you have always believed that everyone should play by the same rules and be judged by the same standards, that would have gotten you labeled a radical 60 years ago, a liberal 30 years ago and a racist today.
Thomas Sowell

It is better to be violent, if there is violence in our hearts, than to put on the cloak of nonviolence to cover impotence.
Mahatma Gandhi

Life without liberty is like a body without spirit.
Khalil Gibran

A healthy democracy requires a decent society; it requires that we are honorable, generous, tolerant and respectful.
Charles W. Pickering

A diplomat is a person who can tell you to go to hell in such a way that you actually look forward to the trip.
Caskie Stinnett

Democracy is when the indigent, and not the men of property, are the rulers.
Aristotle

I am extraordinarily patient, provided I get my own way in the end.
Margaret Thatcher

A liberal is a man or a woman or a child who looks forward to a better day, a more tranquil night, and a bright, infinite future.
Leonard Bernstein

Conservatives are not necessarily stupid, but most stupid people are conservatives.
John Stuart Mill

Politics is war without bloodshed, while war is politics with bloodshed.
Mao Tse-Tung

A leader in the Democratic Party is a boss, in the Republican Party he is a leader.
Harry S. Truman

The good news is that, according to the Obama administration, the rich will pay for everything. The bad news is that, according to the Obama administration, you're rich.
P. J. O'Rourke

I don't make jokes. I just watch the government and report the facts.
Will Rogers

Apparently, a democracy is a place where numerous elections are held at great cost without issues and with interchangeable candidates.
Gore Vidal

A liberal is a man who is willing to spend somebody else's money.
Carter Glass

Politics is not a game. It is an earnest business.
Winston Churchill

Hell, I never vote for anybody, I always vote against.
W. C. Fields

Half of the American people have never read a newspaper. Half never voted for President. One hopes it is the same half.
Gore Vidal

If we desire respect for the law, we must first make the law respectable.
Louis D. Brandeis

I would remind you that extremism in the defense of liberty is no vice! And let me remind you also that moderation in the pursuit of justice is no virtue.
Barry Goldwater

My brother Bob doesn't want to be in government - he promised Dad he'd go straight.
John F. Kennedy

A conservative is a man who just sits and thinks, mostly sits.
Woodrow Wilson

Free speech is not to be regulated like diseased cattle and impure butter. The audience that hissed yesterday may applaud today, even for the same performance.
William O. Douglas

Power tends to corrupt and absolute power corrupts absolutely.
Lord Acton

Conservative, n: A statesman who is enamored of existing evils, as distinguished from the Liberal who wishes to replace them with others.
Ambrose Bierce

Politics has become so expensive that it takes a lot of money even to be defeated.
Will Rogers

America's present need is not heroics but healing; not nostrums but normalcy; not revolution but restoration.
Warren G. Harding

All the president is, is a glorified public relations man who spends his time flattering, kissing, and kicking people to get them to do what they are supposed to do anyway.
Harry S. Truman

An idea not coupled with action will never get any bigger than the brain cell it occupied.
Arnold H. Glasow

Democracy is being allowed to vote for the candidate you dislike least.
Robert Byrne

Ninety percent of the politicians give the other ten percent a bad reputation.
Henry A. Kissinger

In politics the middle way is none at all.
John Adams

I love power. But it is as an artist that I love it. I love it as a musician loves his violin, to draw out its sounds and chords and harmonies.
Napoleon Bonaparte

Republicans have nothing but bad ideas and Democrats have no ideas.
Lewis Black

Politics, it seems to me, for years, or all too long, has been concerned with right or left instead of right or wrong.
Richard Armour

Bad politicians are sent to Washington by good people who don't vote.
William E. Simon

The person who has nothing for which he is willing to fight, nothing which is more important than his own personal safety, is a miserable creature and has no chance of being free unless made and kept so by the exertions of better men than himself.
John Stuart Mill

Republicans are men of narrow vision, who are afraid of the future.
Jimmy Carter

A politician will do anything to keep his job - even become a patriot.
William Randolph

I have a fantasy where Ted Turner is elected President but refuses because he doesn't want to give up power.
Arthur C. Clarke

When bad men combine, the good must associate; else they will fall one by one, an unpitied sacrifice in a contemptible struggle.
Edmund Burke

Pollution is nothing but the resources we are not harvesting. We allow them to disperse because we've been ignorant of their value.
R. Buckminster Fuller

If nominated, I will not run; if elected, I will not serve.
William Tecumseh Sherman

Hell hath no fury like a bureaucrat scorned.
Milton Friedman

A conservative is one who admires radicals centuries after they're dead.
Leo Rosten

You may think the president is all-powerful, but he is not. He needs a lot of guidance from the Lord.
Barbara Bush

Every politician should have been born an orphan and remain a bachelor.
Lady Bird Johnson

He who knows how to flatter also knows how to slander.
Napoleon Bonaparte

Many politicians are in the habit of laying it down as a self-evident proposition that no people ought to be free till they are fit to use their freedom. The maxim is worthy of the fool in the old story who resolved not to go into the water till he had learned to swim.
Thomas B. Macaulay

Perseverance is the hard work you do after you get tired of doing the hard work you already did.
Newt Gingrich

There are many men of principle in both parties in America, but there is no party of principle.
Alexis de Tocqueville

Instead of giving a politician the keys to the city, it might be better to change the locks.
Doug Larson

Politics: A strife of interests masquerading as a contest of principles. The conduct of public affairs for private advantage.
Ambrose Bierce

Conservatives define themselves in terms of what they oppose.
George Will

Our whole constitutional heritage rebels at the thought of giving government the power to control men's minds.
Thurgood Marshall

A war for a great principle ennobles a nation.
Albert Pike

Inflation is as violent as a mugger, as frightening as an armed robber and as deadly as a hit man.
Ronald Reagan

Politicians also have no leisure, because they are always aiming at something beyond political life itself, power and glory, or happiness.
Aristotle

The largest party in America, by the way, is neither the Democrats nor the Republicans. It's the party of non-voters.
Robert Reich

Every man who repeats the dogma of Mill that one country is no fit to rule another country must admit that one class is not fit to rule another class.
B. R. Ambedkar

When buying and selling are controlled by legislation, the first things to be bought and sold are legislators.
P. J. O'Rourke

Whenever men take the law into their own hands, the loser is the law. And when the law loses, freedom languishes.
Robert Kennedy

The activist is not the man who says the river is dirty. The activist is the man who cleans up the river.
Ross Perot

We would all like to vote for the best man but he is never a candidate.
Kin Hubbard

Liberalism is trust of the people tempered by prudence. Conservatism is distrust of the people tempered by fear.
William E. Gladstone

Do you ever get the feeling that the only reason we have elections is to find out if the polls were right?
Robert Orben

Whenever a man has cast a longing eye on offices, a rottenness begins in his conduct.
Thomas Jefferson

It is not in the nature of politics that the best men should be elected. The best men do not want to govern their fellowmen.
George MacDonald

For every talent that poverty has stimulated it has blighted a hundred.
John W. Gardner

You have not converted a man because you have silenced him.
John Morley

The beef industry has contributed to more American deaths than all the wars of this century, all natural disasters, and all automobile accidents combined.
Neal Barnard

One of the reasons people hate politics is that truth is rarely a politician's objective. Election and power are.
Cal Thomas

I think it's a terrible shame that politics has become show business.
Sydney Pollack

You cannot spend your way out of recession or borrow your way out of debt.
Daniel Hannan

Freedom of the press is guaranteed only to those who own one.
A. J. Liebling

The revolution is a dictatorship of the exploited against the exploiters.
Fidel Castro

I've been to war, and it's not easy to kill. It's bloody and messy and totally horrifying, and the consequences are serious.
Oliver Stone

When I was a boy I was told that anybody could become President; I'm beginning to believe it.
Clarence Darrow

When one may pay out over two million dollars to presidential and Congressional campaigns, the U.S. government is virtually up for sale.
John W. Gardner

The thing I enjoyed most were visits from children. They did not want public office.
Herbert Hoover

The secret of getting things done is to act!
Dante Alighieri

If you are going to sin, sin against God, not the bureaucracy. God will forgive you but the bureaucracy won't.
Hyman Rickover

The world will never have lasting peace so long as men reserve for war the finest human qualities. Peace, no less than war, requires idealism and self-sacrifice and a righteous and dynamic faith.
John Foster Dulles

'Tis the business of little minds to shrink; but he whose heart is firm, and whose conscience approves his conduct, will pursue his principles unto death.
Thomas Paine

You want a friend in Washington? Get a dog.
Harry S. Truman

The world is governed by opinion.
William Ellery Channing

The successful revolutionary is a statesman, the unsuccessful one a criminal.
Erich Fromm

Principles have no real force except when one is well-fed.
Mark Twain

Confronted with the choice, the American people would choose the policeman's truncheon over the anarchist's bomb.
Spiro T. Agnew

In most places in the country, voting is looked upon as a right and a duty, but in Chicago it's a sport.
Dick Gregory

In order to become the master, the politician poses as the servant.
Charles de Gaulle

Liberalism is, I think, resurgent. One reason is that more and more people are so painfully aware of the alternative.
John Kenneth Galbraith

The idea that you can merchandise candidates for high office like breakfast cereal - that you can gather votes like box tops - is, I think, the ultimate indignity to the democratic process.
Adlai E. Stevenson

If a politician murders his mother, the first response of the press or of his opponents will likely be not that it was a terrible thing to do, but rather that in a statement made six years before he had gone on record as being opposed to matricide.
Meg Greenfield

Turn on to politics, or politics will turn on you.
Ralph Nader

The flood of money that gushes into politics today is a pollution of democracy.
Theodore White

As you make your bed, so you must lie in it.
Daniel J. Boorstin

We didn't actually overspend our budget. The health Commission allocation simply fell short of our expenditure.
Frank Howard Clark

Politics is too serious a matter to be left to the politicians.
Charles de Gaulle

No real social change has ever been brought about without a revolution... revolution is but thought carried into action.
Emma Goldman

When they see me holding fish, they can see that I am comfortable with kings as well as with paupers.
Imelda Marcos

Freedom means the opportunity to be what we never thought we would be.
Daniel J. Boorstin

Radical changes in world politics leave America with a heightened responsibility to be, for the world, an example of a genuinely free, democratic, just and humane society.
Pope John Paul II

I have no ambition to govern men; it is a painful and thankless office.
Thomas Jefferson

Politics is the art of choosing between the disastrous and the unpalatable.
John Kenneth Galbraith

The revenues of Cuban state-run companies are used exclusively for the benefit of the people, to whom they belong.
Fidel Castro

When governments become large, voters cannot exercise close oversight, otherwise known as political power.
Maggie Gallagher

Television is democracy at its ugliest.
Paddy Chayefsky

Democracy is the recurrent suspicion that more than half of the people are right more than half of the time.
E. B. White

Oh, that lovely title, ex-president.
Dwight D. Eisenhower

We have, I fear, confused power with greatness.
Stewart Udall

So long as we have enough people in this country willing to fight for their rights, we'll be called a democracy.
Roger Nash Baldwin

Reporters thrive on the world's misfortune. For this reason they often take an indecent pleasure in events that dismay the rest of humanity.
Russell Baker

The Vice-Presidency is sort of like the last cookie on the plate. Everybody insists he won't take it, but somebody always does.
Bill Vaughan

I do have a political agenda. It's to have as few regulations as possible.
Dan Quayle

Sensible and responsible women do not want to vote. The relative positions to be assumed by man and woman in the working out of our civilization were assigned long ago by a higher intelligence than ours.
Grover Cleveland

The most important political office is that of the private citizen.
Louis D. Brandeis

They say women talk too much. If you have worked in Congress you know that the filibuster was invented by men.
Clare Boothe Luce

We live in a world in which politics has replaced philosophy.
Martin L. Gross

Their very conservatism is secondhand, and they don't know what they are conserving.
Robertson Davies

The politicians were talking themselves red, white and blue in the face.
Clare Boothe Luce

The only difference between the Democrats and the Republicans is that the Democrats allow the poor to be corrupt, too.
Oscar Levant

Tradition means giving votes to the most obscure of all classes, our ancestors. It is the democracy of the dead. Tradition refuses to submit to that arrogant oligarchy who merely happen to be walking around.
Gilbert K. Chesterton

The United States brags about its political system, but the President says one thing during the election, something else when he takes office, something else at midterm and something else when he leaves.
Deng Xiaoping

After much prayerful consideration, I feel that I must say I have climbed my last political mountain.
George C. Wallace

Voters don't decide issues, they decide who will decide issues.
George Will

I think there is one higher office than president and I would call that patriot.
Gary Hart

Frankly, I don't mind not being President. I just mind that someone else is.
Edward Kennedy

I was a woman in a man's world. I was a Democrat in a Republican administration. I was an intellectual in a world of bureaucrats. I talked differently. This may have made me a bit like an ink blot.
Jeane Kirkpatrick

If you don't like the President, it costs you 90 bucks to fly to Washington to picket. If you don't like the Governor, it costs you 60 bucks to fly to Albany to picket. If you don't like me, 90 cents.
Edward Koch

I know many writers who first dictate passages, then polish what they have dictated. I speak, then I polish - occasionally I do windows.
Edward Koch

Voting is a civic sacrament.
Theodore Hesburgh

It has been well said that a hungry man is more interested in four sandwiches than four freedoms.
Henry Cabot Lodge, Jr.

My hope is that 10 years from now, after I've been across the street at work for a while, they'll all be glad they gave me that wonderful vote.
Sandra Day O'Connor

It is difficult to discern a serious threat to religious liberty from a room of silent, thoughtful schoolchildren.
Sandra Day O'Connor

It is a measure of the framers' fear that a passing majority might find it expedient to compromise 4th Amendment values that these values were embodied in the Constitution itself.
Sandra Day O'Connor

You better take advantage of the good cigars. You don't get much else in that job.
Thomas P. O'Neill

Justice, sir, is the great interest of man on earth. It is the ligament which holds civilized beings and civilized nations together.
Daniel Webster

Vote for the man who promises least; he'll be the least disappointing.
Bernard Baruch

He too serves a certain purpose who only stands and cheers.
Henry B. Adams

The end move in politics is always to pick up a gun.
R. Buckminster Fuller

I can't let important policy decisions hinge on the fact that an election is coming up every 90 days.
Gerhard Schroder

In politics nothing is contemptible.
Benjamin Disraeli

In politics it is necessary either to betray one's country or the electorate. I prefer to betray the electorate.
Charles de Gaulle

In a democracy, dissent is an act of faith.
J. William Fulbright

It is our experience that political leaders do not always mean the opposite of what they say.
Abba Eban

Your every voter, as surely as your chief magistrate, exercises a public trust.
Grover Cleveland

I always voted at my party's call, and I never thought of thinking for myself at all.
William Gilbert

I should prefer to have a politician who regularly went to a massage parlour than one who promised a laptop computer for every teacher.
A. N. Wilson

You know they say the most dangerous person of the world is a member of the United States Congress just home from a three-day fact-finding trip.
Johnny Isakson

Our party is a diverse one, as is my home state of Illinois.
Dick Durbin

What politicians want to create is irreversible change because when you leave office someone changes it back again.
Estelle Morris

And after I make a lot of money, I'll be able to afford running for office.
Christy Romano

When the body of the people is possessed of the supreme power, it is called a democracy.
Charles de Secondat

POWER

Nearly all men can stand adversity, but if you want to test a man's character, give him power.
Abraham Lincoln

Knowledge is power.
Francis Bacon

Knowledge will give you power, but character respect.
Bruce Lee

Being powerful is like being a lady. If you have to tell people you are, you aren't.
Margaret Thatcher

Never underestimate the power of human stupidity.
Robert A. Heinlein

Power is the great aphrodisiac.
Henry A. Kissinger

All the forces in the world are not so powerful as an idea whose time has come.
Victor Hugo

Every man builds his world in his own image. He has the power to choose, but no power to escape the necessity of choice.
Ayn Rand

Never allow a person to tell you no who doesn't have the power to say yes.
Eleanor Roosevelt

The less effort, the faster and more powerful you will be.
Bruce Lee

Will power is to the mind like a strong blind man who carries on his shoulders a lame man who can see.
Arthur Schopenhauer

Power concedes nothing without a demand. It never did and it never will.
Frederick Douglass

To achieve, you need thought. You have to know what you are doing and that's real power.
Ayn Rand

Power is given only to those who dare to lower themselves and pick it up. Only one thing matters, one thing; to be able to dare!
Fyodor Dostoevsky

What it lies in our power to do, it lies in our power not to do.
Aristotle

Circumstances are beyond human control, but our conduct is in our own power.
Benjamin Disraeli

The value systems of those with access to power and of those far removed from such access cannot be the same. The viewpoint of the privileged is unlike that of the underprivileged.
Aung San Suu Kyi

The power of the people and the power of reason are one.
Georg Buchner

No one is in control of your happiness but you; therefore, you have the power to change anything about yourself or your life that you want to change.
Barbara de Angelis

Character is power.
Booker T. Washington

Power is always dangerous. Power attracts the worst and corrupts the best.
Edward Abbey

If you realized how powerful your thoughts are, you would never think a negative thought.
Peace Pilgrim

But to me nothing - the negative, the empty - is exceedingly powerful.
Alan Watts

Money is power, and in that government which pays all the public officers of the states will all political power be substantially concentrated.
Andrew Jackson

A man's true state of power and riches is to be in himself.
Henry Ward Beecher

Make the best use of what is in your power, and take the rest as it happens.
Epictetus

You only have power over people so long as you don't take everything away from them. But when you've robbed a man of everything, he's no longer in your power - he's free again.
Aleksandr Solzhenitsyn

Self-reverence, self-knowledge, self-control; these three alone lead one to sovereign power.
Alfred Lord Tennyson

I was now resolved to do everything in my power to defeat the system.
Oskar Schindler

Capitalism works better from every perspective when the economic decision makers are forced to share power with those who will be affected by those decisions.
Barney Frank

Truth is powerful and it prevails.
Sojourner Truth

The most common way people give up their power is by thinking they don't have any.
Alice Walker

Justice and power must be brought together, so that whatever is just may be powerful, and whatever is powerful may be just.
Blaise Pascal

Nobody is as powerful as we make them out to be.
Alice Walker

Love him or hate him, Trump is a man who is certain about what he wants and sets out to get it, no holds barred. Women find his power almost as much of a turn-on as his money.
Donald Trump

Creativity is the power to connect the seemingly unconnected.
William Plomer

It is folly for a man to pray to the gods for that which he has the power to obtain by himself.
Epicurus

Immense power is acquired by assuring yourself in your secret reveries that you were born to control affairs.
Andrew Carnegie

Question: Why are we Masters of our Fate, the captains of our souls? Because we have the power to control our thoughts, our attitudes. That is why many people live in the withering negative world. That is why many people live in the Positive Faith world.
Alfred A. Montapert

Do not pray for tasks equal to your powers. Pray for powers equal to your tasks.
Phillips Brooks

Getting and spending, we lay waste our powers.
William Wordsworth

The greatest power is often simple patience.
E. Joseph Cossman

Vote: the instrument and symbol of a freeman's power to make a fool of himself and a wreck of his country.
Ambrose Bierce

Our sense of power is more vivid when we break a man's spirit than when we win his heart.
Eric Hoffer

There is no meaning to life except the meaning man gives his life by the unfolding of his powers.
Erich Fromm

Knowledge is the most democratic source of power.
Alvin Toffler

Every crisis offers you extra desired power.
William Moulton Marston

My relationship to power and authority is that I'm all for it. People need somebody to watch over them. Ninety-five percent of the people in the world need to be told what to do and how to behave.
Arnold Schwarzenegger

Never forget that the most powerful force on earth is love.
Nelson Rockefeller

Sooner or later, man has always had to decide whether he worships his own power or the power of God.
Arnold J. Toynbee

Sir, I am no sycophant or worshipper of power anywhere.
Benjamin F. Wade

When you start to develop your powers of empathy and imagination, the whole world opens up to you.
Susan Sarandon

Never go backward. Attempt, and do it with all your might. Determination is power.
Charles Simmons

Arbitrary power is like most other things which are very hard, very liable to be broken.
Abigail Adams

The rules have changed. True power is held by the person who possesses the largest bookshelf, not gun cabinet or wallet.
Anthony J. D'Angelo

Ironically, women who acquire power are more likely to be criticized for it than are the men who have always had it.
Carolyn Heilbrun

There is that in the glance of a flower which may at times control the greatest of creation's braggart lords.
John Muir

The advertisers who believe in the selling power of jingles have never had to sell anything.
David Ogilvy

The eye sees what it brings the power to see.
Thomas Carlyle

There is no power on earth that can neutralize the influence of a high, simple and useful life.
Booker T. Washington

Silence is the ultimate weapon of power.
Charles de Gaulle

The only way to predict the future is to have power to shape the future.
Eric Hoffer

Women have to harness their power - its absolutely true. It's just learning not to take the first no. And if you can't go straight ahead, you go around the corner.
Cher

Next to power without honor, the most dangerous thing in the world is power without humor.
Eric Sevareid

Man's greatness lies in his power of thought.
Blaise Pascal

Power is dangerous unless you have humility.
Richard J. Daley

There is no force so powerful as an idea whose time has come.
Everett Dirksen

Moral power is probably best when it is not used. The less you use it the more you have.
Andrew Young

The purpose of getting power is to be able to give it away.
Aneurin Bevan

Power has only one duty - to secure the social welfare of the People.
Benjamin Disraeli

Power is the most persuasive rhetoric.
Friedrich Schiller

There are two ways of attaining an important end, force and perseverance; the silent power of the latter grows irresistible with time.
Sophie Swetchine

An alliance with a powerful person is never safe.
Phaedrus

Unlimited power corrupts the possessor.
William Pitt

Will power is only the tensile strength of one's own disposition. One cannot increase it by a single ounce.
Cesare Pavese

In my opinion, most of the great men of the past were only there for the beer - the wealth, prestige and grandeur that went with the power.
A. J. P. Taylor

Ambition is the immoderate desire for power.
Baruch Spinoza

There is something about inside information which seems to paralyse a man's reasoning powers.
Bernard Baruch

The law has no power over heroes.
Charlotte Lennox

Power without a nation's confidence is nothing.
Catherine II

Power in America today is control of the means of communication.
Theodore White

Power, after love, is the first source of happiness.
Stendhal

America has a critical role to play as the most powerful member of the world community.
Adam Schiff

Personality has power to uplift, power to depress, power to curse, and power to bless.
Paul Harris

I cured with the power that came through me.
Black Elk

No matter what has happened, you too have the power to enjoy yourself.
Allen Klein

Throughout history, great leaders have known the power of humor.
Allen Klein

The greatest power is not money power, but political power.
Walter Annenberg

The way to have power is to take it.
Boss Tweed

Power ought to serve as a check to power.
Charles de Secondat

I believe in the power of weakness.
Pat Buckley

The real problem is that the way that power is given out in our society pits us against each other.
Anita Hill

Politics is not about power.
Paul Wellstone

People who are in power make their arrangements in secret, largely as a way of maintaining and furthering that power.
Don DeLillo

People who are powerless make an open theater of violence.
Don DeLillo

Prestige is the shadow of money and power.
C. Wright Mills

The greater the power, the more dangerous the abuse.
Edmund Burke

Excessive fear is always powerless.
Aeschylus

Each underestimates her own power and overestimates the other's.
Deborah Tannen

Public misbehavior by the famous is a powerful teaching tool.
Bill O'Reilly

What is genius but the power of expressing a new individuality?
Elizabeth Barrett Browning

The only power you have is the word no.
Frances McDormand

Power and position often make a man trifle with the truth.
George A. Smith

The world itself is the will to power - and nothing else! And you yourself are the will to power - and nothing else!
Friedrich Nietzsche

Power acquired by violence is only a usurpation, and lasts only as long as the force of him who commands prevails over that of those who obey.
Denis Diderot

Power is action; the electoral principle is discussion. No political action is possible when discussion is permanently established.
Honore De Balzac

A true king is neither husband nor father; he considers his throne and nothing else.
Pierre Corneille

Power is paradoxical.
Friedrich Durrenmatt

Whoever is new to power is always harsh.
Aeschylus

Those who desire to rise as high as our human condition allows, must renounce intellectual pride, the omnipotence of clear thinking, belief in the absolute power of logic.
Alexis Carrel

RELIGION

I believe in Christianity as I believe that the sun has risen: not only because I see it, but because by it I see everything else.
C. S. Lewis

Aim at heaven and you will get earth thrown in. Aim at earth and you get neither.
C. S. Lewis

This is my simple religion. There is no need for temples; no need for complicated philosophy. Our own brain, our own heart is our temple; the philosophy is kindness.
Dalai Lama

I would rather live my life as if there is a God and die to find out there isn't, than live my life as if there isn't and die to find out there is.
Albert Camus

Heaven is under our feet as well as over our heads.
Henry David Thoreau

There is no need for temples, no need for complicated philosophies. My brain and my heart are my temples; my philosophy is kindness.
Dalai Lama

I like your Christ, I do not like your Christians. Your Christians are so unlike your Christ.
Mahatma Gandhi

Question with boldness even the existence of a God; because, if there be one, he must more approve of the homage of reason, than that of blind-folded fear.
Thomas Jefferson

Just as a candle cannot burn without fire, men cannot live without a spiritual life.
Buddha

I love you when you bow in your mosque, kneel in your temple, pray in your church. For you and I are sons of one religion, and it is the spirit.
Khalil Gibran

You cannot believe in God until you believe in yourself.
Swami Vivekananda

If Jesus had been killed twenty years ago, Catholic school children would be wearing little electric chairs around their necks instead of crosses.
Lenny Bruce

You can safely assume that you've created God in your own image when it turns out that God hates all the same people you do.
Anne Lamott

Isn't it enough to see that a garden is beautiful without having to believe that there are fairies at the bottom of it too?
Douglas Adams

When the missionaries came to Africa they had the Bible and we had the land. They said "Let us pray." We closed our eyes. When we opened them we had the Bible and they had the land.
Desmond Tutu

Eskimo: "If I did not know about God and sin, would I go to hell?" Priest: "No, not if you did not know." Eskimo: "Then why did you tell me?"
Annie Dillard

I do not feel obliged to believe that the same God who has endowed us with sense, reason, and intellect has intended us to forgo their use.
Galileo Galilei

It is wonderful how much time good people spend fighting the devil. If they would only expend the same amount of energy loving their fellow men, the devil would die in his own tracks of ennui.
Helen Keller

Prayer does not change God, but it changes him who prays.
Soren Kierkegaard

I prayed for twenty years but received no answer until I prayed with my legs.
Frederick Douglass

Just in terms of allocation of time resources, religion is not very efficient. There's a lot more I could be doing on a Sunday morning.
Bill Gates

Religion is what keeps the poor from murdering the rich.
Napoleon Bonaparte

We must respect the other fellow's religion, but only in the sense and to the extent that we respect his theory that his wife is beautiful and his children smart.
H. L. Mencken

Human beings must be known to be loved; but Divine beings must be loved to be known.
Blaise Pascal

Born again?! No, I'm not. Excuse me for getting it right the first time.
Dennis Miller

Creationists make it sound as though a 'theory' is something you dreamt up after being drunk all night.
Isaac Asimov

I never knew how to worship until I knew how to love.
Henry Ward Beecher

If a man would follow, today, the teachings of the Old Testament, he would be a criminal. If he would follow strictly the teachings of the New, he would be insane.
Robert Green Ingersoll

God made everything out of nothing, but the nothingness shows through.
Paul Valery

Let your religion be less of a theory and more of a love affair.
Gilbert K. Chesterton

A just laicism allows religious freedom. The state does not impose religion but rather gives space to religions with a responsibility toward civil society, and therefore it allows these religions to be factors in building up society.
Joseph Ratzinger

It is now quite lawful for a Catholic woman to avoid pregnancy by a resort to mathematics, though she is still forbidden to resort to physics or chemistry.
H. L. Mencken

No man ever believes that the Bible means what it says: He is always convinced that it says what he means.
George Bernard Shaw

Doubt is part of all religion. All the religious thinkers were doubters.
Isaac Bashevis Singer

Morality is of the highest importance - but for us, not for God.
Albert Einstein

If I had to choose a religion, the sun as the universal giver of life would be my god.
Napoleon Bonaparte

It's wonderful to climb the liquid mountains of the sky. Behind me and before me is God and I have no fears.
Helen Keller

He hoped and prayed that there wasn't an afterlife. Then he realized there was a contradiction involved here and merely hoped that there wasn't an afterlife.
Douglas Adams

I don't believe in God but I'm very interested in her.
Arthur C. Clarke

One man's theology is another man's belly laugh.
Robert A. Heinlein

Theology is never any help; it is searching in a dark cellar at midnight for a black cat that isn't there. Theologians can persuade themselves of anything.
Robert A. Heinlein

The Christian resolution to find the world ugly and bad has made the world ugly and bad.
Friedrich Nietzsche

Just as the soul fills the body, so God fills the world. Just as the soul bears the body, so God endures the world. Just as the soul sees but is not seen, so God sees but is not seen. Just as the soul feeds the body, so God gives food to the world.
Marcus Tullius Cicero

The more powerful and original a mind, the more it will incline towards the religion of solitude.
Aldous Huxley

We are always on the anvil; by trials God is shaping us for higher things.
Henry Ward Beecher

The glory of Christianity is to conquer by forgiveness.
William Blake

If the grandfather of the grandfather of Jesus had known what was hidden within him, he would have stood humble and awe-struck before his soul.
Khalil Gibran

When lip service to some mysterious deity permits bestiality on Wednesday and absolution on Sunday, cash me out.
Frank Sinatra

We are punished by our sins, not for them.
Elbert Hubbard

Religion is essentially the art and the theory of the remaking of man. Man is not a finished creation.
Edmund Burke

More and more people care about religious tolerance as fewer and fewer care about religion.
Alexander Chase

The Bible looks like it started out as a game of Mad Libs.
Bill Maher

Jim Bakker spells his name with two k's because three would be too obvious.
Bill Maher

There seems to be a terrible misunderstanding on the part of a great many people to the effect that when you cease to believe you may cease to behave.
Louis Kronenberger

Why should we take advice on sex from the pope? If he knows anything about it, he shouldn't!
George Bernard Shaw

This is God's world, not Satan's. Christians are the lawful heirs, not non-Christians.
Gary North

Our Father and Our God, unto thee, O Lord we lift our souls.
William Pennington

Religion is the idol of the mob; it adores everything it does not understand.
Frederick II

Prayer is the spirit speaking truth to Truth.
Philip James Bailey

Where it is a duty to worship the sun it is pretty sure to be a crime to examine the laws of heat.
John Morley

The Bible is literature, not dogma.
George Santayana

If I had been the Virgin Mary, I would have said "No."
Margaret Smith

Recounting of a life story, a mind thinking aloud leads one inevitably to the consideration of problems which are no longer psychological but spiritual.
Paul Tournier

I was raised Catholic, but my father's people were Methodist, so we went to both churches.
Aaron Neville

Krishna children were taught that in the spiritual world there were no parents, only souls and hence this justified their being kept out of view from others, cloistered in separate buildings and sheltered from the evil material world.
Mary Garden

The Sabbath is a weekly cathedral raised up in my dining room, in my family, in my heart.
Anita Diament

The Godhead consists of the Father, the Son, and the Holy Spirit. The Father is a material being.
Orson Pratt

The emphasis on the birth of Christ tends to polarize our pluralistic society and create legal and ethnic belligerence.
John Clayton

Muslims must believe that all power, success and victory comes from God alone.
Abu Bakar Bashir

We must seek the loving-kindness of God in all the breadth and open-air of common life.
George A. Smith

SCIENCE

Only two things are infinite, the universe and human stupidity, and I'm not sure about the former.
Albert Einstein

Our scientific power has outrun our spiritual power. We have guided missiles and misguided men.
Martin Luther King, Jr.

Aerodynamically, the bumble bee shouldn't be able to fly, but the bumble bee doesn't know it so it goes on flying anyway.
Mary Kay Ash

A scientific truth does not triumph by convincing its opponents and making them see the light, but rather because its opponents eventually die and a new generation grows up that is familiar with it.
Max Planck

Touch a scientist and you touch a child.
Ray Bradbury

Science investigates religion interprets. Science gives man knowledge which is power religion gives man wisdom which is control.
Martin Luther King, Jr.

Bad times have a scientific value. These are occasions a good learner would not miss.
Ralph Waldo Emerson

No amount of experimentation can ever prove me right; a single experiment can prove me wrong.
Albert Einstein

A fact is a simple statement that everyone believes. It is innocent, unless found guilty. A hypothesis is a novel suggestion that no one wants to believe. It is guilty, until found effective.
Edward Teller

The most exciting phrase to hear in science, the one that heralds new discoveries, is not 'Eureka!' but 'That's funny...'
Isaac Asimov

Anybody who has been seriously engaged in scientific work of any kind realizes that over the entrance to the gates of the temple of science are written the words: 'Ye must have faith.'
Max Planck

A year spent in artificial intelligence is enough to make one believe in God.
Alan Perlis

Science is a way of thinking much more than it is a body of knowledge.
Carl Sagan

Research is what I'm doing when I don't know what I'm doing.
Wernher von Braun

The saddest aspect of life right now is that science gathers knowledge faster than society gathers wisdom.
Isaac Asimov

The best scientist is open to experience and begins with romance - the idea that anything is possible.
Ray Bradbury

You cannot feed the hungry on statistics.
Heinrich Heine

Each problem that I solved became a rule, which served afterwards to solve other problems.
Rene Descartes

It is a good morning exercise for a research scientist to discard a pet hypothesis every day before breakfast. It keeps him young.
Konrad Lorenz

The scientific theory I like best is that the rings of Saturn are composed entirely of lost airline luggage.
Mark Russell

Science and technology revolutionize our lives, but memory, tradition and myth frame our response.
Arthur M. Schlesinger

The great tragedy of science - the slaying of a beautiful hypothesis by an ugly fact.
Thomas Huxley

Few tragedies can be more extensive than the stunting of life, few injustices deeper than the denial of an opportunity to strive or even to hope, by a limit imposed from without, but falsely identified as lying within.
Stephen Jay Gould

Science does not know its debt to imagination.
Ralph Waldo Emerson

We can lick gravity, but sometimes the paperwork is overwhelming.
Wernher von Braun

Science is the great antidote to the poison of enthusiasm and superstition.
Adam Smith

The folly of mistaking a paradox for a discovery, a metaphor for a proof, a torrent of verbiage for a spring of capital truths, and oneself for an oracle, is inborn in us.
Paul Valery

If an elderly but distinguished scientist says that something is possible, he is almost certainly right; but if he says that it is impossible, he is very probably wrong.
Arthur C. Clarke

Your theory is crazy, but it's not crazy enough to be true.
Niels Bohr

Science has made us gods even before we are worthy of being men.
Jean Rostand

We are born at a given moment, in a given place and, like vintage years of wine, we have the qualities of the year and of the season of which we are born. Astrology does not lay claim to anything more.
Carl Jung

There are no shortcuts in evolution.
Louis D. Brandeis

Inanimate objects can be classified scientifically into three major categories; those that don't work, those that break down and those that get lost.
Russell Baker

Adventure upon all the tickets in the lottery, and you lose for certain; and the greater the number of your tickets the nearer your approach to this certainty.
Adam Smith

For NASA, space is still a high priority.
Dan Quayle

If a man's wit be wandering, let him study the mathematics.
Francis Bacon

Half of the modern drugs could well be thrown out of the window, except that the birds might eat them.
Martin Henry Fischer

Every great advance in science has issued from a new audacity of imagination.
John Dewey

If we wish to make a new world we have the material ready. The first one, too, was made out of chaos.
Robert Quillen

The fewer the facts, the stronger the opinion.
Arnold H. Glasow

Science is wonderfully equipped to answer the question "How?" but it gets terribly confused when you ask the question "Why?"
Erwin Chargaff

The doctor has been taught to be interested not in health but in disease. What the public is taught is that health is the cure for disease.
Ashley Montagu

He is so old that his blood type was discontinued.
Bill Dana

Nothing has such power to broaden the mind as the ability to investigate systematically and truly all that comes under thy observation in life.
Marcus Aurelius

Facts are the air of scientists. Without them you can never fly.
Linus Pauling

When I investigate and when I discover that the forces of the heavens and the planets are within ourselves, then truly I seem to be living among the gods.
Leon Battista Alberti

Anyone who attempts to generate random numbers by deterministic means is, of course, living in a state of sin.
John von Neumann

Nothing in education is so astonishing as the amount of ignorance it accumulates in the form of inert facts.
Henry B. Adams

There is a single light of science, and to brighten it anywhere is to brighten it everywhere.
Isaac Asimov

The nineteenth century believed in science but the twentieth century does not.
Gertrude Stein

Nothing in the universe can travel at the speed of light, they say, forgetful of the shadow's speed.
Howard Nemerov

The distance between insanity and genius is measured only by success.
Bruce Feirstein

What is a scientist after all? It is a curious man looking through a keyhole, the keyhole of nature, trying to know what's going on.
Jacques Yves Cousteau

Anthropology was the science that gave her the platform from which she surveyed, scolded and beamed at the world.
Jane Howard

A satellite has no conscience.
Edward R. Murrow

From now on we live in a world where man has walked on the Moon. It's not a miracle; we just decided to go.
Tom Hanks

The cloning of humans is on most of the lists of things to worry about from Science, along with behaviour control, genetic engineering, transplanted heads, computer poetry and the unrestrained growth of plastic flowers.
Lewis Thomas

When I find myself in the company of scientists, I feel like a shabby curate who has strayed by mistake into a room full of dukes.
W. H. Auden

I hate facts. I always say the chief end of man is to form general propositions - adding that no general proposition is worth a damn.
Oliver Wendell Holmes

I believe in general in a dualism between facts and the ideas of those facts in human heads.
George Santayana

There is one thing even more vital to science than intelligent methods; and that is, the sincere desire to find out the truth, whatever it may be.
Charles Pierce

I see nothing in space as promising as the view from a Ferris wheel.
E. B. White

The next major explosion is going to be when genetics and computers come together. I'm talking about an organic computer - about biological substances that can function like a semiconductor.
Alvin Toffler

Science is organized common sense where many a beautiful theory was killed by an ugly fact.
Thomas Huxley

The science of today is the technology of tomorrow.
Edward Teller

Men love to wonder, and that is the seed of science.
Ralph Waldo Emerson

In science, "fact" can only mean "confirmed to such a degree that it would be perverse to withhold provisional assent." I suppose that apples might start to rise tomorrow, but the possibility does not merit equal time in physics classrooms.
Stephen Jay Gould

The radical novelty of modern science lies precisely in the rejection of the belief... that the forces which move the stars and atoms are contingent upon the preferences of the human heart.
Walter Lippmann

Science is a first-rate piece of furniture for a man's upper chamber, if he has common sense on the ground floor.
Oliver Wendell Holmes

In all science, error precedes the truth, and it is better it should go first than last.
Hugh Walpole

Science never solves a problem without creating ten more.
George Bernard Shaw

Leave the atom alone.
E. Y. Harburg

Whenever anyone says, 'theoretically,' they really mean, 'not really.'
Dave Parnas

Scientific theory is a contrived foothold in the chaos of living phenomena.
Wilhelm Reich

It will free man from the remaining chains, the chains of gravity which still tie him to this planet.
Wernher von Braun

I am not a scientist. I am, rather, an impresario of scientists.
Jacques Yves Cousteau

Polygraph tests are 20th-century witchcraft.
Sam Ervin

Take young researchers, put them together in virtual seclusion, give them an unprecedented degree of freedom and turn up the pressure by fostering competitiveness.
James D. Watson

People think of the inventor as a screwball, but no one ever asks the inventor what he thinks of other people.
Charles Kettering

Anthropology demands the open-mindedness with which one must look and listen, record in astonishment and wonder that which one would not have been able to guess.
Margaret Mead

Science is simply common sense at its best, that is, rigidly accurate in observation, and merciless to fallacy in logic.
Thomas Huxley

We seem to have a compulsion these days to bury time capsules in order to give those people living in the next century or so some idea of what we are like.
Alfred Hitchcock

Nobody climbs mountains for scientific reasons. Science is used to raise money for the expeditions, but you really climb for the hell of it.
Edmund Hillary

Bush reiterated his stand to conservatives opposing his decision on stem cell research. He said today he believes life begins at conception and ends at execution.
Jay Leno

There was no "before" the beginning of our universe, because once upon a time there was no time.
John D. Barrow

Sadly, embryonic stem cell research is completely legal in this country and has been going on at universities and research facilities for years.
Mike Pence

Some dreamers demand that scientists only discover things that can be used for good.
John Charles Polanyi

The scientist is motivated primarily by curiosity and a desire for truth.
Irving Langmuir

Scientists worldwide agree that the reduction needed to stabilize the climate is actually more like 80 percent.
Donella Meadows

SOCIETY

It is no measure of health to be well adjusted to a profoundly sick society.
Jiddu Krishnamurti

An armed society is a polite society. Manners are good when one may have to back up his acts with his life.
Robert A. Heinlein

Think what a better world it would be if we all, the whole world, had cookies and milk about three o'clock every afternoon and then lay down on our blankets for a nap.
Barbara Jordan

The trouble with the rat race is that even if you win, you're still a rat.
Lily Tomlin

A people that values its privileges above its principles soon loses both.
Dwight D. Eisenhower

We have a system that increasingly taxes work and subsidizes nonwork.
Milton Friedman

You must not lose faith in humanity. Humanity is an ocean; if a few drops of the ocean are dirty, the ocean does not become dirty.
Mahatma Gandhi

The society which scorns excellence in plumbing as a humble activity and tolerates shoddiness in philosophy because it is an exalted activity will have neither good plumbing nor good philosophy: neither its pipes nor its theories will hold water.
John W. Gardner

Do not waste your time on Social Questions. What is the matter with the poor is Poverty; what is the matter with the rich is Uselessness.
George Bernard Shaw

If a man walks in the woods for love of them half of each day, he is in danger of being regarded as a loafer. But if he spends his days as a speculator, shearing off those woods and making the earth bald before her time, he is deemed an industrious and enterprising citizen.
Henry David Thoreau

I am as frustrated with society as a pyromaniac in a petrified forest.
A. Whitney Brown

No society can surely be flourishing and happy, of which the far greater part of the members are poor and miserable.
Adam Smith

The most dangerous creation of any society is the man who has nothing to lose.
James A. Baldwin

A free society is one where it is safe to be unpopular.
Adlai E. Stevenson

Formerly, when religion was strong and science weak, men mistook magic for medicine; now, when science is strong and religion weak, men mistake medicine for magic.
Thomas Szasz

Civilization is unbearable, but it is less unbearable at the top.
Timothy Leary

The danger of the past was that men became slaves. The danger of the future is that man may become robots.
Erich Fromm

In these times you have to be an optimist to open your eyes when you awake in the morning.
Carl Sandburg

How can a society that exists on instant mashed potatoes, packaged cake mixes, frozen dinners, and instant cameras teach patience to its young?
Paul Sweeney

Society honors its living conformists and its dead troublemakers.
Mignon McLaughlin

Punishment is now unfashionable... because it creates moral distinctions among men, which, to the democratic mind, are odious. We prefer a meaningless collective guilt to a meaningful individual responsibility.
Thomas Szasz

There is more to life than

increasing its speed.
Mahatma Gandhi

Life was a lot simpler when what we honored was father and mother rather than all major credit cards.
Robert Orben

Cockroaches and socialites are the only things that can stay up all night and eat anything.
Herb Caen

Neither the life of an individual nor the history of a society can be understood without understanding both.
C. Wright Mills

I think this society suffers so much from too much freedom, too many rights that allow people to be irresponsible.
Boyd Rice

You can find your way across this country using burger joints the way a navigator uses stars.
Charles Kuralt

Society has always seemed to demand a little more from human beings than it will get in practice.
George Orwell

Suburbia is where the developer bulldozes out the trees, then names the streets after them.
Bill Vaughan

What is the use of a house if you haven't got a tolerable planet to put it on?
Henry David Thoreau

Perhaps in time the so-called Dark Ages will be thought of as including our own.
Georg C. Lichtenberg

The wise person often shuns society for fear of being bored.
Jean de la Bruyere

One of the definitions of sanity is the ability to tell real from unreal. Soon we'll need a new definition.
Alvin Toffler

Man is the animal that intends to shoot himself out into interplanetary space, after having given up on the problem of an efficient way to get himself five miles to work and back each day.
Bill Vaughan

It is not a fragrant world.
Raymond Chandler

A pure democracy is a society consisting of a small number of

citizens, who assemble and administer the government in person.
James Madison

Most of the change we think we see in life is due to truths being in and out of favor.
Robert Frost

Normal social behavior requires that we be able to recognize identities in spite of change. Unless we can do so, there can be no human society as we know it.
Kenneth L. Pike

Society is one vast conspiracy for carving one into the kind of statue likes, and then placing it in the most convenient niche it has.
Randolph Bourne

The world is governed more by appearance than realities so that it is fully as necessary to seem to know something as to know it.
Daniel Webster

The enemy of society is middle class and the enemy of life is middle age.
Orson Welles

The human race's prospects of survival were considerably better when we were defenceless against tigers than they are today when we have become defenceless against ourselves.
Arnold J. Toynbee

The first principle of a free society is an untrammeled flow of words in an open forum.
Adlai E. Stevenson

Some people strengthen the society just by being the kind of people they are.
John W. Gardner

Exclusiveness in a garden is a mistake as great as it is in society.
Alfred Austin

Our society is not a community, but merely a collection of isolated family units.
Valerie Solanas

Good-looking individuals are treated better than homely ones in virtually every social situation, from dating to trial by jury.
Martha Beck

Society is based on the assumption that everyone is

alike and no one is alive.
Hugh Kingsmill

Our individual lives cannot, generally, be works of art unless the social order is also.
Charles Horton Cooley

Usually, terrible things that are done with the excuse that progress requires them are not really progress at all, but just terrible things.
Russell Baker

The function of the press in society is to inform, but its role in society is to make money.
A. J. Liebling

What can you say about a society that says that God is dead and Elvis is alive?
Irv Kupcinet

Today the world changes so quickly that in growing up we take leave not just of youth but of the world we were young in.
Peter Medawar

You can't make up anything anymore. The world itself is a satire. All you're doing is recording it.
Art Buchwald

It seems a long time since the morning mail could be called correspondence.
Jacques Barzun

To give aid to every poor man is far beyond the reach and power of every man. Care of the poor is incumbent on society as a whole.
Baruch Spinoza

The key to organizing an alternative society is to organize people around what they can do, and more importantly, what they want to do.
Abbie Hoffman

People are going to behave however the social norms permit, and beyond that.
Max Cannon

In our society leaving baby with Daddy is just one step above leaving the kids to be raised by wolves or apes.
Al Roker

Marriage cannot be severed from its cultural, religious and natural roots without weakening the good influence of society.
Jack Kingston

Society is the union of men and not the men themselves.
Charles de Secondat

It is good for society to have this introspection.
Jacques Verges

We must stop thinking of the individual and start thinking about what is best for society.
Hillary Clinton

Women with money and women in power are two uncomfortable ideas in our society.
Candace Bushnell

SPORTS

I've missed more than 9000 shots in my career. I've lost almost 300 games. 26 times, I've been trusted to take the game winning shot and missed. I've failed over and over and over again in my life. And that is why I succeed.
Michael Jordan

When the going gets weird, the weird turn pro.
Hunter S. Thompson

I want to rip out his heart and feed it to Lennox Lewis. I want to kill people. I want to rip their stomachs out and eat their children.
Mike Tyson

As athletes, we're used to reacting quickly. Here, it's 'come, stop, come, stop.' There's a lot of downtime. That's the toughest part of the day.
Michael Jordan

A good hockey player plays where the puck is. A great hockey player plays where the puck is going to be.
Wayne Gretzky

You can't put a limit on anything. The more you dream, the farther you get.
Michael Phelps

Good, better, best. Never let it rest. Until your good is better and your better is best.
Tim Duncan

If winning isn't everything, why do they keep score?
Vince Lombardi

Adversity causes some men to break; others to break records.
William Arthur Ward

Show me a good loser, and I'll show you a loser.
Vince Lombardi

It's just a job. Grass grows, birds fly, waves pound the sand. I beat people up.
Muhammad Ali

Half the lies they tell about me aren't true.
Yogi Berra

I'm tired of hearing about money, money, money, money, money. I just want to play the game, drink Pepsi, wear Reebok.
Shaquille O'Neal

I went to a fight the other night, and a hockey game broke out.
Rodney Dangerfield

My motto was always to keep swinging. Whether I was in a slump or feeling badly or having trouble off the field, the only thing to do was keep swinging.
Hank Aaron

Golf is a good walk spoiled.
Mark Twain

Many men go fishing all of their lives without knowing that it is not fish they are after.
Henry David Thoreau

Thus so wretched is man that he would weary even without any cause for weariness... and so frivolous is he that, though full of a thousand reasons for weariness, the least thing, such as playing billiards or hitting a ball, is sufficient enough to amuse him.
Blaise Pascal

Don't look back. Something might be gaining on you.
Satchel Paige

All hockey players are bilingual. They know English and profanity.
Gordie Howe

Just play. Have fun. Enjoy the game.
Michael Jordan

Serious sport has nothing to do with fair play. It is bound up with hatred, jealousy, boastfulness, disregard of all rules and sadistic pleasure in witnessing violence. In other words, it is war minus the shooting.
George Orwell

People ask me what I do in winter when there's no baseball. I'll tell you what I do. I stare out the window and wait for spring.
Rogers Hornsby

Gold medals aren't really made of gold. They're made of sweat, determination, and a hard-to-find alloy called guts.
Dan Gable

Winning is habit. Unfortunately, so is losing.
Vince Lombardi

These are my new shoes. They're good shoes. They won't make you rich like me, they won't make you rebound like me, they definitely won't make you handsome like me. They'll only make you have shoes like me. That's it.
Charles Barkley

Hockey is a sport for white men. Basketball is a sport for black men. Golf is a sport for white men dressed like black pimps.
Tiger Woods

Most people never run far enough on their first wind to find out they've got a second.
William James

Baseball players are smarter than football players. How often do you see a baseball team penalized for too many men on the field?
Jim Bouton

I see great things in baseball. It's our game - the American game.
Walt Whitman

Baseball happens to be a game of cumulative tension but football, basketball and hockey are played with hand grenades and machine guns.
John Leonard

Approach the game with no preset agendas and you'll probably come away surprised at your overall efforts.
Phil Jackson

I am building a fire, and everyday I train, I add more fuel. At just the right moment, I light the match.
Mia Hamm

A lifetime of training for just ten seconds.
Jesse Owens

Baseball is the only field of endeavor where a man can succeed three times out of ten and be considered a good performer.
Ted Williams

Football is an incredible game. Sometimes it's so incredible, it's unbelievable.
Tom Landry

It's good sportsmanship to not pick up lost golf balls while they are still rolling.
Mark Twain

Basketball is like war in that offensive weapons are developed first, and it always takes a while for the defense to catch up.
Red Auerbach

You win some, lose some, and wreck some.
Dale Earnhardt

Academe, n.: An ancient school where morality and philosophy were taught. Academy, n.: A modern school where football is taught.
Ambrose Bierce

The only time my prayers are never answered is on the golf course.
Billy Graham

Champions keep playing until they get it right.
Billie Jean King

You wouldn't have won if we'd beaten you.
Yogi Berra

I always turn to the sports pages first, which records people's accomplishments. The front page has nothing but man's failures.
Earl Warren

God made me fast. And when I run, I feel His pleasure.
Eric Liddell

Fans don't boo nobodies.
Reggie Jackson

Baseball is a game where a curve is an optical illusion, a screwball can be a pitch or a person, stealing is legal and you can spit anywhere you like except in the umpire's eye or on the ball.
James Patrick Murray

Success is where preparation and opportunity meet.
Bobby Unser

Baseball is almost the only orderly thing in a very unorderly world. If you get three strikes, even the best lawyer in the world can't get you off.
Bill Veeck

If you meet the Buddha in the lane, feed him the ball.
Phil Jackson

I guess there is nothing that will get your mind off everything like golf. I have never been depressed enough to take up the game, but they say you get so sore at yourself you forget to hate your enemies.
Will Rogers

Give me golf clubs, fresh air and a beautiful partner, and you can keep the clubs and the fresh air.
Jack Benny

Fishing is much more than fish. It is the great occasion when we may return to the fine simplicity of our forefathers.
Herbert Hoover

Baseball has the great advantage over cricket of being sooner ended.
George Bernard Shaw

I know I am getting better at golf because I am hitting fewer spectators.
Gerald R. Ford

If you drink don't drive. Don't even putt.
Dean Martin

Have you ever noticed what golf spells backwards?
Al Boliska

Bobby Knight told me this: 'There is nothing that a good defense cannot beat a better offense.' In other words a good offense wins.
Dan Quayle

Some people are born on third base and go through life thinking they hit a triple.
Barry Switzer

Do you know what my favorite part of the game is? The opportunity to play.
Mike Singletary

You know it's going to hell when the best rapper out there is white and the best golfer is black.
Charles Barkley

Boxing has become America's tragic theater.
Joyce Carol Oates

Sports do not build character. They reveal it.
Heywood Broun

If you watch a game, it's fun. If you play it, it's recreation. If you work at it, it's golf.
Bob Hope

I don't want to play golf. When I hit a ball, I want someone else to go chase it.
Rogers Hornsby

Trying to sneak a fastball past Hank Aaron is like trying to sneak the sunrise past a rooster.
Joe Adcock

It's a round ball and a round bat, and you got to hit it square.
Pete Rose

Baseball is drama with an endless run and an ever-changing cast.
Joe Garagiola

The integrity of the game is everything.
Peter Ueberroth

Nobody's a natural. You work hard to get good and then work to get better. It's hard to stay on top.
Paul Coffey

If a tie is like kissing your sister, losing is like kissing you grandmother with her teeth out.
George Brett

You can't win unless you learn how to lose.
Kareem Abdul-Jabbar

I won't predict anything historic. But nothing is impossible.
Michael Phelps

The only way to prove that you're a good sport is to lose.
Ernie Banks

You don't play against opponents, you play against the game of basketball.
Bobby Knight

Nobody roots for Goliath.
Wilt Chamberlain

Reverse every natural instinct and do the opposite of what you are inclined to do, and you will probably come very close to having a perfect golf swing.
Ben Hogan

If you think it's hard to meet new people, try picking up the wrong golf ball.
Jack Lemmon

Skiing combines outdoor fun with knocking down trees with your face.
Dave Barry

I don't know why people question the academic training of an athlete. Fifty percent of the doctors in this country graduated in the bottom half of their classes.
Al McGuire

If you got the game, you got the game. That's why Tiger Woods is out there playing golf with Greg Norman.
Shaquille O'Neal

The two most important things in life are good friends and a strong bullpen.
Bob Lemon

Hitting is timing. Pitching is upsetting timing.
Warren Spahn

It is almost impossible to remember how tragic a place the world is when one is playing golf.
Robert Wilson Lynd

If a lot of people gripped a knife and fork the way they do a golf club, they'd starve to death.
Sam Snead

Golf is a game in which you yell "fore," shoot six, and write down five.
Paul Harvey

The game of golf would lose a great deal if croquet mallets and billiard cues were allowed on the putting green.
Ernest Hemingway

Don't play too much golf. Two rounds a day are plenty.
Harry Vardon

The difference between the old ballplayer and the new ballplayer is the jersey. The old ballplayer cared about the name on the front. The new ballplayer cares about the name on the back.
Steve Garvey

When I was 40, my doctor advised me that a man in his 40s shouldn't play tennis. I heeded his advice carefully and could hardly wait until I reached 50 to start again.
Hugo Black

If a man watches three football games in a row, he should be declared legally dead.
Erma Bombeck

Life is about timing.
Carl Lewis

All sports for all people.
Pierre de Coubertin

Gray skies are just clouds passing over.
Frank Gifford

Sometimes in football you have to score goals.
Thierry Henry

One man practicing sportsmanship is far better than a hundred teaching it.
Knute Rockne

Baseball life is a tough life on the family.
Nolan Ryan

I went through baseball as "a player to be named later."
Joe Garagiola

One thing you learned as a Cubs fan: when you bought you ticket, you could bank on seeing the bottom of the ninth.
Joe Garagiola

The bell that tolls for all in boxing belongs to a cash register.
Bob Verdi

Wrestling is ballet with violence.
Jesse Ventura

Most ball games are lost, not won.
Casey Stengel

If I weren't earning $3 million a year to dunk a basketball, most people on the street would run in the other direction if they saw me coming.
Charles Barkley

I had pro offers from the Detroit Lions and Green Bay Packers, who were pretty hard up for linemen in those days. If I had gone into professional football the name Jerry Ford might have been a household word today.
Gerald R. Ford

You can make a lot of money in this game. Just ask my ex-wives. Both of them are so rich that neither of their husbands work.
Lee Trevino

What's unfortunate about buying a pitcher for $12 million is that he carries no warranty.
Bob Verdi

Bulls do not win bull fights. People do.
Norman Ralph Augustine

You know they're not going to lose 162 consecutive games.
Harry Caray

The trouble with jogging is that the ice falls out of your glass.
Martin Mull

What's a good tournament for him? Winning it. He's good enough.
Greg Norman

There isn't a flaw in his golf or his makeup. He will win more majors than Arnold Palmer and me combined. Somebody is going to dust my records. It might as well be Tiger, because he's such a great kid.
Jack Nicklaus

He has the finest, fundamentally sound golf swing I've ever seen.
Jack Nicklaus

He's going to be around a long, long time, if his body holds up. That's always a concern with a lot of players because of how much they play. A lot of guys can't handle it. But it looks like he can.
Jack Nicklaus

He hits it long. His shoulders are impressively quick through the ball. That's where he's getting his power from. He's young and has great elasticity.
Nick Faldo

He's got everything. He' not a great player yet because he hasn't won any major championships, but it's a matter of time. He's an outstanding talent. I didn't realize how tall he is.
Nick Price

Overall the fundamentals seem to be there and he's obviously got a very mature head on his shoulders. He's got a kind of presence.
Nick Price

He hits the ball a long way and he knows how to win.
Gary McCord

He's got an overall flair for the game. It looks to me like he really loves what he does and he can't wait to get up in the morning, go hit some balls and go play.
Gary McCord

You spend a good piece of your life gripping a baseball and in the end it turns out that it was the other way around all the time.
Jim Bouton

There are two theories on hitting the knuckleball. Unfortunately, neither of them works.
Charley Lau

Eighteen holes of match play will teach you more about your foe than 18 years of dealing with him across a desk.
Grantland Rice

Golf appeals to the idiot in us and the child. Just how childlike golf players become is proven by their frequent inability to count past five.
John Updike

Golf is a day spent in a round of strenuous idleness.
William Wordsworth

What other people may find in poetry or art museums, I find in the flight of a good drive.
Arnold Palmer

I regard golf as an expensive way of playing marbles.
Gilbert K. Chesterton

If you are going to throw a club, it is important to throw it ahead of you, down the fairway, so you don't have to waste energy going back to pick it up.
Tommy Bolt

Golf is played by twenty million mature American men whose wives think they are out having fun.
Jim Bishop

I play in the low 80s. If it's any hotter than that, I won't play.
Joe E. Lewis

Golf is a game in which one endeavors to control a ball with implements ill adapted for the purpose.
Woodrow Wilson

The difference in golf and government is that in golf you can't improve your lie.
George Deukmejian

Pro football is like nuclear warfare. There are no winners, only survivors.
Frank Gifford

The fewer rules a coach has, the fewer rules there are for players to break.
John Madden

Baseball is a public trust. Players turn over, owners turn over and certain commissioners turn over. But baseball goes on.
Peter Ueberroth

There was endless action - not just football, but sailboats, tennis and other things: movement. There was endless talk - the ambassador at the head of the table laying out the prevailing wisdom, but everyone else weighing in with their opinions and taking part.
Charles Spalding

Football is violence and cold weather and sex and college rye.
Roger Kahn

I was showing early symptoms of becoming a professional baseball man. I was lying to the press.
Roger Kahn

Tennis is a perfect combination of violent action taking place in an atmosphere of total tranquillity.
Billie Jean King

I'll let the racket do the talking.
John McEnroe

I'd just as soon play tennis with the net down.
Robert Frost

Other sports play once a week but this sport is with us every day.
Peter Ueberroth

New Yorkers love it when you spill your guts out there. Spill your guts at Wimbledon and they make you stop and clean it up.
Jimmy Connors

Play is the only way the highest intelligence of humankind can unfold.
Joseph Chilton Pearce

Perhaps the single most important element in mastering the techniques and tactics of racing is experience. But once you have the fundamentals, acquiring the experience is a matter of time.
Greg LeMond

Tennis and golf are best played, not watched.
Roger Kahn

Any time Detroit scores more than 100 points and holds the other team below 100 points they almost always win.
Doug Collins

The triple is the most exciting play in baseball. Home runs win a lot of games, but I never understood why fans are so obsessed with them.
Hank Aaron

I'm not buddy-buddy with the players. If they need a buddy, let them buy a dog.
Whitey Herzog

Many baseball fans look upon an umpire as a sort of necessary evil to the luxury of baseball, like the odor that follows an automobile.
Christy Mathewson

You always get a special kick on opening day, no matter how many you go through. You look forward to it like a birthday party when you're a kid. You think something wonderful is going to happen.
Joe DiMaggio

Olympism is the marriage of sport and culture.
Juan Antonio Samaranch

You don't suffer, kill yourself and take the risks I take just for money. I love bike racing.
Greg LeMond

The only thing a golfer needs is more daylight.
Ben Hogan

Relax? How can anybody relax and play golf? You have to grip the club, don't you?
Ben Hogan

I'm a competitive person and I love the challenge of mastering new things.
Sasha Cohen

My family knew, but most of the sporting world did not realize that my right hand been some 75% paralyzed.
Bill Toomey

I started playing ball when I was a kid. My dad was a pro ball player and he passed on his knowledge to me.
Kurt Russell

Sports are a microcosm of society.
Billie Jean King

SUCCESS

A successful man is one who can lay a firm foundation with the bricks others have thrown at him.
David Brinkley

I've failed over and over and over again in my life and that is why I succeed.
Michael Jordan

Always bear in mind that your own resolution to succeed is more important than any other.
Abraham Lincoln

In order to succeed, your desire for success should be greater than your fear of failure.
Bill Cosby

I don't know the key to success, but the key to failure is trying to please everybody.
Bill Cosby

Don't aim for success if you want it; just do what you love and believe in, and it will come naturally.
David Frost

If at first you don't succeed, try, try again. Then quit. There's no point in being a damn fool about it.
W. C. Fields

Develop success from failures. Discouragement and failure are two of the surest stepping stones to success.
Dale Carnegie

Defeat is not the worst of failures. Not to have tried is the true failure.
George Edward Woodberry

Success is to be measured not so much by the position that one has reached in life as by the obstacles which he has overcome.
Booker T. Washington

Action is the foundational key

to all success.
Pablo Picasso

I honestly think it is better to be a failure at something you love than to be a success at something you hate.
George Burns

Failure is success if we learn from it.
Malcolm Forbes

Formula for success: rise early, work hard, strike oil.
J. Paul Getty

Formal education will make you a living; self-education will make you a fortune.
Jim Rohn

Try not to become a man of success, but rather try to become a man of value.
Albert Einstein

Success is a lousy teacher. It seduces smart people into thinking they can't lose.
Bill Gates

Belief in oneself is one of the most important bricks in building any successful venture.
Lydia M. Child

No man succeeds without a good woman behind him. Wife or mother, if it is both, he is twice blessed indeed.
Harold MacMillan

Success consists of going from failure to failure without loss of enthusiasm.
Winston Churchill

Winning isn't everything, it's the only thing.
Vince Lombardi

Success is getting what you want. Happiness is wanting what you get.
Dale Carnegie

Don't confuse fame with success. Madonna is one; Helen Keller is the other.
Erma Bombeck

In order to succeed you must fail, so that you know what not to do the next time.
Anthony J. D'Angelo

The most important single ingredient in the formula of success is knowing how to get along with people.
Theodore Roosevelt

I couldn't wait for success, so I went ahead without it.
Jonathan Winters

The ladder of success is best climbed by stepping on the

rungs of opportunity.
Ayn Rand

Diligence is the mother of good fortune.
Benjamin Disraeli

Flaming enthusiasm, backed up by horse sense and persistence, is the quality that most frequently makes for success.
Dale Carnegie

Most people give up just when they're about to achieve success. They quit on the one yard line. They give up at the last minute of the game one foot from a winning touchdown.
Ross Perot

Success is falling nine times and getting up ten.
Jon Bon Jovi

If you want to achieve things in life, you've just got to do them, and if you're talented and smart, you'll succeed.
Juliana Hatfield

Success is simple. Do what's right, the right way, at the right time.
Arnold H. Glasow

What is success? I think it is a mixture of having a flair for the thing that you are doing; knowing that it is not enough, that you have got to have hard work and a certain sense of purpose.
Margaret Thatcher

After I won the Oscar, my salary doubled, my friends tripled, my children became more popular at school, my butcher made a pass at me, and my maid hit me up for a raise.
Shirley Jones

Success seems to be largely a matter of hanging on after others have let go.
William Feather

There is only one success - to be able to spend your life in your own way.
Christopher Morley

One secret of success in life is for a man to be ready for his opportunity when it comes.
Benjamin Disraeli

Success in almost any field depends more on energy and drive than it does on intelligence. This explains why we have so many stupid leaders.
Sloan Wilson

Success is a science; if you have the conditions, you get

the result.
Oscar Wilde

Success without honor is an unseasoned dish; it will satisfy your hunger, but it won't taste good.
Joe Paterno

In this world it is not what we take up, but what we give up, that makes us rich.
Henry Ward Beecher

Success isn't a result of spontaneous combustion. You must set yourself on fire.
Arnold H. Glasow

How can they say my life is not a success? Have I not for more than sixty years got enough to eat and escaped being eaten?
Logan P. Smith

It's our nature: Human beings like success but they hate successful people.
Carrot Top

The measure of success is not whether you have a tough problem to deal with, but whether it is the same problem you had last year.
John Foster Dulles

The successful man will profit from his mistakes and try again in a different way.
Dale Carnegie

Success is blocked by concentrating on it and planning for it... Success is shy - it won't come out while you're watching.
Tennessee Williams

Success is how high you bounce when you hit bottom.
George S. Patton

Success is dependent on effort.
Sophocles

The thermometer of success is merely the jealousy of the malcontents.
Salvador Dali

Obedience is the mother of success and is wedded to safety.
Aeschylus

The common idea that success spoils people by making them vain, egotistic and self-complacent is erroneous; on the contrary it makes them, for the most part, humble, tolerant and kind.
W. Somerset Maugham

Success has a simple formula: do your best, and people may

like it.
Sam Ewing

Success is like death. The more successful you become, the higher the houses in the hills get and the higer the fences get.
Kevin Spacey

Success is often the result of taking a misstep in the right direction.
Al Bernstein

Success is that old ABC - ability, breaks, and courage.
Charles Luckman

The toughest thing about success is that you've got to keep on being a success.
Irving Berlin

Those who have succeeded at anything and don't mention luck are kidding themselves.
Larry King

The man who has done his level best... is a success, even though the world may write him down a failure.
B. C. Forbes

Nothing recedes like success.
Walter Winchell
It's not enough that I should succeed - others should fail.
David Merrick

Pray that success will not come any faster than you are able to endure it.
Elbert Hubbard

Success is simply a matter of luck. Ask any failure.
Earl Wilson

Sometimes I worry about being a success in a mediocre world.
Lily Tomlin

Success is the one unpardonable sin against our fellows.
Ambrose Bierce

Success to me is having ten honeydew melons and eating only the top half of each slice.
Barbra Streisand

Success is the progressive realization of predetermined, worthwhile, personal goals.
Paul J. Meyer

The one phrase you can use is that success has a thousand fathers, and failure is an orphan.
Alan Price

TECHNOLOGY

It has become appallingly obvious that our technology has exceeded our humanity.
Albert Einstein

Any sufficiently advanced technology is indistinguishable from magic.
Arthur C. Clarke

The first rule of any technology used in a business is that automation applied to an efficient operation will magnify the efficiency. The second is that automation applied to an inefficient operation will magnify the inefficiency.
Bill Gates

Everybody gets so much information all day long that they lose their common sense.
Gertrude Stein

Do you realize if it weren't for Edison we'd be watching TV by candlelight?
Al Boliska

People who are really serious about software should make their own hardware.
Alan Kay

Getting information off the Internet is like taking a drink from a fire hydrant.
Mitchell Kapor

The world is very different now. For man holds in his mortal hands the power to abolish all forms of human poverty, and all forms of human life.
John F. Kennedy

Bill Gates is a very rich man today... and do you want to know why? The answer is one word: versions.
Dave Barry

All of the books in the world contain no more information than is broadcast as video in a single large American city in a single year. Not all bits have equal value.
Carl Sagan

The march of science and technology does not imply growing intellectual complexity in the lives of most people. It often means the opposite.
Thomas Sowell

The internet is a great way to get on the net.
Bob Dole

The Internet treats censorship as a malfunction and routes around it.
John Perry Barlow

Technological progress has merely provided us with more efficient means for going backwards.
Aldous Huxley

Civilization advances by extending the number of important operations which we can perform without thinking of them.
Alfred North Whitehead

The typewriting machine, when played with expression, is no more annoying than the piano when played by a sister or near relation.
Oscar Wilde

For a successful technology, reality must take precedence over public relations, for Nature cannot be fooled.
Richard P. Feynman

Soon silence will have passed into legend. Man has turned his back on silence. Day after day he invents machines and devices that increase noise and distract humanity from the essence of life, contemplation, meditation.
Jean Arp

Men have become the tools of their tools.
Henry David Thoreau

Globalization, as defined by rich people like us, is a very nice thing... you are talking about the Internet, you are talking about cell phones, you are talking about computers. This doesn't affect two-thirds of the people of the world.
Jimmy Carter

If we continue to develop our technology without wisdom or prudence, our servant may prove to be our executioner.
Omar N. Bradley

Building technical systems involves a lot of hard work and specialized knowledge: languages and protocols, coding and debugging, testing and refactoring.
Jesse James Garrett

The real problem is not whether machines think but whether men do.
B. F. Skinner

I am sorry to say that there is too much point to the wisecrack that life is extinct on other planets because their scientists were more advanced than ours.
John F. Kennedy

Champagne, if you are seeking the truth, is better than a lie detector. It encourages a man to be expansive, even reckless, while lie detectors are only a challenge to tell lies successfully.
Graham Greene

There are three roads to ruin; women, gambling and technicians. The most pleasant is with women, the quickest is with gambling, but the surest is with technicians.
Georges Pompidou

It's impossible to move, to live, to operate at any level without leaving traces, bits, seemingly meaningless fragments of personal information.
William Gibson

Congress will pass a law restricting public comment on the Internet to individuals who have spent a minimum of one hour actually accomplishing a specific task while on line.
Andy Grove

Real programmers can write assembly code in any language.
Larry Wall

Building one space station for everyone was and is insane: we should have built a dozen.
Larry Niven

Humanity is acquiring all the right technology for all the wrong reasons.
R. Buckminster Fuller

If it keeps up, man will atrophy all his limbs but the push-button finger.
Frank Lloyd Wright

One machine can do the work of fifty ordinary men. No machine can do the work of one extraordinary man.
Elbert Hubbard

Technology... is a queer thing. It brings you great gifts with one hand, and it stabs you in the back with the other.
Carrie P. Snow

Doing linear scans over an associative array is like trying to club someone to death with a loaded Uzi.
Larry Wall

The newest computer can merely compound, at speed, the oldest problem in the relations between human beings, and in the end the communicator will be confronted with the old problem, of what to say and how to say it.
Edward R. Murrow

We are the children of a technological age. We have found streamlined ways of doing much of our routine work. Printing is no longer the only way of reproducing books. Reading them, however, has not changed.
Lawrence Clark Powell

Microsoft isn't evil, they just make really crappy operating systems.
Linus Torvalds

We will create a civilization of the Mind in Cyberspace. May it be more humane and fair than the world your governments have made before.
John Perry Barlow

I have an almost religious zeal... not for technology per se, but for the Internet which is for me, the nervous system of mother Earth, which I see as a living creature, linking up.
Dan Millman

I think it is inevitable that people program poorly. Training will not substantially help matters. We have to learn to live with it.
Alan Perlis

Technology has to be invented or adopted.
Jared Diamond

Defect-free software does not exist.
Wietse Venema

It may not always be profitable at first for businesses to be online, but it is certainly going to be unprofitable not to be online.
Esther Dyson

You affect the world by what you browse.
Tim Berners-Lee

Sites need to be able to interact in one single, universal space.
Tim Berners-Lee

The Internet is the most important single development in the history of human communication since the invention of call waiting.
Dave Barry

We need a data network that can easily carry voice, instead of what we have today, a voice network struggling to carry data.
Reed Hundt

Microsoft is engaging in unlawful predatory practices that go well beyond the scope of fair competition.
Orrin Hatch

Gates is the ultimate programming machine. He believes everything can be defined, examined, reduced to essentials, and rearranged into a logical sequence that will achieve a particular goal.
Stewart Alsop

What the country needs are a few labor-making inventions.
Arnold H. Glasow

The only thing that I'd rather own than Windows is English, because then I could charge you two hundred and forty-nine dollars for the right to speak it.
Scott McNealy

The Internet is so big, so powerful and pointless that for some people it is a complete substitute for life.
Andrew Brown

Inventor: A person who makes an ingenious arrangement of wheels, levers and springs, and believes it civilization.
Ambrose Bierce

Technology is the knack of so arranging the world that we don't have to experience it.
Max Frisch

The system of nature, of which man is a part, tends to be self-balancing, self-adjusting, self-cleansing. Not so with technology.
E. F. Schumacher

It is questionable if all the mechanical inventions yet made have lightened the day's toil of any human being.
John Stuart Mill

The most important and urgent problems of the technology of today are no longer the satisfactions of the primary needs or of archetypal wishes, but the reparation of the evils and damages by the technology of yesterday.
Dennis Gabor

We've arranged a civilization in which most crucial elements profoundly depend on science and technology.
Carl Sagan

Telephone, n. An invention of the devil which abrogates some of the advantages of making a disagreeable person keep his distance.
Ambrose Bierce

Television is a medium because anything well done is rare.
Fred Allen

Technology is so much fun but we can drown in our technology. The fog of information can drive out knowledge.
Daniel J. Boorstin

I just invent, then wait until man comes around to needing what I've invented.
R. Buckminster Fuller

For my confirmation, I didn't get a watch and my first pair of long pants, like most Lutheran boys. I got a telescope. My mother thought it would make the best gift.
Wernher von Braun

The research rat of the future allows experimentation without manipulation of the real world. This is the cutting edge of modeling technology.
John Spencer

It is only when they go wrong that machines remind you how powerful they are.
Clive James

Technology is a gift of God. After the gift of life it is perhaps the greatest of God's gifts. It is the mother of civilizations, of arts and of sciences.
Freeman Dyson

What's sort of interesting about the whole public relations disaster that is the Net, in some ways, is that the fundamentals are really good.
Meg Whitman

Just as we could have rode into the sunset, along came the Internet, and it tripled the significance of the PC.
Andy Grove

People are stunned to hear that one company has data files on 185 million Americans.
Ralph Nader

Leaders have to act more quickly today. The pressure comes much faster.
Andy Grove

I think complexity is mostly sort of crummy stuff that is there because it's too expensive to change the interface.
Jaron Lanier

Relying on the government to protect your privacy is like asking a peeping tom to install your window blinds.
John Perry Barlow

The Internet is a telephone system that's gotten uppity.
Clifford Stoll

Cyberspace. A consensual hallucination experienced daily by billions of legitimate operators, in every nation, by children being taught mathematical concepts.
William Gibson

The 'Net is a waste of time, and that's exactly what's right about it.
William Gibson

The protean nature of the computer is such that it can act like a machine or like a language to be shaped and exploited.
Alan Kay

Style used to be an interaction between the human soul and tools that were limiting. In the digital era, it will have to come from the soul alone.
Jaron Lanier

The Linux philosophy is 'Laugh in the face of danger'. Oops. Wrong One. 'Do it yourself'. Yes, that's it.
Linus Torvalds

The machine does not isolate man from the great problems of nature but plunges him more deeply into them.
Antoine de Saint-Exupery

I used to think that cyberspace was fifty years away. What I thought was fifty years away, was only ten years away. And what I thought was ten years away... it was already here. I just wasn't aware of it yet.
Bruce Sterling

In software systems it is often the early bird that makes the worm.
Alan Perlis

We're still in the first minutes of the first day of the Internet revolution.
Scott Cook

Making duplicate copies and computer printouts of things no one wanted even one of in the first place is giving America a new sense of purpose.
Andy Rooney

Technology is making gestures precise and brutal, and with them men.
Theodor Adorno

What new technology does is create new opportunities to do a job that customers want done.
Tim O'Reilly

I think people have a vague sense that the television system is changing.
Michael K. Powell

The telephone is a 100-year-old technology. It's time for a change. Charging for phone calls is something you did last century.
Niklas Zennstrom

Our technological powers increase, but the side effects and potential hazards also escalate.
Alvin Toffler

The Web as I envisaged it, we have not seen it yet. The future is still so much bigger than the past.
Tim Berners-Lee

TEEN

It takes courage to grow up and become who you really are.
e. e. cummings

As a teenager I was so insecure. I was the type of guy that never fitted in because he never dared to choose. I was convinced I had absolutely no talent at all. For nothing. And that thought took away all my ambition too.
Johnny Depp

The greatest day in your life and mine is when we take total responsibility for our attitudes. That's the day we truly grow up.
John C. Maxwell

We never really grow up, we only learn how to act in public.
Bryan White

A fairly bright boy is far more intelligent and far better company than the average adult.
John B. S. Haldane

Being a teenager is an amazing time and a hard time. It's when you make your best friends - I have girls who will never leave my heart and I still talk to. You get the best and the worst as a teen. You have the best friendships and the worst heartbreaks.
Sophia Bush

My kids idea of a hard life is to live in a house with only one phone.
George Foreman

Growing up, I didn't have a lot of toys, and personal entertainment depended on individual ingenuity and imagination - think up a story and go live it for an afternoon.
Terry Brooks

Adolescents are not monsters. They are just people trying to learn how to make it among the adults in the world, who are probably not so sure themselves.
Virginia Satir

To an adolescent, there is nothing in the world more embarrassing than a parent.
Dave Barry

As a teenager you are at the last stage in your life when you will be happy to hear that the phone is for you.
Fran Lebowitz

You have teenagers thinking they're going to make millions as NBA stars when that's not realistic for even 1 percent of them. Becoming a scientist or engineer is.
Dean Kamen

Growing up, I've enjoyed hunting with my father.
Dale Earnhardt

Adolescence is just one big walking pimple.
Carol Burnett

All teenagers have this desire to somehow run away.
Joan Chen

Adolescence isn't just about prom or wearing sparkly dresses.
Jena Malone

Maturity is only a short break in adolescence.
Jules Feiffer

As I've said many times, the single most oppressed class in America right now is the teenager.
Joe Bob Briggs

Friendships in childhood are usually a matter of chance, whereas in adolescence they are most often a matter of choice.
David Elkind

Children, even infants, are capable of sympathy. But only after adolescence are we capable of compassion.
Louise J. Kaplan

Your modern teenager is not about to listen to advice from an old person, defined as a person who remembers when there was no Velcro.
Dave Barry

Heredity is what sets the parents of a teenager wondering about each other.
Laurence J. Peter

When I look in the mirror I see the girl I was when I was growing up, with braces, crooked teeth, a baby face and a skinny body.
Heather Locklear

Youth is the trustee of

prosperity.
Benjamin Disraeli

At the age of 16 I was already dreaming of having a baby because I felt myself to be an adult, but my mum forbid it. Right now, I feel like a teenager and I want to have fun for one or two more years before starting a family.
Milla Jovovich

I spent the first fourteen years of my life convinced that my looks were hideous. Adolescence is painful for everyone, I know, but mine was plain weird.
Uma Thurman

Teenagers today are more free to be themselves and to accept themselves.
John Knowles

Everybody is a teenage idol.
Barry Gibb

Trouble is, kids feel they have to shock their elders and each generation grows up into something harder to shock.
Ben Lindsey

I was a quiet teenager, introverted, full of angst.
Nigella Lawson

The most important role models should and could be parents and teachers. But that said, once you're a teenager you've probably gotten as much of an example from your parents as you're going to.
Andrew Shue

I have always had a sense that we are all pretty much alone in life, particularly in adolescence.
Robert Cormier

I mean, I'm pretty good in real life, but sometimes people seem surprised that I'm like a normal teenager and wear black nail polish and I'm just a little bit more edgy than the person I play on television.
Brittany Snow

I think you go through a period as a teenager of being quite cool and unaffected by things.
Miranda Otto

I think there's a time in your life where you don't feel like you fit in. I think everyone has that when you're a teenager, especially, and especially in the society we live in.
Matthew Vaughn

Can you imagine young people nowadays making a study of trigonometry for the fun of it? Well I did.
Clyde Tombaugh

I think growing up is difficult and it's a process that I'm always interested in, with kids and adults, they are often on two different universes.
Alice Hoffman

I'm a teenager, but I'm independent - I have my own apartment, I have my own life. And I think I have learned more than any of those teenagers have in school. I learned to be responsible, leaving my family and coming here alone.
Adriana Lima

But when I was a teenager, the idea of spending the rest of my life in a factory was real depressing. So the idea that I could become a musician opened up some possibilities I didn't see otherwise.
Wayne Kramer

When I was a teenager, I read a lot of Poe.
Dario Argento

I was a handful growing up.
Olivia Wilde

I wanted to be with the kind of people I'd grown up with, but you can't go back to them and be one of them again, no matter how hard you try.
Ethel Waters

Time scoots along pretty fast when you grow up.
Alan Ladd

My teenage years were exactly what they were supposed to be. Everybody has their own path. It's laid out for you. It's just up to you to walk it.
Justin Timberlake

I liked being a teenager, but I would not go back for all the tea in China.
Rob Lowe

Growing up, I wanted desperately to please, to be a good girl.
Claire Danes

I got through my teen years by being a bit of a clown.
Diane Cilento

I grew up in a house where nobody had to tell me to go to school every day and do my homework.
Constance Baker Motley

If you just watch a teenager, you see a lot of uncertainty.
Jamie Lee Curtis

Well, I could do it for a day, but I wouldn't want to be a teenager again. I really wouldn't.
Jamie Lee Curtis

This generation has given up on growth. They're just hoping for survival.
Penelope Spheeris

I have this sense that I didn't really start growing up until my twenties.
Winona Ryder

You've got to grow up sometime.
Winona Ryder

Adolescence is a new birth, for the higher and more completely human traits are now born.
G. Stanley Hall

Adolescence is when girls experience social pressure to put aside their authentic selves and to display only a small portion of their gifts.
Mary Pipher

Adolescence is the conjugator of childhood and adulthood.
Louise J. Kaplan

Teenagers who are never required to vacuum are living in one.
Fred G. Gosman

The toddler must say no in order to find out who she is. The adolescent says no to assert who she is not.
Louise J. Kaplan

So many people try to grow up too fast, and it's not fun! You should stay a kid as long as possible!
Vanessa Hudgens

TIME

Let him who would enjoy a good future waste none of his present.
Roger Babson

The best thing about the future is that it comes one day at a time.
Abraham Lincoln

Clocks slay time... time is dead as long as it is being clicked off by little wheels; only when the clock stops does time come to life.
William Faulkner

Lost time is never found again.
Benjamin Franklin

If you don't have time to do it right, when will you have time to do it over?
John Wooden

We must use time wisely and forever realize that the time is always ripe to do right.
Nelson Mandela

Time is money.
Benjamin Franklin

Time is the coin of your life. It is the only coin you have, and only you can determine how it will be spent. Be careful lest you let other people spend it for you.
Carl Sandburg

Time changes everything except something within us which is always surprised by change.
Thomas Hardy

I must govern the clock, not be governed by it.
Golda Meir

It is my feeling that Time ripens all things; with Time all things are revealed; Time is the father of truth.
Francois Rabelais

Men talk of killing time, while time quietly kills them.
Dion Boucicault

Finding some quiet time in your life, I think, is hugely important.
Mariel Hemingway

Waste your money and you're only out of money, but waste your time and you've lost a part of your life.
Michael LeBoeuf

Know how to live the time that is given you.
Dario Fo

For disappearing acts, it's hard to beat what happens to the eight hours supposedly left after eight of sleep and eight of work.
Doug Larson

The future is something which everyone reaches at the rate of 60 minutes an hour, whatever he does, whoever he is.
C. S. Lewis

Time is what we want most, but what we use worst.
William Penn

Everything happens to everybody sooner or later if there is time enough.
George Bernard Shaw

You can never plan the future by the past.
Edmund Burke

The time I kill is killing me.
Mason Cooley

Time = Life, Therefore, waste your time and waste of your life, or master your time and master your life.
Alan Lakein

Both young children and old people have a lot of time on their hands. That's probably why they get along so well.
Jonathan Carroll

Until you value yourself, you won't value your time. Until you value your time, you will not do anything with it.
M. Scott Peck

And when is there time to remember, to sift, to weigh, to estimate, to total?
Tillie Olsen

Time moves in one direction, memory in another.
William Gibson

By the time we've made it, we've had it.
Malcolm Forbes

You may delay, but time will not.
Benjamin Franklin

Time goes, you say? Ah, no! alas, time stays, we go.
Henry Austin Dobson

You must have been warned against letting the golden hours slip by; but some of them are golden only because we let them slip by.
James M. Barrie

What then is time? If no one asks me, I know what it is. If I wish to explain it to him who asks, I do not know.
Saint Augustine

Day, n. A period of twenty-four hours, mostly misspent.
Ambrose Bierce

I took some time out for life.
James L. Brooks

I want to go ahead of Father Time with a scythe of my own.
H. G. Wells

So during those first moments of the day, which are yours and yours alone, you can circumvent these boundaries and concentrate fully on spiritual matters. And this gives you the opportunity to plan the time management of the entire day.
Menachem Mendel Schneerson

But time growing old teaches all things.
Aeschylus

Time has been transformed, and we have changed; it has advanced and set us in motion; it has unveiled its face, inspiring us with bewilderment and exhilaration.
Khalil Gibran

Time is the wisest counselor of all.
Pericles

Lose not yourself in a far off time, seize the moment that is thine.
Friedrich Schiller

Work is hard. Distractions are plentiful. And time is short.
Adam Hochschild

Time is the school in which we learn, time is the fire in which we burn.
Delmore Schwartz

The clock talked loud. I threw it away, it scared me what it talked.
Tillie Olsen

Time is but the stream I go a-fishing in.
Henry David Thoreau

Well-timed silence is the most commanding expression.
Mark Helprin

Much may be done in those little shreds and patches of time which every day produces, and which most men throw away.
Charles Caleb Colton

Time brings all things to pass.
Aeschylus

The trouble with our times is that the future is not what it used to be.
Paul Valery

Time is the longest distance between two places.
Tennessee Williams

The present is a point just passed.
David Russell

Time is the father of truth, its mother is our mind.
Giordano Bruno

When in doubt, take more time.
John Zimmerman

My time is now.
John Turner

Time makes heroes but dissolves celebrities.
Daniel J. Boorstin

Time has a way of demonstrating that the most stubborn are the most intelligent.
Yevgeny Yevtushenko

People who cannot find time for recreation are obliged sooner or later to find time for illness.
John Wanamaker

Time is a dressmaker specializing in alterations.
Faith Baldwin

There's time enough, but none to spare.
Charles W. Chesnutt

Wisdom is the power to put our time and our knowledge to the proper use.
Thomas J. Watson

Time does not change us. It just unfolds us.
Max Frisch

We are time's subjects, and time bids be gone.
William Shakespeare

Time, whose tooth gnaws away everything else, is powerless against truth.
Thomas Huxley

TRAVEL

It is better to travel well than to arrive.
Buddha

Though we travel the world over to find the beautiful, we must carry it with us or we find it not.
Ralph Waldo Emerson

The World is a book, and those who do not travel read only a page.
Saint Augustine

What does it mean to pre-board? Do you get on before you get on?
George Carlin

I've always enjoyed traveling and having experience with different cultures and different people. But it's also a wonderful thing to be able to benefit and enable research, not only in our country but around the world.
Laurel Clark

We wander for distraction, but we travel for fulfillment.
Hilaire Belloc

One travels more usefully when alone, because he reflects more.
Thomas Jefferson

In America there are two classes of travel - first class, and with children.
Robert Benchley

Never go on trips with anyone you do not love.
Ernest Hemingway

To the lover of wilderness, Alaska is one of the most wonderful countries in the world.
John Muir

A man travels the world in search of what he needs and returns home to find it.
George Edward Moore

He travels the fastest who travels alone.
Rudyard Kipling

No one realizes how beautiful it is to travel until he comes home and rests his head on his old, familiar pillow.
Lin Yutang

We travel, some of us forever, to seek other states, other lives, other souls.
Anais Nin

To travel is to discover that everyone is wrong about other countries.
Aldous Huxley

I travel not to go anywhere, but to go. I travel for travel's sake. The great affair is to move.
Robert Louis Stevenson

Airplane travel is nature's way of making you look like your passport photo.
Al Gore

Certainly, travel is more than the seeing of sights; it is a change that goes on, deep and permanent, in the ideas of living.
Miriam Beard

Why, I'd like nothing better than to achieve some bold adventure, worthy of our trip.
Aristophanes

The traveler was active; he went strenuously in search of people, of adventure, of experience. The tourist is passive; he expects interesting things to happen to him. He goes "sight-seeing."
Daniel J. Boorstin

You define a good flight by negatives: you didn't get hijacked, you didn't crash, you didn't throw up, you weren't late, you weren't nauseated by the food. So you are grateful.
Paul Theroux

Travel, in the younger sort, is a part of education; in the elder, a part of experience.
Francis Bacon

I love short trips to New York; to me it is the finest three-day town on earth.
James Cameron

I am not a great cook, I am not a great artist, but I love art, and I love food, so I am the perfect traveller.
Michael Palin

Just got back from a pleasure trip: I took my mother-in-law to the airport.
Henny Youngman

I dislike feeling at home when I am abroad.
George Bernard Shaw

When I go on Japanese Airlines, I really love it because I like Japanese food.
Phil Collins

The traveler sees what he sees, the tourist sees what he has come to see.
Gilbert K. Chesterton

Travel becomes a strategy for accumulating photographs.
Susan Sontag

Travelers never think that they are the foreigners.
Mason Cooley

Airline travel is hours of boredom interrupted by moments of stark terror.
Al Boliska

Like all great travelers, I have seen more than I remember, and remember more than I have seen.
Benjamin Disraeli

Travel can be one of the most rewarding forms of introspection.
Lawrence Durrell

Travel is glamorous only in retrospect.
Paul Theroux

I never make a trip to the United States without visiting a supermarket. To me they are more fascinating than any fashion salon.
Wallis Simpson

Travel, which was once either a necessity or an adventure, has become very largely a commodity, and from all sides we are persuaded into thinking that it is a social requirement, too.
Jan Morris

Traveling is seeing; it is the implicit that we travel by.
Cynthia Ozick

A wise traveler never despises his own country.
William Hazlitt

It is not fit that every man should travel; it makes a wise man better, and a fool worse.
William Hazlitt

Tourists don't know where they've been, travelers don't know where they're going.
Paul Theroux

Traveling is the ruin of all happiness! There's no looking at a building after seeing Italy.
Fanny Burney

Everyone carries his own inch rule of taste, and amuses himself by applying it, triumphantly, wherever he travels.
Henry B. Adams

Our deeds still travel with us from afar, and what we have been makes us what we are.
George Eliot

Travelers repose and dream among my leaves.
William Blake

You know more of a road by having traveled it than by all the conjectures and descriptions in the world.
William Hazlitt

Traveling, you realize that differences are lost: each city takes to resembling all cities, places exchange their form, order, distances, a shapeless dust cloud invades the continents.
Italo Calvino

You get educated by traveling.
Solange Knowles

The world is a country which nobody ever yet knew by description; one must travel through it one's self to be acquainted with it.
Lord Chesterfield

The trouble with travelling back later on is that you can never repeat the same experience.
Michael Palin

If you travel first class, you think first class and you are more likely to play first class.
Ray Floyd

When the traveler goes alone he gets acquainted with himself.
Liberty Hyde Bailey

I think a major element of jetlag is psychological. Nobody ever tells me what time it is at home.
David Attenborough

My wife and I have so much fun when we travel and find anything... like stray cats and squirrels.
Eric Roberts

I get pretty much all the exercise I need walking down airport concourses carrying bags.
Guy Clark

On long haul flights I always drink loads and loads of water and eat light and healthy food.
Lisa Snowdon

A journey by Sea and Land, Five Hundred Miles, is not undertaken without money.
Lewis Hallam

My parents and my grandfather on my mom's side would travel the earth. They went to Australia and China, and they went to probably every soccer game I ever played.
Brandi Chastain

The attention of a traveler, should be particularly turned, in the first place, to the various works of Nature, to mark the distinctions of the climates he may explore, and to offer such useful observations on the different productions as may occur.
William Bartram

When I'm in London I do have the convenience of being close to St James Park which is also good for me because it gives me an excuse to get out and get some much needed exercise!
David Blunkett

The hardest part is to travel, and to be away from your family.
Glenn Tipton

No matter where I've been overseas, the food stinks, except in Italy.
Carmen Electra

Travelling expands the mind rarely.
Hans Christian Andersen

The time to enjoy a European trip is about three weeks after unpacking.
George Ade

Reminds me of my safari in Africa. Somebody forgot the corkscrew and for several days we had to live on nothing but food and water.
W. C. Fields

In both business and personal life, I've always found that travel inspires me more than anything else I do. Evidence of the languages, cultures, scenery, food, and design sensibilities that I discover all over the world can be found in every piece of my jewelry.
Ivanka Trump

TRUST

Love all, trust a few, do wrong to none.
William Shakespeare

For every good reason there is to lie, there is a better reason to tell the truth.
Bo Bennett

A lie can travel half way around the world while the truth is putting on its shoes.
Charles Spurgeon

Never trust anyone completely but God. Love people, but put your full trust only in God.
Lawrence Welk

Learning to trust is one of life's most difficult tasks.
Isaac Watts

To be trusted is a greater compliment than being loved.
George MacDonald

A man who trusts nobody is apt to be the kind of man nobody trusts.
Harold MacMillan

The trust of the innocent is the liar's most useful tool.
Stephen King

Depend upon yourself. Make your judgment trustworthy by trusting it. You can develop good judgment as you do the muscles of your body - by judicious, daily exercise. To be known as a man of sound judgment will be much in your favor.
Grantland Rice

I can trust my friends These people force me to examine myself, encourage me to grow.
Cher

A half truth, like half a brick, is always more forcible as an argument than a whole one. It carries better.
Stephen Leacock

The more you trust your intuition, the more empowered you become, the stronger you become, and the happier you become.
Gisele Bundchen

Don't trust anyone over 30.
Pat Boone

I always trust my gut reaction; it's always right.
Kiana Tom

Someone who thinks the world is always cheating him is right. He is missing that wonderful feeling of trust in someone or something.
Eric Hoffer

You can't trust water: Even a straight stick turns crooked in it.
W. C. Fields

How can people trust the harvest, unless they see it sown?
Mary Renault

I would rather trust a woman's instinct than a man's reason.
Stanley Baldwin

Never trust anyone who wants what you've got. Friend or no, envy is an overwhelming emotion.
Eubie Blake

Never be afraid to trust an unknown future to a known God.
Corrie Ten Boom

Trust yourself. Create the kind of self that you will be happy to live with all your life. Make the most of yourself by fanning the tiny, inner sparks of possibility into flames of achievement.
Golda Meir

Trust your hunches. They're usually based on facts filed away just below the conscious level.
Joyce Brothers

Trust is to human relationships what faith is to gospel living. It is the beginning place, the foundation upon which more can be built. Where trust is, love can flourish.
Barbara Smith

It's a delight to trust somebody so completely.
Jeff Goldblum

If we really want to be full and generous in spirit, we have no choice but to trust at some level.
Rita Dove

I have to trust what I do and then do it.
Ednita Nazario

Few delights can equal the presence of one whom we trust utterly.
George MacDonald

Trust yourself, then you will know how to live.
Johann Wolfgang von Goethe

Trust your own instinct. Your mistakes might as well be your own, instead of someone else's.
Billy Wilder

I believe fundamental honesty is the keystone of business.
Harvey S. Firestone

I never trusted good-looking boys.
Frances McDormand

I get along with guys; most of my friends are guys. It's easier to trust men sometimes. I only have a few close girlfriends that I trust.
Paris Hilton

You can't trust anybody with power.
Newt Gingrich

Men are able to trust one another, knowing the exact degree of dishonesty they are entitled to expect.
Stephen Leacock

In these times, God's people must trust him for rest of body and soul.
David Wilkerson

Trust yourself, you know more than you think you do.
Benjamin Spock

When I get logical, and I don't trust my instincts - that's when I get in trouble.
Angelina Jolie

Trust should be the basis for all our moral training.
Robert Baden-Powell

Trust in yourself. Your perceptions are often far more accurate than you are willing to believe.
Claudia Black

You have got to discover you, what you do, and trust it.
Barbra Streisand

I repeat... that all power is a trust; that we are accountable for its exercise; that from the people and for the people all springs, and all must exist.
Benjamin Disraeli

Put your trust in the Lord and go ahead. Worry gets you no place.
Roy Acuff

Trust in what you love, continue to do it, and it will take you where you need to go.
Natalie Goldberg

Men trust their ears less than their eyes.
Herodotus

Never trust sheep.
Ryan Stiles

Trust your ability!
Itzhak Perlman

Who would not rather trust and be deceived?
Eliza Cook

Trust in God - she will provide.
Emmeline Pankhurst

Trust everybody, but cut the cards.
Finley Peter Dunne

Trust no friend without faults, and love a woman, but no angel.
Doris Lessing

Trust not too much to appearances.
Virgil

Would you want to do business with a person who was 99% honest?
Sydney Madwed

Whoever has trusted a woman has trusted deceivers.
Hesiod

Trust is a great force multiplier.
Tom Ridge

We must trust our own thinking. Trust where we're going. And get the job done.
Wilma Mankiller

Trusting your individual uniqueness challenges you to lay yourself open.
James Broughton

WAR

Every gun that is made, every warship launched, every rocket fired, signifies in the final sense a theft from those who hunger and are not fed, those who are cold and are not clothed.
Dwight D. Eisenhower

We shall defend our island, whatever the cost may be, we shall fight on the beaches, we shall fight on the landing grounds, we shall fight in the fields and in the streets, we shall fight in the hills; we shall never surrender.
Winston Churchill

He who joyfully marches to music in rank and file has already earned my contempt. He has been given a large brain by mistake, since for him the spinal cord would suffice.
Albert Einstein

If we don't end war, war will end us.
H. G. Wells

War is an ugly thing, but not the ugliest of things. The decayed and degraded state of moral and patriotic feeling which thinks that nothing is worth war is much worse.
John Stuart Mill

The object of war is not to die for your country but to make the other bastard die for his.
George S. Patton

In peace, sons bury their fathers. In war, fathers bury their sons.
Herodotus

All war is deception.
Sun Tzu

When the rich wage war, it's the poor who die.
Jean-Paul Sartre

War will exist until that distant day when the conscientious objector enjoys the same reputation and prestige that the warrior does today.
John F. Kennedy

Never in the field of human conflict was so much owed by so many to so few.
Winston Churchill

It is forbidden to kill; therefore all murderers are punished unless they kill in large numbers and to the sound of trumpets.
Voltaire

A soldier will fight long and hard for a bit of colored ribbon.
Napoleon Bonaparte

Never think that war, no matter how necessary, nor how justified, is not a crime.
Ernest Hemingway

One of the greatest casualties of the war in Vietnam is the Great Society... shot down on the battlefield of Vietnam.
Martin Luther King, Jr.

I must study politics and war that my sons may have liberty to study mathematics and philosophy.
John Adams

War does not determine who is right - only who is left.
Bertrand Russell

In modern war... you will die like a dog for no good reason.
Ernest Hemingway

All wars are civil wars, because all men are brothers.
Francois Fenelon

It is well that war is so terrible. We should grow too fond of it.
Robert E. Lee

The best weapon against an enemy is another enemy.
Friedrich Nietzsche

Yesterday, December seventh, 1941, a date which will live in infamy, the United States of America was suddenly and deliberately attacked by naval and air forces of the Empire of Japan.
Franklin D. Roosevelt

Mankind must put an end to war before war puts an end to mankind.
John F. Kennedy

Ours is a world of nuclear giants and ethical infants. We know more about war that we know about peace, more about killing that we know about living.
Omar N. Bradley

Older men declare war. But it is the youth that must fight and die.
Herbert Hoover

I'm fed up to the ears with old men dreaming up wars for young men to die in.
George McGovern

The release of atomic energy has not created a new problem. It has merely made more urgent the necessity of solving an existing one.
Albert Einstein

There is no instance of a nation benefitting from prolonged warfare.
Sun Tzu

If it's natural to kill, how come men have to go into training to learn how?
Joan Baez

In my dreams I hear again the crash of guns, the rattle of musketry, the strange, mournful mutter of the battlefield.
Douglas MacArthur

I have never advocated war except as a means of peace.
Ulysses S. Grant

There will one day spring from the brain of science a machine or force so fearful in its potentialities, so absolutely terrifying, that even man, the fighter, who will dare torture and death in order to inflict torture and death, will be appalled, and so abandon war forever.
Thomas A. Edison

There is no avoiding war; it can only be postponed to the advantage of others.
Niccolo Machiavelli

I have not yet begun to fight!
John Paul Jones

It seems like such a terrible shame that innocent civilians have to get hurt in wars, otherwise combat would be such a wonderfully healthy way to rid the human race of unneeded trash.
Fred Woodworth

Only the dead have seen the end of the war.
George Santayana

The direct use of force is such a poor solution to any problem, it is generally employed only by small children and large nations.
David Friedman

Ten soldiers wisely led will beat a hundred without a head.
Euripides

One may know how to gain a victory, and know not how to use it.
Pedro Calderon de la Barca

The first casualty when war comes is truth.
Hiram Johnson

Man has no right to kill his brother. It is no excuse that he does so in uniform: he only adds the infamy of servitude to the crime of murder.
Percy Bysshe Shelley

You can't say civilization don't advance... in every war they kill you in a new way.
Will Rogers

When the war of the giants is over the wars of the pygmies will begin.
Winston Churchill

Sweat saves blood.
Erwin Rommel

The military don't start wars. Politicians start wars.
William Westmoreland

The basic problems facing the world today are not susceptible to a military solution.
John F. Kennedy

We are going to have peace even if we have to fight for it.
Dwight D. Eisenhower

An unjust peace is better than a just war.
Marcus Tullius Cicero

I do not believe that the men who served in uniform in Vietnam have been given the credit they deserve. It was a difficult war against an unorthodox enemy.
William Westmoreland

There was never a good war, or a bad peace.
Benjamin Franklin

No country can act wisely simultaneously in every part of the globe at every moment of time.
Henry A. Kissinger

A visitor from Mars could easily pick out the civilized nations. They have the best implements of war.
Herbert V. Prochnow

What is human warfare but just this; an effort to make the laws of God and nature take sides with one party.
Henry David Thoreau

It has too often been too easy for rulers and governments to incite man to war.
Lester B. Pearson

Wars have never hurt anybody except the people who die.
Salvador Dali

War grows out of the desire of the individual to gain advantage at the expense of his fellow man.
Napoleon Hill

War is only a cowardly escape from the problems of peace.
Thomas Mann

Patriots always talk of dying for their country and never of killing for their country.
Bertrand Russell

What is the use of physicians like myself trying to help parents to bring up children healthy and happy, to have them killed in such numbers for a cause that is ignoble?
Benjamin Spock

Sometime they'll give a war and nobody will come.
Carl Sandburg

We have war when at least one of the parties to a conflict wants something more than it wants peace.
Jeane Kirkpatrick

War is hell.
William Tecumseh Sherman

The power to wage war is the power to wage war successfully.
Charles Evans Hughes

The Establishment center... has led us into the stupidest and cruelest war in all history. That war is a moral and political disaster - a terrible cancer eating away at the soul of our nation.
George McGovern

War makes thieves and peace hangs them.
George Herbert

You can no more win a war than you can win an earthquake.
Jeannette Rankin

War would end if the dead could return.
Stanley Baldwin

John Dalton's records, carefully preserved for a century, were destroyed during the World War II bombing of Manchester. It is not only the living who are killed in war.
Isaac Asimov

The way to win an atomic war is to make certain it never starts.
Omar N. Bradley

There is nothing that war has ever achieved that we could not better achieve without it.
Havelock Ellis

War is not an adventure. It is a disease. It is like typhus.
Antoine de Saint-Exupery

We are all tourists in history, and irony is what we win in wars.
Anatole Broyard

War is a series of catastrophes which result in victory.
Albert Pike

War is the unfolding of miscalculations.
Barbara Tuchman

To walk through the ruined cities of Germany is to feel an actual doubt about the continuity of civilization.
George Orwell

The scenes on this field would have cured anybody of war.
William Tecumseh Sherman

We have been travelling through a cloud. The sky has been dark ever since the war began.
Black Kettle

It was definitely a part of our life. I mean, my mom had both her brothers and her fiancee in Vietnam at the same time, so it wasn't just my dad's story, it was my mom's story too. And we definitely grew up listening to the stories.
Vanessa Kerry

When the question arose whether I, as a member of the royal family, should take part in active combat in the Falklands, there was no question in her mind, and it only took her two days to sort the issue.
Prince Andrew

WEDDING

My advice to you is get married: if you find a good wife you'll be happy; if not, you'll become a philosopher.
Socrates

A wedding anniversary is the celebration of love, trust, partnership, tolerance and tenacity. The order varies for any given year.
Paul Sweeney

I was married by a judge. I should have asked for a jury.
Groucho Marx

A bride at her second marriage does not wear a veil. She wants to see what she is getting.
Helen Rowland

It's a funny thing that when a man hasn't anything on earth to worry about, he goes off and gets married.
Robert Frost

Love is the master key that opens the gates of happiness.
Oliver Wendell Holmes

A wedding is just like a funeral except that you get to smell your own flowers.
Grace Hansen

I have great hopes that we shall love each other all our lives as much as if we had never married at all.
Lord Byron

The real act of marriage takes place in the heart, not in the ballroom or church or synagogue. It's a choice you make - not just on your wedding day, but over and over again - and that choice is reflected in the way you treat your husband or wife.
Barbara de Angelis

Christmas carols always brought tears to my eyes. I also cry at weddings. I should have cried at a couple of my own.
Ethel Merman

When it's over, I want to say: all my life I was a bride married to amazement. I was the bridegroom, taking the world into my arms.
Mary Oliver

An invitation to a wedding invokes more trouble than a summons to a police court.
William Feather

A young bride is like a plucked flower; but a guilty wife is like a flower that had been walked over.
Honore de Balzac

I remember when I was in school, they would ask, 'What are you going to be when you grow up?' and then you'd have to draw a picture of it. I drew a picture of myself as a bride.
Gwen Stefani

Bride: A woman with a fine prospect of happiness behind her.
Ambrose Bierce

The chain of wedlock is so heavy that it takes two to carry it - and sometimes three.
Heraclitus

I don't know nothing about no marriages or nothing. I ain't even never been to a wedding.
Mike Epps

The first thing I did when I sold my book was buy a new wedding ring for my wife and asked her to marry me all over again.
Nicholas Sparks

I think that weddings have probably been crashed since the beginning of time. Cavemen crashed them. You go to meet girls. It makes sense.
Christopher Walken

The trouble with wedlock is that there's not enough wed and too much lock.
Christopher Morley

Women who marry early are often overly enamored of the kind of man who looks great in wedding pictures and passes the maid of honor his telephone number.
Anna Quindlen

The Wedding March always reminds me of the music played when soldiers go into battle.
Heinrich Heine

Never get married in the morning - you never know who you might meet that night.
Paul Hornung

When the wedding march sounds the resolute approach, the clock no longer ticks, it tolls the hour. The figures in the aisle are no longer individuals, they symbolize the human race.
Anne Morrow Lindbergh

Wedding: the point at which a man stops toasting a woman and begins roasting her.
Helen Rowland

That is ever the way. 'Tis all jealousy to the bride and good wishes to the corpse.
James M. Barrie

I am about to be married, and am of course in all the misery of a man in pursuit of happiness.
Lord Byron

A gloomy guest fits not a wedding feast.
Friedrich Schiller

In Hollywood, brides keep the bouquets and throw away the groom.
Groucho Marx

Saw a wedding in the church. It was strange to see what delight we married people have to see these poor fools decoyed into our condition.
Samuel Pepys

No jealousy their dawn of love overcast, nor blasted were their wedded days with strife; each season looked delightful as it past, to the fond husband and the faithful wife.
James Beattie

Getting married, for me, was the best thing I ever did. I was suddenly beset with an immense sense of release, that we have something more important than our separate selves, and that is the marriage. There's immense happiness that can come from working towards that.
Nick Cave

Of course, I do have a slight advantage over the rest of you. It helps in a pinch to be able to remind your bride that you gave up a throne for her.
King Edward VIII

In my 50s I'll be dancing at my children's weddings.
Michael J. Fox

O month when they who love must love and wed.
Helen Hunt Jackson

I'm one of those people who has always been a bridesmaid.
Piper Laurie

I really did put up all my wedding pictures on my website. And I swear to you, my wedding pictures got downloaded just as much as my bikini pictures.
Cindy Margolis

When I decided to get married at 40, I couldn't find a dress with the modernity or sophistication I wanted. That's when I saw the opportunity for a wedding gown business.
Vera Wang

When I design a wedding dress with a bustle, it has to be one the bride can dance in. I love the idea that something is practical and still looks great.
Vera Wang

The one thing that I'm in charge of in this wedding is the food.
Rob Mariano

In the '50s, a lot of girls never saw beyond the wedding day.
Helen Reddy

There's a higher form of happiness in commitment. I'm counting on it.
Claire Forlani

I want the big drama. I always said I don't want a wedding I want a parade.
Star Jones

You may invite the entire 35th Division to your wedding if you want to. I guess it's going to be yours as well as mine. We might as well have the church full while we are at it.
Bess Truman

It was only literally hours after the wedding when he felt he didn't have to keep up the facade.
Trisha Goddard

When he came back from downtown, he had forgotten to bring his license, his identification, the $2 for the wedding license. So we got married two days later.
Eydie Gorme

I sang a song at my sister's wedding. My mother forced me into that, too. But that one felt all right.
Adam Sandler

A person's character is but half formed till after wedlock.
Charles Simmons

I chose my wife, as she did her wedding gown, for qualities that would wear well.
Oliver Goldsmith

I'd imagine my wedding as a fairy tale... huge, beautiful and white.
Paris Hilton

WISDOM

Do not go where the path may lead, go instead where there is no path and leave a trail.
Ralph Waldo Emerson

By three methods we may learn wisdom: First, by reflection, which is noblest; Second, by imitation, which is easiest; and third by experience, which is the bitterest.
Confucius

A good head and a good heart are always a formidable combination.
Nelson Mandela

A wise man is superior to any insults which can be put upon him, and the best reply to unseemly behavior is patience and moderation.
Moliere

A fool flatters himself, a wise man flatters the fool.
Edward G. Bulwer-Lytton

The only true wisdom is in knowing you know nothing.
Socrates

Adopt the pace of nature: her secret is patience.
Ralph Waldo Emerson

If you're trying to achieve, there will be roadblocks. I've had them; everybody has had them. But obstacles don't have to stop you. If you run into a wall, don't turn around and give up. Figure out how to climb it, go through it, or work around it.
Michael Jordan

Winners never quit and quitters never win.
Vince Lombardi

A mistake is simply another way of doing things.
Katharine Graham

Always keep an open mind and a compassionate heart.
Phil Jackson

I'd rather regret the things I've done than regret the things I haven't done.
Lucille Ball

If you talk to a man in a language he understands, that goes to his head. If you talk to him in his language, that goes to his heart.
Nelson Mandela

Experience is not what happens to you; it's what you do with what happens to you.
Aldous Huxley

A man begins cutting his wisdom teeth the first time he bites off more than he can chew.
Herb Caen

Discipline is the bridge between goals and accomplishment.
Jim Rohn

As you walk down the fairway of life you must smell the roses, for you only get to play one round.
Ben Hogan

Climb the mountains and get their good tidings.
John Muir

Honesty is the first chapter in the book of wisdom.
Thomas Jefferson

The teacher who is indeed wise does not bid you to enter the house of his wisdom but rather leads you to the threshold of your mind.
Khalil Gibran

Be happy. It's one way of being wise.
Sidonie Gabrielle Colette

Give me a lever long enough and a fulcrum on which to place it, and I shall move the world.
Archimedes

It's not what you look at that matters, it's what you see.
Henry David Thoreau

Every man is a damn fool for at least five minutes every day; wisdom consists in not exceeding the limit.
Elbert Hubbard

Common sense in an uncommon degree is what the world calls wisdom.
Samuel Taylor Coleridge

A poem begins in delight and ends in wisdom.
Robert Frost

Cleverness is not wisdom.
Euripides

The art of being wise is the art of knowing what to overlook.
William James

Honesty is the best policy.
Benjamin Franklin

If you only have a hammer, you tend to see every problem as a nail.
Abraham Maslow

Obstacles are those frightful things you see when you take your eyes off your goal.
Henry Ford

When written in Chinese, the word "crisis" is composed of two characters. One represents danger and the other represents opportunity.
John F. Kennedy

The less you talk, the more you're listened to.
Abigail Van Buren

Don't follow any advice, no matter how good, until you feel as deeply in your spirit as you think in your mind that the counsel is wise.
Joan Rivers

Reality is merely an illusion, albeit a very persistent one.
Albert Einstein

We should not judge people by their peak of excellence; but by the distance they have traveled from the point where they started.
Henry Ward Beecher

From the errors of others, a wise man corrects his own.
Publilius Syrus

In every walk with nature one receives far more than he seeks.
John Muir

All this worldly wisdom was once the unamiable heresy of some wise man.
Henry David Thoreau

Wisdom, compassion, and courage are the three universally recognized moral qualities of men.
Confucius

Better mad with the rest of the world than wise alone.
Baltasar Gracian

Wise sayings often fall on barren ground, but a kind word is never thrown away.
Arthur Helps

There is a wisdom of the head, and a wisdom of the heart.
Charles Dickens

Good nature is worth more than knowledge, more than money, more than honor, to the persons who possess it.
Henry Ward Beecher

Wisdom begins in wonder.
Socrates

Don't taunt the alligator until after you've crossed the creek.
Dan Rather

The best way to predict the future is to invent it.
Alan Kay

Turn your wounds into wisdom.
Oprah Winfrey

It's better to be a lion for a day than a sheep all your life.
Elizabeth Kenny

Nobody can give you wiser advice than yourself.
Marcus Tullius Cicero

Does wisdom perhaps appear on the earth as a raven which is inspired by the smell of carrion?
Friedrich Nietzsche

It is a characteristic of wisdom not to do desperate things.
Henry David Thoreau

It requires wisdom to understand wisdom: the music is nothing if the audience is deaf.
Walter Lippmann

To be satisfied with a little, is the greatest wisdom; and he that increaseth his riches, increaseth his cares; but a contented mind is a hidden treasure, and trouble find eth it not.
Akhenaton

When it is obvious that the goals cannot be reached, don't adjust the goals, adjust the action steps.
Confucius

The more sand that has escaped from the hourglass of our life, the clearer we should see through it.
Jean Paul

A prudent question is one-half of wisdom.
Francis Bacon

Wisdom is the reward you get for a lifetime of listening when you'd have preferred to talk.
Doug Larson

He who lives by the crystal ball soon learns to eat ground glass.
Edgar R. Fiedler

It is a common experience that a problem difficult at night is resolved in the morning after the committee of sleep has worked on it.
John Steinbeck

Never tell people how to do things. Tell them what to do and they will surprise you with their ingenuity.
George S. Patton

We are made wise not by the recollection of our past, but by the responsibility for our future.
George Bernard Shaw

Better be wise by the misfortunes of others than by your own.
Aesop

He dares to be a fool, and that is the first step in the direction of wisdom.
James Huneker

Ignorant men raise questions that wise men answered a thousand years ago.
Johann Wolfgang von Goethe

Almost every wise saying has an opposite one, no less wise, to balance it.
George Santayana

Knowledge comes, but wisdom lingers.
Alfred Lord Tennyson

Nine-tenths of wisdom is being wise in time.
Theodore Roosevelt

It is better to risk starving to death then surrender. If you give up on your dreams, what's left?
Jim Carrey

If you want to be found stand where the seeker seeks.
Sidney Lanier

Never let a fool kiss you, or a kiss fool you.
Joey Adams

It takes a great man to give sound advice tactfully, but a greater to accept it graciously.
Logan P. Smith

It is the nature of the wise to resist pleasures, but the foolish to be a slave to them.
Epictetus

Repeat anything often enough and it will start to become you.
Tom Hopkins

Patience is the companion of wisdom.
Saint Augustine

In seeking wisdom thou art wise; in imagining that thou hast attained it - thou art a fool.
Lord Chesterfield

Winning is not everything, but wanting to win is.
Vince Lombardi

The greatest obstacle to discovery is not ignorance - it is the illusion of knowledge.
Daniel J. Boorstin

You have to find out what's right for you, so it's trial and error. You are going to be all right if you accept realistic goals for yourself.
Teri Garr

I didn't get where I am today by worryin' about how I'd feel tomorrow.
Ron White

Honesty is the rarest wealth anyone can possess, and yet all the honesty in the world ain't lawful tender for a loaf of bread.
Josh Billings

Wisdom doesn't necessarily come with age. Sometimes age just shows up all by itself.
Tom Wilson

There are three faithful friends - an old wife, an old dog, and ready money.
Benjamin Franklin

The truth is not for all men, but only for those who seek it.
Ayn Rand

Some folks are wise and some are otherwise.
Tobias Smollett

He who devotes sixteen hours a day to hard study may become at sixty as wise as he thought himself at twenty.
Mary Wilson Little

To conquer fear is the beginning of wisdom.
Bertrand Russell

The young man knows the rules, but the old man knows the exceptions.
Oliver Wendell Holmes

It is much more difficult to measure nonperformance than performance.
Harold S. Geneen

Memory is the mother of all

wisdom.
Aeschylus

You can't sweep other people off their feet, if you can't be swept off your own.
Clarence Day

We can't command our love, but we can our actions.
Arthur Conan Doyle

Wisdom stands at the turn in the road and calls upon us publicly, but we consider it false and despise its adherents.
Khalil Gibran

The older I grow the more I distrust the familiar doctrine that age brings wisdom.
H. L. Mencken

Nature and books belong to the eyes that see them.
Ralph Waldo Emerson

Counsel woven into the fabric of real life is wisdom.
Walter Benjamin

Wisdom is found only in truth.
Johann Wolfgang von Goethe

Wisdom is not wisdom when it is derived from books alone.
Horace

Public opinion is no more than this: what people think that other people think.
Alfred Austin

Learning sleeps and snores in libraries, but wisdom is everywhere, wide awake, on tiptoe.
Josh Billings

No man was ever wise by chance.
Lucius Annaeus Seneca

It is impossible to love and to be wise.
Francis Bacon

When I can look life in the eyes, grown calm and very coldly wise, life will have given me the truth, and taken in exchange - my youth.
Sara Teasdale

The wisdom of the wise and the experience of the ages are perpetuated by quotations.
Benjamin Disraeli

Man is only great when he acts from passion.
Benjamin Disraeli

The end of wisdom is to dream high enough to lose the dream in the seeking of it.
William Faulkner

Of prosperity mortals can never have enough.
Aeschylus

People don't notice whether it's winter or summer when they're happy.
Anton Chekhov

The wheel that squeaks the loudest is the one that gets the grease.
Josh Billings

The doors of wisdom are never shut.
Benjamin Franklin

If you believe the doctors, nothing is wholesome; if you believe the theologians, nothing is innocent; if you believe the military, nothing is safe.
Lord Salisbury

Start wide, expand further, and never look back.
Arnold Schwarzenegger

It has long been an axiom of mine that the little things are infinitely the most important.
Arthur Conan Doyle

Self-suggestion makes you master of yourself.
W. Clement Stone

Wisdom is always an overmatch for strength.
Phil Jackson

It is the neglect of timely repair that makes rebuilding necessary.
Richard Whately

What is man's ultimate direction in life? It is to look for love, truth, virtue, and beauty.
Shinichi Suzuki

Who is wise in love, love most, say least.
Alfred Lord Tennyson

The future has already arrived. It's just not evenly distributed yet.
William Gibson

Perspective is worth 80 IQ points.
Alan Kay

The truest wisdom is a resolute determination.
Napoleon Bonaparte

Wise kings generally have wise counselors; and he must be a wise man himself who is capable of distinguishing one.
Diogenes

It is astonishing with how little wisdom mankind can be governed, when that little wisdom is its own.
William Ralph Inge

Wisdom is knowing what to do next; virtue is doing it.
David Starr Jordan

Never does nature say one thing and wisdom another.
Juvenal

It is great folly to wish to be wise all alone.
Francois de La Rochefoucauld

In action a great heart is the chief qualification. In work, a great head.
Arthur Schopenhauer

The opportunity for brotherhood presents itself every time you meet a human being.
Jane Wyman

Wise men make more opportunities than they find.
Francis Bacon

Few of the many wise apothegms which have been uttered have prevented a single foolish action.
Thomas B. Macaulay

Wisdom begins at the end.
Daniel Webster

Wisdom is the quality that keeps you from getting into situations where you need it.
Doug Larson

Wisdom outweighs any wealth.
Sophocles

Wisdom is a sacred communion.
Victor Hugo

Wisdom is the supreme part of happiness.
Sophocles

Virtues are acquired through endeavor, which rests wholly upon yourself.
Sidney Lanier

Rarely promise, but, if lawful, constantly perform.
William Penn

The wisdom of the wise is an uncommon degree of common sense.
Dean Inge

The difference between chirping out of turn and a faux pas depends on what kind of a bar you're in.
Wilson Mizner

Life is a travelling to the edge of knowledge, then a leap taken.
David Herbert Lawrence

Tis but a part we see, and not
a whole.
Alexander Pope

WOMEN

I don't know who invented high heels, but all women owe him a lot.
Marilyn Monroe

Ah, women. They make the highs higher and the lows more frequent.
Friedrich Nietzsche

Women don't want to hear what you think. Women want to hear what they think - in a deeper voice.
Bill Cosby

Women have always been the strong ones of the world. The men are always seeking from women a little pillow to put their heads down on. They are always longing for the mother who held them as infants.
Coco Chanel

Women who seek to be equal with men lack ambition.
Timothy Leary

When women go wrong, men go right after them.
Mae West

Clever and attractive women do not want to vote; they are willing to let men govern as long as they govern men.
George Bernard Shaw

No doubt exists that all women are crazy; it's only a question of degree.
W. C. Fields

I don't know why women want any of the things men have when one the things that women have is men.
Coco Chanel

Man does not control his own fate. The women in his life do that for him.
Groucho Marx

Men and women belong to different species and communications between them is still in its infancy.
Bill Cosby

I always play women I would date.
Angelina Jolie

Women cannot complain about men anymore until they start getting better taste in them.
Bill Maher

I do not wish women to have power over men; but over themselves.
Mary Wollstonecraft Shelley

Women think with their whole bodies and they see things as a whole more than men do.
Dorothy Day

Being a sex symbol has to do with an attitude, not looks. Most men think it's looks, most women know otherwise.
Kathleen Turner

Women hold up half the sky.
Mao Tse-Tung

I like intelligent women. When you go out, it shouldn't be a staring contest.
Frank Sinatra

All women should know how to take care of children. Most of them will have a husband some day.
Franklin P. Jones

America is a land where men govern, but women rule.
John Mason Brown

I've yet to be on a campus where most women weren't worrying about some aspect of combining marriage, children, and a career. I've yet to find one where many men were worrying about the same thing.
Gloria Steinem

I never realized until lately that women were supposed to be the inferior sex.
Katharine Hepburn

I measure the progress of a community by the degree of progress which women have achieved.
B. R. Ambedkar

Plain women know more about men than beautiful women do.
Katharine Hepburn

Men are governed by lines of intellect - women: by curves of emotion.
James Joyce

Men are April when they woo, December when they wed. Maids are May when they are maids, but the sky changes when they are wives.
William Shakespeare

Speaking very generally, I find that women are spiritually, emotionally, and often physically stronger than men.
Gary Oldman

Some of us are becoming the men we wanted to marry.
Gloria Steinem

Women, can't live with them, can't live without them.
Desiderius Erasmus

I think that maybe if women and children were in charge we would get somewhere.
James Thurber

In love, women are professionals, men are amateurs.
Francois Truffaut

If women were particular about men's characters, they would never get married at all.
George Bernard Shaw

For women's tears are but the sweat of eyes.
Juvenal

Women need real moments of solitude and self-reflection to balance out how much of ourselves we give away.
Barbara de Angelis

You see a lot of smart guys with dumb women, but you hardly ever see a smart woman with a dumb guy.
Erica Jong

Women have simple tastes. They get pleasure out of the conversation of children in arms and men in love.
H. L. Mencken

If men knew all that women think, they would be twenty times more audacious.
Alphonse Karr

There is a physical relationship with a woman that you don't have with anybody else, but that's not about love. Love is a spiritual thing.
Ziggy Marley

Men should only believe half of what women say. But which half?
Jean Giraudoux

You can tell the strength of a nation by the women behind its men.
Benjamin Disraeli

Men are by nature merely indifferent to one another; but women are by nature enemies.
Arthur Schopenhauer

I'm not denyin' the women are foolish. God Almighty made 'em to match the men.
George Eliot

Women want mediocre men, and men are working to be as mediocre as possible.
Margaret Mead

In our society, the women who break down barriers are those who ignore limits.
Arnold Schwarzenegger

I demanded more rights for women because I know what women had to put up with.
Evita Peron

All issues are women's issues - and there are several that are just women's business.
Eddie Bernice Johnson

I think that women just have a primeval instinct to make soup, which they will try to foist on anybody who looks like a likely candidate.
Dylan Moran

All women's issues are to some degree men's issues and all men's issues are to some degree women's issues because when either sex wins unilaterally both sexes lose.
Warren Farrell

Women are incredible in groups together. Terrifying. Men have nothing on them.
Michael Hutchence

And I think women have come a very, very long way, but they have a long way to go.
Lara Flynn Boyle

In life, single women are the most vulnerable adults. In movies, they are given imaginary power.
Elizabeth Wurtzel

I grew up in the Bronx where you would stay up late with your girlfriends, just being silly in our bedrooms, whatever. And I was always the clown.
Jennifer Lopez

The test of civilization is its estimate of women.
George William Curtis

The most virtuous women have something within them, something that is never chaste.
Honore de Balzac

What we women need to do, instead of worrying about what we don't have, is just love what we do have.
Cameron Diaz

Friends are generally of the same sex, for when men and women agree, it is only in the conclusions; their reasons are always different.
George Santayana

Men are allowed to have passion and commitment for their work... a woman is allowed that feeling for a man, but not her work.
Barbra Streisand

They say that women talk too much. If you have worked in Congress you know that the filibuster was invented by men.
Clare Boothe Luce

Wives are young men's mistresses, companions for middle age, and old men's nurses.
Francis Bacon

The first problem for all of us, men and women, is not to learn, but to unlearn.
Gloria Steinem

A homely face and no figure have aided many women heavenward.
Minna Antrim

Nature makes woman to be won and men to win.
George William Curtis

Men mourn for what they have lost; women for what they ain't got.
Josh Billings

I owe nothing to Women's Lib.
Margaret Thatcher

I'm surrounded by very powerful women and very progressive men.
Christie Hefner

A lot of women say they love being pregnant, but I wasn't such a big fan.
Marion Jones

What bugs me is that movies don't reflect how interesting and vibrant women are. We don't treasure women as they get older.
Jill Clayburgh

There's no evidence whatsoever that men are more rational than women. Both sexes seem to be equally irrational.
Albert Ellis

Some women feel the best cure for a broken heart is a new beau.
Gene Tierney

I think women are excellent social critics.
Laurie Anderson

Women get more unhappy the more they try to liberate themselves.
Brigitte Bardot

When women are encouraged to be competitive, too many of them become disagreeable.
Benjamin Spock

I will not say that women have no character; rather, they have a new one every day.
Heinrich Heine

Women, like men, should try to do the impossible. And when they fail, their failure should be a challenge to others.
Amelia Earhart

In politics women type the letters, lick the stamps, distribute the pamphlets and get out the vote. Men get elected.
Clare Boothe Luce

Women always excel men in that sort of wisdom which comes from experience. To be a woman is in itself a terrible experience.
H. L. Mencken

Charm, in most men and nearly all women, is a decoration.
E. M. Forster

You women could make someone fall in love even with a lie.
Georg Buchner

This man is frank and earnest with women. In Fresno, he's Frank and in Chicago he's Ernest.
Henny Youngman

Whether women are better than men I cannot say - but I can say they are certainly no worse.
Golda Meir

When men reach their sixties and retire, they go to pieces. Women go right on cooking.
Gail Sheehy

Why is it men are permitted to be obsessed about their work, but women are only permitted to be obsessed about men?
Barbra Streisand

Women are the real architects of society.
Cher

The only really happy folk are married women and single men.
H. L. Mencken

Men and women, women and men. It will never work.
Erica Jong

Women love always: when earth slips from them, they take refuge in heaven.
George Sand

Women have been called queens for a long time, but the kingdom given them isn't worth ruling.
Louisa May Alcott

Intimacies between women often go backwards, beginning in revelations and ending in small talk.
Elizabeth Bowen

Single women have a dreadful propensity for being poor. Which is one very strong argument in favor of matrimony.
Jane Austen

The trouble with life is that there are so many beautiful women and so little time.
John Barrymore

The sight of women talking together has always made men uneasy; nowadays it means rank subversion.
Germaine Greer

Women like to sit down with trouble - as if it were knitting.
Ellen Glasgow

Only men who are not interested in women are interested in women's clothes. Men who like women never notice what they wear.
Anatole France

The appalling thing is the degree of charity women are capable of. You see it all the time... love lavished on absolute fools. Love's a charity ward, you know.
Lawrence Durrell

When anything goes, it's women who lose.
Camille Paglia

In too many instances, the march to globalization has also meant the marginalization of women and girls. And that must change.
Hillary Clinton

You can't raise the standard of women's morals by raising their pay envelope. It lies deeper than that.
Billy Sunday

Women like myself, CEOs, can pave the way for more women to get to the top.
Andrea Jung

Women will never be as successful as men because they have no wives to advise them.
Dick Van Dyke

It is little men know of women; their smiles and their tears alike are seldom what they seem.
Amelia Barr

I don't love dolls. I love women. I love their bodies.
John Galliano

Women are women, and hurray for that.
John Galliano

Women don't realize how powerful they are.
Judith Light

Emancipation of women has made them lose their mystery.
Grace Kelly

Women are the first to jump on what is fashionable.
Gavin DeGraw

Years ago women of my size were considered royalty.
Camryn Manheim

Women have a favorite room, men a favorite chair.
Bern Williams

Women today have more of an overview of their lives and how marriage is or is not a part of it.
Helen Reddy

The only people you can really share certain things with in secret are your girlfriends.
Shirley Knight

We're getting ready to take over the world. My group of girlfriends - we're renegades.
Lisa Bonet

Women hear rhythm differently than men.
Elvis Costello

Women may not have it easy, but we are given a fairer chance to reach for the top.
Jessica Savitch

Women have a predestination to suffering.
Bela Lugosi

On the whole, I think women wear too much and are to fussy. You can't see the person for all the clutter.
Julie Andrews

Women want love to be a novel, men a short story.
Daphne du Maurier

I always say God should have given women one extra decade at least, especially if you want a family. You're trying to pack a lot in.
Christine Baranski

My advantage as a woman and a human being has been in having a mother who believed strongly in women's education. She was an early undergraduate at Oxford, and her own mother was a doctor.
Antonia Fraser

I'll always prefer to play with women and hang out with women, and I'll always be a feminist.
Courtney Love

I think today women are very scared to celebrate themselves, because then they just get labeled.
Charlize Theron

People don't want to see women doing things they don't think women should do.
Joan Jett

To understand how any society functions you must understand the relationship between the men and the women.
Angela Davis

Women are clear-headed, they are more creative and for this reason, sometimes, also more fragile.
Emma Bonino

Were there no women, men might live like gods.
Thomas Dekker

Relationships are made of talk - and talk is for girls and women.
Deborah Tannen

The women's movement completely changed attitudes all over the world in ways we'll never be able to count.
Holly Near

Women are frightening. If you get to 41 as a man, you're quite battle-scarred.
Hugh Grant

Women need not always keep their mouths shut and their wombs open.
Emma Goldman

Women have this obsession with shoes.
Alexandra Paul

Women are naturally secretive, and they like to do their own secreting.
Arthur Conan Doyle

Women in love are less ashamed than men. They have less to be ashamed of.
Ambrose Bierce

One can find women who have never had one love affair, but it is rare indeed to find any who have had only one.
Francois de La Rochefoucauld

There are few virtuous women who are not bored with their trade.
Francois de La Rochefoucauld

Women hate everything which strips off the tinsel of sentiment, and they are right, or it would rob them of their weapons.
George Byron

The labor of women in the house, certainly, enables men to produce more wealth than they otherwise could; and in this way women are economic factors in society. But so are horses.
Charlotte Perkins Gilman

The house a woman creates is a Utopia. She can't help it - can't help trying to interest her nearest and dearest not in happiness itself but in the search for it.
Marguerite Duras

A man who graduated high in his class at Yale Law School and made partnership in a top law firm would be celebrated. A man who invested wisely would be admired, but a woman who accomplishes this is treated with suspicion.
Barbra Streisand

Women's Lib? Oh, I'm afraid it doesn't interest me one bit. I've been so liberated it hurts.
Lucille Ball

I believe women still face a glass ceiling that must be shattered.
Andrew Cuomo

You're not working with models, you're working with real women who have, like, anatomy. Models do not have anatomy.
Isaac Mizrahi

It's incredibly unfair. You don't see a lot of 60-year-old women with 20-year-old men onscreen.
George Clooney

WORK

Choose a job you love, and you will never have to work a day in your life.
Confucius

All labor that uplifts humanity has dignity and importance and should be undertaken with painstaking excellence.
Martin Luther King, Jr.

Opportunity is missed by most people because it is dressed in overalls and looks like work.
Thomas A. Edison

By working faithfully eight hours a day you may eventually get to be boss and work twelve hours a day.
Robert Frost

The only place success comes before work is in the dictionary.
Vince Lombardi

All things are difficult before they are easy.
Thomas Fuller

Hard work spotlights the character of people: some turn up their sleeves, some turn up their noses, and some don't turn up at all.
Sam Ewing

The harder I work, the luckier I get.
Samuel Goldwyn

Nothing will work unless you do.
Maya Angelou

A man's work is nothing but this slow trek to rediscover, through the detours of art, those two or three great and simple images in whose presence his heart first opened.
Albert Camus

Far and away the best prize that life has to offer is the chance to work hard at work worth doing.
Theodore Roosevelt

The brain is a wonderful organ; it starts working the moment you get up in the morning and does not stop until you get into the office.
Robert Frost

Anyone who can walk to the welfare office can walk to work.
Al Capp

Find a job you like and you add five days to every week.
H. Jackson Brown, Jr.

Be regular and orderly in your life, so that you may be violent and original in your work.
Gustave Flaubert

There is no substitute for hard work.
Thomas A. Edison

It's a shame that the only thing a man can do for eight hours a day is work. He can't eat for eight hours; he can't drink for eight hours; he can't make love for eight hours. The only thing a man can do for eight hours is work.
William Faulkner

I can't imagine anything more worthwhile than doing what I most love. And they pay me for it.
Edgar Winter

Work is the curse of the drinking classes.
Oscar Wilde

Work is love made visible. And if you cannot work with love but only with distaste, it is better that you should leave your work and sit at the gate of the temple and take alms of those who work with joy.
Khalil Gibran

The taxpayer - that's someone who works for the federal government but doesn't have to take the civil service examination.
Ronald Reagan

Nothing ever comes to one, that is worth having, except as a result of hard work.
Booker T. Washington

If you don't want to work you have to work to earn enough money so that you won't have to work.
Ogden Nash

And to get real work experience, you need a job, and most jobs will require you to have had either real work experience or a graduate degree.
Donald Norman

Laziness may appear attractive, but work gives satisfaction.
Anne Frank

Going to work for a large company is like getting on a train. Are you going sixty miles an hour or is the train going sixty miles an hour and you're just sitting still?
J. Paul Getty

Do not hire a man who does your work for money, but him who does it for love of it.
Henry David Thoreau

I think the person who takes a job in order to live - that is to say, for the money - has turned himself into a slave.
Joseph Campbell

Work is a necessary evil to be avoided.
Mark Twain

There is joy in work. There is no happiness except in the realization that we have accomplished something.
Henry Ford

The best preparation for good work tomorrow is to do good work today.
Elbert Hubbard

After two weeks of working on a project, you know whether it will work or not.
Bill Budge

America believes in education: the average professor earns more money in a year than a professional athlete earns in a whole week.
Evan Esar

When your work speaks for itself, don't interrupt.
Henry J. Kaiser

Management is nothing more than motivating other people.
Lee Iacocca

To find out what one is fitted to do, and to secure an opportunity to do it, is the key to happiness.
John Dewey

Work is a necessity for man. Man invented the alarm clock.
Pablo Picasso

It is your work in life that is the ultimate seduction.
Pablo Picasso

Ya gots to work with what you gots to work with.
Stevie Wonder

I have always argued that change becomes stressful and overwhelming only when you've lost any sense of the constancy of your life. You need firm ground to stand on. From there, you can deal with that change.
Richard Nelson Bolles

Work is accomplished by those employees who have not yet reached their level of incompetence.
Laurence J. Peter

Opportunities are usually disguised as hard work, so most people don't recognize them.
Ann Landers

As I understand it, sport is hard work for which you do not get paid.
Irvin S. Cobb

There are one hundred men seeking security to one able man who is willing to risk his fortune.
J. Paul Getty

Without work, all life goes rotten. But when work is soulless, life stifles and dies.
Albert Camus

Every noble work is at first impossible.
Thomas Carlyle

Because I have work to care about, it is possible that I may be less difficult to get along with than other women when the double chins start to form.
Gloria Steinem

Nothing is work unless you'd rather be doing something else.
George Halas

To find joy in work is to discover the fountain of youth.
Pearl S. Buck

Teaching was the hardest work I had ever done, and it remains the hardest work I have done to date.
Ann Richards

Work expands so as to fill the time available for its completion.
C. Northcote Parkinson

Life grants nothing to us mortals without hard work.
Horace

If Botticelli were alive today he'd be working for Vogue.
Peter Ustinov

Dreaming in public is an important part of our job description, as science writers, but there are bad dreams as well as good dreams. We're dreamers, you see, but we're also realists, of a sort.
William Gibson

The only thing that overcomes hard luck is hard work.
Harry Golden

The supreme accomplishment is to blur the line between work and play.
Arnold J. Toynbee

To be a poet is a condition, not a profession.
Robert Frost

Work is not man's punishment. It is his reward and his strength and his pleasure.
George Sand

The more I want to get something done, the less I call it work.
Richard Bach

We work to become, not to acquire.
Elbert Hubbard

Plans are only good intentions unless they immediately degenerate into hard work.
Peter Drucker

When a man tells you that he got rich through hard work, ask him: 'Whose?'
Don Marquis

O man you are busy working for the world, and the world is busy trying to turn you out.
Abu Bakr

Be open to the amazing changes which are occurring in the field that interest you.
Leigh Steinberg

Work, look for peace and calm in work: you will find it nowhere else.
Dmitri Mendeleev

If you put all your strength and faith and vigor into a job and try to do the best you can, the money will come.
Lawrence Welk

I'm working myself to death.
Alan Ladd

Work isn't to make money; you work to justify life.
Marc Chagall

Most people treat the office manual the way they treat a software manual. They never look at it.
James Levine

There is a vast world of work out there in this country, where at least 111 million people are employed in this country alone - many of whom are bored out of their minds. All day long.
Richard Nelson Bolles

Men for the sake of getting a living forget to live.
Margaret Fuller

When more and more people are thrown out of work, unemployment results.
Calvin Coolidge

Unemployment is capitalism's way of getting you to plant a garden.
Orson Scott Card

Management must manage!
Harold S. Geneen

Managers in all too many American companies do not achieve the desired results because nobody makes them do it.
Harold S. Geneen

Work alone is noble.
Thomas Carlyle

I met an American woman and got married so I had to get a job.
Walter Wager

It can be liberating to get fired because you realize the world doesn't end. There's other ways to make money, better jobs.
Ron Livingston

Printed in Great Britain
by Amazon